3604626577

Canterbury Christ Church
University College

LIBRARY

7 DAY LOAN *

This item must be returned (or renewed) on or before
the last date indicated below.

* NB: A fine will be charged for late return

	6 MAY 2002	- 4 MAR 2004
9 MAR 2000	17 DEC 2002	24 MAR 2004
		31/3/04
	10 JAN 2003	16/4/04
23 MAR 2000		
	28 APR 2003	26 APR 2004
21 MAR 2001	- 6 MAY 2003	
		- 2 JAN 2008
12 APR 2001	14 MAR 2006	18 JAN 2009

18 MAR 2002

WITHDRAWN

D1421432

WILKIE COLLINS

An Illustrated Guide

WILKIE COLLINS

⤙ An Illustrated Guide ⤚

ANDREW GASSON

Consultant Editor: Catherine Peters

Oxford New York

OXFORD UNIVERSITY PRESS

1998

Oxford University Press, Great Clarendon Street, Oxford OX2 6DP

Oxford New York

Athens Auckland Bangkok Bogota Bombay Buenos Aires Calcutta
Cape Town Chennai Dar es Salaam Delhi Florence Hong Kong Istanbul
Karachi Kuala Lumpur Madrid Melbourne Mexico City Mumbai
Nairobi Paris São Paolo Singapore Taipei Tokyo Toronto Warsaw
and associated companies in Berlin Ibadan

Oxford is a registered trade mark of Oxford University Press

© Andrew Gasson 1998

The moral rights of the author have been asserted

First published 1998

All rights reserved. No part of this publication may be reproduced,
stored in a retrieval system, or transmitted, in any form or by any means,
without the prior permission in writing of Oxford University Press.
Within the UK, exceptions are allowed in respect of any fair dealing for the
purpose of research or private study, or criticism or review, as permitted
under the Copyright, Designs and Patents Act 1988, or in the case of
reprographic reproduction in accordance with the terms of the licences
issued by the Copyright Licensing Agency. Enquiries concerning
reproduction outside these terms and in other countries should be
sent to the Rights Department, Oxford University Press,
at the address above

British Library Cataloguing in Publication Data

Data available

Library of Congress Cataloging in Publication Data

Data available

ISBN 0–19–866215–7

1 3 5 7 9 10 8 6 4 2

Printed in Great Britain
on acid-free paper by
Butler & Tanner Ltd
Frome, Somerset

**CANTERBURY CHRIST
CHURCH COLLEGE**

360462 6577

John Smith & Son	12/1/99
823. 8	£19.99
COC	

⇌ CONTENTS ⇌

✠ PREFACE ✠

I FIRST READ Wilkie Collins in the early 1970s when, except for *The Moonstone* and *The Woman in White*, all his other books were out of print. My search for the more elusive works of this important but at that time neglected author introduced me to the bygone world of Victorian fiction—the world of periodicals, three-deckers, decorated cloth, yellowbacks and paper wrappers. I soon realised that Collins's own publishing history was representative of nineteenth century book production in general.

Similarly, a study of Collins's unconventional life provides an overview of the cultural side of Victorian England. Because of his family background, profession and association with Dickens, Collins's circle of friends included many pre-eminent figures of the day. He knew the major writers as well as a host of minor novelists. His friends and acquaintances included some of the foremost artists, playrights, theatrical personalities, musicians, publishers, physicians and society figures of the time. Collins's unorthodox lifestyle reveals a cynical view of the Victorian establishment combined with a sense of humour and a profound understanding for many of the then prevailing social injustices. These attitudes are reflected in his books, which display an unusually sympathetic treatment of women's rights, disabled people, servants and animals.

During the last twenty-five years nearly all of Collins's works have reappeared in the bookshops from which they had mostly been absent since the turn of the century. An enormous revival of interest has been accompanied by two recent biographies as well as radio, television, cinema and theatrical productions. Wilkie has returned—and mainly in cheap editions, which would have pleased him immensely.

Wilkie Collins: An Illustrated Guide aims to present concise details of Collins's life and works as well as introducing just some of his large circle of friends and associates. Plot summaries are provided for most of his stories, followed by details of their publishing history. There is a strong bibliographical emphasis throughout to provide clear identification of the first English, US and other key editions, as well as information not included in existing sources—for example on translations and pirated editions.

The Guide is copiously illustrated to help recreate Collins's world, to assist the collector in identifying bibliographical points, and to show the work of several leading illustrators of the day. Many of the pictures are unique to this volume.

APG

⇌ ACKNOWLEDGEMENTS ⇌

'Wherever the story touches on questions connected with Law, Medicine, or Chemistry, it has been submitted, before publication, to the experience of professional men.' (Armadale)

I MUST first thank Catherine Peters who has far surpassed her role as consultant editor in terms of time, effort and contributions to the text. She has given me the benefit of her considerable literary experience as well as generously allowing me access to the research notes for her own biography of Collins. I am indebted to Faith Clarke for permission to quote unpublished manuscript material and for making available personal family photographs. Both William Clarke, with his boundless enthusiasm for any project connected with Wilkie, and Professor William Baker of Northern Illinois University considerately allowed me to see the draft manuscript for their *Letters of Wilkie Collins* due to be published in late 1998. I am also grateful to Professor Ira Nadel of the University of British Columbia for his helpful advice on several entries including that for *Iolâni*; Paul Lewis for many bibliographical research details which corrected some of the myths concerning Collins's early periodical publication; Dr H. Jonathan Kersely and Dr John Glyn for suggestions on Collins's ocular and health problems; Doreen Berger for her genealogical advice; Kirsten Hüttner and Irina Rozhkova for providing details of German and Russsian translations; Dr Jacob Harskamp of the British Library and Drs Marieke van Delft of the National Library of the Netherlands for information on Dutch editions; and to all those other librarians, archivists, book and ephemera dealers, too numerous to mention, who have unearthed scarce Collins material as well as providing the benefit of their own particular expertise.

Any mistakes or omissions, however, I must claim as my own. 'I leave my book', as Collins wrote in *The Fallen Leaves*, 'to make its appeal to the reading public on such merits as it may possess.'

APG

⊰ THE MAIN WORKS OF WILKIE COLLINS ⊱

TITLE	PUBLISHER	DATE
After Dark	Smith, Elder	1856
Antonina	Bentley	1850
Armadale	Smith, Elder	1866
Basil	Bentley	1852
The Black Robe	Chatto & Windus	1881
Blind Love	Chatto & Windus	1890
The Dead Secret	Bradbury & Evans	1857
The Evil Genius	Chatto & Windus	1886
The Fallen Leaves	Chatto & Windus	1879
The Frozen Deep and Other Stories	Bentley	1874
The Guilty River	Arrowsmith	1886
The Haunted Hotel	Chatto & Windus	1879
Heart and Science	Chatto & Windus	1883
Hide and Seek	Bentley	1854
Ioláni	Princeton University Press	1998
'I Say No'	Chatto & Windus	1884
Jezebel's Daughter	Chatto & Windus	1880
The Law and the Lady	Chatto & Windus	1875
The Lazy Tour of Two Idle Apprentices	Chapman & Hall	1890
The Legacy of Cain	Chatto & Windus	1889
Little Novels	Chatto & Windus	1887
Man and Wife	Ellis	1870
Memoirs of the Life of William Collins, Esq. R.A.	Longman	1848
Miss or Mrs? and Other Stories in Outline	Bentley	1873
The Moonstone	Tinsley	1868
Mr Wray's Cash-Box	Bentley	1852
My Miscellanies	Sampson Low	1863
The New Magdalen	Bentley	1873
No Name	Sampson Low	1862
Poor Miss Finch	Bentley	1872
The Queen of Hearts	Hurst & Blackett	1859
Rambles Beyond Railways	Bentley	1851
A Rogue's Life	Bentley	1879
The Two Destinies	Chatto & Windus	1876
The Woman in White	Sampson Low	1860

See PERIODICALS, PLAYS, PUBLISHERS, SHORT STORIES.

CHRONOLOGY

YEAR	DATE	EVENTS
1824	8 Jan.	Born at 11 New Cavendish Street, Marylebone
1826		Family moves to Hampstead Green
1828	25 Jan.	Brother, Charles Allston Collins born
1829	Summer	Family visits Boulogne
1829	Sept.	Family moves to Hampstead Square
1830		Family moves to Porchester Terrace, Bayswater
1835	Jan.	Attends school at the Maida Hill Academy
1836	Sept.	Family visits France and Italy until August 1838
1838	Aug.	Moves to 20 Avenue Road and attends Cole's private boarding-school in Highbury
1840	Summer	Family moves to 85 Oxford Terrace, Bayswater
1841	Jan.	Apprenticed to Antrobus & Co., tea merchants
1842	June–July	Visits Scotland with his father, William Collins
1843	Aug.	First signed publication 'The Last Stage Coachman', *Illuminated Magazine*
1844		Writes *Ioláni*
1844		Visits France with Charles Ward
1845		*Ioláni* rejected; visits Paris on his own
1846		Visits Belgium with Charles Ward
1846	May	Enters Lincoln's Inn to study law
1847	17 Feb.	Death of William Collins
1847		Visits Normandy with Charles Ward
1848	Summer	Family moves to Blandford Square
1848	Nov.	First book published: *Memoirs of the Life of William Collins, Esq., R.A.*
1849	Summer	Exhibits *The Smuggler's Retreat* at the Royal Academy Summer Exhibition
1849		Visits France with Charles Ward
1850	26 Feb.	*A Court Duel* at the Soho Theatre
1850	27 Feb.	First novel: *Antonina*
1850	Summer	Moves with his mother to 17 Hanover Terrace
1850	July–Aug.	Walking tour of Cornwall with Henry Brandling
1851	30 Jan.	*Rambles Beyond Railways*
1851	Mar.	Meets Dickens
1851	Mar.	First contribution to *Bentley's Miscellany*, 'The Twin Sisters'
1851	16 May	Acts with Dickens in *Not So Bad as We Seem*
1851	27 Sept.	First contribution to *The Leader*
1851	21 Nov.	Called to the Bar
1851	17 Dec.	*Mr Wray's Cash-Box*
1852	24 Apr.	First contribution to *Household Words*, 'A Terribly Strange Bed'
1852	16 Nov.	*Basil*
1853	May–June	Early attack of illness
1853	July–Sept.	Stays with Dickens in Boulogne
1853	Oct.–Dec.	Tours Switzerland and Italy with Dickens and Augustus Egg

Chronology

1854		Joins the Garrick Club
1854	6 June	*Hide and Seek*
1854	July–Aug.	Stays with Dickens in Boulogne
1854	Dec.	First contribution to a Christmas number, 'A Stolen Letter' in *Household Words*
1855	Feb.	Illness during trip to Paris with Dickens
1855	16 June	*The Lighthouse* performed at Tavistock House
1855	Sept.	Sails with Pigott to the Scilly Isles
1855	Nov.	Critical review of Collins by Émile Forgues
1855	22 Dec.	First non-fiction piece for *Household Words*, 'The Cruise of the Tomtit'
1856	Feb.	First collection of stories, *After Dark*
1856	1–29 Mar.	*A Rogue's Life* serialized in *Household Words*
1856	June	Approached by Tauchnitz to publish *After Dark* on the Continent
1856	Sept.	Moves to 2 Harley Place
1856	Oct.	Joins permanent staff of *Household Words*
1857	3 Jan.	*The Dead Secret* begins serialization in *Household Words*
1857	24 Jan.	First serialization in *Harper's Weekly*, *The Dead Secret*
1857	6 Jan.	*The Frozen Deep* performed at Tavistock House
1857	June	Critical review of Collins by Yates in *The Train*
1857	June	*The Dead Secret* (book)
1857	10 Aug.	*The Lighthouse* opens at the Olympic Theatre
1857	21 Aug.	*The Frozen Deep* performed in Manchester
1857	7 Sept.	Leaves with Dickens for walking tour in Cumberland
1857	3–31 Oct.	'The Lazy Tour of Two Idle Apprentices'
1857	Dec.	Collaboration with Dickens: 'The Perils of Certain English Prisoners'
1858		First French translation, *The Dead Secret*
1858	July–Aug.	First visit to Broadstairs, Kent
1858	Sept.	Resigns from the Garrick Club
1858	11 Oct.	*The Red Vial* opens at the Olympic Theatre
1859	Jan.	Living with Caroline Graves, in Albany Street
1859	Spring	Moves to 2A New Cavendish Street
1859	Oct.	*The Queen of Hearts*
1859	26 Nov.	*The Woman in White* begins in *All the Year Round*
1859	Dec.	Moves to 12 Harley Street
1860	Jan.	Negotiates with Sampson Low for future publication
1860	17 July	Charles Collins marries Kate Dickens
1860	Aug.	*The Woman in White* (book)
1860	22 Aug.	Opens bank account at Coutts
1861	Jan.	Resigns from *All the Year Round*
1861	16 Apr.	Elected to the Athenaeum
1861	Aug.	Visits Whitby with Caroline Graves
1862	15 Mar.	*No Name* begins in *All the Year Round*
1862	July–Oct.	Rents the Fort House in Broadstairs
1862	Dec.	*No Name* (book)
1863	Apr.	Visits Aix-la-Chapelle
1863	Aug.	Visits the Isle of Man with Caroline and her daughter
1863	Nov.	*My Miscellanies*
1863	Dec.	Visits Italy for three months with Caroline
1864	Summer	Probably meets Martha Rudd in Great Yarmouth

1864	Nov.	*Armadale* begins in *The Cornhill*
1864	Dec.	Moves to 9 Melcombe Place
1864	Dec.	*Armadale* saves *Harper's Monthly* from closure
1865		Smith, Elder acquire Collins's copyrights
1865	Mar.	Resigns a second time from the Garrick Club
1865	12 Apr.	Takes the chair at the Royal General Theatrical Fund
1866	Apr.	Visits Paris with Frederick Lehmann
1866	May–June	*Armadale* (book)
1866	Oct.	Visits Italy with Edward Pigott
1866	27 Oct.	*The Frozen Deep* at The Olympic
1867	Sept.	Moves to 90 Gloucester Place
1867	9 Nov.	Visits Liverpool to see Dickens off to America
1867	Dec.	Collaborates again with Dickens 'No Thoroughfare' in *All the Year Round*
1867	26 Dec.	*No Thoroughfare* at the Adelphi Theatre
1868	4 Jan.–8 Aug.	*The Moonstone* serialized in *All the Year Round*
1868		Martha Rudd (as Mrs Dawson) installed at 33 Bolsover Street
1868	19 Mar.	Death of Harriet Collins, his mother
1868	July	*The Moonstone* (book)
1868	29 Oct.	Witnesses Caroline Graves marry Joseph Clow
1869	29 Mar.	*Black and White* opens at the Adelphi Theatre
1869	4 July	Elder daughter, Marian Dawson, born
1869	20 Nov.	*Man and Wife* begins in *Cassell's Magazine*
1870	9 June	Death of Dickens
1870	June	*Man and Wife* (book)
1871	Apr.	Caroline Graves returns to Gloucester Place
1871	14 May	Younger daughter, Harriet Dawson, born
1871	9 Oct.	*The Woman in White* opens at the Olympic Theatre
1871	Sept.	*Poor Miss Finch* begins in *Cassell's Magazine*
1871	25 Dec.	'Miss or Mrs?' in *The Graphic*
1872	26 Jan.	*Poor Miss Finch* (book)
1872	Oct.	*The New Magdalen* begins in *Temple Bar*
1872	3 Feb.	'The Novelist Who Invented Sensation' in *Vanity Fair*
1873	17 Jan.	*Miss or Mrs? and Other Stories*
1873	22 Feb.	*Man and Wife* opens at the Prince of Wales Theatre
1873	9 Apr.	Charles Collins dies
1873	17 May	*The New Magdalen* (book)
1873	19 May	*The New Magdalen* opens at the Olympic
1873	25 Sept.	Arrives in New York for American reading tour
1873	10 Nov.	Attends first night of *The New Magdalen* in New York
1874	7 Mar.	Leaves Boston for England
1874		Moves Martha Rudd to Taunton Place
1874	26 Sept.	*The Law and the Lady* begins in *The Graphic*
1874	2 Nov.	*The Frozen Deep and Other Stories*
1874	25 Dec.	Son, William Charles Collins Dawson, born
1875		Chatto & Windus become Collins's main English publishers
1875	Feb.	*The Law and the Lady* (book)
1875		Visits Italy with Frith
1876	Jan.–Sept.	*The Two Destinies* in *Temple Bar*
1876	15 Apr.	*Miss Gwilt* opens at the Globe Theatre

Chronology

1876	Aug.	*The Two Destinies* (book)
1877	2 July	'Mr Percy and the Prophet' in *All the Year Round*
1877	29 Aug.	*The Dead Secret* at the Lyceum Theatre
1877		Replaces Tindell with Henry Bartley as solicitor
1877	17 Sept.	*The Moonstone* opens at the Olympic Theatre
1877	Dec.	'My Lady's Money' in *The Illustrated London News*
1878		Disagreement with Harpers
1878	June–Nov.	*The Haunted Hotel* in *Belgravia Magazine*
1878	Nov.	*The Haunted Hotel* (book)
1879	1 Jan.	*The Fallen Leaves* begins in *The World*
1879	7 Apr.	*A Rogue's Life* (book)
1879	July	*The Fallen Leaves* (book)
1879	Sept.	Begins dealings with Tillotson with syndication of *Jezebel's Daughter*
1880	Mar.	*Jezebel's Daughter* (book)
1880	2 Oct.	*The Black Robe* begins syndication
1881	Apr.	*The Black Robe* (Book)
1881	Dec.	Approaches A. P. Watt to become his literary agent
1882	Aug.	*Heart and Science* begins in *Belgravia*
1883	Apr.	*Heart and Science* (book)
1883	9 June	*Rank and Riches* at the Adelphi Theatre
1883	Dec.	Resumes relations with Harpers; 'I Say No' begins in *Harper's Weekly*
1884		Founder member of the Society of Authors
1884	Jan.–Dec.	'I Say No' serialized in *London Society*
1884	Oct.	'I Say No' (book)
1885	June	Begins correspondence with Nannie Wynne
1885	28 Aug.	Tommie, Collins's dog, dies
1885	30 Oct.	Copyright performance of *The Evil Genius*
1885	Dec.	*The Evil Genius* begins syndication
1886	Sept.	*The Evil Genius* (book)
1886	15 Nov.	*The Guilty River*
1887	May	*Little Novels*
1888	Feb.	Moves from Gloucester Place to 82 Wimpole Street
1888	Feb.	*The Legacy of Cain* begins syndication with Tillotson
1888	Nov.	*The Legacy of Cain* (book)
1889	30 June	Suffers a stroke
1889	23 Sept.	Dies at 82 Wimpole Street
1889	27 Sept.	Funeral at Kensal Green
1889	July–Dec.	*Blind Love* in *The Illustrated London News*
1889	24 Oct.	Auction sale of furniture and effects
1890	Jan.	*Blind Love* (book)
1890	20 Jan.	Auction sale of library
1890	22 Feb.	Auction sale of pictures and drawings
1890		*The Lazy Tour of Two Idle Apprentices* (book)
1895	June	Death of Caroline Graves; buried in Wilkie's grave
1919		Death of Martha Rudd
1998		*Iolàni* finally published

⫷ SHORT REFERENCES USED IN THE TEXT ⫸

Brussel (1935)   Brussel, I. R., *Anglo-American First Editions 1826–1900: East to West*, London 1935;
                       reprinted, New York 1981

Clarke (1988)   Clarke, W. M., *The Secret Life of Wilkie Collins*, London 1988; reprinted, Stroud
                       1996

Collins, W., *Memoirs* Collins, W. W., *Memoirs of the Life of William Collins, Esq., R. A.* (2 vols),
                       London 1848

de la Mare (1932)   de la Mare, W., 'The Early Novels of Wilkie Collins', in *The Eighteen Sixties*,
                       edited by John Drinkwater, Cambridge 1932

Ellis (1931)   Ellis, S. M., *Wilkie Collins, Le Fanu and Others*, London 1931

Gasson (1980)   Gasson, A., 'Wilkie Collins: A Collector's and Bibliographer's Challenge', *The
                       Private Library*, Third Series 3: 2 (Summer 1980), 51–77

Harper (1912)   Harper, J. H., *The House of Harper*, New York and London 1912

IELM   *Index of English Literary Manuscripts, iv: (1800–1900)*, compiled by B. Rosen-
                       baum and P. White, London and New York 1982

Lehmann (1908)   Lehmann, R. C., *Memories of Half a Century*, London 1908

Letters   *The Letters of Wilkie Collins* edited by W. Baker and W. M. Clarke (2 vols), Lon-
                       don 1998

Page (1974)   Page, N. (editor), *Wilkie Collins: The Critical Heritage*, London 1974

Parrish (1940)   Parrish, M. L., with E. V. Miller, *Wilkie Collins and Charles Reade: First Editions
                       Described with Notes*, London 1940; reprinted, New York 1968

PELCD   *The Pilgrim Edition of the Letters of Charles Dickens* (12 vols), Oxford

Peters (1991)   Peters, C., *The King of Inventors*, London 1991; paperback 1992

Reeve (1906)   Reeve, W., 'Recollections of Wilkie Collins', *Chambers's Journal*, 9 (June 1906),
                       458–61

Robinson (1951)   Robinson, K., *Wilkie Collins: A Biography*, London 1951; reprinted 1974

Sadleir (1951)   Sadleir, M., *XIX Century Fiction: A Bibliographical Record Based on His Own Col-
                       lection* (2 vols), London 1951; reprinted, New York 1969

WCS   The Wilkie Collins Society

WCSJ   *The Wilkie Collins Society Journal*

⇸ NOTE TO THE READER ⇷

Entries are arranged in letter-by-letter alphabetical order up to the first punctuation in the headword. Cross-references are indicated by an asterisk or by the use in brackets of 'See' followed by the entry title, or part of it, in small capitals. Occasionally, 'See also' is used at the end of an entry to inform the reader of related subjects.

As entries are provided for all of the main works (see p.xi for listing), these are not generally cross-referenced unless they elucidate a particular point. Cross-references appear only where they are likely to amplify the entry being read, and are not given in all instances where a headword appears in the text.

Most of Collins's short stories are listed under the name by which they are best known. Entries for main works consist of a general contextual introduction, then a plot summary (marked by ●◆), followed by a bibliographical summary of publishing history which includes periodical, first English, main one-volume English and first US publication, and translations where known.

Where financial sums are mentioned in the text, these can be multiplied by approximately 40 to give a rough equivalent to modern values.

As a useful starting point, and as a biographical summary, it is suggested that readers consult the WILKIE COLLINS entry first.

WILKIE COLLINS
An Illustrated Guide

THEATRE ROYAL ADELPHI.

SOLE PROPRIETOR AND MANAGER, MR. BENJAMIN WEBSTER.

Licensed by the Lord Chamberlain to Mr. BENJAMIN WEBSTER, Actual and Responsible Manager. Kennington Park.

Directress, - Mrs. ALFRED MELLON.

Mr. FECHTER
As OBENREIZER.

Mr. B. WEBSTER
As JOEY LADLE.

TRIUMPHANT SUCCESS
OF

THE NEW AND ORIGINAL DRAMA,

By CHARLES DICKENS & WILKIE COLLINS, Esqs.,

Dramatised from their Christmas Story of

NO THOROUGHFARE!

IN WHICH WILL APPEAR

Mr. FECHTER,

Miss CARLOTTA LECLERCQ,

Mrs. ALFRED MELLON,   Mrs. BILLINGTON,   Mrs. H. LEWIS,

Mr. BILLINGTON,   Mr. HENRY NEVILLE,   Mr. G. BELMORE,

Mr. R. PHILLIPS,   Mr. C. J. SMITH,   and   Mr. BENJAMIN WEBSTER.

MONDAY, FEB. 10th, 1868, & DURING THE WEEK,

At SEVEN o'clock, the Screaming NEW and ORIGINAL FARCE, by HARRY LEMON, Esq., called

UP FOR THE CATTLE SHOW.

Gabriel Marlow, — (a Lawyer)		Mr. C. J. SMITH,
John Liston, (his Clerk) Mr. BRANSCOMBE,	Paul Granville, Mr. W. H. EBURNE,	
Peter Strollop, —		Mr. G. BELMORE,
Clerk, Mr. BRANSCOMBE,	Servant, Mr HITCHENSON,	
Cecilia Marlow, (Marlow's Daughter) Miss HARRIS,	Phœbe Bingley, Miss EMILY PITT,	

After which will be presented, with SPLENDID NEW SCENERY and EFFECTS, at a Quarter to Eight,

A NEW AND ORIGINAL DRAMA,

By CHARLES DICKENS and WILKIE COLLINS, Esqs. (Dramatised from their Great Christmas Story in "All the Year Round") entitled

NO THOROUGHFARE.

The New Scenery and Effects by **Mr. T. GRIEVE and SON.**

The Appointments by Mr. T. IRELAND and Assistants.   The Machinery by Mr. CHARKER and Assistants.

The Costumes by Mrs. AULPH, Miss RAYNER and Assistants.   Gas Arrangements by Mr. G. BASTARD.

The Incidental Music composed and arranged by Mr. E. ELLIS.   And the Piece produced under the direction of

MR. FECHTER.

THE OVERTURE.

PERIOD   -   -   OCTOBER, 1847.

London Time by the Great Clock of St. Paul's, Ten at Night.

Scene—EXTERIOR OF THE

HOSPITAL FOR FOUNDLING CHILDREN.

The Veiled Lady, ...   Mrs. BILLINGTON.

Sarah (otherwise Sally) Goldstraw   ..   ..   Mrs. ALFRED MELLON.

Ablewhite, Godfrey The true villain of *The Moonstone*, originally conceived by Collins as a clergyman, but modified to a hypocritical philanthropist, the darling of pious old ladies. Ablewhite embezzles £20,000 from a trust fund to pay for his mistress and her villa, taking the stolen diamond from Franklin *Blake and pledging it to save himself from ruin. He unsuccessfully tries to marry his cousin Rachel *Verinder for money and is finally murdered by the Indians when they recover the diamond.

Adelphi, Theatre Royal London theatre in the *Strand specializing in melodrama; staged three plays by Collins and several by *Dickens. 'Adelphi Drama' was considered less sophisticated than that of its rival, the *Olympic. The manager in the 1860s was Benjamin *Webster, whom Collins praised in a deliberately back-handed way in 'A Breach of British Privilege' (*Household Words*, 19 March 1859). Collins's dramatizations were: *No Thoroughfare* (26 December 1867, for 200 performances); *Black and White* (with Charles *Fechter) (29 March 1869 for 60 performances); and *Rank and Riches* (9 June 1883).

After Dark Collins's first collection of six short stories, published in 1856, and consisting of 'The Traveller's Story of A *Terribly Strange Bed', 'The Lawyer's Story of A *Stolen Letter', 'The French Governess's Story of *Sister Rose', 'The Angler's Story of The *Lady of Glenwith Grange', 'The Nun's Story of *Gabriel's Marriage', and 'The Professor's Story of The *Yellow Mask'. All but the fourth had previously been published in *Household Words*.

Collins provides a narrative framework, 'Leaves from Leah's Diary', set in 1827. Leah Kerby's husband, William, is a poor travelling portrait-painter forced to abandon his profession for six months in order to save his sight. Leah realizes that if she acts as amanuensis William can support them by turning author. This situation may have been prompted by a period of eye-trouble suffered by Collins's father. In the preface to *After Dark*, Collins also acknowledges the painter W. S. Herrick as his source for the facts on which 'A Terribly Strange Bed' and 'The Yellow Mask' are based. See Appendix A for illustration of MS.

Serialization. For first publication see individual stories.
Book publication
1st edn. 2 vols, *Smith, Elder, London 1856. Dark grey-green cloth, covers blocked in blind, spines lettered in gilt, pale yellow endpapers. Half-title in each vol. Published in Feb. 1856. Variant binding in paper boards, half cloth, with white endpapers.
Vol I viii + 316 pp. 16 pp publisher's catalogue bound in at end (dated Jan., Feb. or Apr. 1856).
Vol II (iv) + 324 pp. Publisher's advertisement occupies p (323).
1-vol edns. Smith, Elder 1859–90 (with 5 illustrations [by A. B. Houghton]); *Chatto & Windus 1890–1925.
1st US edn. Dick & Fitzgerald, New York [1856].
Translations. German, Lemgo 1859; Polish, Lwow 1871; Dutch, The Hague 1876.

'Air and the Audience, The: Considerations on the Atmospheric Influences of Theatres' Light-hearted essay comparing poorly ventilated English theatres lit with gas, and the effect this had on the alertness of the audience, with their healthier American counterparts. Collins refused to have gas in his own house in *Gloucester Place.

Written in 1881 (?) and first published in 1885 by Allen Thorndike Rice of New York. Reprinted with a foreword by John Balance in The *Mask of October 1924 as 'The Use of Gas in Theatres'. More recently edited with notes and commentary by Steve Farmer in the WCSJ (6, 1986, pp 19–26).

Aix-la-Chapelle (now Aachen).
'The famous physician got rid of him in no time—sent him abroad to boil himself in foreign baths' (*Blind Love*).
Spa town in Germany near the border with Belgium. Visited by Collins for his *health in April 1863. To avoid the uncomfortable routine of rising at seven and gulping hot water on an empty stomach, Collins sent a carrier to the spring with a stoppered bottle and drank the water 'horizontally in bed'. He submitted to afternoon baths in the hot sulphur spring, being 'all over sulphur, inside and out', and the overall effect of the treatment proved encouraging. More particularly, Collins enjoyed the Hotel Nuellan's excellent cellar and Parisian cuisine which encouraged his 'natural gluttony by a continuous succession of *entrées* which are to be eaten but not described'. Lehmann (1908), 44–6.

Aldborough [Aldeburgh]. Suffolk town used as the seaside setting for much of *No Name*. During his research for the novel, Collins stayed in Aldeburgh with Caroline *Graves in 1861.

Aldersley, Frank Leading character in The *Frozen Deep (1857), engaged to Clara Burnham. Played by Collins opposite Charles *Dickens's Richard *Wardour.

(facing) Programme for the Adelphi production of *No Thoroughfare*
(above) Cover of the Smith Elder 1876 yellowback edition of *After Dark*

'Alicia Warlock' US title of 'The *Dream Woman', included in *Alicia Warlock (A Mystery) and Other Stories*, Gill, Boston 1875. The edition also contains: 'A Sane Madman' (see 'MAD MARRIAGE, A'), 'The *Fatal Cradle', '*Blow Up with the Brig!'; together with 'The Queen's Revenge', 'My Black Mirror', 'Mrs Badgery' and 'Memoirs of an Adopted Son' from *My Miscellanies* (1863).

Alicia Warlock is the revised name of the ostler's wife, originally called Rebecca Murdoch in the 1855 version of the story.

All the Year Round (1859–95). Weekly periodical founded and edited by *Dickens. It succeeded and incorporated *Household Words* following a personal disagreement with his former partners, *Bradbury & Evans. Dickens owned three-quarters and W. H. *Wills, continuing as sub-editor, one quarter. Collins was a member of the staff until January 1862, returning temporarily in 1868 because of Wills's illness.

All the Year Round followed the style of *Household Words* as a family paper for the middle classes. Dickens changed the emphasis so that each number featured a serialized full-length novel, no longer anonymous, and also contained a short story. Inevitably there was less space for social comment, and because of his other commitments Dickens's distinctive editorial style was less obvious.

The original series of *All the Year Round* ran for 501 numbers from 30 April 1859 until 28 November 1868, with a New Series commencing on 5 December. The paper had been widely advertised and proved an immediate success. Circulation reached 100,000 within a few weeks and eventually achieved 300,000 for special issues. The regular numbers cost 2*d*. each and consisted of twenty-four pages. They were also available in monthly parts at 11*d*. and biannual bound volumes at 5*s*. 6*d*. There were eight extra *Christmas numbers.

Dickens arranged for the simultaneous publication of *All the Year Round* in the USA, using stereotype plates. He also sold via *Sampson Low the rights for *Harpers to publish in their own papers all articles except stories taking longer than three months to serialize. Charles Dickens Junior worked on the magazine from September 1868 and became sole

proprietor and editor from January 1871.

Between 1859 and 1861, Collins regularly contributed articles to *All the Year Round*, several of which were reprinted in *My Miscellanies* (1863). He also collaborated with Dickens for the Christmas numbers of 1859, 1860, 1861 and 1867; and published '*Percy and the Prophet' in the New Series (2 July 1877).

More significantly, *All the Year Round* published three of Collins's major novels. In 1859 Dickens needed an exciting serial to follow his own relatively short *A Tale of Two Cities*. He had enough confidence in Collins to ask him to undertake this and the result was *The Woman in White* (26 Nov. 1859–25 Aug. 1860). It established Collins's reputation and from the open-

Offices of *All the Year Round* at 26 Wellington Street off the Strand

ing numbers sales of the magazine began to rise. *All the Year Round* also serialized *No Name* (15 Mar. 1862–17 Jan. 1863) and *The Moonstone* (4 Jan.–8 Aug. 1868). The publisher, *Tinsley, recollected that 'During the run of *The Moonstone* as a serial there were scenes in Wellington Street that doubtless did the author's and publisher's hearts good. And especially when the serial was nearing its ending, on publishing days there would be quite a crowd of anxious readers waiting for the new number.'

Other contributors included *Bulwer-Lytton, *Charles Collins, *Fitzgerald,

Mrs Gaskell, *Reade, *Sala and *Yates.

Lehmann, R. C., *Charles Dickens as Editor*, London 1912.

Oppenlander, E. A., *Dickens' 'All the Year Round': Descriptive Index and Contributor List*, Troy, NY, 1984.

Allonby Coastal town in *Cumberland on the Solway Firth, visited by Collins and *Dickens on their walking tour in 1857. They arrived in time for lunch on 9 September and stopped for two nights before going on to Doncaster. They stayed at *The Ship*, described by Dickens as 'a capital little homely inn looking out upon the sea . . . a clean nice place in a rough wild country'. The landlord was Benjamin Partridge whose immensely fat wife was 'very obliging and comfortable'. It is in Allonby, in 'The *Lazy Tour of Two Idle Apprentices', that Collins as Thomas *Idle engages in autobiographical reflections.

    PELCD.

amateur theatricals One of Collins's favourite social recreations as a young man. After his family moved to Blandford Square in 1838, their back drawing room became known as the 'Theatre Royal'. Collins produced there Sheridan's *The Rivals*, and later described an amateur production of the play in **No Name* (1862). The young ladies and gentlemen accepted 'all the other responsibilities, incidental to creating a dramatic world out of a domestic chaos. Having accustomed themselves to the breaking of furniture and staining of walls—to thumping, hammering, and screaming'. He also pro-

duced Goldsmith's *The Good-Natur'd Man* on 19 June 1849, acting with his brother, *Frith and *Millais, and writing a new verse prologue to the play. The costumes were designed by Edward *Ward whose wife, Henrietta, later recalled how, in spite of Wilkie's characteristic efforts at peacemaking, both the leading lady and man resigned because they detested one another.

The following year Collins became more ambitious, translating *A *Court Duel* from the French. One public charity performance was given at the Soho Theatre on 26 February 1850. The cast included Charles *Collins, who took the lead, and Henry *Brandling. Wilkie himself took the small part of a courtier. *A Court Duel* was followed by James Kenny's farce, *Raising the Wind*, in which Wilkie played the lead.

Amateur theatricals brought Collins into contact with *Dickens in 1851. Planning the production of *Not So Bad as We Seem* in aid of the Guild of Literature and Art, Dickens wrote to Augustus *Egg on 8 March:

'I think *you* told *me* that Mr Wilkie Collins would be glad to play any part in Bulwer's Comedy; and I think *I* told *you* that I considered him a very desirable recruit. There is a Valet, called (as I remember) Smart—a small part, but, what there is of it, decidedly good . . .. Will you undertake to ask him if I shall cast him in this part? If yes, I will call him to the reading on Wednesday . . .. I knew his father well, and should be very glad to know him.'

The first performance took place on 16 May 1851 in the converted drawing room of Devonshire House before the Queen

Programme for the 1865 amateur production of *The Lighthouse*

and Prince Consort. At the Duke of Devonshire's request, the play was repeated on 27 May together with Mark *Lemon's farce *Mr Nightingale's Diary* in which Collins played the part of Lithers, the landlord. He subsequently travelled with Dickens's troupe to Bristol and with the provincial tour early the following year to Manchester, where the audience reached nearly three thousand, and to *Liverpool where Collins also acted in Charles Mathews' *Used Up*.

In early 1855, Collins briefly assumed the stage name 'Wilkini Collini' when he appeared as 'Gobbler' in the Twelfth Night children's pantomime put on by the Dickens family. Later that year he wrote *The *Lighthouse*. Dickens masterminded its production at *Tavistock House from 16 June, and subsequently at Campden House. The play featured Collins as Martin Gurnock, Dickens as Aaron Gurnock, and Augustus Egg, Mark Lemon and Georgina *Hogarth. The next joint production was *The *Frozen Deep* in January 1857, also staged at Tavistock House, followed by performances at the Gallery of Illustration and the Manchester Free Trade Hall. Collins

Innkeeper's book for *The Ship*, Allonby, where Collins stayed with Dickens in September 1857: showing their expenses for lunch, dinner, board, and breakfast

appeared in two farces which made up the programme, *Animal Magnetism* and *Uncle John*.

Ainger, A., *Lectures and Essays*, 2 vols, London 1905: ii. 203–8.

Dexter, W., 'For One Night Only: Dickens's Appearances as an Amateur Actor', *Dickensian*, 36 (1 Sept. 1940), 195–201.

Fitz-Gerald, S. J. A., *Dickens and the Drama*, London 1910.

Ward, Mrs E. M., *Memories of Ninety Years*, edited by I. G. McAllister, London 1924, 52.

America

'I have been enjoying myself among the most hospitable people in the world.' (*The Evil Genius*)

Collins made a reading tour of the USA and Canada from September 1873 to March 1874. Wybert *Reeve, who was to accompany him, was delayed and Collins sailed by himself from Liverpool on 13 September 1873. The s.s. *Algeria* stopped at Queenstown, Ireland, and arrived in New York on 25 September. He was met by Charles *Fechter who escorted him to the Westminster Hotel where he stayed in the suite Dickens had once occupied. Fechter also introduced him to the gastronomic delights of New York, including soft-shell crab. Collins's godson, Frank *Ward, accompanied him for most of the tour; Collins found him invaluable as both secretary and companion. Ward normally worked for Sebastian *Schlesinger, with whom Collins became friends for the rest of his life.

On 27 September the Lotos Club of New York gave a brilliant reception and dinner for Collins. The evening was presided over by Whitelaw Reid, US Ambassador to London, and in response to his welcoming speech Collins expressed his grateful thanks for this recognition of English literature. Collins was also entertained by his US publishers, *Harpers, letting them know in advance that he could drink only very dry champagne. To celebrate the visit, Harpers issued an Illustrated Library Edition of his novels with a facsimile dedication 'to The American People'.

The readings featured an adaptation of 'The *Dream Woman' and the hectic tour began with visits to New York State; cities included Albany (8 October), Rochester, Troy and Syracuse. Collins went on to Philadelphia (17 October) where he stayed with Fechter and met the publisher George Childs. He was back in

WILKIE COLLINS'S NOVELS.

HARPER'S ILLUSTRATED LIBRARY EDITION.
12mo, Cloth, $1.25 per Volume.

ARMADALE.
BASIL.
HIDE-AND-SEEK.
THE NEW MAGDALEN.
NO NAME.
QUEEN OF HEARTS.
MY MISCELLANIES.

MAN AND WIFE.
POOR MISS FINCH.
THE MOONSTONE.
THE WOMAN IN WHITE.
THE DEAD SECRET.
AFTER DARK, and Other Stories.
ANTONINA.

THE LAW AND THE LADY.

PUBLISHED BY HARPER & BROTHERS, NEW YORK.

(above) Dedication by Collins for the Harper's Illustrated Library Edition of his novels produced for his American reading tour in 1873–4
(right) Portrait by Halpin used for Collins's American editions published by Harpers

New York, however, on 22 October for a breakfast banquet given by William *Seaver. The tour continued to Boston, for a reading at the Music Hall on 30 October, on to Cambridge the following day and back to New York for rehearsals of *The *New Magdalen*. The play opened at *Daly's Broadway Theatre on 10 November and was followed by a reading the next day at Association Hall. In mid-November, Collins travelled south to Baltimore and Washington (which he didn't care for), returning to the St James's Hotel, Boston, on 13 December. By this time he had written the first part of '*John Jago's Ghost', derived from a true story he had heard at Troy. Wybert Reeve opened in a two-week run of *The Woman in White* on 15 December.

The following week Collins departed for Montreal and Toronto where he was entertained for Christmas by his Canadian publishers, *Hunter Rose. There was a reading on Boxing Day after which Collins left for Niagara. The cold, dry weather had helped his *gout but he was worried that the Falls would create problems. In the event, he wrote 'No words can tell how these wonderful Falls astonished and impressed me. It is well worth the voyage from England to see Niagara alone.'

The tour continued with Buffalo (2 January 1874), Cleveland, Ohio (8 January),

Sandusky, Ohio (9 January) and on by sleeping car to Chicago's Sherman House Hotel by 17 January. Attendances proved disappointing and the Music Hall was only half-full. The discomfort of travelling long distances by train forced Collins to abandon an idea of venturing further west to visit cousins in San Francisco. He therefore returned via Detroit and Rochester, arriving on 27 January in Boston for another round of dinners. He met literary figures such as Mark Twain, H. W. Longfellow, and Oliver Wendell Holmes who recited a tribute in verse. Collins adapted *The *Frozen Deep* for his farewell performances and dedicated the English book edition to Holmes. February was spent in further readings and a return visit to New York. He sat for the photographer *Sarony, and on his final night in the city met Fechter for a farewell dinner.

Collins sailed from Boston on the s.s. *Parthia* on 7 March, arriving in Liverpool eleven days later. He had intended staying in America until the end of March but, as he wrote to Childs, 'letters from home have obliged me to hasten my departure . . . and I had no other choice than to get back and attend to some business which was all going wrong in my absence'. Overall, Collins regarded the tour as a great success. He earned some £2,500 from his readings: had his health been strong enough it could have been much more.

Collins, W., introduction to *The Frozen Deep*, London 1874.
Harper (1912), 343–8.
The Poems of Oliver Wendell Holmes, Boston 1875.
Lehmann (1908), 67.
Reeve (1906).
Walford, L. B., *Memories of Victorian London*, London 1912, 207–9.
Letters.

Andersen, Hans Christian (1805–75).
Danish author of fairy-tales. Overstayed his welcome with *Dickens at *Gad's Hill in the summer of 1857. Collins was also a guest and presented him with a copy of *The Dead Secret*. Andersen in turn wished to translate the dramatic version of *The *Frozen Deep*. Collins satirized Andersen in 'The Bachelor Bedroom', **All the Year Round*, 6 August 1859; reprinted in **My Miscellanies* (1863).

Lohrli, A., 'Herr von Müffe', *Dickensian*, 62 (Jan. 1966), 5–13.

Anderson, Mary de Navarro (1859–1940).
American classical actress famed for her beauty. Appeared at the *Lyceum for three seasons (1883–4, 1884–5 and 1887–8) and became as popular in England as in the USA. Retired early from the stage in 1899. Met Collins in 1883 during her first London season and remained a close friend for the rest of his life. Collins in 1885 wanted to write a play for her based on American history but the idea never came to fruition. Her autobiography, *A Few Memories* (New York 1896), contains several letters from Collins and anecdotes about him.

animals and pets

'There are periods in a man's life when he finds the society that walks on four feet a welcome relief from the society that walks on two.' (*The Fallen Leaves*)

Collins was a great animal-lover and there were invariably pets in *Gloucester Place. His much loved dog, *Tommie, appeared in '*My Lady's Money' and Collins even kept a note in his travelling desk, along with other anniversaries, that Tommie died on 28 August 1885. Cats were also great favourites and there was often one in the household. Collins admired their characteristics, noting in *The New Magdalen* 'the cat is a sleek and splendid creature' and referring to a 'subtle cat-like courage' in '*Sister Rose'. Mannion in *Basil* has 'a large black cat . . . basking luxuriously in the heat of the fire' and Snooks, a real cat owned by the Collins family when Wilkie was a young man, features by name in *Hide and Seek*.

John *Herncastle in *The Moonstone* lives as a recluse with his animals and *Fosco in *The Woman in White* is constantly surrounded by his birds and mice. Describing the injured spaniel in the same book, Marian *Halcombe's diary records 'The misery of a weak, helpless, dumb creature is surely one of the sad-

Mary Anderson, American actress renowned for her beauty

dest of all the mournful sights which this world can show.' In *The Fallen Leaves* Collins notes 'the insatiable Anglo-Saxon delight in killing birds' and Allan *Armadale observes 'I could enjoy a ride on horseback without galloping after a wretched stinking fox or a distracted little hare.'

Heart and Science (1883) supported the anti-vivisection movement to which Collins alludes in the preface. During his research he wrote to Surgeon-General Gordon 'I am endeavouring to add my small contribution in aid of the good cause by such means as Fiction will permit.' In 1884, mentioning a cheap one-volume reprint to Miss Frances Power Cobbe, Collins added 'What little I have been able to do towards helping this good cause is in a fair way, I hope, of appealing to a large audience.'

Letters.

'Anne Rodway, The Diary of' See 'DIARY OF ANNE RODWAY, THE'.

Antonina; or The Fall of Rome. A Romance of the Fifth Century
Collins's first published novel. Dedicated to Lady Chantrey, wife of William *Collins's friend, the sculptor Sir Francis Legatt Chantrey (1791–1841). *Antonina* was begun in April 1846, delayed for a year during the writing of *Memoirs of the Life of William Collins, Esq., R.A.*, and published in 1850. It is written in a laborious, deliberately florid style using detail from

Title-page by John Gilbert for the Sampson Low edition of *Antonina* in 1861

Gibbon's *Decline and Fall of the Roman Empire* and modelled on *Bulwer-Lytton's *The Last Days of Pompeii* (1834). The plot is absurd, and many passages read like a cross between a guide-book to ancient Rome, based on Collins's visit in 1837, and a description of his father's paintings. Other sections, particularly the more horrific and violent, are vividly written and there are already indications of Collins's interest in physical handicap and abnormal states of mind, and his dislike of all forms of extremism. The conflict between the imaginative and artistic Antonina and her stern father is reworked to better effect in Collins's next novel, *Basil*. *Antonina* received good reviews, sold well and was reprinted throughout Collins's lifetime and into the twentieth century.

The plot revolves around two separate but related struggles: that of the old pagan and new Christian religions, seen as equally destructive, embodied in the opposing characters of Ulpius and Numerian; and that of the strong figure of the Goth, Goisvintha (modelled on Norna in *Scott's *The Pirate*), seeking revenge against the weak heroine, Antonina.

➡ In the Rome of AD 408, the young Antonina lives with her father Numerian, zealous in his aims to restore the Christian faith to its former ideals. Numerian's steward, Ulpius, brought up in the old religion, secretly lives only to restore the forbidden gods of pagan sacrifice. Vetranio, their wealthy neighbour, has designs on the innocent Antonina. When they are surprised by Numerian in an apparently compromising situation, Antonina flees outside the city walls just before Rome is blockaded by the encircling army of the Goths.

Antonina is captured by the chieftain, Hermanric, who falls in love with her. His sister, Goisvintha, was the sole survivor of a Roman massacre in which her children perished and has vowed revenge on Rome and its people. She attempts to kill Antonina but is prevented by Hermanric who allows Antonina to escape. During the weeks of the siege, she lives in a deserted farmhouse, visited nightly by Hermanric. Goisvintha betrays her brother to the Huns who kill him, while Antonina escapes for a second time.

Ulpius, meanwhile, has discovered a breach in the city wall and attempts to betray Rome to Alaric in exchange for his destruction of the Christian religion. Alaric is interested only in humbling his enemies into surrender and seizing a large tribute of gold. Returning towards the city, Ulpius discovers Antonina and accompanies her to Rome where she finds her overjoyed but starving father. Antonina begs the last morsels of food from Vetranio at a macabre and suicidal 'Banquet of Famine', preventing him from making a funeral pyre of his palace.

Goisvintha, ever more obsessed with revenge, smuggles her way into Rome to seek out Antonina. Father and daughter take refuge in a disused pagan temple, inhabited by the now totally deranged Ulpius. Before he can sacrifice Antonina to the old gods, she is stabbed by the pursuing Goisvintha who is lured to her own death in a mechanical booby-trap. The raving Ulpius reveals that he is Numerian's long-lost brother and barricading himself in the temple is burned to death among his idols by the Christian priests. Antonina has been rescued and after recovering from her wound lives peacefully with her father, happily tending Hermanric's grave. The repentant Vetranio retires to the country.

Book publication
1st edn. 3 vols, Richard *Bentley, London 1850. Cream embossed cloth, spines lettered in gilt, yellow endpapers printed with publisher's advertisements. Half-title in each vol. Published 27 Feb. 1850.
Vol I (xvi) + 296 pp.
Vol II (viii) + 324 pp. Publisher's advertisements occupy pp (323–4).
Vol III (viii) + 340 pp. Publisher's advertisements occupy pp (339–40).
Other 3-vol edns. [May] 1850, 2nd edn (revised with revised preface); 1853, using 1st-edn sheets.
1-vol edns. *Sampson Low (new preface and illustrated title by John *Gilbert) 1861–5; *Smith, Elder 1865–72; *Chatto & Windus (with 8 illustrations by Alfred Concanen) 1875–1908.
1st US edn. *Harpers, New York 1850.
Translation. German, Leipzig 1850.

Antrobus, Edmund Edward
(1806–86). London tea merchant and writer on social problems who employed the young Collins as a clerk from 1841 to 1846. Antrobus's father was a director of *Coutts Bank and the position was probably secured for Wilkie through the

influence of his father's friend, Charles *Ward. William *Collins painted a group portrait of Antrobus's three children for the sum of 200 guineas; the picture, *Scene at Aberystwyth*, was exhibited at the Royal Academy summer exhibition in 1842.

The offices of Antrobus & Co. were at 446 *Strand, close to Coutts at 440. There were several publishers in the area, including *Chapman & Hall, and the offices of *The *Illustrated London News*, **Punch*, and Douglas *Jerrold's *The *Illuminated Magazine* which published 'The *Last Stage Coachman' in 1843. During office hours Collins wrote epic poems, tragedies, comedies and fiction, including his Polynesian novel **Ioláni*; but he always claimed in later life that when detected in this activity he had been able to show that all his allotted clerical tasks had been completed. Antrobus also allowed him liberal time off to travel. Collins finally left Antrobus & Co. in 1846 to study law at *Lincoln's Inn.

Collins drew on his time with Antrobus for scenes in **Hide and Seek* (1854), in which the reluctant Zachary Thorpe complains 'You wouldn't like being forced into an infernal tea-shop, when you wanted to be an artist'; and 'Here I have been for the last three weeks at a Tea Broker's office in the city . . . . I don't want to be respectable and I hate commercial pursuits.'

Collins, W., *Memoirs*.
Healey, E., *Coutts & Co 1692–1992: The Portrait of a Private Bank*, London 1992.
**Illustrated London News*, 15 May 1886, p 512; 4 Sept. 1886, 268.

Appleton, D. & Co. New York publishing house founded in 1825. Issued **Basil* in 1853; and **A Rogue's Life* and 'The *Yellow Mask' in the New Handy-Volume Series (1879). Published **Blind Love* in the Town and Country Library (1890).

Appleton's Journal, a general literary magazine, published a biographical and critical piece on Collins, 3 September 1870. It includes a description by Collins of his first novel, **Ioláni*, and his unsuccessful attempts to have it published.

Archer, Frank (Arnold, Frank Bishop) (d. 1917 aged 72). English actor who played Julian Gray in the original production of *The *New Magdalen* at the *Olympic in 1873. Collins selected Archer on the recommendation of the *Bancrofts and was enthusiastic about his performance. Archer declined to join the 1875 revival at the Charing Cross Theatre but played the part again at the Novelty during 1884. He was particularly grateful for Collins's advice on story writing and they remained friends for over twenty years. Their last meeting was at *Gloucester Place in December 1887.

Archer, F., *An Actor's Notebook*, London 1912.

(*left*) Frank Archer, the actor
(*right*) Title-page to the 1869 Smith, Elder one-volume edition of *Armadale*

Armadale (book).

'I was wondering . . . whether there is such a thing as chance.'

Collins's longest novel, published in 1866 and dedicated to John *Forster. The story spans two generations of the Armadale families and the complex plot combines several of Collins's favourite themes, including the *supernatural, *identity, murder and *detection. A stage version of *Armadale* was published in 1866 to protect dramatic *copyright. Collins noted in an appendix that he had carefully researched certain aspects of the novel: 'Wherever the story touches on questions connected with Law, Medicine, or Chemistry, it has been submitted, before publication, to the experience of professional men.' The Ladies' Toilette Repository of Mrs *Oldershaw was based on the Bond Street beauty parlour of the infamous Madame Rachel Leverson, and Lydia *Gwilt's criminal past is partly drawn from the famous trial for murder of Madeleine Smith.

Collins wrote in the preface 'Viewed by the Clap-trap morality of the day, this may be a very daring book. Judged by the Christian morality which is of all time, it is simply a book daring enough to speak the truth.' The critics rose to the challenge. *The Spectator* (9 June 1866) considered it 'a discordant mosaic instead of a harmonious picture' and its heroine 'a woman fouler than the refuse of the streets'. *The Saturday Review* (16 June 1866) remarked on Collins's 'strange capacity for weaving extraordinary plots. *Armadale*, from beginning to end, is a lurid labyrinth of improbabilities.' H. F. *Chorley in *The Athenaeum* (2 June 1866) described the book as 'a sensation novel with a vengeance', with 'one of the most hardened female villains whose devices and desires have ever blackened fiction'. In the twentieth century T. S. *Eliot wrote 'The one of Collins's novels which we should choose as the most typical, or as the best of the more typical, and which we should recommend as a specimen of the melodramatic fiction of the epoch, is *Armadale*. It has no merit beyond melodrama, and it has every merit that melodrama can have.' More recent critics, however, have seen psychological depth and complexity as well as melodrama in the novel.

➾ In the Swiss town of Wildbad during 1832, Allan Armadale makes a deathbed confession of murder, written down by the only other British visitor, Mr Neal. The document is sent to Armadale's executors, to be given to his son when he comes of age, warning him never to contact people connected with the confession.

The dying man was born in Barbados and inherited the estate of his godfather, his father's cousin, on the condition that he changed his name to that of Allan Armadale, his godfather's disgraced natural son. After receiving the inheritance, Armadale had fallen in love with the portrait of Jane Blanchard, daughter of a family friend then staying in Madeira. But before he could sail to meet her, he was poisoned by his clerk, Fergus Ingleby. By the time he reached Jane she had married Ingleby, deceiving her father with a letter forged by her young maid. Ingleby was really the disgraced Allan Armadale, marrying Jane in revenge for the loss of his birthright. The married couple escaped on a timber-ship, ironically called *La Grâce de Dieu*, but Armadale followed them disguised as a crew member. The ship was partially wrecked during a hurricane and although Armadale saved Jane, he locked her husband in a cabin, leaving him to drown. Armadale departed for Trinidad where he married a half-caste woman who named their son Allan. Just before coming to Wildbad for his rapidly failing health, Armadale learned that Jane also had an infant son called Allan *Armadale.

The main story begins in 1851 when Jane's son, Allan Armadale, has by a series of accidents inherited the Blanchard family estate at *Thorpe Ambrose, Norfolk. In the intervening years he has been brought up in the West Country by his reclusive mother and the Revd Decimus Brock who knows there is an undisclosed family secret. Shortly after a visit by her former maid to extort money, Jane has died leaving Brock to look after her son. Allan, naïve and immature, takes everything at face value and acts totally on impulse.

Before he takes up his inheritance at Thorpe Ambrose, Allan arranges a sailing trip with his only friend, the dark and mysterious Ozias *Midwinter. While cruising round the Isle of *Man Midwinter receives the letter written by his father in Wildbad nineteen years earlier—he is in fact the other Allan Armadale in the second generation. He shows the document to Brock, also on the trip, and reveals the story of his earlier life. Midwinter had been ill-treated after his mother married Mr Neal. Escaping from school, he took up with a gipsy whose name he was happy to borrow. When the gipsy died, Midwinter continued the hard life of a vagabond, working as a servant, a seaman, and an usher in a school. Dismissed from this last post because of serious illness, he was rescued by Allan Armadale, the first person ever to treat him with kindness.

Midwinter burns the letter, pledging to keep its secrets from Allan, while Brock returns to Somerset now confident that Midwinter will protect his friend. They borrow a boat from the local doctor, Mr Hawbury, and become stranded on board the nearby wreck of the old timber-ship, *La Grâce de Dieu*. Allan falls asleep and dreams of a drowning man, followed by three other visions: the shadow of a woman by a pool at sunset; the shadow of a man with a broken statue; and a man and woman passing him a glass, after which he faints. Midwinter is convinced the dream is supernatural while the doctor argues a rational explanation for all of the predictions.

Allan, now 22, takes up residence at Thorpe Ambrose and innocently upsets the entire neighbourhood as well as offending the family lawyer, Mr Darch. To replace him Allan engages Mr *Pedgift and his son who recommend the elderly Mr Bashwood to teach Midwinter the duties of steward. Bashwood is experienced in this role but lost his previous position when bankrupted by a disreputable son, currently working as a private enquiry agent. The steward's cottage is occupied by Major Milroy, his bedridden wife and their daughter Eleanor (Neelie) *Milroy with whom Allan immediately falls in love.

Jane Blanchard's former maid, the beautiful, red-headed Lydia Gwilt, hears about the inheritance from an old accomplice, Mrs Oldershaw, who encourages her to marry Allan for his money. Miss Gwilt, with the help of false references from Mrs Oldershaw, becomes governess to Miss Milroy. She first meets Allan at Hurle Mere on the Norfolk Broads and although Midwinter realizes she has fulfilled the first vision of the dream both he and Allan fall in love with her. Even the timid Bashwood is besotted with Miss Gwilt and agrees to act as her spy at Thorpe Ambrose.

Mrs Milroy is obsessively jealous of the governess and tricks Allan into making enquiries about Miss Gwilt's references. The resulting scandal puts him in an even worse light with his neighbours and Pedgift resigns when Allan declines to take his advice. Allan also quarrels with Midwinter and when a statuette is knocked over the second vision of the dream is fulfilled. Miss Gwilt realizes there is no chance of marrying Allan and when Midwinter reveals that his true name is also Allan Armadale she conceives a new plot. She has fallen in love with Midwinter, and if she marries him under his real name and can contrive that Allan leaves Thorpe Ambrose and should somehow die, she can return as his widow using the marriage certificate as evidence of her claim on the estate.

Allan goes to London to consult a new lawyer and Miss Gwilt arranges to travel in the same railway compartment. They are spotted by Bashwood, now so jealous that he employs his son to investigate Miss Gwilt's background. They learn that twenty-five years earlier she had been brought up by Mrs Oldershaw before Jane Blanchard took her abroad as a maid. To avoid further scandal after the death of Ingleby, the Blanchards sent her to be educated in France where she took up with a Russian card-sharper. She trapped a rich Englishman called Waldron into marriage but poisoned him when she was suspected of having an affair with a Cuban, Captain Manuel. She was tried and convicted of murder but the case caused such a public outcry that the sentence was quashed and she served just two years in prison for theft. On release, the Cuban married her bigamously but abandoned her after spending the money from Waldron's will. She returned to Mrs Oldershaw who ran a beauty parlour in association with the shady Dr Downward.

Back in London, Miss Gwilt reconciles Midwinter and Allan and secretly marries Midwinter. Needing Allan to keep away from Thorpe Ambrose, she encourages him to see Brock in Somerset and then to visit Naples where she will be living with her husband. Two months later Allan arrives in Italy and one evening after the opera faints when given a drink, so fulfilling the third vision from the dream. Miss Gwilt is approached at the same time by Manuel who tries to blackmail her for money. Instead she arranges for him to captain Allan's new yacht, knowing that the Cuban will rob and kill him.

Miss Gwilt returns to London and enlists the help of Dr Downward. Under the alias Le Doux, he is opening a private sanatorium in *Hampstead where she pretends to be a patient in order to avoid Midwinter. Miss Gwilt sees a newspaper report that Allan's yacht has been sunk and writes to Thorpe Ambrose as his widow. She once again makes use of Bashwood and he informs her that Allan has been miraculously saved and is on his way back to England. Late at night, under the pretext of seeing Miss Milroy, Bashwood lures Allan and Midwinter to the sanatorium where the doctor offers them accommodation. Downward has shown Miss Gwilt the means of killing Allan by filling his room with a deadly gas which leaves no trace; he will seem to have died from natural causes. Midwinter senses that something is wrong and finding an excuse to change rooms is overcome by the gas. Miss Gwilt suddenly realizes her mistake. She still loves Midwinter and drags his unconscious body into the corridor. When she is certain he will live, she writes a confession before killing herself with the poison.

Midwinter allows the world to think Miss Gwilt died naturally while Bashwood loses his reason. Allan marries Miss Milroy leaving Midwinter convinced that the visions were in fact meant to bring the two Armadales closer together.

Serialization. *Cornhill, Nov. 1864–June 1866; *Harper's New Monthly Magazine, Dec. 1864–July 1866.
Book publication
1st English edn. 2 vols, *Smith, Elder, London 1866. Red-brown cloth, front covers blocked in gilt and blind, spines lettered in gilt, pale yellow endpapers. No half-titles. Twenty illustrations by George H. Thomas, nine in vol I and eleven in vol II. Published in June 1866 (advertised as for sale on 18 May).
Vol I (viii) + 304 pp.
Vol II (iv) + 372 pp.
2nd and 3rd edns, 2 vols, 1866.
1-vol edns. Smith, Elder 1867–90; *Chatto & Windus 1891–1920; Dover, New York 1977; World's Classics 1989 (critical edn, edited by C. Peters); Folio Society 1992; Penguin 1995 (critical edn).
1st US edn. *Harpers, New York 1866 (adver-

tised as for sale on 26 May).
Translations. German, Leipzig 1866, 1878; Russian, St Petersburg 1871; Dutch, The Hague 1866, 1875.
Ellis (1931), 37.
Gasson (1980), 67–8.
Page (1974), 145–60.

Armadale (play). Stage adaptation of the novel, written in 1866 to protect dramatic *copyright but never produced. Collins collaborated with *Régnier for an intended French version but ultimately staged the play in England as *Miss Gwilt.* The revised plot had Lydia *Gwilt as a more sympathetic character and Dr Downward as the main villain. It was first performed at the Alexandra Theatre, *Liverpool, 9 December 1875 and opened in London at the *Globe Theatre on 15 April 1876. The part of Mr Darch was played by A. W. *Pinero and the title role by Ada *Cavendish. She also took the play to New York, opening at Wallack's Theatre on 5 June 1879. A *parody entitled *The Gwilty Governess and the Downey Doctor* was staged at Brighton in July 1876.

Armadale: A Drama in Three Acts was 'Published for the Author' in an edition of 25 copies (*Smith, Elder, London 1866, 1 vol, 76 pp, pink paper wrappers). *Miss Gwilt: A Drama in Five Acts* was never published but 'Printed for performance at the Theatre only' (1875, 1 vol, 104 pp, paper wrappers with blue spine).

Armadale, Allan The fair hero of *Armadale* (1866) who inherits *Thorpe Ambrose from the family of his mother, Jane Blanchard. Kept in ignorance that his own father was murdered by *Midwinter's father on *La Grâce de Dieu.* Good-natured, naïve and impulsive, Allan is the object of Lydia *Gwilt's unsuccessful machinations first to marry and then to kill him for money.

Arrowsmith, J. W. (d. 1913). Bristol publisher of *The *Guilty River* as 'Arrowsmith's Christmas Annual' for 1886; re-issued as no. 19 in the 'Bristol Library', 1887. Arrowsmith liked the story and, having printed a large edition, launched it with advertising on posters, shopcards and 'sandwich men'. Although 20,000 copies sold in a week, Arrowsmith never-

theless complained to A. P. *Watt in 1889 that he still had 25,000 copies left.

Athenaeum London club founded in 1824 by *Scott, Davy, Faraday and others for those associated with literature, science and the arts. William *Collins and David *Wilkie were founder members. Named after the Roman Athenaeum of Hadrian.

Collins was elected on 16 April 1861 under Rule II of the club by invitation of the General Committee for 'persons of distinguished eminence in Science, Literature or the Arts'. He was proposed by Richard Monckton Milnes, MP (later Lord Houghton). The entrance fee was £30 and the annual subscription £7.

Collins remained a member until his death in 1889, seconding Charles *Kent in 1880 and Frederick *Lehmann in 1886. In the latter case he was too ill to attend for the ballot and confessed that he had not entered the club for many years. The Athenaeum currently holds the copy of Michael Kelly's *Reminiscences with Original Anecdotes* (1826) from Collins's library, with his annotations.

Atlantic Monthly, The New England literary journal, founded in 1857. First published Collins's 'The *Biter Bit' under the title 'Who is the Thief?' in April 1858.

auctions After his death on 23 September 1889, the majority of Collins's manu-

Front cover to later re-issue of *The Guilty River*, published by J. W. Arrowsmith

CATALOGUE

OF

THE COLLECTION OF

MODERN PICTURES,

Water-Colour Drawings, & Engravings,

OF

WILKIE COLLINS,

DECEASED;

Portraits by G. Romney and others,

THE PROPERTY OF

JOHN CARWARDINE, ESQ.,

DECEASED;

ALSO,

PICTURES FROM THE COLLECTIONS

OF

LORD ACTON,

AND THE

RT. HON. E. PLEYDELL BOUVERIE,

DECEASED;

WHICH

Will be Sold by Auction, by

MESSRS. CHRISTIE, MANSON & WOODS,

AT THEIR GREAT ROOMS,

8, KING STREET, ST. JAMES'S SQUARE,

On SATURDAY, FEBRUARY 22, 1890,

AT ONE O'CLOCK PRECISELY.

——⚬✦⚬——

May be viewed Two days preceding, and Catalogues had, at Messrs. CHRISTIE, MANSON and WOODS' Offices, 8, *King Street, St. James's Square, S.W.*

Auction catalogue of Collins's pictures, sold by Christie, Manson & Woods, 22 February 1890

short stories by Collins. *The Woman in White* includes a note in Collins's hand describing its book publication on 16 August 1860 (see illustration on p. 159).

Sotheby, 14 July 1898. Lots 596–602, 'Original Manuscripts of Wilkie Collins' Plays'.

Hodgson & Co, 6–7 Dec. 1923. Lots 213–44, 'Original MSS of Novels and Plays by William Wilkie Collins'. (Several lots from earlier sales.)

Australia Collins never visited Australia but it provided a convenient destination for various characters. Several of his works, including *The Frozen Deep*, *The Law and the Lady* and *The Two Destinies*, were published in Melbourne. Collins was always careful that any part-publication should never precede that in England. After the death of his local agent, *Biers, he wrote to Wybert *Reeve in July 1886 about *The Evil Genius*: 'My new novel—now shortly to be published in book-form—has appeared previously in various newspapers, and the speculator, purchasing all serial rights in England and the Colonies (for the largest sum that I have ever received), managed Australian publication himself.' Wybert Reeve also produced his own stage adaptation of *No Name* for the Australian theatre.

At least two titles, *Heart and Science* (1883) and *Little Novels* (1887) were published by George Robertson of Melbourne 'by special arrangement with the proprietors of the English Copyright'. Robertson (1825–98) was a bookseller and publisher who opposed the admission of American *pirated editions. He installed a lithographic plant and bindery, and imported the stereotype plates of overseas books for which he had secured the local rights. In 1872 he moved to a large warehouse, appropriately located in Little Collins Street.

Australia is mentioned in several Collins stories. Frank Softly in *A Rogue's Life* is transported there and, although they were never written, Collins intended a further series of adventures in Australia. Noah Truscott in 'The *Diary of Anne Rodway' (1856) is also transported and Magdalen helps her maid, Louisa, emigrate there in *No Name* (1862). *Letters*.

scripts, books, pictures and effects were sold at the following auctions:

Catalogue of the Sale of the Furniture of the Late Wilkie Collins, Walter Holcombe, 24 Oct. 1889.

Catalogue of the Interesting Library of Modern Books of the Late Wilkie Collins, Esq., Puttick and Simpson, 20 Jan. 1890. 246 Lots. Includes numerous presentation copies; Mejan's *Recueil des causes célèbres; Ellis's Polynesian Researches*, source for *Ioláni; Byron's *Life, Letters, and Journals;* Defoe's *Life and Adventures of Robinson Crusoe;* *Brandling's *Views in the North of France;* Nordhoff's *Communistic Societies of the United States*, used for *The

Fallen Leaves; and Kelly's *Reminiscences with Original Anecdotes,* now in the *Athenaeum library.

Catalogue of the Collection of Modern Pictures, Water-Colour Drawing & Engraving, of Wilkie Collins, Deceased. Christie, Manson & Woods, 22 Feb. 1890. 66 Lots, 24 by William *Collins; others by Charles *Collins, J. E. *Millais, A. *Geddes, J. *Linnell and Mrs *Carpenter.

Catalogue of the Original Manuscripts, by Charles Dickens and Wilkie Collins. Sotheby, Wilkinson & Hodge, 18 June 1890. Includes *The Frozen Deep* (play and book), *The Perils of Certain English Prisoners,* and 29 manuscripts of novels and

Balzac, Honoré de (1799–1850). French novelist and author of the *Comédie Humaine*, a series of interconnected novels and stories written between 1827 and 1847. Conceived as a fictional representation of French society, the books also demonstrate Balzac's interest in the supernatural and mysterious.

Collins greatly admired Balzac, considering him, along with *Scott and *Cooper, one of his three 'Kings of Fiction'. He also called him one of the great geniuses 'who leave their mark ineffaceably on the literature of their age'. Collins's translation of 'Épisode sous la Terreur' was published as 'The *Midnight Mass'. His library contained the 45-volume complete edition of Balzac's works (Paris 1859–69).

See also FRENCH LITERATURE.

Collins, W., 'Portrait of an Author, Painted by his Publisher', *All the Year Round*, 18 and 25 June 1859; reprinted in *My Miscellanies* (1863).

Bancroft, Sir Squire (1841–1926) and **Lady Marie Effie**, née Wilton (1839–1921). Joint actor-managers of the *Prince of Wales Theatre. Marie Wilton and Squire Bancroft had similar backgrounds in comedy and married in 1867. Gradu-

ally they turned to more serious drama with *Man and Wife* as their first such venture. They became firm friends with Collins from their early negotiations in 1871. The Bancrofts moved to the larger Haymarket Theatre in July 1880 but retired from management in 1885. Their artistic and administrative reforms helped to make the theatre world more respectable.

The Bancrofts were also technical innovators. Electric light was used for the first time on the English stage to create a storm scene in *Man and Wife*, and the scenery gave the illusion of moving clouds. Marie and Squire Bancroft took the small parts of Blanche Lundie and Dr Speedwell. They seriously considered playing Miss Clack and Sergeant *Cuff in *The Moonstone* but decided it was too melodramatic for the Prince of Wales.

The Bancrofts wrote three volumes of reminiscences which include correspondence with Collins. They also describe the production of *Man and Wife*, Collins's first-night nerves, and his use of *opium.

Bancroft, M. and S., *Mr and Mrs Bancroft: On and off the Stage* (2 vols), London 1888.
Bancroft, M. and S., *The Bancrofts: Recollections of Sixty Years*, London 1909.
Bancroft, S., *Empty Chairs*, London 1925.

Doris Bartley as Doris Beresford, her stage name

Bartley, Doris Elizabeth (Dah), (Doris Beresford) (b. 1879). Eldest daughter of Harriet Elizabeth and Henry Powell *Bartley; Collins's god-daughter. Musical comedy actress with the stage name Doris Beresford. Played the leading role in *My Girl*, 1899. Joined George Edwardes' Gaiety Theatre appearing in *The Messenger Boy*, *The Toreador* and *The Orchid*. Married actor Louis Bishop and subsequently Ivo Locke, a mining engineer, in 1910.

Doris was followed on to the musical stage by her three sisters, Cecile Marguerite (Cissie), Evelyn Beatrice (Bollie, stage name Eve Bevington) and Iris Dora.

Bartley, Harriet Elizabeth (Carrie) née Graves (1851–1905). Only child of *Caroline and George Graves, her mother's first husband; dedicatee of *The Legacy of Cain* (1888). 'Elizabeth Harriet' on her birth certificate ('Lizzie'), she inverted her name to 'Harriet Elizabeth' during the 1870s and signed herself 'Harriet E. L. Graves'. She lost her father before she was a year old and was about 7

Marie Bancroft

Squire Bancroft as Dr Speedwell in *Man and Wife*

when her mother and Wilkie began living together. Collins, who referred to her as his 'godchild', treated her as an adopted daughter and always called her 'Carrie'. Charles *Dickens referred to her as 'The Butler'. Wilkie took care to see she had a happy childhood and Carrie became extremely fond of him. As she grew

(top) Harriet Bartley in the late 1870s
(above) Letter written by Harriet Bartley in 1889, after Collins's death, signed as his adopted daughter and amanuensis

up she often acted as his amanuensis. Her handwriting appears for the first time in the manuscript of *The Moonstone*, when Collins was ill and in too much pain to write himself. After this she often wrote from his dictation and continued to do so after her marriage. Caroline married Joseph *Clow in 1868 and Carrie, aged 17½, remained with Wilkie.

In 1878 Carrie married Henry Powell *Bartley, a solicitor who subsequently acted for Collins. They had five daughters (one of whom died in infancy) but the marriage was not happy. Henry Bartley was a dishonest spendthrift who dissipated most of the property left by Collins. He then abandoned his family, leaving his wife and children in poverty, dependent on the charity of his mother. Carrie was reduced to selling her mementoes of Wilkie Collins such as his travelling writing desk—bought by A. P. *Watt in 1901, four years before her death.
    Clarke (1988).
    Peters (1991).

Bartley, Henry Powell (1854–97). Son-in-law of Caroline *Graves, married Harriet Graves in March 1878. Henry Bartley succeeded William *Tindell as Collins's solicitor in 1877. He practised at Somerset Street, Portman Square, a few hundred yards from Collins's home in *Gloucester Place. Together with Sebastian *Schlesinger and Frank *Beard, Bartley became co-executor of Collins's *will.

Bartley had been a visitor to *Ramsgate both before and after his marriage to Harriet. He shared Collins's love of *sailing and moored his yacht, *Doris*, in the harbour there. Bartley received several large cheques from Collins, and in 1893 sold the 1850 *Millais portrait to the National Portrait Gallery to raise funds. Ultimately Bartley's extravagant lifestyle destroyed the inheritance that Collins had so carefully worked out for his two 'families'. Bartley died of cancer in Guildford in August 1897.
    Clarke (1988).

Basil: A Story of Modern Life Novel published in 1852 and dedicated to Charles *Ward. Collins's second full-length work of fiction and first contemporary novel. In the introduction, he warns the reader that he has 'not hesitated to violate the conventionalities of sentimental fiction'. *Basil* is sometimes

regarded as an early example of, if not the first, *sensation novel. The author also declares his interest in drama, 'Believing that the Novel and the Play are twin-sisters in the family of Fiction'.

Collins claimed that the main event of the story was founded on a fact within his own knowledge. This could be the secret marriage, based on that of *Edward and *Henrietta Ward. It might possibly refer more closely to Collins, since throughout the book there are links to his own life. Basil, like Collins, has a snobbish father who misunderstands him, and chooses the Bar as a stepping-stone to literature. He has travelled on the Continent to research locations for his partly written historical romance. Basil follows Margaret Sherwin to her home just north of Regent's Park, close to where Collins lived in *Hanover Terrace during 1852. The later chapters are set in *Cornwall with descriptive writing familiar to readers of *Rambles Beyond Railways*, published the year before.

Basil received a mixed reception. Collins's literary friends gave good reviews and *Dickens wrote 'the story contains admirable writing' and 'I have made Basil's acquaintance with great gratification.' The *Athenaeum*, however, called *Basil* 'a tale of criminality, almost revolting from its domestic horrors' and the *Westminster Review* described it as 'absolutely disgusting'. Mrs *Oliphant later called the novel 'a revolting story' and the critics harked back to it even in their obituaries of Collins. The *Daily News* termed it 'a domestic story of a somewhat revolting kind' and claimed, quite erroneously, that Collins 'was not long in perceiving and repenting the errors of taste' and was 'accustomed to buy up and destroy a copy of the three volume edition if it came his way.' In an addition to the preface for the 1862 edition, Collins stoutly defended the 'purity' of the novel and maintained that 'Slowly and surely, my story forced its way through all adverse criticism, to a place in the public favour which it has never lost since.' However, he did shorten the text with hundreds of small amendments and one or two longer cuts which toned down the violence of the original version.
    ➤ Basil is the younger son of a proud, stern father and comes of an ancient, noble family. He has a devoted younger sister, Clara, and a wild but good-natured

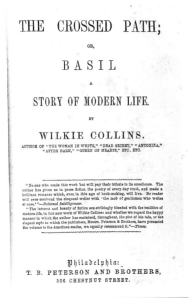

Title-page to the 1860 American edition of *Basil* published by Peterson as *The Crossed Path*

older brother, Ralph. Travelling home, on impulse by omnibus, Basil falls in love at first sight with Margaret Sherwin, a linen-draper's daughter. He follows her home to the newly built suburbs north of Regent's Park and, after contriving a meeting, asks her father for permission to marry; but because of his own father's certain opposition, the marriage should be kept secret. Mr Sherwin agrees on condition that the marriage takes place within the week but is not consummated for one year, since Margaret is only just seventeen. The delay will give Basil time to persuade his father to accept the marriage, and he cannot be forced to withdraw from it. The marriage duly takes place and Basil spends the next few months visiting Margaret every evening under the supervision of the mildly deranged Mrs Sherwin. He tries unsuccessfully to improve Margaret's mind and after overhearing two of her tantrums begins to doubt her character.

Sherwin's confidential clerk, Robert Mannion, returns from a business trip to France. Mannion's previous background is cloaked in secrecy and he has a strange power over the family. Nevertheless, he professes friendship and uses his influence for Basil's benefit. After a strained visit to his father's country house, Basil returns to find both Margaret and Man-

nion changed. On the evening before his year's 'probation' is completed, Basil is disconcerted that Margaret has gone to a party and will be escorted home by Mannion. He decides to collect her himself but sees her leave early with his rival. Basil follows them to a hotel and through a thin partition wall hears Mannion seduce Margaret. Basil waits and attacks Mannion, hurling him to the ground with such force that he is permanently disfigured and loses the sight of one eye. Basil collapses into delirium.

On recovering, he realizes that Margaret is as much to blame as Mannion, despite threatening letters from Sherwin defending her. Basil confesses the ignoble marriage to his father who disowns him, tearing his name from the record in the family Bible. Mannion writes from hospital, revealing his secret past. When his father, a gentleman who lived beyond his means, was to be hanged for forgery, Basil's father, Mannion's patron, refused to intervene. Mannion had lived a miserable existence under assumed names until a friend arranged employment with Sherwin where he made himself indispensable. He had watched Margaret develop and despite her deceitful nature regarded her as his prize. Basil's marriage had compounded the family offence and Mannion resolved to take revenge by ruining his happiness and reputation.

Ralph returns from the Continent and visits Sherwin to buy his silence. He fortuitously obtains a letter written by Mannion which confirms Margaret's guilt. Margaret, visiting Mannion in hospital, contracts typhus from which she dies. Basil sees her when she is at the point of death, forgives her and leaves London for Cornwall. Mannion forces him to leave the fishing village where he is staying and confronts him on the cliff tops. While gloating over his revenge, Mannion falls to his death on the rocks below. The shock causes Basil to collapse. He is brought back to London by Ralph and Clara and reconciled with his father. After writing his history, Basil retires to the country to live quietly with Clara.

Book publication

1st edn. 3 vols, Richard *Bentley, London 1852. Blue cloth, covers blocked in blind, spines lettered in gilt. Red-brown endpapers. Half-title in vol I. Published 16 Nov. 1852. Variant binding issued simultaneously in paper boards, half cloth, with white endpapers.

Vol I 300 pp (6–21 paginated in roman numerals; text on pp (25)–300).

Vol II (ii) + 304 pp.

Vol III (ii) + 302 pp.

1-vol edns. James *Blackwood, London 1856; *Sampson Low 1862; *Smith, Elder 1865–72; *Chatto & Windus 1875–1910. Dover, New York 1980; World's Classics 1990 (critical edition, edited by D. Goldman).

US edns. *Appleton, New York 1853; *Peterson, Philadelphia [1860] (as *The Crossed Path*).

Daily News, 24 Sept. 1889, p 6.

Page (1974).

Goldman, D., introduction to World's Classics edition of *Basil*, Oxford 1990.

Beard, Francis Carr (Frank), FRCS (1814–93). Collins's doctor and close friend for thirty years; dedicatee of *No Name*, and co-executor of his will. Beard qualified as a general practitioner and practised first at 215 Oxford Street and later at 44 Welbeck Street, close to Collins in *Gloucester Place and *Wimpole Street. His older brother, Thomas, was known as 'Dickens's earliest friend' and Beard was doctor to the Dickens household from 1859. Beard first attended Collins in 1861, and prescribed *laudanum for his 'rheumatic *gout'. He also treated Caroline *Graves, and Collins's mother in her last illness. Collins frequently asked his advice on medical points for his novels and even accompanied him to a running track when writing *Man and Wife.

Beard occasionally acted as amanuensis when Collins's eyes were bandaged because of gout and he was unable to write. In October 1868, he was a witness with Collins at Caroline Grave's wedding to Joseph *Clow. Collins's last note in September 1889 ('I am dying—old friend') was addressed to Beard.

Francis Beard's son, Nathaniel, became chief clerk of *Bentley's in its later years. He included several personal anecdotes about Collins in 'Some Recollections of Yesterday', *Temple Bar, 102 (July 1894), 315–39.

Belgravia: A London Magazine (1866–99). Illustrated monthly published by John Maxwell. The most important contributor was Mary *Braddon who founded the magazine and edited it until 1876 when it was sold to *Chatto & Windus. She described it as 'The best bait for the shillings of Brixton and Bow'. Its companion was the *Belgravia Annual*, published at Christmas. Authors included *Besant, *Harte, Hardy, Ouida, and Collins who contributed the following novels and short stories:

Belgravia
'The Captain's Last Love', Jan. 1877.
The Haunted Hotel, June–Nov. 1878.
'How I Married Him', Jan. 1882.
Heart and Science, Aug. 1882–June 1883.
'An Old Maid's Husband', Jan. 1887.

Belgravia Annual
'A Shocking Story', 1878.
'Your Money or Your Life', 1881.

Belinfante Brothers Dutch publishers in The Hague, issuing *Man and Wife* in their periodical *Stuivers Magazyn* in 1870. Holland was one of the last countries to implement international *copyright and in November 1869 Belinfante applied to *Cassells for the stereotype plates, or 'clichés' of the illustrations, for

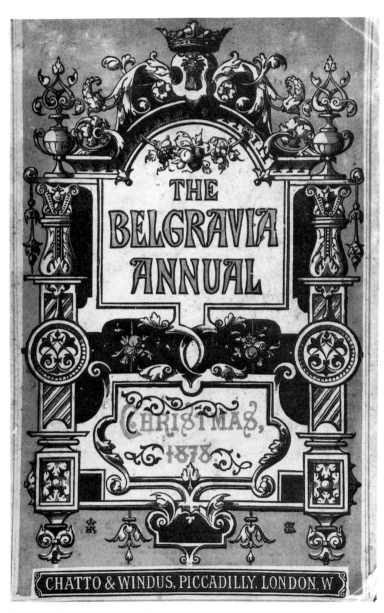

The 1878 issue of the *Belgravia Annual* which published 'A Shocking Story'

Man and Wife. Cassells referred them to Collins and Belinfante duly wrote to 'Madame Wilkie Collins' applying for access to the plates. In return they offered only a copy of the magazine, to which Collins replied:

The trumpet of Fame, gentlemen, has played the wrong tune in your ears. I am not the charming person whom you suppose me to be. I wear trowsers; I have a vote for Parliament; I possess a beard; in two dreadful words, I am—a Man. . . . I observe with profound surprise and regret that your request for permission to publish my book in Holland, in your magazine, is not accompanied by the slightest hint of any intention on your part of paying for the privilege. All that you offer me is a copy of the magazine. What am I to do with a copy of the magazine? I don't understand Dutch. All that I can do is to look at your magazine, and mourn over my own neglected education.

Collins went on to suggest they should in honour make some payment, however small, and pointed out that Baron *Tauchnitz always did so. Belinfante's reply, sticking to their original position, then evoked a more indignant response from Collins:

What am I to say to men who acknowledge that they . . . derive profit from publishing my book, and who, owning this, not only repudiate the bare idea of being under any pecuniary obligations toward me as the writer of the book, but shamelessly assert their own act of spoliation to be a right—because no law happens to exist which prohibits that act as a wrong? . . . What is to prevent men who trade on such principles as these from picking my pocket if they see their way to making a profit out of my handkerchief?

He warned them that he would openly expose 'the principles on which Dutch publishers trade' by sending the correspondence to an English newspaper, in order to deter 'other persons of larcenous literary habits'. The correspondence was published in both *The Echo* and *Harper's Weekly* and produced an unexpectedly positive result. On 30 November Collins wrote to the editor of *The Echo*, 'Messrs. Belinfante Brothers concede the point . . . they consent to recognise my moral claim on them, as author, by giving me a share in the profits produced by my book.' Belinfante also agreed to treat other English authors in the same way.

The principle mattered to Collins more than the money. He wrote to Cassells in July 1871:

LA DYNASTIE DES BENTLEY

Edward   Samuel   Richard senior   George   Richard junior

The Bentley Dynasty

Belinfante Brothers have made a noble effort. They have sent me as the purchase-money for *Man and Wife* the sum of one hundred guilders—amounting in English money to between £8 and £9! As they have never hitherto paid sixpence to any other author (but a Dutchman) in this civilised universe, I feel bound to consider myself as the object of an act of extraordinary munificence.

Belinfante therefore published *Man and Wife* with Collins's full approval. Between 1875 and 1877 they issued thirteen of his works in a special 'Collins-editie' and by 1885 had published a total of twenty-five titles, including 'The Dead Alive' (1874), *The Haunted Hotel* (1879), *The Black Robe* (1881), *'I Say No'* (1884) and 'The Girl at the Gate' (1885).

> Flower, D., 'Authors and Copyright in the Nineteenth Century, with Unpublished Letters from Wilkie Collins', *Book-Collector's Quarterly*, no. 7 (July–Sept. 1932), 1–35. *Brinkmans Cumulatieve Catalogus* (Dutch National Bibliography).
> *The Echo*, 24 Nov. 1869 (p 3) and 1 Dec. 1869 (p 3).

Bentley, Richard & Son Nineteenth-century publishers, founded in 1829 as a partnership between Richard Bentley (1794–1871) and Henry Colburn. After an acrimonious three years, Colburn left at the termination of their agreement in 1832. Bentley continued to run the firm from the offices in New Burlington Street. He created the Standard Novels and Romances, a series that eventually ran to 127 titles, and also founded *Bentley's Miscellany* in 1837.

Collins's connection with Richard Bentley began with the publication of *Antonina* (27 February 1850). It was followed by *Rambles Beyond Railways* (30 January 1851), *Mr Wray's Cash-Box* (December 1851), *Basil* (16 November 1852) and *Hide and Seek* (6 June 1854). Collins also made several contributions to the *Miscellany*.

In 1853, Bentley tried to change the market for first editions, at that time sold in three volumes at 31s. 6d. The price was dictated by the *circulating libraries and Bentley wanted to reduce it to 10s. 6d. Collins enthusiastically agreed to participate for his next novel although the plan never proceeded. It was also intended that *Basil* should appear in Bentley's Railroad Library (Bentley's Shilling Series) during 1854 but the title was bought by James *Blackwood.

The business had suffered for several years from financial problems that came to a head in the 1850s. Bentley sold the *Miscellany* in 1854 and invited authors to buy back their copyrights. Collins declined *Antonina* and *Basil* for £200, even on deferred terms, since his own finances were strained after his trip to *Italy and sales of *Hide and Seek* were proving slow.

George Bentley (1828–95) joined his father in the firm during 1845. He first made contact with Collins in 1851 and regularly invited him to his Wednesday evening soirées. In 1863 he called Collins the 'King of inventors'. Richard Bentley was injured in a railway accident in 1867 after which George took over the management of the business. In 1871 he hoped that Collins could influence *Forster whose biography George felt misrepre-

sented the earlier quarrel between Dickens and Richard Bentley.

After an interval of eighteen years, Collins returned to Richard Bentley & Son with the publication of *Poor Miss Finch* (January 1872). Collins's negotiations with the firm had always involved hard bargaining but in this instance he showed great fairness. The novel was still running in *Cassell's Magazine* when it was offered to *Mudie and *Smith. They realized that it would soon be available much more cheaply as a single volume bound up from parts from Cassell and placed a negligible order for the *threedecker. Collins immediately offered to refund half the money Bentley had paid him.

Bentley published *Miss or Mrs?* and *The New Magdalen* during 1873 and *The Frozen Deep and Other Stories* in 1874. The last two titles followed successful serialization in *Temple Bar*. Collins also negotiated with Bentley to issue his earlier works in a 6s. edition but eventually accepted a better offer from *Chatto. Bentley's final Collins publication was *A Rogue's Life* in 1879.

George Bentley's son, also Richard (1854–1936), became an active partner in 1884. He ran the firm for its last five years until selling it to Macmillan in 1898 for £8,000. The chief clerk in the later years was Frank *Beard's son, Nathaniel.

> Chesnau, E., *Richard Bentley and Son*, privately printed 1886. (Reprinted from *Le Livre* of October 1885, with some additional notes.)
> Gettman, R. A., *A Victorian Publisher: A Study of the Bentley Papers*, Cambridge 1960.
> Sadleir, M., 'The Camel's Back' in *Nineteenth Century Essays*, Oxford 1948, 127–32.

Bentley's Miscellany (1837–68). Influential literary magazine noted mainly for its fiction, founded in 1837 by Richard *Bentley. Its first editor was *Dickens who had agreed to contribute two novels. The first of these, *Oliver Twist*, was published in 1837–8 but Dickens fell out with Bentley during 1839 over both payment and editorial interference. He subsequently called him 'the Burlington Street Brigand'. W. Harrison Ainsworth succeeded Dickens, secretly purchasing the *Miscellany* for £1,700 in 1854. He remained editor until 1868 when it was absorbed into *Temple Bar*. Collins contributed the following stories and essays. (The payments noted are derived from the Bentley Papers held in the British Library.)

'The *Twin Sisters', Mar. 1851 (£8 17s. 6d.)

'A Pictorial Tour to St George Bosherville', May 1851 (£10 10s. 2d.)

'The Exhibition of the Royal Academy', June 1851 (£6 18s. 0d.) (See the PRE-RAPHAELITE BROTHERHOOD.)

'The Picture Galleries of England 1, The Earl of Ellesmere's Collection', July 1851 (£6 11s. 0d.)

'The Picture Galleries of England 2, Northumberland House and Syon House', Aug. 1851 (£7 4s. 6d.)

'The Picture Galleries of England 3, Dulwich Gallery', Oct. 1851 (£5 11s. 6d.)

'A *Passage in the Life of Mr Perugino Potts', Feb. 1852 (£7 17s. 6d.)

'The *Midnight Mass', June 1852 (£5 5s. 0d.) (a translation with possible assistance by Collins of *Balzac's story 'Episode sous la Terreur').

'*Nine O'Clock', Aug. 1852 (£8 4s. 0d.)

Benzon, Elizabeth (Lizbeth). Sister of Frederick *Lehmann and friend of Collins. Married to Ernst Benzon of the engineering firm Naylor Vickers. They lived at 10 Kensington Palace Gardens where they entertained literary, artistic and musical friends. Elizabeth was a music lover and fine amateur singer. Collins attended a concert with her in February 1869 and confided his attempts to give up *opium.

Lehmann, J., *Ancestors and Friends*, London 1962.

Letters.

Beresford, Doris See BARTLEY, DORIS ELIZABETH.

Berger, Francesco (1834–1933). Popular composer and pianist. Friend of George *Critchett, Collins's ophthalmologist, and a member of Dickens's amateur theatrical troupe. He wrote the music for The *Lighthouse in 1855 and his overture to The *Frozen Deep (1857), dedicated to Dickens, was published as part of the fund-raising for Douglas *Jerrold's widow.

Berger, F., *Reminiscences, Impressions and Anecdotes*, London 1913, 18–40.

Besant, Sir Walter (1836–1901). English novelist and essayist. Social reformer and founder of the *Society of Authors in 1884. Collaborated with James Rice on several best-selling novels from 1871 until Rice's death in 1882. Besant contributed twelve Christmas numbers to *All the Year Round* from 1876 to 1887, the first six also with Rice.

In August 1889, Collins realized that he was too ill to finish *Blind Love, then being serialized in the *Illustrated London News. Collins suggested that A. P. *Watt should approach Besant, a long-standing friend and popular novelist: 'if he has the time I think he will do it . . . he knows that I would do the same for him if he were in my place.' Besant agreed to complete the novel and received Collins's working notes. He was surprised to find they represented a detailed scenario with fragments of dialogue already inserted. Besant was 'careful to adhere faithfully and exactly to the plot, scene by scene, down to the smallest detail as it was laid down by the author'. He later persuaded Andrew *Chatto to allow him 'to write a preface stating my share in the book . . . to give the real facts of the case'.

Preface to *Blind Love* (1890).

Wolff, R. L., *Nineteenth-Century Fiction: A Bibliographical Catalogue*, 5 vols, New York and London 1981, 257.

Betteredge, Gabriel In *The Moonstone*, faithful old House-steward of Lady Julia Verinder. Likeable pipe-smoking eccentric who guides his life by constant reference to *Robinson Crusoe*. With his detailed knowledge of the family history, the principal narrator of the story.

Biers, H. (d. 1886). Friend of Collins, and his agent in *Australia. Biers settled in Melbourne and was given a power of attorney for Australia and New Zealand in December 1875. He arranged the publication of The *Two Destinies (1876), *Heart and Science (1883), *'I Say No' (1884) and probably other stories. Collins acknowledged Biers's 'unremitting devotion' to his literary interests for over twenty years and after Biers's death in 1886 A. P. *Watt was asked to handle the Australian rights.

Letters.

Francesco Berger

MR. WALTER BESANT

Sir Walter Besant, from a drawing in 1888

'Biter Bit, The' Short story originally published as 'Who is the Thief?' in *The *Atlantic Monthly*, April 1858; reprinted in *The *Queen of Hearts* (1859) as 'Brother Griffith's Story of The Biter Bit'. Early example of a humorous *detective story, featuring a comically inept detective and other features of the genre.

➥ Mathew Sharpin is seconded from his position as a lawyer's clerk to the Detective Police. He bungles an investigation into Mr Yatman's stolen banknotes while mistakenly pursuing an eloping couple. To the gratification of his superiors who have been promoted on merit, they are easily able to deduce from his rambling reports that the true culprit is the extravagant Mrs Yatman.

Black and White: A Love Story in Three Acts Play written by Collins from an idea by Charles *Fechter who suggested the outline of the first two acts. With Fechter's agreement, Collins provided the ending, developed the characters and wrote the dialogue. The story is set in Trinidad in 1830 and treats the theme of slavery. The English villain, Stephen Westcraft, competes with the Count de Layrac for the hand of an heiress, Miss Milburn. He discovers that the Count is actually of mixed race and legally a slave. He buys him at auction but

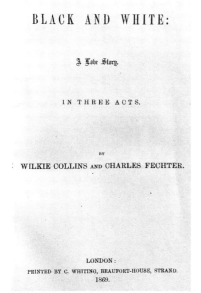

Title-page to the printed version of the play *Black and White*, written by Collins and Charles Fechter in 1869

by another technicality the Count is freed. Fechter played the part of Maurice de Layrac. His leading lady, Carlotta Leclerq, took the part of Miss Milburn.

The play opened at the *Adelphi on 29 March 1869 and ran for about sixty nights followed by an unsuccessful provincial tour. Collins considered it a better play than *No Thoroughfare* but felt it achieved only limited success because English audiences had been saturated with adaptations of *Uncle Tom's Cabin*. *Black and White* was also staged at the Globe Theatre, Boston, from 26 December 1870. In England the play was printed for acting purposes by C. Whiting but never published (56 pp, white paper wrappers). It also appeared in de Witt's Acting Plays (no 296), New York [nd].

'Black Cottage, The' Short story originally published as 'The Siege of the Black Cottage' in *Harper's New Monthly Magazine*, Feb. 1857; reprinted in *The *Queen of Hearts* (1859) as 'Brother Owen's Story of the Black Cottage'.

➥ Bessie is a stonemason's daughter left alone in her cottage on the moors one night to look after a valuable pocketbook. She successfully protects herself, the money and Polly, the cat, from two violent burglars. An early example by Collins of a courageous and resourceful female character.

Black Robe, The

'True remorse depends, to my mind, on a man's accurate knowledge of his own motives.'

Anti-Jesuit novel published in 1881 which elaborates on a theme first used in 'The *Yellow Mask' (1855). In both, a high-ranking Catholic priest schemes to recover property he considers to belong rightfully to the Church. Mr Murthwaite, the renowned traveller from *The Moonstone* (1868), makes a very brief appearance as does Dr Wybrow, first seen in *The Haunted Hotel* (1879). Collins wrote to William *Winter in September 1881 that it was thought in 'Roman Catholic countries as well as Protestant England, to be the best thing I have written for some time. And it is especially memorable to me as having produced a freely offered gift of forty pounds from one of the pirates on the American side!!!' The pirate was probably George Munro of the *Seaside Library.

Binding of the 1881 first edition of *The Black Robe*, published by Chatto & Windus

➥ Lewis Romayne, accompanied by his old friend Major Hynd, is in Boulogne to see his dying aunt. He is involved in a quarrel over a card game, challenged to a duel and accidentally kills his opponent. The plaintive screams of the dead Frenchman's younger brother afterwards haunt Romayne for ever.

Distracted with remorse, Romayne returns first to London and then to his Yorkshire home, Vange Abbey, confiscated at the dissolution of the monasteries and given to one of his ancestors by Henry VIII. Even at Vange he still hears the French boy's voice and escapes to London to visit another old friend, Lord Loring, head of a prominent Catholic family. Staying with Lady Loring is Stella Eyrecourt who falls in love with Romayne. Father Benwell, the Lorings' spiritual adviser, is determined to convert Romayne and restore Vange to the Church with the help of the young priest Arthur Penrose.

Romayne, vulnerable and still troubled by the duel, sends Major Hynd to enquire about the Frenchman's family, now living in London, hoping he can at least assist them financially. He also confides in Penrose who, despite his ulterior motives, forms a genuine friendship with Romayne and accepts that marriage to Stella, though she is a Protestant, is best for his long-term happiness.

Benwell plans to undermine the marriage and introduces Romayne to the wealthy Bernard Winterfield who he knows has a past connection with Stella. When Stella's worldly mother is taken ill Benwell meets her physician, Dr Wybrow, who innocently mentions Stella's earlier romance with Winterfield. Wybrow also talks of a deranged French boy (in fact the duellist's brother) found with papers stolen from Winterfield. Benwell agrees to return the documents but first breaks the seal to discover they contain a confession from Winterfield's separated wife Emma, now dead, a circus performer and a drunkard. Jealous of his love for Stella, Emma arranged for a false announcement of her death to be put in the papers, and then greeted him outside the church after the bigamous marriage ceremony. Stella was immediately removed by her relatives and the marriage hushed up.

Penrose is called to Rome and then sent to a mission in America. Benwell resolves to manage Romayne's conversion himself and succeeds where Penrose failed. Romayne, not knowing that Stella is pregnant, goes to a retreat where Benwell cleverly manoeuvres him into leaving Vange Abbey to the Church in his will. Benwell also tells Romayne that in the eyes of the Church he is still a single man. Winterfield's registry office wedding to his first wife, though legal, is not recognized by the Catholic authorities. His second marriage to Stella, although annulled by the courts, is irrevocably recognized by the Church. Romayne's own marriage to Stella is therefore void and he is free to fulfil his vocation to become a priest.

Stella leaves England to live with her mother in Paris. Winterfield, still in love with Stella, is anxious to avoid any further scandal. He therefore takes a long sailing trip to the East, returning via Rome where he learns that Romayne has made rapid advancement in the church because of his diplomatic skills. Reading a report in *The Times* by Mr Murthwaite that Penrose is held captive by American Indians, Winterfield embarks on a successful rescue.

Romayne has been promoted to an ecclesiastical post in Paris but, knowing he is dying, consents for the first time to see Stella and his son. Benwell brings Romayne's family lawyer to his death-bed to

confirm the validity of the will and ensure that the Church can inherit Vange. In his last moments, Romayne finally acknowledges his love for his wife and child and the will is destroyed. The inheritance passes to his family and not to the Church. Stella fulfils Romayne's final wish and marries Winterfield.

Serialization. The Sheffield and Rotherham Independent Supplement, 2 Oct. 1880–26 Mar. 1881 ('Specially written for The Independent'), and several other provincial newspapers; *The *Canadian Monthly*, Nov. 1880–June 1881.

Book publication

1st edn. 3 vols, *Chatto & Windus, London 1881. Black cloth, covers blocked in white, spines lettered in gilt. Blue and white floral endpapers. Half-title in each vol. Published in April 1881.

Vol I viii (numbered vi) + 320 pp.

Vol II viii (numbered vi) + 296 pp.

Vol III viii (numbered vi) + 272 pp. Publisher's advertisements occupy pp (267–72). 32 pp publisher's catalogue dated Mar. 1881 bound in at end.

2nd edn, 3 vols, 1881.

1-vol Chatto & Windus edns 1884–1901; Sutton, Stroud 1994.

1st US edn. *Seaside Library, New York 1881.

Translations. Russian, St Petersburg 1881, 1882; German, Berlin 1882.

Blackwater Park In *The Woman in White*, the Hampshire home of Sir Percival *Glyde. According to Collins's '*Rem-

The first one-volume edition of *Basil* published as a YELLOWBACK by James Blackwood in 1856

iniscences of a Story-Teller' (*Universal Review*, June 1888), the description of the overgrown estate was so realistic that he received an indignant letter complaining that he had written about his correspondent's own property.

Blackwood, James London publisher in Paternoster Row; no connection to the Edinburgh firm. Purchased *Basil at a Southgate & Barrett auction of *Bentley's Railway Library and published the first one-volume edition in November 1856 in Blackwood's London Library, a small-format series of *yellowbacks relying mainly on reprints.

Topp, C. W., *Victorian Yellowbacks & Paperbacks, 1849–1905*, i (George Routledge), Denver, Colo., 1993, 474.

Blake, Franklin In *The Moonstone*, cousin of Rachel *Verinder; on his return from a continental education responsible for presenting the diamond to her. Takes it under influence of *opium and ultimately marries Rachel when investigations confirm his innocence.

Blind Love

'The blind love that had so cruelly misled her.'

Collins's last novel, finished after his death by Walter *Besant. Collins planned the whole work and was able to complete the first forty-eight chapters (weekly parts 1–18, to 2 November 1889). Besant finished the remainder from Collins's comprehensive notes, and explained the circumstances in his preface. *Blind Love* was the third title for the story, originally known as 'Iris' and as late as May 1889 called 'The Lord Harry'.

The plot is based on the *Von Scheurer insurance fraud although the actual crime forms only the latter half of the book. It uses many details from the case, including the *Paris setting, the substituted *identity of the victim, a servant who reveals the fraud and the suicide of the main proponent. It also touches on the highly topical issues of Irish Home Rule and Fenian terrorism.

The novel charts the moral decline of the central male character, Lord Harry Norland. His unstable personality veers from fervent idealism, which implicates him in a political murder, to suicidal despair; then to involvement in a sordid insurance fraud, also resulting in murder.

He is finally killed by the Fenian terrorists whose cause he had supported. The virtuous Iris is blinded to his faults and insidiously corrupted by her love for him until she discovers the true enormity of his crime. Then 'The blind love fell from her—it was dead at last; but it left her bound to the man by a chain which nothing could break; she was in her right senses; she saw things as they were; but the knowledge came too late.' The insurance fraud is similar to that in *The Haunted Hotel* (1879) and the determined maid Fanny, eavesdropping on the plotting Vimpany and Lord Harry, recalls Marian *Halcombe spying on *Fosco and *Glyde in *The Woman in White* (1860). Lord Harry's suicide attempt may have been suggested by the death of Collins's old friend Edward *Ward, who cut his throat in a fit of depression in 1879.

➡ Iris Henley is at odds with her father because she refuses to marry Hugh Mountjoy, nephew of her Irish godfather. She is in love with the wild Lord Harry Norland, a friend of Hugh's brother, Arthur. Harry has joined the Invincibles, an Irish political secret society, which assassinates Arthur despite Harry's attempted warnings. Harry, saved from betrayal by Iris, vows revenge on his friend's murderer. Iris returns to England, breaking her journey to stay with Mrs Vimpany, wife of an unsuccessful, avaricious doctor. Mrs Vimpany has been secretly paid by Harry to keep a watch on Iris.

Iris quarrels once again with her father because she still refuses to marry Hugh. She engages a new maid, Fanny Mere, who becomes her friend and ally. Walking across Hampstead Heath, they find Lord Harry with his throat cut. He has attempted to commit suicide, leaving a note for Iris professing his love but owning that he has gambled away the last of his money. Harry's life is saved by Dr Vimpany who has separated from his wife and moved to *Hampstead. Harry and Iris marry, and her father cuts her out of his will. Harry takes out life insurance for £15,000.

The couple start married life in a cottage near Paris where they are joined by Dr Vimpany. Both Harry and the doctor are in serious financial difficulties and in desperation Harry agrees to an insurance fraud. Vimpany searches the Paris hospitals for a patient with a strong resem-

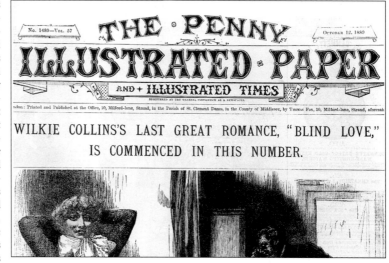

(top) *Blind Love* serialized in *The Penny Illustrated Newspaper* in October 1889
(above) Part of Walter Besant's preface to the book edition of *Blind Love* in 1890

blance to Harry. He finds the consumptive Oxbye who accepts the offer of a supposed new treatment in Harry's cottage. Iris has returned to London; but the resourceful Fanny remains behind as a nurse, spying on behalf of her mistress. Contrary to expectations, Oxbye makes a steady recovery and Fanny realizes that something is wrong when she is dismissed in favour of a new nurse who doesn't know the patient. She hides in the sick room and sees Vimpany poison

Oxbye while Harry looks on. The dead Oxbye is photographed as evidence of Lord Harry's death, and buried in the local cemetery.

Iris returns to Paris and assumes Oxbye has died of natural causes. Against her better instincts she is drawn into the conspiracy to claim the insurance money as Harry's widow. They travel to Louvain in Belgium under a false name, causing the faithful Fanny to lose touch with her mistress. However, after speaking with the new nurse Fanny works out the truth, returns to London to write down all she knows of the affair and sends her testimony to Iris *poste restante* in Brussels.

Iris sees the family lawyer who settles the insurance claim on her behalf. She takes £5,000 which Harry had borrowed from her, pays off Vimpany with £2,000 and opens a bank account with the balance in the name of William Linville. Iris and Harry live an unhappy, reclusive existence in Louvain and are about to leave for America when Iris receives Fanny's testimony. Jolted back to reality, Iris realizes that Oxbye was poisoned. She recovers her moral principles and leaves Harry for ever to make what redress she can. She repays the £5,000 to the insurance company which also accepts Harry's proposal to return £8,000 if no proceedings are taken against his wife. The lawyers pay the remaining £2,000 which is reimbursed by Hugh Mountjoy. Iris accepts Hugh's offer of his remote cottage in Scotland.

Harry travels openly to Ireland, knowing that he will be killed by the Invincibles, and is shot by the man who killed Arthur. Mrs Vimpany, now living with Iris and Fanny, receives a blackmail note from her husband, but he is drowned on the way to their cottage before he can carry out any threats. Iris finally agrees to marry Hugh Mountjoy.

Serialization. **Illustrated London News*, 6 July–28 Dec. 1889; the *Penny Illustrated Paper*, from 12 Oct. 1889.

Book publication

First edn. 3 vols, *Chatto & Windus, London 1890. Blue cloth, covers blocked in black, spines lettered in gilt, grey and white floral endpapers. Half-title in each volume. Sixteen wood engravings by A. Forestier (7 in vol I, 2 in vol II, 7 in vol III). Published in Jan. 1890.

Vol I (xii) + 304 pp.

Vol II (viii) + 304 pp. 32 pp publisher's catalogue dated Oct. 1889 bound in at end.

Vol III (viii) + 316.

Second edn, 3 vols, 1890.

1-vol edns. Chatto & Windus 1890–1910. Dover, New York 1986.

1st US edns. *Appleton's Town and Country Library, New York 1890; Hurst, New York, 1890.

Translation. German, Stuttgart 1890.

'Blow up with the Brig!' Short story originally published as 'The Ghost in the Cupboard Room', Chapter 5 of 'The Haunted House', the *Christmas num-

Cover to the *Boy's Own Paper* which published 'Victims of Circumstances' in 1886 and 1887

ber of **All the Year Round* for December 1859; subsequently included in **Miss or Mrs? and Other Stories in Outline* (1873).

➥ An old sea captain tells how as a young sailor in the early 1800s he joined the crew of a brig carrying gunpowder to revolutionaries in South America. The ship was betrayed to the Spanish enemy by the local pilot and all on board were murdered except the narrator. He was tied up and left to watch a candle burn-

ing down to a fuse laid to gunpowder, intended to blow up the brig. The sailor was saved at the last moment but haunted for the rest of his life by the ghost of a bedroom candlestick.

Boulogne First visited by Collins as a child in 1829 when his family spent a six-week holiday there, and in September 1836 on their way through *France to *Italy. Collins spent several summer holi-

Henry Brandling's illustration of Looe in Cornwall for *Rambles Beyond Railways*, published in 1851

days with *Dickens at Boulogne, beginning with an invitation in July 1853 to the Villa des Moulineaux. The time was to be used to 'write no end of Basils' and to plan their joint trip to Italy. The following July Collins joined Dickens in the Villa du Camp de Droite and during August 1856 returned with him to the Villa des Moulineaux to begin work on *The Frozen Deep*. In July 1873, Collins stayed in Boulogne on the way to Paris. Boulogne is the setting for the opening chapters of *The Black Robe*.

Boy's Own Paper (1879–1967). Popular boys' weekly magazine, edited by James Macaulay and originally issued at a price of one penny. It published Collins's '*Victims of Circumstances discovered in Records of old Trials' in 1886 and 1887. Other contributors at this time were R. M. Ballantyne, Sir Arthur Conan *Doyle, Talbot Baines Reed and Jules Verne.

Bradbury & Evans London printers and publishers at 11 Bouverie Street. With expertise in large-scale printing and distribution, they dominated serial publishing

from the mid-1840s to the 1850s. The success of *Punch earned them £5,000 a year. They published the majority of *Dickens's fiction after his disagreement with *Chapman & Hall in 1844. Dickens in turn quarrelled with Bradbury & Evans in 1859 when they declined to publish a letter in *Punch* vindicating his matrimonial problems. The partnership for their joint ownership of *Household Words* was dissolved and the firm set up *Once a Week* in competition with *All the Year Round.

Bradbury & Evans were the printers of *Antonina* (1851), *Mr Wray's Cash-Box* (1852) and *Hide and Seek* (1854). They published one Collins novel, The *Dead Secret* (1857), on a shared profits basis. At Dickens's suggestion, Bradbury & Evans took a quarter of the profits rather than the usual one-third. According to Sadleir, the edition of 750 was mismanaged as Bradbury & Evans' distribution was unsuitable for fiction in book form. Unbound sheets were remaindered in the 1870s (see CHAPMAN & HALL).

Sadleir, M., *Trollope: A Bibliography*, London 1928, 254–5.

Sutherland, J.A., *Victorian Novelists and Publishers*, London 1976.

Braddon, Mary Elizabeth (1835 –1915). Novelist and founding editor of *Belgravia* where she sometimes used the pseudonym Babbington White. Lived with and in 1874 married publisher John Maxwell. Miss Braddon was strongly influenced by Collins, *Bulwer-Lytton and French writers, particularly *Balzac. Best known for *Lady Audley's Secret* (1862), she wrote over seventy other *sensation novels.

Miss Braddon emulated Collins, not only in using substituted *identity, but also setting criminal activities in everyday surroundings. In 1887 she acknowledged that she owed *Lady Audley's Secret* to *The Woman in White* and that 'Wilkie Collins is assuredly my literary father.' Collins also became a personal friend. In *Rough Justice* (1898) she introduced Detective Faunce whose novel-reading includes Wilkie Collins, Balzac, *Dickens, Gaboriau and *Scott.

Wolff, R. L., *Sensational Victorian: The Life and Fiction of Mary Elizabeth Braddon*, New York 1979.

Brandling, Henry C. Artist friend of Collins. Accompanied him on his walking tour of Cornwall in July and August of 1850, providing twelve lithographs for *Rambles Beyond Railways*. Brandling was to receive payment of £37 16s. plus £25 for the copyright after sales reached 1,100 copies. The Brandling family came from Newcastle and Collins stayed there with Henry and his sisters in 1852. Brandling had also acted in the 1850 production of A *Court Duel* and published *Views in the North of France* (1848).

Broadstairs Seaside resort in Kent about five miles from *Ramsgate. Collins first stayed there in July and August 1858, using it as a base to sail to Dunkirk with Henry *Bullar and Edward *Pigott. The following summer he rented the isolated Church Hill Cottage for six weeks while writing *The Woman in White* and again visited Broadstairs in July 1861. From July to October 1862 Collins rented the more prestigious *Fort House during the serialization of *No Name*. Broadstairs gave him ample scope to pursue his interest in *sailing. Charles *Collins and other friends were frequent visitors.

Bullar, Henry (1815–70). Long-standing friend and *sailing companion of Wilkie Collins; dedicatee of *My Miscellanies* (1863). Barrister of *Lincoln's Inn and

on the Western circuit. Son of John Bullar of Southampton, a friend of *Harriet and *William Collins and William Collins's executor.

Collins, W., *Memoirs*.

Bulwer-Lytton, Edward George Earle Lytton, First Baron Lytton (1803–73). Prolific writer, dramatist and poet; occasional contributor to *Household Words* and *All the Year Round*. Mutual friend and admirer of *Dickens, literary mentor to Mary *Braddon. Author of *Not So Bad as We Seem* (1851), the comedy written for Dickens's *amateur dramatic company to perform in aid of the Guild of Literature and Art which occasioned Collins's first meeting with Dickens. Bulwer-Lytton had made a disastrous marriage to Rosina Doyle Wheeler who threatened to disrupt the performance. Years later she wrote to Collins complaining that *Fosco was a very poor villain far eclipsed by her own husband. Collins greatly admired Bulwer-Lytton whose Roman novel *The Last Days of Pompeii* (1834) influenced the writing of *Antonina* (1850). Bulwer-Lytton, however, described *The Woman in White* to Frederick *Lehmann as 'great trash'.

Caine, H., *My Story*, London 1908, 335.
Peters (1991), 96–7.

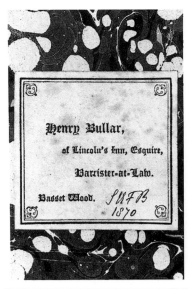

Henry Bullar's bookplate

Burnand, Sir Francis Cowley (1836–1917). Humorous writer and dramatist; regular contributor to *Punch* and its editor 1880–1906. Author of *Mokeanna!* and *Chikkin Hazard* which include *parodies of Collins's titles. These were originally published in *Punch* (7–14 March 1868) as a production of 'The *Sensation Novel Company'.

Caccia, Alberto Collins's Italian translator and agent, living in Florence. In 1875 Caccia managed a production of *The New Magdalen* in which Julian Gray's profession was changed from clergyman to magistrate since a priest could not be depicted on the Italian stage. Caccia was dedicatee of *Jezebel's Daughter* (1880).

Caine, Sir Thomas Henry Hall (1853–1931). Manx novelist, friend and biographer of D. G. Rossetti. Met Collins in the late 1880s and asked his advice on copyright and literary matters. Caine's autobiography repeats several recollections of Collins previously published in *The Globe* (4 October 1889). The anecdotes, not necessarily reliable, include his use of *opium (by the wine-glass), the naming of *The Woman in White* and its popular reception. Collins apparently wrote effusive letters to Caine about his early books but ultimately lost faith in his abilities and preferred *Besant to complete *Blind Love*. Shortly after Collins's death, Caine was criticized by a correspondent to *The *World (16 October 1889) for inaccurate recollections in a number of provincial journals.
See also MAN, ISLE OF.
  Caine, H., *My Story*, London 1908, 327–43.

Canada See AMERICA.

Canadian Monthly and National Review, The (1872–82). Literary magazine published in Toronto, originally by Adam, Stevenson. In July 1878 it became Rose-Belford's *Canadian Monthly*, edited by G. Stewart, Jr. Collins met the publishers during his reading tour of North *America in 1873–4. He contributed the following stories: 'The Dead Alive', Jan.–Feb. 1874; 'The Clergyman's Confession', Aug.–Sept. 1875; *The Haunted Hotel*, July–Dec. 1878; *The Fallen Leaves*, Feb. 1879–Mar. 1880; *The Black Robe*, Nov. 1880–June 1881.
  'Wilkie Collins as a Novelist', a critical article by J. L. Stewart, was published in Nov. 1878.

'Captain's Last Love, The' Short story originally published in *The *Spirit of the Times*, 23 Dec. 1876; and *Belgravia*, Jan. 1877; reprinted in *Little Novels* (1887). Collins sets a story in Polynesia for the first time since his earlier, then unpublished novel, *Ioláni*. The stories are different but have in common a main female character called Aimáta and a powerful high priest. There are also resemblances in the descriptive passages of the scenery.
➤ The *Fortuna* is blown off course in the South Pacific and visits an uncharted Polynesian island. While trading with the local inhabitants, the captain falls in love with the priest's daughter, Aimáta. He plans to bring her to England but she is drowned during a volcanic eruption. The captain now hates the sea and will never marry.

Carpenter, Margaret, née Geddes (1793–1872). Collins's aunt, younger sister of Harriet *Collins. A talented and successful portrait-painter, she was encouraged and supported by Lord and Lady

Radnor while still very young. She moved to London and lived independently from 1812, exhibiting at the *Royal Academy almost every year from 1814 to 1866. In 1817 she married William Hookham Carpenter (1792–1866), later Keeper of Prints and Drawings at the British Museum. They had seven surviving children, three of whom became painters. Their daughter Jane, Wilkie Collins's favourite cousin, married Charles *Ward. Collins acquired Margaret Carpenter's portrait of his mother as a young girl from Jane's daughter, Margaret Ward, when he moved into *Gloucester Place during 1867. Margaret Carpenter's portrait of Collins's paternal grandmother is now in the National Gallery of New Zealand.
  Smith, R. J., 'Margaret Carpenter (1793–1872): A Salisbury Artist Restored', *Hatcher Review*, 4 (Autumn 1993), 2–32.

Carr, John Dickson (1906–77). Prolific writer of detective fiction. Uses Collins in two stories: *The Dead Man's Knock* (1958): features a fictional unrecorded Collins

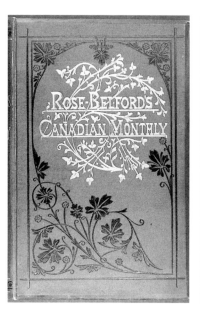

The *Canadian Monthly*, which serialized *The Fallen Leaves* and *The Black Robe*

Collins's picture on the dust-wrapper of John Dickson Carr's *The Hungry Goblin*, 1972

(above left) Man and Wife serialized in Cassell's Magazine, beginning in November 1869
(above right) Ada Cavendish as Mercy Merrick in The New Magdalen

manuscript, letters to Dickens and a locked-room murder; and *The Hungry Goblin* (1972): uses Collins as a character to help solve an 1869 mystery.

> Cooper, J. and Pike, B. A., *Detective Fiction: The Collector's Guide*, 2nd edn, London 1994, 65–74.

Carrock (Carrick) Fell Mountain in *Cumberland where Collins sprained his ankle during his walking tour with *Dickens in 1857. The incident was described in 'The *Lazy Tour of Two Idle Apprentices'.

Cassell's Magazine (1867–74). Successor to *Cassell's Illustrated Family Paper*. Renamed *Cassell's Family Magazine* in 1874. Collins was recruited, together with Sheridan Le Fanu and Charles *Reade, to raise the magazine's standard. After changing a routine clause in the Cassell contract that would have enabled them to alter his text, Collins contributed two novels:

> *Man and Wife*, 37 weekly parts, 20 Nov. 1869–30 July 1870. The story was so popu-

lar that it raised circulation to seventy thousand.

> *Poor Miss Finch*, 2 Sept. 1871–24 Feb. 1872 (SEE BENTLEY, RICHARD & SON).

> Nowell-Smith, S., *The House of Cassell: 1848–1958*, London 1958.

Catherick, Anne The mysterious, simple-minded character who provides the title for *The Woman in White*. Half-sister to Laura *Fairlie to whom she bears a striking resemblance she is confined in an asylum by Sir Percival *Glyde to preserve the secret of his illegitimacy. Dies of a heart condition and buried at Limmeridge in Laura's name.

Cavendish, Ada (Mrs Frank Marshall) (1839–95). Actress-manageress and friend of Collins. Produced *The *New Magdalen* at the *Olympic Theatre in 1873, playing Mercy Merrick opposite Frank *Archer. Subsequently arranged a provincial tour and staged two London revivals, at the Charing Cross Theatre in 1875 and the Novelty in 1884. Played the lead in the 1876 production of *Miss Gwilt* at the *Globe and took the play on tour to New York in 1879.

> Winter, W., *Old Friends*, New York 1909, 377–80.

Chapman & Hall Innovative London publishers at 193 Piccadilly. Founded in 1830 and *Dickens's publishers during his rise to fame. Pioneered monthly shilling numbers (1836), Christmas books (1843) and cheap re-issues (1847). In 1845, they introduced cheap fiction by publishing novels in four monthly parts at three shillings each as an unsuccessful attempt to challenge the *three-decker format imposed by the *circulating libraries. Chapman & Hall published the first English book edition of *The *Lazy Tour of Two Idle Apprentices* in 1890. They also re-issued four Collins titles in secondary bindings during the early 1870s.

Chapman & Hall collaborated with W. H. *Smith on the production of one-volume novels, combining their respective manufacturing and distribution skills. Smith's were therefore keen to stock Chapman & Hall reprints. They bought up remaindered sheets and had them discreetly made up by Chapman & Hall for display and sale in the railway bookstalls. This is the likely explanation for the secondary bindings seen with *The *Dead Secret*, *My Miscellanies*, *The *Frozen Deep* and *The *New Magdalen*. The distinctive characteristics for these re-issues are first edition sheets, Chapman & Hall advertisements on the front and back endpapers, a W. H. Smith embossed blind stamp on the front free endpaper

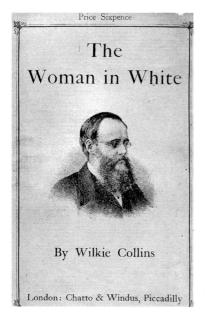

Front cover of the cheap 1894 edition of *The Woman in White* published in paper wrappers by Chatto & Windus

and, in the case of the first three titles, no publisher's imprint on the spine. The probable dates are 1873–4.

Sadleir (1951), ii. 132.

Sutherland, J. A., *Victorian Novelists and Publishers*, London 1976.

Fraser, A., 'Remaindered Books with Chapman & Hall Advertisements', *Antiquarian Book Monthly Review*, 16 (Dec. 1989), 464–5.

Chatto & Windus London publisher noted for its fiction, general literature and quality of book design. The firm was founded in 1855, by John Camden Hotten (1832–73), on the present site of the Ritz Hotel. It later occupied various other addresses in Piccadilly. When Hotten died, his successor was Andrew Chatto (d. 1913 aged 73) who had been with the firm since he was 15. He bought the business from Hotten's widow for £25,000 and was joined in partnership, initially by William Edward Windus who was relatively inactive in the firm, and subsequently by Percy Spalding in 1876. Chatto & Windus issued its first catalogue in July 1874 and bought *Belgravia* in 1876. Chatto was an aggressive publisher but had a reputation for fairness. He acted as his own reader and always negotiated himself with *Mudie's and *Smith's. He retired in 1911.

The firm's authors included Collins, Walter *Besant, Ouida, Charles *Reade, R. L. Stevenson and Anthony *Trollope.

Chatto & Windus became Collins's main publishers, commencing in 1875 with *The Law and the Lady*. *The Haunted Hotel* and *Heart and Science* first appeared in *Belgravia*, together with four of Collins's short stories. Altogether Chatto published twelve first English editions, each book being separately negotiated: *The Law and the Lady* (1875); *The Two Destinies* (1876); *The Haunted Hotel* (1879); *The Fallen Leaves* (1879); *Jezebel's Daughter* (1880); *The Black Robe* (1881); *Heart and Science* (1883); '*I Say No*' (1884); *The Evil Genius* (1886); *Little Novels* (1887); *The Legacy of Cain* (1889); *Blind Love* (1890).

Collins had always been keen to see his books in cheap editions to appeal to the widest possible range of readers. He had previously suggested the idea to George *Smith, who felt it would not be in their joint interests, and to *Bentley who was prepared to proceed. Ultimately, however, Collins reached agreement in November 1874 with Andrew Chatto for a large inclusive payment for a seven-year lease of his available copyrights. Chatto & Windus issued thirteen titles during 1875 in 6s. and 2s. editions. Three copyrights retained by Smith, Elder were excluded. These, together with Bentley's *A *Rogue's Life*, did not appear in Chatto's advertisements until November 1890. They then listed twenty-nine titles which were published in various editions well into the twentieth century. The formats included the superior New Illustrated Library and Piccadilly Novels; 'library' and 'popular editions' in limp cloth; pictorial boards; and eventually paper wrappers at sixpence.

Warner, O., *Chatto & Windus: A Brief Account of the Firm's Origin, History and Development*, London 1973.

Chorley, Henry Fothergill (1808–72). Music and literary critic of *The Athenaeum* from 1833; librettist and unsuccessful novelist. Occasional contributor to *Household Words* and *All the Year Round*. Friend of *Dickens from about 1855, attending Kate *Dickens's wedding to Charles *Collins in 1860. Wrote Dickens's obituary for *The Athenaeum*.

Despite meeting Wilkie Collins at both *Gad's Hill and the *Lehmanns, Chorley and *The Athenaeum* generally published unfavourable reviews of his novels. Chorley's criticism became increasingly severe with age and he was particularly harsh on *Armadale*. He did, however, share Collins's strong dislike of Schumann's *music and Madame Schumann.

Lehmann (1908), 178, 228–35.

Page (1974), 146–8.

Christmas numbers *Household Words* and *All the Year Round* both published extra Christmas numbers. They generally consisted of short stories by various authors linked within a narrative framework. Collins contributed to several numbers and was the only author with whom Dickens regularly collaborated.

Household Words (eight Christmas numbers of thirty-six pages from 1851 to

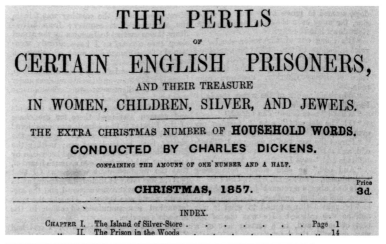

'Perils of Certain English Prisoners', *Household Words* extra Christmas number for 1857

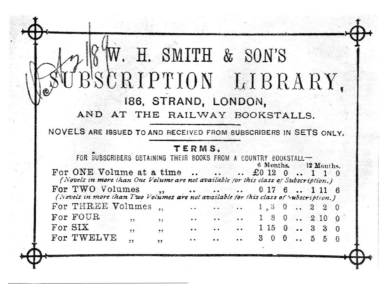

W. H. SMITH & SON'S
SUBSCRIPTION LIBRARY,
186, STRAND, LONDON,
AND AT THE RAILWAY BOOKSTALLS.

NOVELS ARE ISSUED TO AND RECEIVED FROM SUBSCRIBERS IN SETS ONLY.

TERMS.

FOR SUBSCRIBERS OBTAINING THEIR BOOKS FROM A COUNTRY BOOKSTALL—

	6 Months.	12 Months.
For ONE Volume at a time	£0 12 0	1 1 0
(Novels in more than One Volume are not available for this class of Subscription.)		
For TWO Volumes ,, ...	0 17 6	1 11 6
(Novels in more than Two Volumes are not available for this class of Subscription.)		
For THREE Volumes ,, ...	1 3 0	2 2 0
For FOUR ,, ,, ...	1 8 0	2 10 0
For SIX ,, ,, ...	1 15 0	3 3 0
For TWELVE ,, ,, ...	3 0 0	5 5 0

Library label for W. H. Smith's circulating library

1858). Collins contributed:

1854, 'The Fourth Poor Traveller' ('A *Stolen Letter') in 'The Seven Poor Travellers'.

1855, 'The Ostler' ('The *Dream Woman') as the second part of 'The Holly Tree Inn'.

1856, 'John Steadiman's Account' and 'The Deliverance' in 'The *Wreck of the Golden Mary'.

1857, 'The Prison in the Woods' in 'The *Perils of Certain English Prisoners'.

1858, 'Trottles Report'; and (with Dickens) 'Over the Way' and 'Let at Last' in 'A *House to Let'.

All the Year Round (nine Christmas numbers of forty-eight pages from 1859 to 1867). Collins contributed:

1859, 'The Ghost in the Cupboard Room' (*'Blow up with the Brig!') in 'The Haunted House'.

1860, 'The Seafaring Man'; and (with Dickens) 'The Money' and 'The Restitution' in 'A *Message from the Sea'.

1861, 'Picking up Waifs at Sea' ('The *Fatal Cradle') in 'Tom Tiddler's Ground'.

1867, *No Thoroughfare* (with Dickens).

circulating libraries Libraries from which books were borrowed for an annual subscription fee. They existed in Edinburgh during 1725 and in London from 1740 but they particularly flourished in the second half of the nineteenth century. Their success coincided with the

expansion of literacy and prompted Anthony *Trollope in one of his *Four Lectures* of 1870 to say 'We have become a novel-reading people from the Prime Minister down to the last-appointed scullery maid.'

The best known and most powerful were *Mudie's and W. H. *Smith's, with an annual subscription of one guinea per volume, but other libraries included Bull's, Saunders & Otley, Churton's, and Horne & Co. Both Mudie and Smith were deeply religious social reformers with, they considered, a moral responsibility to the public. Collins always resented their dictatorial attitude towards novelists and called them 'the twin tyrants of literature'. He was keen to support any publisher trying to break their stranglehold, allied himself to *Bentley in 1853 and later had discussions for cheap editions with *Smith, Elder and *Chatto & Windus.

All the libraries succeeded by means of the artificial *three-decker system of publishing. When this no longer proved profitable, Mudie's and Smith's warned publishers in 1894 that they would no longer accept high-priced fiction. Against the background of cheap, mass publication and free public libraries, they sealed their own fate and the circulating libraries slowly declined during the twentieth century. The last to close was Boots in 1966.

Griest, G. L., *Mudie's Circulating Library and*

the Victorian Novel, Bloomington, Ind., and Newton Abbot 1970.

'Clergyman's Confession, The'
*Supernatural story originally published in *The *World*, 4–18 Aug. 1875; in the *Canadian Monthly*, Aug.–Sept. 1875; in *Golden Treasures of Poetry, Romance, and Art*, Boston 1876; and in *Papyrus Leaves*, 1880. Reprinted as 'Miss Jéromette and the Clergyman' in *Little Novels* (1887).

➥ The story is told by a clergyman. Before he joined the Church he met and fell in love with Miss Jéromette, a French-woman alone in London. They enter on a relationship but she tells him candidly she loves another man who has deserted her. Miss Jéromette predicts the man will return to her but that she will die young and miserably. To please his dying mother the narrator becomes a clergyman and ends his association with Miss Jéromette. She dies as she predicted, and the clergyman sees a bloodstained apparition at the same time as her death. Although her lover is acquitted of murder for lack of evidence, the clergyman knows for certain who killed her.

Clow, Joseph Charles (d. 1927). Married Caroline *Graves on 29 October 1868, at about the time Martha *Rudd arrived in London. Son of Joseph Clow, a distiller, and his wife Frances of 2 Avenue Road. This overlooked Regent's Park and, ironically, was close to the spot where Collins himself was reputed to have met Caroline (see MILLAIS). The wedding took place at the parish church of St Marylebone with Caroline's daughter and Frank *Beard as witnesses. Collins also attended the ceremony and later that day described it to his sister-in-law, Kate. The marriage lasted for only about two years after which Caroline returned to Wilkie in *Gloucester Place. Clow, however, was still bothering them with correspondence in 1875. He died in 1927 aged 81.

Storey, G., *Dickens and Daughter*, London 1939, 214.

clubs Collins frequented several London clubs, particularly in the 1850s and 1860s, before he was overtaken by the constraints of domestic responsibilities. He was a member of the prestigious *Garrick and *Athenaeum and known at the Junior Athenaeum and Savile. He was also a member of the more informal

Chatto & Windus collected edition issued from
1875

Fielding. Other members of this late-supper club in Covent Garden included G. H. *Lewes, *Pigott, *Thackeray and *Yates. Poor health and pressure of work prevented most of Collins's club activities in later years although he maintained his membership of the Athenaeum until his death in 1889.

Coleridge, Samuel Taylor

(1772–1834). Romantic poet and critic; friend of William *Collins who painted a portrait of Coleridge's daughter, Sara. Wilkie Collins remembered Coleridge often coming to visit his parents, and recalled an exchange between his mother and the poet which made a deep impression on him. Coleridge was in great distress over his craving for *opium and Harriet *Collins responded briskly: 'Mr Coleridge, do not cry; if the opium really does you any good, and you *must* have it, why do you not go and get it?'

Winter, W., *Old Friends*, New York 1909, 213–14.

collaborations The vast majority of Collins's output was individually written. He contributed several stories to the *Christmas numbers of *Household Words* and *All the Year Round*, and also wrote several pieces jointly with *Dickens. Both writers sometimes imitated each other's style and Collins in particular was amused 'to see reviewers point out a passage of mine as an example of Dickens' peculiar vein, and in the next sentence comment on a paragraph of Dickens' as a sample of Wilkie Collins' sensational style'. When Collins was ill and struggling to complete the numbers of *No Name* on time, Dickens offered to write them for him. Collins gratefully declined.

Collaborations with Dickens
Household Words

'The *Wreck of the Golden Mary', extra Christmas number, Dec. 1856 (Part collaboration, part contributions).
'The *Lazy Tour of Two Idle Apprentices', 3–31 Oct. 1857.
'The *Perils of Certain English Prisoners', extra Christmas number, Dec. 1857.
'A Clause for the New Reform Bill', 9 Oct. 1858: attacking tasteless municipal displays for royal visits.

'Dr Dulcamara, MP', 18 Dec. 1858: review criticizing Charlotte Yonge's *Heir of Redclyffe*.
'A House to Let', extra Christmas number, Dec. 1858, 'Let at Last' and 'Over the Way' with Dickens (plus contribution, 'Trottles Report').

All the Year Round

'Occasional Register', 30 Apr. 1859.
'*No Thoroughfare', extra Christmas number, Dec. 1867.

Other Collaborations

Edmund *Yates, 'Occasional Register', *All the Year Round*, 7 May 1859.
Charles *Fechter, *Black and White* (1869).
Walter *Besant, completed *Blind Love* (1890) when Collins became too ill to continue.

collected editions There is no complete edition of Collins's works although there have been several partial collections. *Sampson Low during 1861–2 issued a 'cheap and uniform edition' of six titles with vignette frontispieces by *Gilbert: *Antonina*; *Basil*; *Hide and Seek*; *The Dead Secret*; *The Queen of Hearts*; *The Woman in White*. They added a one-volume edition of *No Name* in 1864 for Low's Favourite Library of Popular Books.

From 1865 *Smith, Elder added the copyright of these works to *After Dark* and *Armadale*, publishing nine titles in various cheap editions, mainly pictorial

boards or limp cloth. The popular edition of 1872 also included *The Moonstone*.

In 1875, *Chatto & Windus acquired the copyright to most of the earlier titles (excluding *Armadale*, *After Dark* and *No Name* which remained with Smith, Elder until 1890, and *Bentley's *A Rogue's Life*); they published the majority of Collins's new works till 1889. Chatto issued several cheap editions from 1875 in various formats, including the New Illustrated Library edition, Piccadilly Novels, and popular editions. By 1890 they had published twenty-nine titles which continued to be issued well into the twentieth century. *Routledge published four works in pictorial boards between 1897 and 1898. On the Continent, *Tauchnitz in the 'Collection of British Authors' published twenty-eight titles in fifty volumes between 1856 and 1890.

In America, *Harpers, New York, were Collins's main publishers. They issued seventeen titles in a variety of formats between 1873 and 1902. Collier, New York, published a thirty-volume edition in 1900 but this is also not complete (reprinted AMS Press, New York 1970). Most of Collins's works were issued in unauthorized editions by *pirates such as the Fireside, *Lovell and *Seaside Libraries (New York); Lakeside Library (Chicago); and *Peterson (Philadelphia).

Modern publishers re-issuing Collins titles include Oxford University Press, Sutton Publishing (Stroud) and Dover (New York), all of whom have also issued

various collections of short stories. The 1994 *Complete Shorter Fiction* (edited by Julian Thompson) includes several works not previously re-issued or which originally appeared in America and had not been published in England.

See also TRANSLATIONS.

Collins, Charles Allston (1828–73). Younger brother of Wilkie Collins; born 25 January 1828 at Pond Street, Hampstead, and named after his father's American painter friend, Washington Allston. Tall and good-looking with red hair and blue eyes, Charles was unlike his brother in character as well as appearance, although they remained close throughout their lives. Charley, as he was known to family and friends, inherited his father's nervous temperament as well as his artistic ability, and suffered from a chronic lack of self-confidence, exacerbated by religious scruples. He never shared the youthful zest for life that was so marked a feature of his brother although as a boy he enjoyed skating and later became a good dancer. He also participated in Wilkie's *amateur theatricals, playing the lead in A *Court Duel.

In 1843 he became a student at the Royal Academy Schools, where he was a contemporary of John *Millais and Holman *Hunt. He was associated with the foundation of the *Pre-Raphaelite Brotherhood although to his great chagrin never admitted to full membership. Nevertheless, he was attacked in the press for *Convent Thoughts*, the Pre-Raphaelite painting he exhibited at the Royal Academy Summer Exhibition of 1851.

Charles Collins was said to have been hopelessly in love with his model for *Convent Thoughts*, Maria Rossetti—the sister of Christina, William and Dante Gabriel Rossetti. Maria did not return his feelings and became a nun in an Anglican order. In about 1856 Charles seems to have become entangled with an 'unsuitable' woman of unknown name. Millais begged Hunt to persuade Charles to give her up. In 1858 he abandoned painting, which he found an increasingly stressful occupation, after struggling for months with *The Electric Telegraph*. He had enthusiastically begun this work on a modern subject but came to feel, quite irrationally, that it plagiarised Millais's ideas. He turned instead to writing. He contributed individual articles to *Household Words*, and three series to *All the Year Round* all later published in book form as *A New Sentimental Journey* (1859), *The Eyewitness* (1860), and *A Cruise upon Wheels* (1863). He also wrote three novels: *Strathcairn* (1864), *The Bar Sinister* (1864) and *At the Bar* (1866).

Charles Collins married *Dickens's younger daughter Kate on 17 July 1860. For her going-away dress the bride wore black and Dickens, who felt the marriage was a disaster, was discovered afterwards sobbing into her wedding-dress. There were rumours, believed by the Dickens family, that Charles was impotent. There were no children of the marriage and Kate later said she wished to obtain a legal separation and could have done so, but that her father would not allow it.

In the last ten years of his life Charles Collins was plagued by emotional problems, as well as physical illness finally diagnosed as stomach cancer. In 1870 Dickens asked him to draw the illustrations for *Edwin Drood* but he was too ill to complete more than the cover of the first number. Charles died on 9 April 1873. Wilkie Collins wrote the entry for the *Dictionary of National Biography*.

Cohen, J. R., *Charles Dickens and His Original Illustrators*, London 1980.

(*above left*) Harriet Collins by John Linnell in 1831
(*above right*) Locket commemorating Harriet
Collins's death in 1868

Meisel, M., 'Fraternity and Anxiety: Charles Allston Collins and the Electric Telegraph', *Notebooks in Cultural Analysis*, 2 (1985), 112–68.

Peters (1991).

Collins, Francis (179?–1833).

Wilkie Collins's uncle, younger brother of William *Collins. A sweet-natured man, very popular with his nephews, he was knowledgeable about art and artists, though without worldly or artistic ambition. He followed his father's occupation of art-dealer and picture restorer. In 1833 he contracted typhus and after lapsing into violent delirium died on 5 October.

Collins, W., *Memoirs*, ii. 29–39.

Collins, Harriet (1790–1868).

Wilkie Collins's mother, born Harriet Geddes on 27 July 1790 at Hagley, Worcestershire. Eldest child of Lieutenant Alexander *Geddes and his wife Harriet (Easton); brought up in genteel poverty at Shute End House, Alderbury, three miles southeast of Salisbury. When her father lost what remained of his inheritance, Harriet intended to become an actress and almost accepted an offer of employment from the manager of the Theatre Royal, Bath. She was instead persuaded to become a governess, teaching first at a school run by a French emigrée in Lon-

don and later in a number of private households in England and Scotland. Her last position was with the May family, of Hale Park, Hampshire.

Harriet met William *Collins through her sister, Margaret *Carpenter, at an artists' ball in London during 1814. They were immediately attracted to each other, but he was in no position to marry and she had no fortune. Eight years later, when William was in Edinburgh recording the visit to Scotland of King George IV, Harriet joined him and they were married there on 18 September 1822, against the wishes of his widowed mother. She relented, however, and on their return they joined *Margaret and *Francis Collins at 11 *New Cavendish Street, where their first son William Wilkie Collins was born in 1824.

Harriet Collins was a devoted wife and mother whose strong personality, at first subordinated to the needs of her husband and two sons, broke free in the long years of her widowhood between 1848 and her death twenty years later. In 1853 she wrote a lively, lightly fictionalized account of her early life, up to the time of her marriage.

Wilkie and his brother Charles *Collins were devoted to Harriet, as were their friends like *Millais and Holman *Hunt, to some of whom she became almost a second mother. She kept house for both sons until 1858 and then just for Charles until his marriage in 1860. Har-

riet retired to Tunbridge Wells where she lived at various addresses, always keeping a room for Wilkie. She died at Bentham Hill Cottage, Southborough, on 19 March 1868. Wilkie, struggling to write *The Moonstone* while suffering from the worst attack of rheumatic *gout he had ever endured, was too ill to visit during her last weeks. Unable to attend her funeral, he was represented by Holman Hunt. Wilkie described Harriet's death as the bitterest affliction of his life.

Collins, Harriet: untitled MS dated '25 April 1853' in HRC, University of Texas at Austin.

Peters (1991).

Information supplied by Richard J. Smith.

Collins, Margaret (d. 1833).

Wilkie Collins's formidable paternal grandmother, a Scotswoman from near Edinburgh. In her later years, increasingly senile and dependent, she lived with her son William *Collins and daughter-in-law Harriet *Collins during much of Wilkie's early childhood, first at *New Cavendish Street and then at 30 Porchester Terrace where she died on 29 December 1833. She is buried in the churchyard of St Mary's Paddington.

Collins, William John Thomas, R.A. (1788–1847).

Wilkie Collins's father; celebrated portrait and landscape painter. Born 18 September 1788 at Great

Titchfield Street, London, the elder son of *William and *Margaret Collins. Showed early artistic promise and was for a time an informal pupil of his father's friend George Morland. In 1807 he was admitted to the *Royal Academy Schools and in the same year had two landscape paintings hung in the Summer Exhibition. In 1809 William Collins won the Academy silver medal for drawing in the life school, and he was just beginning to earn a modest income from painting when his father died bankrupt in 1812. Over the next ten years William Collins steadily consolidated his artistic position. In 1814, the year in which he met his future wife, he was elected an Associate of the Royal Academy and in 1818 sold a landscape painting to the Prince Regent. In 1820 William Collins became a full

William Collins, from *Memoirs of the Life of William Collins, Esq., R. A.*

Academician and in 1822, while in Scotland to record the visit of King George IV to Edinburgh, he at last married Harriet Geddes, against his mother's wishes.

William and Harriet at first lived with his mother and brother, Francis *Collins, at 11 *New Cavendish Street, the birthplace of William Wilkie Collins. The married couple moved in 1826 to Pond Street, *Hampstead, where their younger son Charles Allston *Collins was born. In 1829 they moved to Hampstead Square and the following year settled at 30 Porchester Terrace, Bayswater. During these years William Collins travelled throughout England, usually leaving his family at home, visiting patrons and painting both portraits and landscapes. In 1836, however, in order to broaden his artistic ex-perience, he took his wife and sons abroad for almost two years, travelling through *France and *Italy.

On their return the family moved first to 20 Avenue Road off Regent's Park, then to 85 Oxford Terrace, Bayswater, and finally in 1843 to 1 Devonshire Terrace, Bayswater. William Collins's studio in this house was minutely described in *Hide and Seek.

In the summer of 1842 William Collins visited Scotland with his 18-year-old son Wilkie, travelling through the Highlands and Shetland. William was already ill with heart disease and resigned his appointment as Librarian of the Royal Academy in 1845. He died on 17 February 1847, having had the satisfaction of seeing his elder son show promise as a writer and his younger accepted as a student at the Royal Academy Schools.

William Collins was often accused of snobbery and obsequiousness, but he was generally respected by his friends and acquaintances. These included writers such as *Coleridge and Wordsworth, as well as painters like Sir David *Wilkie after whom Wilkie Collins was named. William was an affectionate father and husband, and a conscientious and hardworking painter, competent rather than inspired. However, he was often bewildered by his ebullient elder son, Wilkie, who in turn disliked his father's anxious snobbery, later satirized in A *Rogue's Life. Wilkie also opposed his father's evangelical religious fervour, a cause of conflict which is recalled in the early scenes of *Hide and Seek. *Memoirs of the Life of William Collins, Esq., R.A. (1848) was Wilkie Collins's first published book.

Collins, William (Senior) (1740–1812). Wilkie Collins's paternal grandfather. From an impoverished Irish Protestant background in County Wicklow, he came to London as a young man and made a precarious living as a picture-dealer and restorer. He had literary ambitions, publishing a number of works including a poem attacking the slave trade. *Memoirs of a Picture* (1805), a lively if incoherent novel, combined fiction with a biography of his friend, the painter George Morland. Its account of faking and shady dealings in the art world together with the improvident and scandalous life of Morland inspired his grandson's A *Rogue's Life in 1856. William Collins Senior died bankrupt in 1812, leaving almost destitute his Scottish wife *Margaret and their two surviving children, *William and *Francis Collins.

Collins, (William) Wilkie (8 Jan. 1824–23 Sept. 1889).

'My life has been rather a strange one.'
(*A Rogue's Life*)

Elder son of *William and *Harriet Collins. Born at 11 *New Cavendish Street, London, 8 January 1824, and christened at the nearby St Marylebone parish church. His middle name was given him in compliment to his godfather, the painter Sir David *Wilkie. As a child he was known as 'Willie', but it was as Wilkie Collins he became known to the reading public. It was typical of his informality that in adult life he was always called Wilkie by his many friends. Though his family lived at various places in *Marylebone, *Hampstead and Bayswater during his childhood, his homes as an adult were all in the Marylebone area.

His appearance was in some respects unusual. He was born with a prominent bulge on the right side of his forehead, visible in some photographs, and his head and shoulders were disproportionately large. He grew to be only five feet six inches tall and had particularly small hands and feet; he could wear women's shoes and gloves. From a child he was short-sighted and portraits from the age of 21 show him wearing spectacles. He had restless tics and mannerisms, often remarked on, and liked to wear flamboyant and unconventional clothes as part of his revolt against Victorian bourgeois habits.

Wilkie's childhood was happy, although slightly overshadowed by the earnest evangelicalism of his parents, particularly his father, reflected in the early chapters of *Hide and Seek* (1854).

Wilkie and Charles Collins aged 9 and 5

Wilkie Collins as a baby, drawn by William Collins

He respected and admired his father, a successful and popular painter, but Wilkie also rebelled against William Collins's snobbishness and conventionality. The unorthodox aspects of Wilkie's later life suggest a reaction against his upbringing. He was devoted to his mother, who taught him his early lessons, and later claimed his literary interests came from her. He also showed signs of artistic talent and had a painting hung in the *Royal Academy Summer Exhibition of 1849; but it was his younger brother Charles *Collins who studied at the Royal Academy Schools and worked for a time as a painter. The two brothers were always good friends, in spite of marked differences in their appearance, beliefs and characters.

From January 1835 Collins attended a day school, the Maida Hill Academy, where he seems to have settled in well, on one occasion winning a prize. His studies were interrupted the following year, when William Collins took his wife and sons to *France and *Italy from September 1836 until August 1838. Collins said of this period of travel, with lengthy stays in *Rome and Naples, that he had learned more in Italy 'which has since been of use to me, among the scenery, the pictures, and the people, than I ever learned at school'. Wilkie and Charles were taken to see the art galleries of *Paris, Florence, Rome and Naples; met many of the artists of the day and began to learn Italian. Collins later recalled that at the age of

12 or 13 he had fallen in love for the first time in Rome with a grown-up woman and to have been furiously jealous of her husband. In a version told to *Dickens and Augustus *Egg he claimed that he had actually seduced her. Other memorable experiences followed in Naples, later used as one of the settings for *Armadale* (1866); and in *Venice, where the family hired 'Beppo', a former employee of Byron, as cook and guide. Collins gave a detailed account of this period of his life in *Memoirs of the Life of William Collins, Esq., R.A.* (1848).

On the family's return to England in August 1838, Collins was sent to a boarding school at 39 Highbury Place, North London, run by the Revd Henry Cole. Here he felt out of place and was often in trouble for laziness and inattention. However, he also began his career as a story-teller to appease the dormitory bully. He later said, 'it was this brute who first awakened in me, his poor little victim, a power of which but for him I might never have been aware. Certainly no-one in my "own home" credited me with it and when I left school I still continued story-telling for my own pleasure.'

He left school in 1841, and was found employment in the firm of *Antrobus & Co, a tea-merchant in the *Strand. He fictionalized his experiences of this office in *Hide and Seek*. Though he found the work boring, and called the office 'the prison at the Strand', he had time to write and scribbled 'tragedies, comedies, epic

Wilkie Collins photographed for *Men of Mark*

poems'. His first signed publication, 'The *Last Stage Coachman' appeared in *The *Illuminated Magazine* in August 1843.

In the summer of 1842 Collins visited Scotland with his father, who had been commissioned to provide the illustrations for the Abbotsford edition of *Scott's novel *The Pirate*, set in Shetland. This was the only time the two were alone together for any extended period and it is evident from their letters that they both enjoyed the experience and got on well together in their travels from Edinburgh to the remote and primitive Highlands and islands.

In the summer of 1844, Collins went abroad for the first time without his parents, staying in Paris for five weeks with Charles *Ward. Paris, where he discovered the delights of gourmet *food and drink, was to remain one of his favourite cities. On his return he began his first novel, *Iolání*, a story set in the South Seas before the coming of the missionaries. This was finished in 1845 and submitted to *Longmans and *Chapman & Hall. It was rejected by both and never published in his lifetime. He later wrote of it: 'My youthful imagination ran riot among the noble savages in scenes which caused the respectable British publisher to declare that it was impossible to put his name on the title page.' In April 1846 he began another historical novel, *Antonina*, set in ancient Rome. His father, impressed by his literary ability and determination, allowed him to leave the firm of Antrobus and Collins was admitted to read *law as a student of *Lincoln's Inn in May 1846. Though he 'ate dinners and kept terms' (then the only prerequisite for qualifying as a barrister) and was called to the Bar in November 1851, he never practised as a lawyer. Collins nevertheless retained a fascination for the complex processes of the law which is reflected in his fiction. He also put his knowledge to practical use when arranging the secret marriage of his friends *Edward and *Henrietta Ward in 1848.

When William Collins died in February 1847, he left enough money to ensure a comfortable life for his widow and relieve his sons from any immediate financial anxieties. Wilkie Collins at once suspended work on the half-finished *Antonina* in order to write his father's biography. *Memoirs of the Life of William Collins, Esq., R.A.*, his first published book, appeared in November 1848 and was well received.

Collins was now living at 38 Blandford Square with his mother and brother. Harriet Collins welcomed her sons' friends to the house and gave informal dinner-parties at which smoking was allowed. Amateur performances of plays by Goldsmith and Sheridan were staged in the back drawing-room. More ambitiously Wilkie translated a French play, *A *Court Duel*, which was given a charity performance by the two brothers and their friends in a public theatre on 26 February 1850. Two days later, *Antonina*, Collins's first published novel, was issued by Richard *Bentley to excellent reviews; a second, revised edition was published three months later. Its success was the deciding factor in Collins's determination to make a career as a writer.

In the summer of 1850 Collins tried his hand for the first and last time as a travel writer. With a painter friend, Henry *Brandling, who supplied the illustrations, he took a walking tour of *Corn-

Painting of Wilkie Collins by J. E. Millais in 1850

wall, writing up their experiences as
Rambles Beyond Railways. On his return
he moved with his mother and brother
into 17 *Hanover Terrace, a large house
overlooking Regent's Park. They lived
here for the next six years, entertaining
frequently and on one occasion giving a
dance for seventy people.

One of the most important relationships of Collins's life began in 1851, when
he was introduced to Dickens by Augustus Egg. Dickens needed an actor to join
his amateur company for his production
of *Not So Bad as We Seem*, a play written by
*Bulwer-Lytton to raise money for the
newly formed charity the Guild of Literature and Art. Collins was offered the
small part of Dickens's valet, which he
accepted with enthusiasm. For most of
the following year Collins was involved in
performances of the play, first in London
and then on a series of countrywide
tours. He continued to write articles for
Bentley's Miscellany and also contributed
regularly to The *Leader*, but did not
begin another novel until 1852.

Though Dickens was twelve years
older than Collins and already a world-
famous author, their acquaintance rapidly
deepened into friendship. For the next
sixteen years Collins was one of Dickens's most favoured companions as well
as a colleague valued for his many contributions to *Household Words* and *All the
Year Round*. The two were in many ways
dissimilar but Dickens found the younger
man's enjoyment of life and disregard for
conventions refreshing; they spent much
time together in London and also travelled in England and on the Continent.
Collins stayed with Dickens and his family at *Broadstairs, *Boulogne and Paris,
and collaborated with him on a number
of literary projects.

The association, which was close
enough to arouse the jealousy of John
*Forster, was of great benefit to Collins,
especially in the early years of their
friendship. Dickens's experience as a
writer and editor, and his excellent critical eye, were mostly a positive influence
on Collins's writing. He was sometimes
alarmed, however, at Collins's refusal to
conform, either in his life or his writing,
to the prudish susceptibilities of the
British public. Dickens once warned

Wilkie Collins by Herbert Watkins in 1864

W. H. *Wills not to leave anything in a Collins article that 'may be sweeping, and unnecessarily offensive to the middle class'. Nevertheless, Dickens was the first to recognize the originality of *Basil*, Collins's earliest novel of contemporary life, which was published by Richard Bentley in 1852. It received mostly hostile reviews for its outspokenness on sexual relations but reviewers acknowledged the quality of the writing. The novel established Collins as a writer of contemporary fiction.

It has been suggested that the plot of *Basil* bears some relation to a secret episode in Collins's own life, and that his failure to marry either of the women with whom he later established long-term relationships was because of a secret marriage when young. There is, however, no evidence for this. Collins had a lifelong aversion to marriage, dating from the 1840s. His own statement in the Preface to *Basil* that the 'main event' of the story was based on 'a fact in real life which had come within my own knowledge' most probably refers to the secret marriage of Edward and Henrietta Ward.

From 1853 Collins was a regular contributor to *Household Words*, while still maintaining his connection with other periodicals. He also began a second novel with a contemporary setting, *Hide and Seek*. Work on this was interrupted by a bout of serious illness in May and June, the first experience of the ill-health that was to dog him for the rest of his life. At the end of July he visited Dickens and his family in Boulogne, and in October he joined Dickens and Augustus Egg for an extensive journey to *Switzerland and Italy.

Collins hoped to make money from the trip by selling articles about his experiences to *Bentley's Miscellany*, but these were not accepted and the only accounts are in his letters and those of Dickens. Both give lively and amusing narratives of their adventures, including a terrifying excursion to Chamonix; coach travel in Italy; a journey in an overcrowded boat from Genoa to Naples and a visit to the opera in Venice.

Hide and Seek, dedicated to Dickens, was published by Bentley in June 1854.

The early part of the novel drew heavily on Collins's own experiences as a child and young man. With less power but far more charm than *Basil*, it was welcomed enthusiastically by reviewers and by Dickens, who now treated Collins on a more equal footing. Their relationship became more intimate and they spent much of their free time together, wandering by night in the less respectable areas of London and Paris, and regularly dining together at Verrey's restaurant in Regent Street. Collins again spent much of this summer with Dickens and his family at Boulogne and had a holiday with Dickens 'en garçon' in Paris during February 1855; unfortunately Collins was ill for much of this trip.

Collins's fascination with the stage, encouraged by his association with Dickens's *amateur theatricals, led him in 1855 to write his first play, *The Lighthouse*. It was staged at *Tavistock House in June. Dickens played the lead and Collins the part of a young lover, with Mamie Dickens as his sweetheart. In September he also experienced for the first time the pleasures of *sailing, which remained a lifelong pastime. With Edward *Pigott he chartered a boat and sailed down the Bristol Channel to the Scilly Isles. The cruise was written up for *Household Words* and appeared in December 1855 as 'The *Cruise of the Tomtit'. Collins discovered that the relaxed life on board ship

suited his unconventional temperament. 'We are a happy, dawdling, undisciplined, slovenly lot' he wrote. 'We have no principles, no respectability, no business, no stake in the country, no knowledge of Mrs. Grundy.'

Collins's next book, *After Dark*, a collection of his short stories with a framing and linking narrative, was published in February 1856. Collins then joined Dickens and his family in Paris, staying next door to them in the rue des Champs Elysées in a miniature pavilion 'like a cottage in a ballet'. However, he was ill for most of his stay, with a serious attack of the arthritic disorder that continued to afflict him for the rest of his life. In spite of this he managed to complete his next story, *A Rogue's Life*, and work out the plot of *The Dead Secret*; to visit the theatres and music-halls with Dickens; and to discover, on a bookstall, the *Recueil des causes célèbres*, which provided the basis of the plot for *The Woman in White*.

On his return to London, Collins was without a home as his mother was about to move house, and he went into lodgings at 22 Howland Street, Fitzroy Square. He was again ill and wrote 'Laid Up in Lodgings', a powerful article for *Household Words* on his unhappy experiences and the unpleasantness of his landlady to her exploited maid-servants. It was very probably at this time that he met Caroline *Graves. However, after a yachting

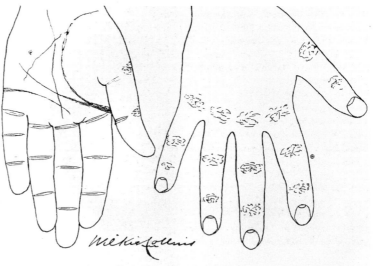

WILKIE **COLLINS**: ARTIST: *NOVELIST*.

The hands of Wilkie Collins from *Celebrated Hands* by Claude Warren, London 1882 trip with Pigott in June and a holiday in Boulogne with Dickens in August he returned to live with his mother and brother at their new home, 2 Harley Place, in September 1856. In the same month Collins was invited to become a member of the regular staff of *Household Words*, at a salary of £5 a week (later raised by £50 a year). He stipulated that his next novel should be advertised under his own name in the magazine. The new arrangement was marked by his first collaboration with Dickens on a *Christmas number for *Household Words*, *The *Wreck of the 'Golden Mary'*.

Collins's next novel, *The Dead Secret*, was serialized in *Household Words* from January to June 1857. When the volume edition appeared in June, Edmund *Yates wrote an article for *The *Train* on Collins's fiction, suggesting it was exceeded only by that of Dickens, *Thackeray and Charlotte Brontë, and that as a story-teller he had no equal among living writers. The year 1857 also saw the writing and production of *The Frozen Deep*, Collins's best-known play, and a successful professional run of *The Lighthouse*. It was also during this year that Dickens moved to *Gad's Hill where Collins was a frequent visitor. An early fellow-visitor, though not a popular one, was Hans *Andersen whom Collins described in a comic article, 'The Bachelor Bedroom', for *All the Year Round* in 1859.

When the four public performances of *The Frozen Deep* at Manchester were over, Dickens, restless and disturbed by his feelings for Ellen Ternan, asked Collins to accompany him on a tour of *Cumberland. This trip provided material for a joint series, 'The *Lazy Tour of Two Idle Apprentices', and another *collaboration followed with 'The *Perils of Certain English Prisoners', the 1857 Christmas number of *Household Words*. The success of *The Frozen Deep* led Collins to experiment further with drama and a new play, *The Red Vial*, with Frederick *Robson in a leading part, was given a professional production at the *Olympic Theatre in October 1858. The audience found the melodrama absurd and the play was taken off after the first night. Collins's published literary work during 1858 consisted of his many contributions to *Household Words*. He was also hard at work planning his next novel, *The Woman in White*. He spent much of the summer in seaside lodgings at Broadstairs and sailed across the Channel with his brother and other friends.

Collins's relationship with Dickens began to diminish somewhat in 1858 although Collins remained on the editorial staff. They both had personal preoccupations. In May, Dickens had parted from his wife and by the end of the year Collins had left his mother and brother. He was now living in lodgings with Caroline Graves and her 7-year-old daughter Harriet, first at 124 Albany Street and, by the spring of 1859, at 2A *New Cavendish Street. Caroline was to live with Wilkie, with one break of about two years, for the rest of his life.

The year 1859 was Collins's *annus mirabilis*. He acquired a settled domestic life, a lifelong companion in Caroline, and an adoptive daughter in Harriet (usually called Carrie) for whom he took complete responsibility; and *The Woman in White*, the novel that was to ensure his enduring fame, began publication in Dickens's new periodical *All the Year Round*.

Collins spent the summer of 1859 with Caroline Graves in Broadstairs, in order to write his novel in peaceful surroundings. He had difficulty at first in naming the book. He recalled how, on a walk to the *North Foreland lighthouse, the awkward stiffness of the lighthouse in the evening light suggested his 'white woman—woman in white!' Dickens agreed with him that it was the perfect title and the story began serialization in November. By Christmas it was the talk of London and it was clear that it would be Collins's greatest success, financially as well as critically. On the strength of this, Collins and Caroline moved to 12 *Harley Street in the spring of 1860. He spent a considerable amount on redecorating and refurbishing their rooms, to make them handsome and comfortable, and employed two servants. While they lived there Caroline was known as 'Mrs Collins' to the landlord with whom they shared the house. Collins finished writing *The Woman in White* on 26 July and gave a party to celebrate. He hired a Genoese chef for the occasion and invited Henry *Bullar, Augustus Egg, Frederick *Lehmann, Holman *Hunt and Edward Ward. He could now afford to indulge his liking for the best food and drink; and for the rest of his life he entertained his friends generously, in an informal and relaxed fashion.

Also in July 1860 Charles Collins was married to Kate *Dickens, Charles Dickens's younger daughter, at Gad's Hill. Her father was against the marriage, feeling that Kate was only marrying to get away from home. He also disapproved of Collins's open liaison with Caroline Graves, calling her 'the (female) skeleton in that house' and hoping Wilkie was not contemplating marriage to her. Collins showed no inclination for marriage although Caroline was introduced to all his close male friends. He travelled openly with her, taking her to Paris in October, travelling first class and staying at the best hotels.

His new financial security and continued ill-health led Collins in January 1861 to resign from the staff of *All the Year Round*, to concentrate on writing his next novel, *No Name*, serialized in the magazine from March 1862. Towards the end of the year, when he was struggling to finish the story, Collins was alarmed by the development of new symptoms added to his now familiar 'rheumatic *gout'. These were probably caused by the *laudanum prescribed by Frank *Beard to ease the pain of his illness. He was to remain dependent on ever-increasing doses of opium for the rest of his life, eventually taking enough to kill anyone not adapted to the drug.

The publisher George Smith of *Smith, Elder, disappointed at missing the chance of publishing *The Woman in White*, made Collins an offer of £5,000 for his next novel, *Armadale*. The increasing severity of his illness led to a postponement and the serialization was not completed until 1866. Collins took the waters at *Aix-la-Chapelle and Wildbad in a vain attempt at a cure. He travelled widely while planning the book and wrote nothing for eighteen months. A visit to the Isle of *Man, one of the settings for *Armadale*, was far too primitive and uncomfortable for his liking. He spent the winter of 1863–4 in Rome, with Caroline and her daughter, for the third extended visit of his life to Italy. Collins celebrated his fortieth birthday there, still refusing to succumb to the 'regular habits and respectable prejudices' of middle age.

In August 1864 Collins took a sailing holiday in Norfolk, another of the settings for *Armadale*. He stayed in Great Yarmouth, and it may have been at this time that he met Martha *Rudd, then aged 19, who had been working as a servant for an innkeeper in the Great

Yarmouth area. There is, however, no definite record of their relationship until 1868.

Armadale began serialization in The *Cornhill* in November 1864 and the following month Collins moved to 9 Melcombe Place, Dorset Square, where Caroline resumed her own name, Mrs Graves. They moved again in 1867 to a larger house, 90 *Gloucester Place, where Collins was to live for over twenty years. He refused to have gas lighting installed, thinking it unhealthy, but the house was otherwise made comfortable and up-to-date.

Collins temporarily took over the editorship of *All the Year Round* in 1867 while Dickens was in America. He also wrote a play that year, *No Thoroughfare*, which proved his first success in the commercial theatre—a professional production of *The Frozen Deep* in 1866 had not been popular since the public found it old-fashioned. He also began to write *The Moonstone*, second only to *The Woman in White* in popularity among his novels, and the forerunner of the classic detective story. Its success is all the more remarkable because it was written at a moment of crisis in Collins's life. His mother became ill at the beginning of 1868 and died in March. Collins, suffering the worst attack of 'rheumatic gout' he had ever had to endure, called her death the bitterest affliction of his life. He was too ill to attend her funeral and for a

while he was even too ill to write *The Moonstone* in his own hand, and had to dictate five pages to Carrie Graves. His suffering, and the laudanum which relieved it, are reflected in the experiences of Ezra *Jennings in the novel.

Collins's relationship with Martha Rudd and the effect this had on Caroline Graves caused further complications during 1868. By now Martha was living in London and, apparently in response to Collins's relationship with her, Caroline married Joseph *Clow on 29 October. Harriet Graves stayed with Collins during her mother's brief marriage, taking over the running of the household with the help of her grandmother, Mary Ann *Graves. Martha, who became pregnant with her first child at around the same time, never lived with Collins. Known as 'Mrs Dawson', she lived at various addresses within walking distance of the house in Gloucester Place, and Collins adopted the alias of 'William *Dawson, barrister-at-law' when he visited her or when he stayed with her in lodgings at *Ramsgate, now his favourite holiday destination. Their first child, Marian, was born 4 July 1869; and their second daughter, Harriet, 14 May 1871. In spite of this 'morganatic marriage' as he called it, Caroline returned to Collins, abandoning her marriage to Clow after about two years. She accepted the situation and Wilkie's children often came to stay with them, both at Gloucester Place and when they

were on holiday at Ramsgate.

Collins's relationship with Dickens apparently cooled in the last two years before Dickens's death in 1870, in part because of Dickens's disparagement of *The Moonstone*, in part because of his expressed irritation at the ineffectuality of his son-in-law, Charles Collins. Charles was in fact suffering from a stomach ailment, finally diagnosed as cancer, from which he died, after much suffering, in 1873.

During the 1870s Collins's attempts to establish himself as a playwright met with increasing success. A dramatization of *The Woman in White*, for which he rewrote much of the action, opened in London in October 1871 and then successfully toured for over a year. He now planned a number of his novels with stage adaptation in mind from the outset. *Man and Wife*, his *didactic novel of 1870 attacking the state of *marriage laws, was first conceived as a play and staged very successfully in 1873. *The New Magdalen*, a plea for sympathy for 'fallen women' and dramatized in the same year, was also extremely popular as a play. Dramatizations of *Armadale* (entitled *Miss Gwilt*) and *The Moonstone* followed in 1876 and 1877. Many of the friends he made in the last twenty years of his life were connected with the theatre. The actor Wybert *Reeve, who played Count *Fosco in *The Woman in White*, and the American actress Mary *Anderson were especial favourites.

In 1873 Collins took up an invitation to tour *America, giving readings from his works. He prepared a special adaptation of 'The *Dream Woman' which took two hours to deliver. He toured the United States and Canada, mostly meeting with appreciative audiences, for the next five months. He enjoyed the cordiality and the free-and-easy manners of the Americans, and made several new friends. Although the climate suited him, the constant travelling was exhausting and he left for home earlier than he had intended, having earned about £2,500. Back in London he found a new home for Martha and his two daughters, a cottage in Taunton Place, at the top of Gloucester Place. It was here that his son, William Charles Collins *Dawson ('Charley'), was born on Christmas Day 1874.

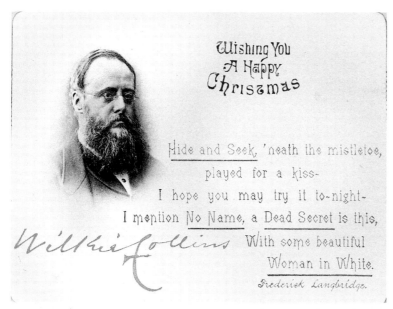

Wishing You
A Happy
Christmas

Hide and Seek, 'neath the mistletoe,
played for a kiss-
I hope you may try it to-night-
I mention No Name, a Dead Secret is this,
With some beautiful
Woman in White.

Frederick Langbridge.

Christmas card featuring Collins's titles.

THE BOOKMAN

WITH PRESENTATION PLATE PORTRAIT
of WILKIE COLLINS

C.W. MUIR.
GISBORNE.
BOOKSELLER STATIONER NEWSAGENT
9d.

JUNE
1912

CONTENTS

Painting of Wilkie Collins by Rudolf Lehmann in 1880

Wilkie Collins photographed in Boston by Warren.

In 1875 Collins's novel *The Law and the Lady* was published by *Chatto & Windus, who subsequently became his main publishers. This proved a highly satisfactory arrangement for Collins. Chatto eventually issued *collected editions of his novels in various formats. In December 1881 he reduced the business burden of his literary affairs when he appointed A. P. *Watt as his agent. Watt rapidly became a personal friend. Collins's last play, *Rank and Riches*, not a dramatization of a novel but an original play, was produced in 1881. Though he had high hopes for it, the play proved a theatrical disaster and he never tried to write another.

Collins's health continued to decline as heart problems, causing him intense pain from angina, were added to his longstanding arthritis. He made attempts, not very successfully, to follow a more ab-

(opposite) Wilkie Collins on the cover of *The Bookman*'s special issue of June 1912

stemious regime but mostly continued to eat and drink more than was good for him, insisting that dry champagne did him no harm. He still continued to write industriously, in order to provide for his two households and educate his children, producing a full-length novel almost every year, as well as short stories, novellas and articles. He continued to feel a close involvement with his writing and his anti-vivisection novel *Heart and Science* so 'mercilessly excited' him that he wrote it week after week without a break. But his work was no longer so popular with the public and Watt sometimes found it difficult to sell.

In 1878 Harriet Graves married a solicitor, Henry Powell *Bartley, and Collins transferred his legal affairs from William *Tindell. Wilkie continued to use Harriet as his amanuensis after her marriage and acted as an affectionate 'grandfather' to her children.

Collins continued to make new friends

in the last years of his life. In addition to younger writers such as Harry *Quilter and Hall *Caine, he made friends with a 12-year-old schoolgirl, Anne ('Nannie') *Wynne. He addressed her—surprisingly for a man so consistently opposed to marriage—as his 'little wife', writing to her regularly during the last four years of his life. Collins's letters to her are among the liveliest he ever wrote, full of gossip about his life and complaints at the state of his health.

In 1887 he was faced with the unwelcome prospect of moving house, when the lease of 90 Gloucester Place ran out and the landlord asked an exorbitant sum to renew it. He found the upper part of a house in *Wimpole Street and moved there in February 1888. He did not live long to enjoy it. In January 1889 he survived a carriage accident on his way home from a dinner-party at Sebastian *Schlesinger's, when he was thrown from a cab in a collision, but in June he

Plaster bas relief of Wilkie Collins made in 1890 by Adolf Rost

suffered a stroke. Although he seemed to be recovering, he arranged for Walter *Besant to complete *Blind Love*, the novel he was writing at the time, in case it should be necessary. By September it was clear that he was dying and an attack of bronchitis led to his death on 23 September 1889. A simple *funeral, attended by Caroline, Harriet Bartley and her husband, but not by Martha or his children, was followed by burial at Kensal Green Cemetery.

'Ask yourself if there is any explanation of the mystery of your own life and death.' (*The Haunted Hotel*)

Considerations on the Copyright Question Addressed to an American Friend

Strongly worded essay in the form of a letter protesting at literary *piracy and the lack of international *copyright in the USA. Noting the 'honourable example' of treaties in Europe, Collins levels the accusation that 'the President and Congress of America remain content to contemplate the habitual perpetration, by American citizens, of the act of theft'. He laments that '. . . *one* American publisher informed a friend of mine that he had "sold one hundred and twenty thousand copies of 'The Woman in White' ". He never sent me sixpence.' Collins concludes, 'I must go back to my regular work, and make money for American robbers, under the sanction of Congress.'

Issued as a 16-page pamphlet, Trübner & Co, London 1880. Also published in the *International Review*, June 1880; reprinted in *The Author*, June 1890.

Cook, Edward Dutton (1829–83).

Dramatic critic of the *Pall Mall Gazette (1867–75) and The *World (1875–83), minor novelist and contributor to the *Dictionary of National Biography*. Regarded as one of the ablest but most difficult critics to please. With the exception of *Man and Wife*, gave generally poor notices of Collins's plays. These are included in Cook's *Nights at the Play* (London 1883).

Cooper, James Fenimore (1789–1851).

American author, the first to become widely popular outside his own country. Best known for the *Leather-stocking Tales* with adventures among frontiersmen and American Indians, full of varied and dramatic incident. Stories included *The Pioneers* (1823) and *The Last of the Mohicans* (1826). Regarded by Collins as one of his three 'Kings of Fiction', along with *Balzac and *Scott, Cooper is a likely influence on the character of Old Mat in *Hide and Seek* (1854).

copyright, dramatic The first statute concerned with stage production was the 1833 Dramatic Copyright Act, promoted by *Bulwer-Lytton, although this gave protection to the author for a limited period only. The subsequent Literary Copyright Act of 1842 still failed to cover performances of dramatization of non-dramatic works. The only way therefore in which a novelist could protect himself from unauthorized stage production was by making his own dramatizations.

It was generally held that if a play were published before being produced, the performing right was lost. Thus *The Frozen Deep* (1857), *Black and White* (1869), *The Moonstone* (1877) and *Rank and Riches* (1883) were all 'printed but not published'; and *Miss Gwilt* was 'Printed for performance at the Theatre only'. Authors also employed actors, usually without costumes or scenery, to give a 'copyright performance' in 'a place of public entertainment'. *The Evil Genius*, for example, was given a single afternoon performance at the Vaudeville on 30 October 1885 to establish Collins's own dramatic copyright.

None of these copyright considerations applied in America where Collins was constantly plagued by *pirated productions and editions of his works.

copyright, international

'...because their government forgets what is due to the honour of a nation.' (*The Evil Genius*)

The question of international copyright became a burning issue in the nineteenth century and Wilkie Collins was at the forefront of demands for reform. In England, the question of literary property had been the cause of much controversy in the second half of the eighteenth century and, although the position of authors gradually improved, they were not finally granted life-time property in their own work until the Act of 1842, after five years of debate initiated by Thomas Noon Talford. The Act granted copyright for forty-two years from the date of publication, or the life of the author plus seven years, whichever was the greater.

An international agreement, the Berne Convention, was arrived at in 1887, but the United States was still governed by its own 1790 Copyright Act. Until 1891 not only did the US Constitution fail to recognize the copyright of overseas authors but the wording of the Fifth Section actively encouraged the reprinting of foreign authors. It afforded no protection to 'any person not a citizen of the United States'. Captain Marryat failed in a test case in 1838 despite having resided in America for twelve months.

Literary *piracy was therefore an accepted way of life for US publishers. They had to choose between paying authors and publishing at high prices or pirating cheap reprints. Eventually, the Americans realized that lack of international copyright was having an unsatisfactory effect on their own literature. Unknown US writers found publication increasingly difficult because of the competition from cheaper books by better-known English authors.

The North American situation became more complicated when US publishers sold reprints of English books across the border in Canada and *vice versa*. Between 1878 and 1884, this predicament caused a disagreement between Collins and his main US publishers, *Harpers.

Collins had similar copyright problems in Europe, exemplified by his correspondence with the Dutch firm *Belinfante Brothers. These difficulties were partially solved by the 1887 international agreement. Collins was nevertheless careful to issue *Chatto & Windus with precise instructions for the correct way of reserving his translation rights and found by experience that the German interpretation of copyright law was far more strict than the French.

Collins was perpetually incensed at the activities of the pirates and became a life-long advocate for international copyright. In 1880 he set out his strong opinions in *Considerations on the Copyright Question Addressed to an American Friend*.

Bossche, C. R. V., 'The Value of Literature: Representations of Print Culture in the Copyright Debate of 1837–1842', *Victorian Studies*, 38 (Autumn 1994), 41–68.

Brussel (1935): introduction by G. Pollard, 3–31.

Exman, E., *The House of Harper*, New York 1967, 48–53.

Mackinnon, Sir Frank, 'Notes on the History of English Copyright' in *The Oxford Companion to English Literature*, compiled and edited by Sir Paul Harvey, revised by Dorothy Eagle, Oxford 1967.

Cornhill Magazine, The (1860–1975). Monthly periodical specializing in high-quality fiction, published by George Smith of *Smith, Elder. Its first editor was *Thackeray, until his sudden death in 1863. Other authors published in *The Cornhill* included George Eliot, Mrs Gaskell, Hardy, *Reade and *Trollope. Collins contributed one novel, *Armadale*.

Smith always regretted missing *The Woman in White* and in July 1861 offered Collins £5,000 for a long story to be published in the magazine. At the time this was the highest sum ever offered for a novel to anyone but Dickens. *Armadale* was originally intended for publication in 1863 but was delayed for nearly two years because of Collins's ill-health and travels in Europe. It was eventually serialized from November 1864 to June 1866. Twenty of the wood engravings by George H. Thomas were used in the book edition.

Cornwall Collins visited Cornwall with his artist friend, Henry *Brandling, in July and August 1850. The story of their walking tour was published as *Rambles*

THE

CORNHILL MAGAZINE.

NOVEMBER, 1864.

Armadale.

BOOK THE FIRST.

CHAPTER I.

THE TRAVELLERS.

IT was the opening of the season of eighteen hundred and thirty-two, at the Baths of WILDBAD.

The evening shadows were beginning to gather over the quiet little German town; and the diligence was expected every minute. Before the door of the principal inn, waiting the arrival of the first visitors of the year, were assembled the three notable personages of Wildbad, accompanied by their wives — the mayor, representing the inhabitants; the doctor, representing the waters; the landlord, representing his own establishment. Beyond this select circle, grouped snugly about the trim little square in front of the inn, appeared the townspeople in general, mixed here and there with the countrypeople in their quaint German costume placidly expectant of the diligence—the men in

VOL. X.—NO. 59.   25.

Armadale, serialized in *The Cornhill* from November 1864

Beyond Railways (1851). Collins subsequently used Cornwall as the setting for the final, dramatic chapters of *Basil* (1852); for Porthgenna Towers where much of the action takes place in *The Dead Secret* (1857); and in 'The *Parson's Scruple' (1859) where the Revd Alfred Carling is Rector of Penliddy.

Court Duel, A Collins's first dramatic adaptation on 26 February 1850, in which he made his first appearance on a public

stage, at the Soho Theatre (previously Miss Kelly's), 73 Dean Street. Advertised in *The Times* of 22 and 26 February, it afforded a wider public audience than that of Collins's earlier *amateur theatricals. He translated from the French a melodrama set in the French court of 1726. The original was by 'Monsieur Lockroy' (J. P. Simon) and Edmond Badon. Charles *Collins played the lead and Wilkie the part of Soubise, a comic courtier. The cast also included Henry

*Brandling and one professional actress, Jane Mordaunt. The play was staged in aid of the Female Emigration Fund which assisted impoverished women to settle in the colonies. This theme later appears in *No Name* (1862) where Magdalen's maid, Louisa, emigrates to *Australia. *A Court Duel* was never published and may have been a collaboration since only one act of the manuscript is in Collins's handwriting.

Parrish (1940), 155.
Peters (1991), 83–4.

Coutts & Co. Private bank located in the *Strand, founded in 1692. Used by the Collins family from 1844 as well as by Charles *Dickens, Frank *Beard, Charles *Fechter and Edward *Pigott. Collins's lifelong friend and financial adviser, *Charles Ward, worked at Coutts but Collins didn't open his own account until he was 36, on 22 August 1860. The eponymous hero of *Armadale* also used Coutts Bank.

See also FINANCES.

Critchett, George (1817–82). Distinguished ophthalmic surgeon, attached to Moorfields and the Middlesex Hospital. Also practised at 21 Harley Street and treated Collins in the 1870s. Known for his kindness and generosity; friend of the *Bancrofts and Francesco *Berger.

Crossed Path, The Title used by T. B. *Peterson of Philadelphia for their 1860 edition of *Basil*.

'Cruise of the Tomtit, The' Collins's first non-fiction article for *Household Words*. Originally published 22 December 1855 and later included in the 1861 edition of *Rambles Beyond Railways*.

Light-hearted account of Collins's sailing trip to the Scilly Isles with Edward *Pigott in September 1855 (identified in the article as Mr Jollins and Mr Migott). They hired a 36-foot cutter, sailing from the Bristol Channel with a professional crew of three brothers. In July 1860, Collins recollected to the Revd Hutchinson Smith 'I well remember my pleasant experience at the Scilly Islands—and the very large part of it for which I was indebted to Mrs Augustus Smith's hospitality and to your kindness in giving my friend Mr Pigott and myself the advantage of your local knowledge.'

Letters.

CHEESE WRING.

The Cheese Wring, one of Henry Brandling's Cornish illustrations to *Rambles Beyond Railways*

Cuff, Sergeant Richard The rose-growing detective sergeant in *The Moonstone*, called in to investigate the theft of the jewel. Cuff originally suspects Rachel *Verinder and later establishes Godfrey *Ablewhite's guilt. His character is based on the real-life Inspector *Whicher, famous for the Constance *Kent Road case;

his appearance on another Scotland Yard detective, Inspector Walker. Cuff is described by Collins as:

A grizzled elderly man, so miserably lean that he looked as if he had not got an ounce of flesh on his bones in any part of him. He was dressed all in decent black, with a white cravat round his neck. His face was as sharp as a hatchet, and the skin of it was as yellow and dry and withered as an autumn leaf. His eyes, of a steely light grey, had a disconcerting trick when they encountered your eyes, of looking as if they expected something more from you than you were aware of yourself. His walk was soft; his voice was melancholy; his long lanky fingers were hooked like claws. He might have been a parson, or an undertaker—or anything else you like, except what he really was.

See also DETECTIVE FICTION.

Cumberland In 1857 Collins and *Dickens made a walking tour in Cumberland, subsequently recounting their adventures in 'The *Lazy Tour of Two Idle Apprentices'. They left London by train for Carlisle on 7 September, travelling another fourteen miles to the village of Hesket Newmarket. Here they stayed at the Queen's Head close to *Carrock Fell. The next day Dickens insisted on climbing the mountain despite bad weather. Their innkeeper guide hadn't been up there for twenty years, Dickens's compass broke and in thick mist they became hopelessly lost near the summit. To make matters worse, the reluctant Collins badly sprained his ankle on the descent. They travelled on to nearby Wigton, where Collins saw a doctor, and then to

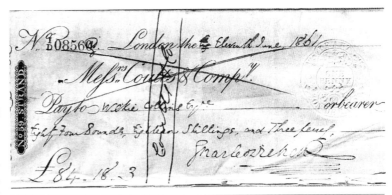

Cheque drawn on Coutts Bank from Charles Dickens to Wilkie Collins in June 1861

*Allonby. After two days they headed, via Carlisle and Lancaster, for Doncaster where from 14 September they stayed at the Angel Hotel. The race meeting was to provide local colour for their *collaboration which they had been writing *en route* and Dickens also calculated on seeing Ellen Ternan at the local theatre. During the third week of September, Dickens returned to London while Collins went on to Scarborough to recuperate.

Cumberland also features in several of Collins's works. It is the location of Limmeridge House in *The Woman in White* (1860); Noel and Magdalen *Vanstone take their honeymoon there in *No Name* (1862), as does Rosamond in 'The *Lady of Glenwith Grange' (1856). In *The Evil Genius* (1886), Catherine Linley takes Kitty to Cumberland with Mrs Presty.

Lehmann, R. C., *Charles Dickens as Editor*, London 1912.

PELCD.

D

Daly, (John) Augustin (1838–99). Distinguished theatre manager and producer in New York. Noted dramatist, translator and critic. In 1870, he asked Collins to adapt *Man and Wife* but, unhappy with the result, Daly produced his own version. Collins was concerned for his reputation although Daly closely followed the original novel. The play was a hit, running at the Fifth Avenue Theatre for ten weeks from 13 September 1870; Collins received $1,000. The same theatre staged *No Name* on 7 June 1871, and Collins collaborated more willingly for the highly successful The *New Magdalen*. This opened on 10 November 1873 at the Broadway Theatre during his reading tour of *America.

Daly was also the first owner of the *Ioláni* manuscript, probably presented to him by Collins during a visit to London in autumn 1878. Daly's company toured England on five occasions and appeared at the *Lyceum in 1888 and 1890. He opened his own theatre in Leicester Square in June 1893.

Daly, J. F., *The Life of Augustin Daly*, New York 1917.

Winter, W., *The Wallet of Time* (2 vols), New York 1913, i. 348–58.

Dawson, Harriet Constance (Hetty) (1871–1955). Younger daughter of Collins and Martha *Rudd, born in Bolsover Street on 14 May 1871. She was educated at the Maria Grey College in Fitzroy Square and in her twenties became a governess for a time. Harriet never married and remained discreetly silent about her famous father. She died in Southend on 6 July 1955.

Dawson, Marian (Tottie) (1869–1955). Elder daughter of Wilkie Collins and Martha *Rudd. An attractive, lively girl, born 4 July 1869 in Bolsover Street. Marian was a frequent visitor to *Gloucester Place and was recorded there in the 1881 census as Collins's daughter. Educated at the Maria Grey College in Fitzroy Square, she became a governess for a while in her

Augustin Daly

twenties. Remaining discreetly silent about her famous father, she never married. With her mother and sister she later moved to Southend, and died at Rochford General Hospital, Essex, 6 April 1955.

Dawson, Martha Name taken by Martha *Rudd during her liaison with Wilkie Collins. From 1868, when she lived in Bolsover Street, she became Mrs William *Dawson.

Dawson, William Identity assumed by Collins to observe the proprieties during his unmarried liaison with Martha *Rudd. When visiting her either in London or during holidays at *Ramsgate, Wilkie Collins became William Dawson, Barrister-at-Law. This is the description given for the registration of his son's birth and all three of his children were brought up with the surname Dawson.

In August 1888 Collins wrote to Sebastian *Schlesinger:

Wilkie Collins, of 82 Wimpole Street has disappeared from this mortal sphere of action, and is replaced by William Dawson, 27 Wellington Crescent, Ramsgate. In plain Eng-

lish, I am here with my 'morganatic family'—and must travel (like the Royal Personages) under an alias—or not be admitted into this respectable house now occupied by my children and their mother.

Dawson, William Charles Collins (Charley) (1874–1913). Son of Wilkie Collins and Martha *Rudd; born in Taunton Place, *Marylebone, 25 December 1874. Tall and good-looking, attended a day school in the City. At 19 Charley joined the South Wales Borderers, rising to sergeant. In 1900 he saw action in South Africa during the Boer War, receiving the Queen's Africa Medal. On leaving the army in 1902, he became a chauffeur and ultimately a motoring expert. Married Florence Sugg and had two children, Helen Martha Dawson (Bobby) (1907–87) and Lionel Charles Dawson (1912–87). In 1913, aged 38, Charley died suddenly of influenza at Southend-on-Sea.

'Dead Alive, The' See 'JOHN JAGO'S GHOST'.

William Charles Collins Dawson (Charley)

'Dead Hand, The' Short story originally published as 'The Double-Bedded Room' in *Household Words*, 10 Oct. 1857; forms the second chapter of 'The *Lazy Tour of Two Idle Apprentices'. Later republished in *The *Queen of Hearts* as 'Brother Morgan's Story of the Dead Hand'. Considered by Thompson to be based on an anecdote in J. G. Lockhart's *Life of Sir Walter Scott* (Edinburgh, 1837–8). The physical description of the 'dead' man, however, was that of a doctor's assistant Collins and Dickens met on their tour. Collins later used his strange appearance for the character of Ezra *Jennings in *The Moonstone*.

➤ Arthur Holliday arrives in Doncaster during the busy September race-week. The only accommodation he can find is a shared room with a body occupying the other bed. His apparently dead companion revives in the night. He has an uncanny resemblance to Arthur and years later is found to be his illegitimate half-brother.

Wilkie Collins: The Complete Shorter Fiction, edited by J. Thompson, London 1995, 257.

Dead Secret, The (book).

'The secret between us will remain a Dead Secret to the end of the world!'

The first full-length novel by Collins specifically written for *serialization. Dedicated to Edward *Pigott. Collins's introduction reveals that he wrote the story to show 'the influence of a heavy responsibility on a naturally timid woman, whose mind was neither strong enough to bear it, nor bold enough to drop it altogether'. The tragic servant figure reappears as Rosanna *Spearman in *The Moonstone*. A blind character is used again, to greater effect, in *Poor Miss Finch*, and Mr Phippen, the hypochondriac friend of Dr Chennery, foreshadows Mr *Fairlie in *The Woman in White* (1860).

➤ In 1829, Mrs Treverton lies dying in Porthgenna Tower on the west coast of *Cornwall. She dictates to her maid, Sarah Leeson, a death-bed confession for her husband, Captain Treverton. Mrs Treverton dies before she can make Sarah swear to give it to the Captain but she has already extracted promises neither to destroy the paper nor to take it away from the house. Sarah therefore hides the confession in the Myrtle Room in the derelict north wing and after leaving a note for the Captain disappears from the house.

Fifteen years later, the young Rosamond Treverton is privately married by Dr Chennery to the blind Leonard Frankland. Chennery is a friend of both families and knows that Leonard's father had bought Porthgenna Tower from the Captain after the death of Mrs Treverton. The Captain had quarrelled with his misanthropic brother, Andrew Treverton, who had insulted the Captain's wife, a former actress. Andrew lives a miserly existence in Bayswater with his equally unpleasant servant, Shrowl.

A few months later, while Rosamond and Leonard are travelling through the Somerset village of West Winston on their way to Porthgenna, Rosamond is taken ill and gives birth prematurely. They engage a temporary nurse, Mrs Jazeph, who alarms Rosamond by her strange behaviour and a warning to keep out of the Myrtle Room. Mrs Jazeph is dismissed and flees to Truro to visit her uncle, Joseph Buschmann. He is delighted to see his niece, in reality Sarah Leeson, after an interval of many years. Uncle Joseph, a passionate lover of Mozart which he plays incessantly on his musical box, plans to help Sarah recover the secret paper from Porthgenna. They gain entrance to the house but before Sarah can reach the letter she faints, terrified by mistaking the wind for a ghost. Sarah leaves Porthgenna and to avoid any further questions loses herself in the anonymity of London.

Dr Chennery writes to Andrew Treverton on Rosamond's behalf to identify the Myrtle Room. Treverton refuses to help but Shrowl sells a copy of the plans and the Dead Secret is revealed. Rosamond is really the illegitimate daughter of Sarah Leeson whose lover, Hugh Polwheal, was killed in a mining accident before they could marry. The childless Mrs Treverton passed off Rosamond as her own, both to preserve the love of her husband and to save Sarah's reputation. Rosamond's inheritance of £40,000, the purchase price of Porthgenna paid by Leonard's father, rightfully belongs to the dead Captain's brother. Andrew Treverton, staggered at finding two people who don't care about money, forces them to take it back. Uncle Joseph has meanwhile traced Sarah so that mother and daughter are reunited. The frail Sarah dies happy in Rosamond's arms, at peace because the ghost which perpetually haunted her has finally disappeared. She is buried in Hugh Polwheal's grave in Porthgenna.

Serialization. *Household Words*, 3 Jan.–13 June 1857; *Harper's Weekly*, 24 Jan.–27 June 1857; Littell's Living Age, Boston, 28 Feb.–18 Jul. 1857.

Book publication

1st edn. 2 vols, *Bradbury & Evans, London 1857. Grey-purple cloth, covers blocked in blind, spines lettered in gilt, cream endpapers. Half-title in vol I. Published between 1 and 14 June 1857. Copies in brown cloth, with yellow endpapers and *Chapman & Hall advertisements are of later issue (1873–4).

Vol I viii + 304 pp.

Vol II (iv) + 332 pp.

1-vol edns. *Sampson Low 1861 (new preface and frontispiece by J. *Gilbert); *Smith, Elder 1865–72; *Chatto & Windus, 1875–1929. Dover, New York 1979; Sutton, Stroud 1986; World's Classics 1997 (critical edition, edited by I. Nadel).

1st US edn. Miller & Curtis, New York 1857.

Translations. Russian, St Petersburg 1857, 1861; French, Paris 1858 (by É.-D. *Forgues); Dutch, Amsterdam 1858; German, Leipzig 1862.

Dead Secret, The (play). Stage version first performed at the Royal *Lyceum Theatre on 29 August 1877. 'Adapted, by the Author's express permission, from the Popular Novel' by E. J. Bramwell. Sarah Leeson was played by Miss Bateman and Shrowle (*sic*) by Arthur *Pinero. A review in *The *World of 5 September extended praise to both Collins and the

THE DEAD SECRET.

BY

WILKIE COLLINS.

IN TWO VOLUMES.

VOL. I.

LONDON:
BRADBURY & EVANS, 11, BOUVERIE STREET.
1857.

The Right of Translation is reserved by the Author.

Title-page to the first edition of *The Dead Secret*

original novel but pronounced the play 'a very poor adaptation' and 'a clumsy melodrama'.

dedications to Collins

Collins and his works inspired at least four nineteenth-century dedications, beginning with James *Payn's *Gwendoline's Harvest* (1870).

Blanche Roosevelt prefaced *Verdi, Milan, and Othello* (1887) 'To Wilkie Collins. My dear friend . . . knowing that the work never would have been written without you, I dedicate it to you.'

J. G. Holmes in *Ghost's Gloom* (1889) wrote 'To Wilkie Collins, Esq., This novel is gratefully dedicated by an admirer of his genius and a recipient of his kindness.'

Hadley Welford dedicated *Whose Deed? A Romance* (1899) 'To the memory of G. H. H. H. and Wilkie Collins.'

TO

WILKIE COLLINS.

MY DEAR FRIEND,

When I left England for Italy, you said, " Do write me all about Verdi, Milan, and the new opera *Othello*." I have taken you at your word ; only the letters, like most feminine epistles, have stretched away into limitless pages, and from a few vagabond sheets have grown into a volume. I am sure you will never again ask a woman to write to you, even from Paradise ; but in the mean time, here is the result of your amiability, and, knowing that the work never would have been written without you, I dedicate it to you. I hope also that it may recall to your mind not alone a composer, a country, and a people whom you have long so professedly admired, but likewise the humble colleague who, with the world, owes you more delightful hours than any pen—not your own—could ever hope to repay.

With expression of sincerest regard,

Affectionately yours,

BLANCHE ROOSEVELT.

Paris, June 1887.

Dedication to Collins in *Verdi, Milan, and Othello* by Blanche Roosevelt (1887)

detective fiction

'Reckoned up is, if you please, detective English for being watched.' (*The Evil Genius*). *The Moonstone*, one of Collins's best-known books, was described by T. S. *Eliot as 'the first and greatest of English detective novels'. Priority is now often given to Felix's *The *Notting Hill Mystery* (1865) but the success of Collins's landmark work gives it a strong claim to have established detective fiction as a genre. It also influenced his successors from *Trollope and Conan *Doyle onwards. *The Moonstone* introduces several classic features of the twentieth-century detective story: a country-house robbery; an 'inside job'; a celebrated policeman with an amiable touch of eccentricity; bungling local constabulary; detective procedures; false suspects; the 'least likely suspect'; a rudimentary 'locked room' murder; a staged reconstruction of the crime; and a final twist in the plot.

Collins's claims in the field of detection extend far beyond *The Moonstone*. 'Firsts' are inevitably difficult to pinpoint, but Ashley makes a convincing case that Collins in his early short stories created the first British detective story, 'A *Stolen Letter' (1854); the first appearance of a police detective, 'A *Terribly Strange Bed' (1852); the first woman detective, 'The *Diary of Anne Rodway' (1856); the first humorous detective story, 'The *Biter Bit' (1858); and even the first canine detective, '*My Lady's Money' (1877).

The Law and the Lady (1875) is notable as a full-length novel featuring a female detective. It also incorporates a courtroom cross-examination and repeats the concept of an alibi previously mentioned in *Poor Miss Finch* (1872). *Man and Wife* (1870) describes another crude but effective 'locked room' murder by Hester Dethridge, and in *The Haunted Hotel* (1879) the murderous Countess Narona is compelled by Destiny to return to the scene of the crime.

Collins uses many other devices which reappear in modern detective thrillers. *The Woman in White* (1860) is perhaps more a mystery novel but has Walter *Hartright jump in a cab to lose his pursuers and later in the story, before setting out to confront *Fosco, he leaves a letter with a third party, to be opened only if he fails to return by a certain time. *Armadale* (1866) begins with a deathbed confession and subsequently involves Pedgift Junior in a series of detective activities. *Midwinter when following Bashwood by cab encourages his driver with 'double your fare, whatever it is', and 'Pedgift's postscript' is a forerunner to the modern Detective Columbo's throw-away parting comment. Oscar in *Poor Miss Finch* sends a message for help written in blood and the subject of insurance fraud appears in both *The Haunted Hotel* and *Blind Love*

(1890). The modern 'murder made to look like suicide' reverses the plots of '*I Say No*' (1884) and *The Law and the Lady* where the apparent crime is ultimately proved to be death by the victim's own hand, similar to Conan Doyle's case of 'Thor Bridge'.

Collins is also precise in the forensic aspects of detection. Hartright examines the grave of Mrs Fairlie for footprints and *Cuff, in *The Moonstone*, tells *Betteredge 'Sand—in respect of its printing off of people's footsteps—is one of the best detective officers I know of.' In *Jezebel's Daughter* (1880) Madame Fontaine examines a layer of dust with a magnifying glass to confirm that a box of poisons has not been tampered with, and Marian *Halcombe in *The Woman in White* is aware that her desk has been secretly examined because it is too tidy. In *The Haunted Hotel* Lord Montbarry's body is disposed of by acid and Henry Westwick uses false teeth taken from the decomposing head as a means of identification.

Throughout his novels, Collins adheres to the modern view of 'fair play' in presenting all the clues to the reader. By using the technique of multiple narratives, however, he reveals the information in his own time, switching narrators if too much would be revealed too soon. Where he might today be criticized by modern crime writers is in his use of the undetectable poison. The deadly gas in *Armadale* 'will tell the whole College of Surgeons nothing'; *Jezebel's Daughter* features a fast-acting untraceable poison, 'The Looking Glass Drops' and a mysterious Hungarian who leaves a suicide note saying 'Let a committee of surgeons and analysts examine my remains. I defy them to discover a trace of the drug that has killed me.' The theme is continued in *The Haunted Hotel* where Baron Rivar 'can set any post-mortem examination at defiance'.

Overall, Collins commands a well-deserved place, between the innovative puzzles of *Poe and the refinements of Conan Doyle. He did not necessarily set out to write detective fiction but proved the formative influence on the genre. As Ashley writes, 'If Conan Doyle was the father of English detective fiction, then Collins was the grandfather.'

Ashley, R., 'Wilkie Collins and the Detective Story', *Nineteenth-Century Fiction*, 6 (June 1951), 47–60.

Ashley, R. *Wilkie Collins*, London 1952, 137.

Spectacles, The' Short ... ginally published in The *Spirit of ... s, 20 Dec. 1879; and in The Bolton ... ournal and other English syndi- ... apers, 20–27 Dec. 1884. Reprinted ... Magic Spectacles' in the *Seaside ... y (25 June 1880, no. 745). Collins ... : 'In England it is to be called The ... s Spectacles . . . but if "the Devil" is ... acred a personage in the U.S., to be ... in this way—then try the weaker ... of The Magic Spectacles.' Collins re- ... sted that this story, along with ... ove's Random Shot' and '*Fie! Fie! or, ... Fair Physician', should not be repub- ... ned after his death.

Brussel (1935), 53–4.

Wilkie Collins: The Complete Shorter Fiction, ed. by Julian Thompson, London 1995, 701.

'Diary of Anne Rodway, The'

Short story originally published in *Household Words 19–26 July 1856; reprinted in The *Queen of Hearts (1859) as 'Brother Owen's Story of Anne Rodway'. Features possibly the first fictional female detective and an early example by Collins of episodic diary narrative. As in much of his work, there is a deformed character.

➡ Set in 1840, Anne Rodway is a poor 'plain needlewoman' whose friend and fellow lodger, Mary Mallinson, is brought home mortally wounded by a blow to the head. Anne follows the clue of a torn cravat clutched in her dying friend's hand and sets out to discover the murderer. She is assisted by her fiancé, Robert, who has just returned from America, and they bring to justice Noah Truscott, the perpetrator of the crime.

Dickens, Charles John Huffham

(1812–70). Collins first met Dickens in the spring of 1851, when they were aged respectively 27 and 39. The introduction came via their mutual friend, Augustus *Egg, who recruited Collins to Dickens's *amateur theatrical company. Dickens, already established as a major novelist, had been editing *Household Words for two years. Collins, apart from his early journalism, had written only the Memoirs of William Collins, Esq., R.A., Rambles Beyond Railways and Antonina.

Collins effectively joined the Dickens circle on 4 March 1851, the date of Dickens's first recorded letter to him, and they met for the first time on 12 March. Collins rehearsed with the rest of Dickens's com-

pany *Bulwer-Lytton's Not So Bad as We Seem, first performed on 16 May in Devonshire House before the Queen and Prince Consort.

Dickens and Collins at once took to each other and a friendship began which lasted until Dickens's death in 1870. *Forster, in his 1873 biography of Dickens, wrote, in one of his few references to Collins in the book, that 'Wilkie Collins became for all the rest of the life of Dickens one of his dearest and most valued friends.' The friendship was rewarding for both men. For Collins, it was immensely flattering to be admitted to terms of intimacy with a man so eminent in his chosen profession; one who was not only a brilliant novelist but a gifted editor, critically acute and generously encouraging to his protégé. Dickens, for his part, found the younger man's disregard of convention and wholehearted enjoyment of life refreshing, and admired his capacity for taking pains with his writing.

Dickens's tenth child was born in 1852, and he was restless and dissatisfied with his marriage. As the only successful member of his family, he was the financial provider for his parents and other relations. He was to some extent trapped by his success as a writer; his relationship with his public depended on fulfilling the expectations he had aroused, and as the

" Familiar in their Mouths as HOUSEHOLD WORDS."
Shakespeare.

On SATURDAY, MARCH 30, will be published, Price Twopence, or stamped for post, Threepence, (also in Monthly Parts).

NO. I. OF

HOUSEHOLD WORDS.

A Weekly Journal,

DESIGNED FOR THE INSTRUCTION AND ENTERTAINMENT OF ALL CLASSES OF READERS.

CONDUCTED BY

CHARLES DICKENS.

LONDON:
OFFICE, 16, WELLINGTON STREET NORTH,
(Where all communications to the Editor must be addressed.)
And Sold by all Booksellers and Newsmen, and at all Railway Stations.

Advertisement for the first number of Dickens's Household Words, 30 March 1851

editor of Household Words he was wary of upsetting the conventional morality of the middle classes. In the company of Collins, who was free from all these constraints, he could escape from the burdens of fame and family.

In addition to performing in Not So Bad as We Seem during 1851 and on a highly successful provincial tour in 1852, Collins stayed with Dickens at Camden Crescent, Dover, in the summer of that year, the first of many such visits to Dickens's homes and holiday houses. Collins, always popular with children, enjoyed the family life that Dickens often found burdensome, and soon established a friendship with Catherine Dickens that survived her later separation from her husband. Dickens, for his part, attended a dance given by Harriet *Collins at *Hanover Terrace in April 1852, described by *Millais, who recalled that Dickens came for about half an hour and officiated as principal carver.

Collins wrote 'A *Terribly Strange Bed', the first of his many contributions to Household Words, in 1852, and was also working on his next full-length novel, Basil, which he completed while staying with Dickens at Dover. Though Dickens admired Basil and appreciated Collins's early journalism, he was careful to consider the susceptibilities of his readers. A few months later, in February 1853, he instructed *Wills to reject Collins's story of hereditary insanity, '*Mad Monkton', fearing readers would object to it.

The association rapidly became one in which work and play were inextricably bound together. Dickens was by this time issuing invitations to Collins to go off on various jaunts which would supply material for Household Words, as well as recreation. They were often to be seen dining together at Verrey's restaurant, where a special table was always reserved for them, and they prowled the night-time streets of London and *Paris together, visiting music- and dance-halls. On 20 December 1853 Dickens wrote from *Tavistock House: 'I am open to any proposal to go anywhere any day or days this week. Fresh air and change in any amount I am ready for. If only I could find an idle man (this is a general observation), he would find the warmest recognition in this direction.' Soon they were planning a longer excursion to *Italy with Augustus Egg.

Scene at Devonshire House at Dickens's production of *Not So Bad as We Seem* in 1851

Meanwhile, Dickens accepted '*Gabriel's Marriage', published in April 1853, and Collins had begun his next novel, *Hide and Seek*. That summer Dickens took his whole family to the Villa des Moulineaux at *Boulogne, and invited Collins at the end of June. Unfortunately Collins suffered his first bout of serious illness that year and was able to travel only at the end of July. He returned to London in September to discuss *Hide and Seek* with *Bentley, accompanying Dickens who was finalizing the arrangements for his just completed *Bleak House*.

The Italian trip began on 10 October. Dickens, the undisputed leader, planned the route which took the three travellers through *France, *Switzerland and Italy. Though Dickens's letters are full of complaints about the irritating habits of his travelling companions, Collins's are enthusiastic and invariably complimentary about Dickens.

The three arrived home in London on 10 December. Dickens began work at the end of January 1854 on *Hard Times*, designed to revive the declining circulation of *Household Words*, while Collins was completing *Hide and Seek*. This was published in June and dedicated to Dickens 'as a token of admiration and affection'. Dickens admired the novel, which he described as 'in some respects masterly'.

Dickens joined the *Garrick Club in the spring of 1854 and Collins became a member shortly after, one indication of the closeness of their lives at this time. In July Dickens was in need of a respite from *Hard Times* and wrote to Collins from Boulogne: 'The interval I propose to pass in a career of amiable dissipation and unbounded license in the metropolis. If you will come and breakfast with me about midnight—anywhere—any day, and go to bed no more until we fly to these pastoral retreats, I shall be delighted to have such a vicious associate.'

Collins returned to Boulogne with Dickens for the rest of July and August. Other visitors were Wills, Egg, C. H. *Townshend and Dickens's oldest friend Thomas Beard, the elder brother of Frank *Beard who became the doctor of both Dickens and Collins.

The 1854 *Christmas number of *Household Words* saw Collins's first collaboration with Dickens. He wrote the fourth story in 'The Seven Poor Travellers', 'A *Stolen Letter', for which he received the sum of £10.

In 1855 Collins was invited for the first time to act in the Twelfth Night children's theatricals at Tavistock House. Around the same time Dickens and Millais dined together at Hanover Terrace—an attempt by Harriet Collins to heal the

breach between Dickens and Collins's *Pre-Raphaelite friends after adverse criticism of their paintings in *Household Words*. Collins then accompanied Dickens to Paris for two weeks in February. They stayed in accommodation arranged by *Régnier, but Collins's enjoyment was limited by another attack of illness.

Collins's next story '*Sister Rose', was published in *Household Words* during April 1855. Dickens considered it 'an excellent story, charmingly written' and the French Revolution background may have had some influence on *A Tale of Two Cities*. Their next joint project was *The Lighthouse*, Collins's first play, produced by Dickens at Tavistock House.

During the summer Collins spent six weeks with Dickens at Folkestone, and planning began for the next Christmas number, 'The Holly Tree Inn'. Collins contributed 'The Ostler' which later became better known as 'The *Dream Woman'.

Dickens and his family spent the winter of 1855–6 in Paris. Collins was invited in January but was delayed by the first of three serious attacks of illness that year and eventually travelled at the end of February. It was during this trip to Paris that he found, while wandering about the streets with Dickens, Méjan's *Recueil des causes célèbres*.

From the spring of 1856 Collins was contributing more frequently to *Household Words*. His earnings were increasing and Dickens wrote to Wills 'I think, in such a case as that of Collins's, the right thing is to give £50 [for *A Rogue's Life*] . . . a careful and good writer on whom we can depend for Xmas Nos. and the like.' By September, Dickens wrote again to Wills with a view to recruiting Collins to the permanent staff. 'I have been thinking a good deal about Collins, and it strikes me that the best thing we can just now do for H.W. is to add him on to Morley, and offer him Five Guineas a week. He is very suggestive, and exceeding quick to take my notions. Being industrious and reliable besides, I don't think we should be at an additional expense of £20 in the year by the transaction.' Dickens preferred Wills to conduct the negotiations rather than '. . . interpose myself in this stage of the business, solely because I think it right that he should consider and decide without any personal influence on my part'. Collins ultimately accepted the appoint-

and wrote to Collins 'Any mad proposal you please will find a wildly insane response in Yours ever, C.D.' and '—if the mind can devise anything sufficiently in the style of sybarite Rome in the days of its culminating voluptuousness, I am your man . . .. If you can think of any tremendous way of passing the night, in the meantime, do. I don't care what it is. I give (for that night only) restraint to the Winds!'

When Dickens's and Collins's mutual friend Douglas *Jerrold died suddenly in June 1857, a revival of *The Frozen Deep* was arranged to contribute to a fund-raising effort for his widow devised by Dickens. After performances in London, the play transferred to Manchester towards the end of August for three public performances with professional women actors who included the young Ellen Ternan. Dickens was soon confiding in Collins 'I have never known a moment's peace or content since the last night of *The Frozen Deep*' and, 'Partly in the grim despair and restlessness of this subsidence from excitement and partly for the sake of *Household Words*, I want to cast about whether you and I can go anywhere—take any tour—see anything—whereon we could write something together . . .. I want to escape from myself . . . my blankness is inconceivable—indescribable—my misery amazing.'

Their 'escape' to *Cumberland in September 1857 was written up as 'The *Lazy Tour of Two Idle Apprentices', published in *Household Words* the following month. The destination was chosen by Dickens, who knew that Ellen's next engagement was in Doncaster. He decided on a walking tour, finishing at Doncaster for the races and the theatre.

Collins received an increase of £50 in his salary after twelve months on the staff of *Household Words*. He collaborated with Dickens on 'The *Perils of Certain English Prisoners', the 1857 Christmas number. The manuscript was bound and presented by Dickens to Collins early the following year, 'Thinking it may one day be interesting to you—say, when you are weak in *both* feet [a reference to the ankle Collins sprained in Cumberland] and when I and Doncaster are quiet and the great race is over—to possess this memorial of our joint Christmas work . . ..'

Spring of 1858 saw the separation, by now inevitable, of Dickens from his wife.

Charles Dickens

ment on the understanding that his name would be advertised in advance for any 'long story'.

The next key event in their association was the production of *The Frozen Deep*. Although the play was written by Collins, it was jointly planned and the Arctic theme decided on as early as March 1856. In July Collins was invited to Boulogne and Dickens wrote 'I am charmed to hear you have discovered so good a notion for the play. Immense excitement is always in action here on the subject, and I don't think Mary and Katey will feel quite safe until you are shut up in the Pavilion on pen and ink.' Both men grew beards for

the play and Dickens was eventually almost living the part of Richard *Wardour. 'Took twenty miles to-day, and got up all Richard's words, to the great terror of Finchley, Neasden and Willesden.' Collins played Wardour's rival Frank *Aldersley and the first performance took place on 6 January 1857.

Dickens took possession of his new house, *Gad's Hill, in February 1857 although he was not able to move in until May. Collins was one of the first visitors, coinciding with Hans Christian *Andersen who overstayed his welcome and was later parodied in Collins's 'The Bachelor Bedroom'. Dickens finished *Little Dorrit*

Collins had become the friend on whom he relied for sympathy in his predicament (though Collins was also one of the few who remained friendly with both Dickens and Catherine). Dickens wrote to him in May, 'Mr Dear Wilkie' [no longer 'My Dear Collins'] 'A thousand thanks for your kind letter. I always feel your friendship very much, and prize it in proportion to the true affection I have for you.'

In July 1858 Dickens and Collins resigned from the Garrick Club in support of Edmund *Yates in what became known as 'The Garrick Club Affair'. Yates, another of Dickens's protégés, was attacked by *Thackeray for publishing gossip he had heard at the Club. Thackeray asked for Yates to be expelled from club membership. The affair caused a rift between Dickens and Thackeray only healed shortly before Thackeray's death.

Collins contributed numerous articles to *Household Words* during 1858, including two lead articles on which he collaborated with Dickens. He suffered another bout of illness and, escaping from the heat of London to recover, spent August in *Broadstairs. A letter from Gad's Hill in September invited him to contribute to the next Christmas number, which ultimately became 'A *House to Let'.

By the beginning of 1859 Dickens had dissolved his partnership with *Bradbury & Evans, and he launched his own paper, *All the Year Round,* on 30 April 1859. Both Collins and his brother made contributions to the early numbers, from May and June respectively. Dickens's opening serial, *A Tale of Two Cities*, was relatively short and he needed to decide fairly soon on its successor. He could have selected an established or 'safe' author but was sufficiently confident of Collins by this time to rely on his writing as well as his friendship.

Collins rose to the occasion, writing to Wills in August 1859 '. . . I *must* stagger the public into attention, if possible, at the outset.' The novel in question was *The Woman in White*, begun during the summer of 1859 at *Broadstairs. Serialization began on 26 November and increased the circulation of the already successful *All the Year Round*. Dickens was enthusiastic about *The Woman in White* and in January 1860 wrote 'There cannot be a doubt that

it is a very great advance on all your former writing. . . .. In character it is excellent . . . *I* know that this is an admirable book, and that it grips the difficulty of the weekly portion and throws them in a masterly style. No one else could do it half so well.'

By the end of 1859, Charles *Collins had also become a regular visitor to Dickens's household. He proposed to Dickens's daughter Kate the following spring.

Dickens might have been happy to forge a closer link with Collins's family, though he found Harriet *Collins irritating, but he was against the marriage because of his son-in-law's 'nervous and delicate health', and because he suspected Kate was marrying him only to get away from home. He did not, however, prevent the wedding, which took place in July 1860 with Forster and Townshend as witnesses.

Charles Collins, Wilkie's brother, and son-in-law to Charles Dickens

At Gad's Hill in September 1860, Dickens made a great bonfire of letters from literary friends, including Collins, which accounts for the one-sided nature of their surviving correspondence. In October, the two writers travelled to the West Country for local colour and collaborated on the next Christmas number, *A *Message from the Sea*, which eventually sold over a quarter of a million copies.

In January 1861, Collins departed from *All the Year Round* after five years on the staff of Dickens's periodicals. With the success of *The Woman in White* he had become a household name in his own right and no longer needed a regular salary with the constraints of weekly contributions. Dickens took his resignation in good part, writing 'I am very sorry that we part company (though only in a literary sense) but I hope we shall work together again one day.' They did not collaborate again until *No Thoroughfare* in 1867, although Collins contributed one story to 'Tom Tiddler's Ground' that Christmas.

Dickens, however, serialized Collins's next novel, *No Name*, which ran for forty-five instalments from March 1862. Dickens made several helpful suggestions while still maintaining his editorial authority. In September he wrote: 'I have gone through the Second Volume at a sitting and I find it *wonderfully fine*. It is as far before and beyond *The Woman in White* as *that* was beyond the wretched common level of fiction-writing.'

The year 1862 was a bad one for Collins's *gout and he was so unwell by October that Dickens, hearing of it from Frank Beard and remembering his own illness during the writing of *Bleak House*, volunteered to help. 'Write to me at Paris at any moment, and say you are unequal to your work, and want me, and I will come to London straight, and do your work. I am quite confident, that with your notes, and a few words of explanation, I could take it up at any time . . . . I hope that the knowledge may be a comfort to you. Call me, and I come.' Collins didn't need to avail himself of this offer and was able to complete the story himself. *No Name* was published in book form in December 1862 and a copy was sent to Gad's Hill in time for New Year's Day. 'Many thanks for the book, the arrival of which has created an immense sensation in this palatial abode. I am delighted (but

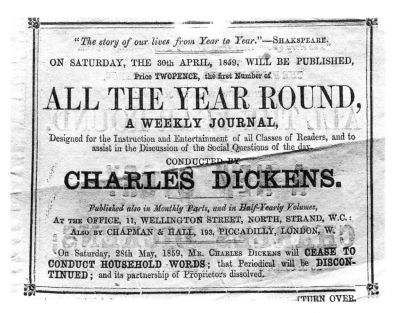

Advertisement for the first number of Charles Dickens's *All the Year Round*, 30 April 1859

not surprised) to hear of its wonderful sale.'

In the same letter Dickens mentions that before going to Paris he will 'vanish into space'. Later, in August 1863, he says '. . . I am thinking of evaporating for a fortnight on the 18th.' These disappearances are discreet references to his continuing association with Ellen Ternan. He was soon to assume the identity of 'Mr Tringham' of Slough, an interesting parallel with Collins's later *alter ego* 'Mr William *Dawson'. By this time Collins and Dickens had rejoined the Garrick Club and proposed Wills for membership. When he was blackballed they both resigned for the second time in March 1865, followed soon after by *Fechter.

The two writers collaborated for the final time during 1867, writing *No Thoroughfare* for the Christmas number. Dickens sailed for *America from Liverpool on 9 November 1867 and Collins travelled north for his farewell party. The year 1867 also saw the serialization of *The Moonstone* in *All the Year Round*. Dickens had written to Wills in June 'It is prepared with extraordinary care, and stands every chance of being a hit. It is in many respects much better than anything he has done.' The following year, however, he wrote to Wills in more critical terms, 'I quite agree with you about "The Moon-

stone". The construction is wearisome beyond endurance, and there is a vein of obstinate conceit in it that makes enemies of readers.'

This criticism has been taken as symptomatic of an estrangement between Dickens and Collins. Yet as recently as December 1867 Dickens had written to Wills with comments such as 'Tell Collins with my love', and in June 1868 still signed himself 'ever affectionately' in a letter enthusiastically discussing the Paris production of *No Thoroughfare*.

There are hints in Dickens's correspondence which suggest that one probable cause of any estrangement was his annoyance at the increasing entanglements of Collins's domestic arrangements. Another cause was Collins's brother. Charles Collins had been struggling since his marriage with the difficulties of earning a living and the early symptoms of stomach cancer. Dickens, apart from employing him on *All the Year Round*, doubled Kate's marriage portion in 1867, and further gave Charles £150 in 1867 and £350 in 1868. He also agreed that Charles should provide the illustrations for *The Mystery of Edwin Drood*. Despite the apparent cooling of their friendship, Collins still visited Gad's Hill for a week in September 1869 and invited Dickens and family that year to the first night of *Black *and White*. Dickens wrote to Wills that the play had real merit, and deserved to run.

In January 1870, Dickens wrote a formal letter, requested by Collins for legal reasons, establishing his copyright to everything by him published in *Household Words* and *All the Year Round*. 'I can have no hesitation in stating . . .. You have the right, hereby freely acknowledged, of disposing of and publishing the same novels, tales, and articles in any way you think proper.' The accompanying, less formal note concludes 'I don't come to see you because I don't want to bother you. Perhaps you may be glad to see me by-and-by. Who knows?' It was apparently the last letter Collins received from Dickens, who died on 9 June 1870. Collins was shocked by the news and, of course, attended the funeral, travelling in the same coach as his brother and Frank Beard. In 1878 he stated that he had been asked to complete *Edwin Drood* but had 'positively refused'. He also refused to publish any reminiscences of Dickens, but did help Georgina *Hogarth with her three-volume edition of Dickens's letters, suggesting a surprising number of omissions which he felt advisable.

Lehmann, R. C., *Charles Dickens as Editor*, London 1912.
PELCD

See also 'THE DICKENS CONNECTION' in the Bibliography.

Dickens, Katherine Elisabeth Macready (Kate or Kitty) (1839–1929) (Mrs Charles Collins; later Mrs Carlo Perugini). Younger daughter of Charles *Dickens; Wilkie Collins's sister-in-law. Kate Dickens had spent a good deal of time with Charles *Collins from the beginning of 1860 when they both sat for *Millais's historical painting, *The Black Brunswicker*. They became engaged in May and married on 17 July 1860. Kate saw marriage to Charles Collins as a way of escaping the unhappy Dickens household and although 'she respected him and considered him the kindest and most sweet-tempered of men, was not in the least in love with him'. After the guests had left, Mamie Dickens came across her weeping father who said tearfully 'But for me, Katey would not have left home.' Frederick *Lehmann considered the marriage an 'infamy' which has been taken as a reference to the possible impotence of Charles Collins.

Kate Dickens

Kate Collins became something of a confidante to Wilkie who visited her immediately after the marriage of Caroline *Graves to Joseph *Clow in 1868. In June 1874, a year after Charles Collins's death, Kate married the painter Carlo Perugini (1839–1918). In later life, as Kate Perugini, she recalled of Wilkie 'I liked him, and my father was very fond of him and enjoyed his company more than that of any other of his friends—Forster was very jealous of their friendship. He had very high spirits and was a splendid companion, but he was as bad as he could be, yet the gentlest and most kind-hearted of men.'

Lehmann, J., *Ancestors and Friends*, London 1962.
Storey, G., *Dickens and Daughter*, London 1939, 105–6, 214.
Wells, P. 'Kate Perugini: Some Observations Arising from a Drawing by Sir Luke Fildes, R.A.', *Dickensian*, 92 (Summer 1996), 111–14.

Dickinson, Frances Vickress, later Elliot (1820–98). Dedicatee (as Mrs Elliot) of *Poor Miss Finch* (1872). Journalist, travel-writer, historian and novelist; a popular writer in her day. Collins introduced her to *Dickens in 1857 when, in *The Frozen Deep*, a substitute actress was wanted for the part of the old nurse, originally played by Janet Wills. Frances Dickinson appeared as 'Mrs Francis' in four performances at the Gallery of Illustration.

Frances Dickinson's experiences probably suggested some aspects of *Man and Wife* (1870), *The Evil Genius* (1886) and the earlier short story, 'The *Parson's Scruple' (1859). In 1845 she left her first husband, losing custody of her four daughters, and resumed her maiden name. A two-year case heard in the Court of Arches, 1846–8, resulted in a judicial separation. In 1855 she finally managed to obtain a Scotch divorce. The case, which proved notorious, turned on the difference between English and Scots law. After another mysterious 'marriage' (probably not legal) she later married, in 1863, the Very Revd Gilbert Elliot, Dean of Bristol. When this marriage also failed, Dickens was asked to mediate between the parties, which he did without success.

Frances Dickinson spent much of her life in Italy, dying in Florence at the house of her daughter who had married an Italian aristocrat.
PELCD, vol viii.
Peters (1991), 173–4, 330–2.

didactic novels Collins's novels of moral purpose are generally considered to date from the 1870s when he came under the influence of Charles *Reade. Didacticism is, perhaps unfairly, held to account for a decline in Collins's later works. *Man and Wife*, attacking *marriage laws and athleticism, was viewed by *Swinburne as 'the first and best' of the didactic novels, although other critics disagreed with his opinion that the story is 'so brilliant in exposition of character, so dexterous in construction of incident'. Hugh Walpole thought Collins 'hampered himself with one of the curses of the "seventies" novel, and that was the quite intolerable demon of Propaganda', while Elwin considered Collins sometimes made his points 'with blows from a clumsy bludgeon'.

Collins used several earlier stories as a form of protest and continued the practice throughout his career with the most overt criticism in his anti-vivisection novel, *Heart and Science* (1883). *The Woman in White* (1860) illustrated the abuses of lunatic asylums, a theme he returned to in 'A *Mad Marriage' (1874) with a direct attack on the Lunacy Commission and the Court of Chancery. *Jezebel's Daughter* (1880), using the character of Jack Straw, made a plea for the humane treatment of lunatics while Mrs

Du Maurier frontispiece to the Chatto & Windus one-volume edition of *The New Magdalen*

Wagner in the same novel argued for equal employment rights for women.

In *No Name* (1862), the plight of Magdalen and Norah Vanstone highlighted the laws on illegitimacy and inheritance. The 'fallen woman' was dealt with in both *The New Magdalen* (1873) and *The Fallen Leaves* (1879). *The Law and the Lady* attacked the Scottish Not Proven verdict while *The Evil Genius* (1886) considered the effect of the divorce laws on the custody of children.

In a more general way, Collins's novels suggest a sympathetic approach towards the handicapped, for example with the deaf-mute Madonna in *Hide and Seek* (1854) and blind Lucilla in *Poor Miss Finch* (1872).

> Elwin, M., 'Wilkie Collins' in *Victorian Wallflowers*, London 1934, 221.
> Walpole, H., 'Novelists of the "Seventies"' in *The Eighteen-Seventies*, edited by H. Granville-Barker, Cambridge 1929, 31.

Doyle, Sir Arthur Conan (1859–1930). Author best known for his detective, Sherlock Holmes. Collins was acknow- ledged in Conan Doyle's own notebooks as one influence that helped create his detective. Holmes emulates many of the features of both Sergeant *Cuff in *The Moonstone* (1868) and the pipe-smoking Old Sharon in '*My Lady's Money' (1877). In the latter story, Felix Sweetsir's 'exhaustive system of reasoning' is remarkably like Holmes' dictum that 'when you have eliminated the impossible, whatever remains, *however improbable*, must be the truth' ('The Red-Headed League'). The notion of a 'three-pipe problem' (*The Sign of Four*) was introduced by Uncle Joseph in *The Dead Secret* (1857).

The brilliant success of Holmes was achieved by applying observation, reason and deduction, characteristics foreshadowed in Collins's *detective fiction. In *The Moonstone*, Sergeant Cuff proves an early exponent of the magnifying glass and correctly predicts the course of the investigation; the theme of cursed treasure reappears in *The Sign of Four*; and the young clerk, Gooseberry, acts like one of Holmes' Baker Street Irregulars.

Lambert, G., *The Dangerous Edge*, London 1975, 36.

'Dream Woman, The' Supernatural short story originally published as 'The Ostler', second part of 'The Holly Tree Inn', the extra *Christmas number of *Household Words* for December 1855. Later included in The *Queen of Hearts* as 'Brother Morgan's Story of the Dream Woman'. Adapted by Collins for his reading tour of *America and enlarged within a narrative framework for The *Frozen Deep and Other Stories* (1874).

➽ Isaac Scatchard, an itinerant ostler, wakes on the night of his birthday to see the apparition of a woman trying to stab him with a clasp knife. Seven years later he marries Rebecca Murdoch, against the wishes of his mother who recognizes her from Isaac's description as the dream woman. Rebecca takes to drink and fulfils the prophecy by attacking him on his birthday. She disappears and Isaac can never again sleep at night for fear she will return to kill him.

'Duel in Herne Wood, The' Short story originally published in The *Spirit of the Times*, 22 December 1877. Reprinted in the *Seaside Library (vol 44, no. 905), 1880; and as 'Miss Bertha and the Yankee' in *Little Novels* (1887).

➽ Captain Stanwick and Lionel Varleigh are old friends but after falling out over their attentions to Bertha Laroche fight an illegal duel in Herne Wood. Stanwick wrongly thinks he has killed Varleigh and goes mad, killing himself with a razor, when his supposed victim returns like an apparition from the dead. Varleigh is acquitted of murder and marries Bertha.

du Maurier, George Louis Palmella (Kicky) (1834–96). Black-and-white artist, cartoonist and regular contributor to *Punch. Author of *Trilby* and *Peter Ibbetson*; grandfather of Daphne du Maurier. *Illustrator of *The Moonstone*, *Poor Miss Finch*, *The New Magdalen* and *The Frozen Deep* in the *Chatto & Windus collected edition of 1875.

Egg, Augustus Leopold, R.A. (1816–63). Painter of popular works in contemporary and historical genres. Friend of Collins and his family, introducing Wilkie to *Dickens in 1851. Egg had private means and entertained at his house in Bayswater friends who included William *Frith, Douglas *Jerrold, Leech, Macready and Edward *Ward.

Egg joined Dickens's *amateur theatrical company in 1848. He sketched the costume designs for the 1851 production of *Not So Bad as We Seem* and suggested to Dickens that Collins would be willing to take the part of his valet in the play. Egg toured with the company in 1852 and 1857, and acted in the 1855 production of *The *Lighthouse.*

In 1853 he travelled to *Italy with Collins and Dickens, acquiring the nickname 'The Colonel' ('Kernel') on the journey. Egg was in love with Georgina *Hogarth and proposed to her in 1852 but was refused. He eventually married Esther Brown in 1860 but mysteriously kept her hidden. After his death memoirs of Egg omitted all mention of his marriage.

Egg visited Wilkie and Caroline at Albany Street during 1859 and stayed with them at *Broadstairs in 1862. Soon after, he went abroad for his health but died the following March in Algiers.

Eliot, Thomas Stearns (1888–1965). Author of 'Wilkie Collins and Charles Dickens', *Times Literary Supplement*, 4 Aug. 1927; reprinted in *Selected Essays: 1917–1932*, London 1932. The essay forms the basis for Eliot's introduction to *The Moonstone*, World's Classics, 1928. Together with Dorothy L. *Sayers and Walter de la Mare, he is one of the few major figures of English literature in the early part of the twentieth century to have recognized Collins's achievements. Eliot described *The Moonstone* as 'the first and greatest of English detective novels'. He praised *The Haunted Hotel*, considered *The Woman in White* 'the greatest of Collins's novels' and of *Armadale* wrote 'It has no merit beyond melodrama, and it has every merit that melodrama can have.'

Elliotson, John (1791–1868). Professor of Medicine in the University of London (1831–8) and one of the founders of University College Hospital. Celebrated both for his pioneering clinical work (on heart disease and hay fever) and for his unconventional and pseudo-scientific treatments. Elliotson founded the Phrenological Society but is better known for his popular interest in mesmerism (hypnotism) which he shared with *Townshend and *Dickens. He was one of the first surgeons to operate using hypnosis as a form of anaesthesia but

Augustus Egg, from a sketch by W. P. FRITH

MAN AND WIFE.

A Novel.

BY

WILKIE COLLINS.

" May I not write in such a style as this?
In such a method too, and yet not miss
My end, thy good? Why may it not be done?
Dark clouds bring waters, when the bright bring none."
JOHN BUNYAN'S *Apology for his Book.*

IN THREE VOLUMES.

VOL. I.

LONDON:
F. S. ELLIS, 33, KING STREET, COVENT GARDEN.
1870.

[*The Right of Translation is Reserved ; and the Right of Dramatic Adaptation has been secured by the Author.*]

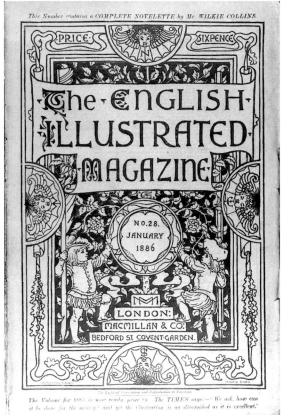

(*above left*) Title-page to the scarce first edition of *Man and Wife* published by F. S. Ellis in 1870
(*above right*) The January 1886 issue of *The English Illustrated Magazine*, which published 'The Poetry Did It'

concern among his colleagues about his unconventional practices led to his forced resignation from his Chair during 1838. In 1849 Elliotson saved the life of *Thackeray who dedicated *Pendennis* to him the following year.

Collins was well acquainted with Elliotson who in 1863 tried, unsuccessfully, to use hypnotism as a substitute for *laudanum to control the pain of his rheumatic *gout. Ezra *Jennings in *The Moonstone* (1868) calls Elliotson 'one of the greatest of English physiologists' and uses a case history in Elliotson's *Human Physiology* as his inspiration for the attempt to find the missing diamond by administering a second dose of opium to Franklin *Blake.

Ellis, Frederick Startridge (1830–1901). London publisher and distinguished antiquarian bookseller. Noted for his association with William Morris, D. G. Rossetti and Morris's Kelmscott Press. F. S. Ellis & Co, at 33 King Street, Covent Garden, published *Man and Wife* in 1870, on a 10 per cent commission of gross receipts. The firm was an unlikely choice by Collins since the book was apparently their only novel, but author and publisher had in common aesthetic and anti-athletic opinions. The current rarity of the first edition is due to its publication by a small, specialized publisher unsuited to distribute a work of fiction. Collins accused Ellis of keeping the publication 'as profound a secret as he can'.

Sadleir (1951), i. 376.

English Illustrated Magazine, The
(1883–1913). Monthly literary magazine published by Macmillan. Authors included Gosse, Jefferies, Mrs *Oliphant and *Swinburne; illustrators, Walter Crane, Carlo Perugini (Kate *Dickens's second husband), Alma-Tadema and Louis Wain. Collins contributed two short stories: 'The *Girl at the Gate', Jan.–Feb. 1885; and 'The *Poetry Did It. An Event in the Life of Major Evergreen', Jan. 1886.

Every Saturday Weekly paper published in Boston by Ticknor & Fields. Its contents were taken from English and European periodicals. The extra Christmas number for 1867 consisted of '*No Thoroughfare', printed using advance sheets from *All the Year Round.

Evil Genius, The: A Domestic Story
(book). Novel published in 1886, dedicated to William Holman *Hunt, treating the related themes of divorce and child-custody. The story was ahead of its time in presenting both the wife and the mistress of an adulterous husband in a sympathetic light and concentrating the reader's attention on the plight of the child involved in the break-up of a marriage. The 'evil genius' of the title is an interfering mother-in-law. Collins unexpectedly upholds double standards in a

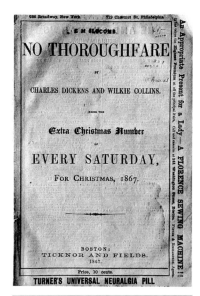

US edition of 'No Thoroughfare' published in *Every Saturday*, December 1867

passage added shortly before publication, claiming that a husband's adultery should not, by itself, be sufficient grounds for divorce, and ends the novel with a reconciliation and remarriage. Collins also used the plot for a dramatic version with the same title. He wrote the book and play simultaneously and traces of his method can be detected in the novel which has an unusually high proportion of dialogue. The play, tauter and in some ways more effective than the book, was never performed, though it was given a single reading for the purpose of establishing dramatic *copyright.

•◦ After a traumatic childhood and youth, Sydney Westerfield is rescued from the drudgery of teaching in her aunt's school by becoming the governess of Kitty, only child of Herbert and Catherine Linley. Herbert and Sydney fall in love and matters are brought to a crisis by the meddling of Mrs Presty, Catherine Linley's mother. Sydney leaves the household but is brought back when Kitty becomes seriously ill, pining for her beloved governess. The situation deteriorates further and Catherine leaves her husband. To avoid custody of the child being given to Herbert, she goes into hiding with her mother and Kitty, obtaining a divorce under Scottish law. Kitty, however, is miserable. She misses her father and her governess—she is told her father is dead—and lacks companions because other children are not allowed to play with the child of divorced parents.

Matters are further complicated by the introduction of a friend of Sydney's dead father, Captain Bennydeck, who is searching for her. He falls in love with Catherine but withdraws a proposal of marriage when he learns she is divorced. A somewhat contrived happy ending is brought about when Sydney, tormented by her guilty conscience, leaves Herbert and the Linleys are reunited by Kitty and remarry. Sydney becomes Captain Bennydeck's secretary and the reader is left with the expectation that they will marry.

Serialization. First published in the *Leigh Journal and Times*, 11 Dec. 1885–30 Apr. 1886; the *Bolton Weekly Journal* (12 Dec. 1885–1 May 1886) and several other *Tillotson syndicated newspapers.

Book publication

1st English edn. 3 vols, *Chatto & Windus, London 1886. Dark green cloth, front covers blocked in black, spines lettered in gilt, grey and white floral endpapers. Half-title in each vol. Published between 1 and 15 Sept. 1886.

Vol I viii + 284 pp.

Vol II vi + 304 pp.

Vol III vi + 266 pp. 32 pp publisher's catalogue dated May 1886 bound in at end.

The Prologue was published separately with the same title, Bolton [1885], 24 pp, buff paper wrappers.

1-vol edns. Chatto & Windus 1887–99. Broadview Press, Ontario, 1994 (critical edition, edited by G. Law); Sutton, Stroud 1995.

1st US edns (precede English). *Harper's Handy Series, (no. 72) New York 1886 (first book publication); Donnelley's Lakeside Edition, Chicago 1886; Lovell's Library (vol 14, no. 722), New York 1886; *Seaside Library (vol 102, no. 2069), New York 1886. *Translations.* German, Berlin 1887; Russian, 1887.

Brussel (1935).

Evil Genius, The: A Drama in Four Acts (play).

Stage version written at the same time as the novel. Though the play is one of Collins's better works for the theatre, it was never produced except for a single afternoon performance at the Vaudeville Theatre, 30 October 1885, purely to establish Collins's dramatic *copyright. Managements were probably wary of it because of the theme of divorce. No published version exists although acting copies appeared at the 1898 Sotheby's *auction.

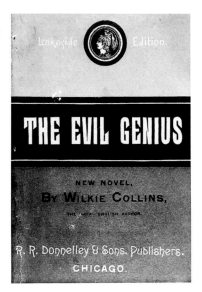

Cover of *The Evil Genius*, published in paper wrappers in Donnelley's Lakeside Library, 1886

F

Fairlie, Frederick

'It is the grand misfortune of my life that nobody will let me alone.'

Eccentric valetudinarian in *The Woman in White*. Lives in seclusion at Limmeridge House with his jewels, coins and art treasures. Uncle and guardian to Laura *Fairlie who is placed in jeopardy through his selfish inactivity. The character is described as 'a bundle of nerves made up to look like a man' and is probably based on Collins's friend, C. H. *Townshend.

Fairlie, Laura

Fair-haired, blue-eyed token heroine of *The Woman in White*. Half-sister to her double, Anne *Catherick, and to Marian *Halcombe. Basically a weak character, married to Sir Percival *Glyde who, with the assistance of Count *Fosco, steals both her fortune and her *identity. Ultimately saved by, and marries, the hero, Walter *Hartright.

Fallen Leaves, The: *First Series*. Novel

published in 1879, dedicated to Caroline [*Graves]. The 'Fallen Leaves' of the title are 'The people who have drawn blanks in the lottery of life . . . the friendless and the lonely, the wounded and the lost'. The novel was not well received and a planned *Second Series*, showing an unconventional marriage failing because of outside pressures, was never written.

The novel follows the fortunes of four women, all in one way or another 'fallen leaves', who are linked by their relationships with the hero, Amelius Goldenheart, and also by secrets from the past. Their histories are looked at from two perspectives: that of the ruthless capitalist society of England in which they live, and that of the Christian Socialism of the hero who has been brought up in a Utopian community in America. Collins modelled his description on the Oneida

communities of New England, in which sexual relationships were not restricted to marriage but had to be sanctioned by the elders. One of the leading themes of the novel is the difficulty of creating relationships between men and women which are neither hypocritical nor exploitative. Unfortunately the novel is not well constructed, and the importance of Collins's message is lost in a convoluted and extravagant plot. It relies heavily on coincidence and the writing is moralistic and melodramatic.

➤ Amelius Goldenheart is in exile from his Utopian community because of an unsanctioned relationship with an older English woman who has suffered some mysterious tragedy in her earlier life— she is the first of the 'fallen leaves'. He

Envelope sending weekly parts of *The Fallen Leaves* to C. Thomas of Robson the printers

comes to London with a letter of introduction to the villainous John Farnaby, and is captivated by Farnaby's niece Regina to whom, after some complications, he becomes engaged. Mrs Farnaby, a woman who 'lives in some secret hell of her own making, and longs for the release of death' enlists his help to look for the illegitimate daughter she lost sixteen years earlier. Farnaby had seduced his employer's daughter in order to force her into marriage and further his own career, but when the baby was born he kidnapped it and gave it to a baby-farmer.

On the streets of London, Amelius is accosted by a 16-year-old prostitute, Simple Sally, and takes her home with him to save her from a life on the streets. They live together as brother and sister, but when Regina discovers her presence she rejects Amelius, breaking off their engagement. Sally turns out to be Mrs Farnaby's long-lost child and they are reunited at Mrs Farnaby's deathbed. Amelius and Sally then marry. The 'Second Series' was intended to follow the course and breakdown of their marriage.

Serialization. The *World, 1 Jan.–23 July 1879; and in The *Canadian Monthly, Feb. 1879–Mar. 1880.

Book publication

1st edn. 3 vols, *Chatto & Windus, London 1879. Olive-brown cloth, covers blocked and lettered in black, spines lettered in gilt, blue and black floral endpapers. Half-title in each vol. Published between 1 and 16 July 1879.

Vol I (viii) + 276 pp.

Vol II (iv) + 272 pp. 40 pp publisher's catalogue dated May 1879 bound in at end.

Vol III (iv) + 296 pp.

1-vol edns. Chatto & Windus 1880–99. Sutton, Stroud 1994.

1st US edn. Included in Collier *collected edition (vol 21), 1900.

Rose-Belford, Toronto 1879.

Translations. German, Berlin 1880; Russian, Moscow 1880.

'Family Secret, The' Short story originally published as 'Uncle George; or, the Family Mystery' in The National Magazine, November 1856. Reprinted in The *Queen of Hearts (1859) as 'Brother Griffith's Story of the Family Secret'.

➥ Charley, the narrator, spends many years trying to discover the family secret from his relatives. He finally learns by chance that his beautiful young sister died when Uncle George, a doctor, performed a rash operation to remove an unsightly tumour from her neck.

'Fatal Cradle, The: Otherwise the Heartrending Story of Mr Heavysides'

'My weight has been the grand misfortune of my life.'

Short story first published as 'Picking up Waifs at Sea', Chapter 4 of 'Tom Tiddler's Ground', the extra *Christmas number of *All the Year Round for December 1861. Subsequently included in *Miss or Mrs? and Other Stories in Outline (1873).

➥ Humorous tale of two babies born simultaneously on a crowded ship bound for Australia. One is the eighth child of a poor family, the Heavysides, the other the first-born of a well-to-do couple, the Smallchilds. Their identities become confused when they are placed in the same makeshift cradle and the captain, after trying several unsuccessful methods, finally allocates them by weight, giving the heavier baby to the heavier woman. The narrator claims his life has been blighted by the captain's mistaken choice.

'Fatal Marriage, A' See 'MAD MARRIAGE, A'.

'Fauntleroy' Short story originally published in *Household Words, 13 Nov. 1858, as 'A Paradoxical Experience'. Reprinted in The *Queen of Hearts (1859) as 'Brother Morgan's Story of Fauntleroy'. Also included in Remember: A Keepsake, New York [1874] and in Readings and Recitations from Modern Authors, Chicago 1890.

Henry Fauntleroy (1785–1824) was the last man hanged in England for forgery. A middle-aged merchant, Mr Trowbridge, tells the other side of the story. The forger not only helped him as a young man start in business but also protected his interests when the bank that Fauntleroy ruined was forced to close.

Fechter, Charles Albert (1824–79). English-French actor, born in London and brought up in Boulogne. Friend of *Dickens and Collins, who saw him on the *Paris stage in the 1850s. Collins met him in London during 1860 when Fechter appeared in an English translation of Ruy Blas. Collins became a regular visitor to Fechter's home in St John's Wood, the

Charles Fechter, the actor

scene of informal gastronomic excesses (see also FOOD AND DRINK).

In 1869, they collaborated on Collins's play Black and White. Fechter suggested the outline of the first two acts while Collins provided the ending, characters and dialogue. Fechter played the part of the French Count de Layrac. He also starred in London and New York as Obenreizer in the more succesful No Thoroughfare, written by Collins and Dickens at *Gad's Hill in the Swiss chalet given to Dickens by Fechter in 1865. A French version, L'Abîme, was jointly written by Fechter and Dickens. Fechter left England for *America at the end of 1869 and was the first to greet Collins when he disembarked at New York for his reading tour. Collins stayed with him in Pennsylvania and they met for the last time in New York before Collins's return to London. Once the idol of the London and Paris stages—Collins thought his Hamlet the only true one he had ever seen in thirty-five years' playgoing—Fechter was not wholly successful in America and died neglected and embittered.

Collins wrote a candid account of Fechter describing both his acting skills and personal shortcomings. 'Ungovernable temper was the curse of Fechter's life' and, according to Dickens, he had 'a perfect genius for quarrelling'. Fechter was financially irresponsible, at times owing Collins and more particularly Dickens large sums of money. Collins also described Fechter's legendary stage-fright but glossed over his last years which included a bigamous marriage to actress Lizzie Price and a lonely decline into alcoholism.

Peters (1991), 360–1.
'Wilkie Collins's Recollections of Charles Fechter' in Kate Field, *Charles Albert Fechter*, Boston 1882, 154–73.

'Fie! Fie! Or the Fair Physician'

Short story first published simultaneously in the special Christmas supplement to *The Pictorial World* and in *The *Spirit of the Times*, 23 Dec. 1882; reissued in the *Seaside Library (no. 1587) Apr. 1883. Not published in England during Collins's lifetime and listed among the works he did not wish republished after his death.

See also 'LOVE'S RANDOM SHOT'.

film versions The following film versions of Collins's works have been located:

Armadale (1916). Directed by Richard Garrick.

Costume design by Milo Anderson for Sidney Greenstreet as Count Fosco in the 1948 film version of *The Woman in White*

Basil (1997). Directed by Radha Bharadwaj; with Derek Jacobi, Jared Leto, Christian Slater and Clair Forlani.

The Dead Secret (1913). Directed by Stanner E. V. Taylor.

The Moonstone (1909 and 1915) silent versions; (USA, 1934) directed by Reginald Barker and set in the twentieth century. Apart from the title, bears almost no resemblance to the Collins original.

The New Magdalen (1910, 1912, 1913, 1914) silent versions.

'She Loves and Lies' (USA, 1920). Directed by Chester Withey.

'A Terribly Strange Bed' (Poland, 1968). Directed by Witold Lesiewicz.

The Woman in White (Great Britain, 1929). Directed by Herbert Wilcox. (The last of several silent versions from 1912 with various titles such as *The Dream Woman* and *Twin Pawns*.)

Crimes at the Old Dark House (Great Britain, 1939). Directed by George King and very loosely based on *The Woman in White*. The film is a convenient vehicle for melodramatic horror star Tod Slaughter.

The Woman in White (USA, 1948). Directed by Peter Godfrey. Stars Sidney Greenstreet as a convincing Count Fosco, Eleanor Parker as Laura *Fairlie and Ann (sic) *Catherick, and Gig Young as Walter *Hartright. James Agee, the film critic and screen-writer, summed it up with: 'The Wilkie Collins novel is given the studious, stolid treatment ordinarily reserved for the ritual assassination of a great classic. This is not intended as a recommendation.'

See also TELEVISION ADAPTATIONS.

Hubin, A. J., *Crime Fiction: A Comprehensive Bibliography, 1749–1990* (2 vols), New York 1994, 180–1.

finances

'I am not rich enough to care about money.' (*Poor Miss Finch*)

Collins's bank account at *Coutts & Co was opened in August 1860 and earnings during 1860–1 were £1,223. His peak year was 1868–9, receiving (with capital from Harriet *Collins) over £6,000. The periods of greatest regular income were 1867–8 and 1877–8, approximately £3,000–£4,000. From 1879 to 1889 his income reduced to an average of £2,500. These figures can be multiplied by about forty to equate with modern values. Collins's accounts also show regular payments to Caroline *Graves and Martha

*Rudd, together with subscriptions and household expenses.

Clarke (1988), 228–9.

'First Officer's Confession, The'

Short story published in *The *Spirit of the Times* and *Bow Bells*, New York, 24 Dec. 1887. Reprinted for the first time in *Wilkie Collins: The Complete Shorter Fiction* (edited by J. Thompson, London 1995).
➥ First officer Evan Fencote proposes to Mira Ringmore, a transatlantic passenger visiting her English aunt, Miss Urban. Finding Mira living as Mrs Motherwell, Evan is reassured to discover that she is pretending to be the mother of her aunt's illegitimate son after Miss Urban had been tricked into a bigamous marriage.

Fitzgerald, Percy Hetherington

(1834–1925). Biographer and friend of *Dickens, although Fitzgerald professed a closeness not acknowledged in Dickens's own letters. Novelist, journalist and reviewer; regular contributor to *Household Words* and *All the Year Round*. Collins first met Fitzgerald at a dinner party given by *Wills when, so Fitzgerald claimed, Collins described 'in his fluent, dramatic way, how he was subject to a curious ghostly influence, having often the idea that "someone was standing behind him", and he was tempted to look round constantly'.

In both *Memoirs of an Author* (1895) and *Memories of Charles Dickens* (1913), Fitzgerald criticized Collins's novels, his stage reading ability and more particularly his influence on Dickens. The tone of the later book is more antagonistic.

food and drink

'Properly pursued, the Art of Cookery allows of no divided attention.' (*The Law and the Lady*)

Food and drink were two of Collins's pleasures in life from a young age. From his first trips to *Paris, he acquired the taste for French dishes and always tended to denigrate both English cooking and plain food. Italian cooking he described as 'more fanciful than the English and more solid than the French' ('My Black Mirror', *Household Words*, 6 Sept. 1856). Food features in the novels, from *Antonina* (1850) where Vetranio is 'the author of some of the most celebrated sauces of the age' including the 'Nightingale

Sauce' and accuses women of being 'culpably deficient in gastronomic enthusiasm', to *Blind Love* (1890) in which the landlady produces food 'cooked to a degree of imperfection only attained in an English kitchen'.

During the 1860s, Collins was a regular visitor to informal dinners at Charles *Fechter's house where they had 'every variety of French cookery'. They 'twice put the inexhaustible resources of Gastronomic France to the test by dining on one article of food only': 'a potato dinner in six courses and an egg dinner in eight courses'. Fechter's cook was a 'great culinary artist' but Collins had to advise Frederick *Lehmann in 1869 not to employ her because she had done 'all sorts of dreadful things'. He confessed his own style of cooking was expensive since he regarded meat 'simply as a material for sauces', a view repeated by Miserrimus Dexter in *The Law and the Lady* (1875) where 'a man who eats a plain joint is only one remove from a cannibal—or a butcher'. Allan *Armadale, however, declares that his notion of good feeding is 'Lots of strong soup, and joints done with gravy in them'.

Collins's own cooking was sometimes far from successful. On one occasion he collaborated with Frank *Beard to prepare a 'Don Pedro pie' which used so much garlic that they both took to their beds and were ill for several days. Another time, in February 1880, he wrote to Nina Lehmann 'Oh! I was foolish enough to eat slices of plain joints for two days following. The bilious miseries that followed proved obstinate until I most fortunately ate some *pâté de foie gras*. The cure was instantaneous—and lasting.'

Collins also had firm views on alcohol, convinced that he would not exacerbate his *gout if he drank only the very driest champagne, warning *Harpers in advance of this during his *American tour in 1873. He regularly ordered cases of 'Vin Brut' and Ribera sherry (which he couldn't drink) from Beechens, Yaxley, his wine merchants, and allowed them to use one of his letters as a testimonial. In *Heart and Science* (1883), Mr Gallilee remarks 'Isn't a pint of champagne nice drinking, this hot weather?' and Miserrimus Dexter calls Burgundy 'the King of Wines' and Clos Vougeot 'the King of Burgundies'. In *Blind Love*, however, the villainous Dr Vimpany observes 'if there is a poison which undermines the sources of life . . . it is alcohol'.

Collins's gastronomic excesses must have contributed to his poor *health and gout in particular. It was only during his last few years that rather unwillingly he attempted to control his eating habits. In 1864, Beard had put him on a light diet and even when he visited *Aix-la-Chapelle for his health he allowed the hotel's Parisian cook to encourage his 'natural gluttony'.

Beard, N., 'Some Recollections of Yesterday', *Temple Bar*, 102 (July 1894), 315–39.
Lehmann (1908), 46.

Forgues, Émile-D. (1813–83). French critic and translator. Dedicatee of *The *Queen of Hearts* (1859) in grateful recognition for his positive essay on Collins in *La *Revue des deux mondes* of 1855. This 34-page early critical examination of Collins anticipated his later success. It discussed *Memoirs of the Life of William Collins, Esq., R.A.*, *Antonina*, *Basil*, *Hide and Seek* and *The Lighthouse*. Forgues also translated *The Lighthouse*, *The Dead Secret*, *The Woman in White* and *No Name*.

Collins, W., Preface to *The Queen of Hearts* (1859).
'Études sur le Roman Anglais: William Wilkie Collins', *La Revue des deux mondes*, 2e série, Nov. 1855, 815–48.
Page (1974), 11–12, 62–6.

Forster, John (1812–76). Friend of *Dickens for over thirty years and his principal contemporary biographer. Editor and historian, Forster met Dickens in 1836. He became his adviser in both literary and personal affairs and was ultimately appointed co-executor. Forster originally owned an eighth part of *Household Words* to which he made occasional contributions. He relinquished his share in 1856 because of friction with *Wills, the sub-editor.

Collins apparently enjoyed a cordial relationship with Forster for several years, seeing him at Dickens's house and during *amateur theatricals. The dour and pompous Forster, however, became increasingly jealous of the younger, more exuberant writer's influence. Collins for his part felt no ill-feeling and dedicated *Armadale* (1866) to Forster 'in affectionate remembrance of a friendship which is associated with some of the happiest years of my life'. After Dickens's death, Collins and Forster became increasingly remote.

Collins was impressed with the first volume of *The Life of Charles Dickens*, thanking Forster in November 1872 for 'the most masterly biographical story you have ever told'. George Bentley at this time felt that Forster's *Life* would misrepresent the quarrel between his father, Richard *Bentley, and Dickens in 1837–8. Collins unsuccessfully interceded with Forster to destroy the correspondence and omit it from his biography. The later volumes deliberately ignored Collins and prompted him to describe the book as 'The Life of John Forster, with notices of Dickens.' Collins's frank views on both Dickens's work and Forster are preserved in an article in *The *Pall Mall Gazette* (20 Jan. 1890): 'Wilkie Collins about Charles Dickens, from a Marked Copy of Forster's "Dickens"' (excerpts reprinted in Robinson (1951), 258–9).

Forster, J., *The Life of Charles Dickens* (3 vols), London 1872–4.
Ley, J. W. T., *The Dickens Circle: A Narrative of the Novelist's Friendships*, London 1919.
Lohrli (1973), 274–6.

Fort House Stark-looking mansion on the cliffs at *Broadstairs, now called 'Bleak House' because of its association with *Dickens. Collins rented the house with Caroline Graves from July to October 1862. It provided both a quiet place for working on the serialization of *No Name* (1862) and ample accommodation for the frequent visitors. These included Charles *Ward, Frank *Beard and Augustus *Egg, as well as *Bullar and *Pigott for the *sailing.

Fosco, Count Isidor Ottavio Baldassare Italian count and true villain of *The Woman in White*. Described by Marian *Halcombe as 'a man who could tame anything'; immensely fat, yet strangely attractive, with a remarkable likeness to Napoleon and with unfathomable grey eyes of extraordinary expression and power. Married to Eleanor Fairlie who stands to inherit £10,000 on the death of her niece, Laura *Fairlie. When *Glyde fails to force Laura to sign away her fortune, Fosco conceives the plan to put her in an asylum with the identity of Anne *Catherick. Fosco is ultimately killed in Paris as a traitor to the secret Brotherhood. Archetypal 'fat-man', intellectual criminal.

MUSICAL DEDICATIONS: *The Fosco Galop*

1878 and sold Leslie the serial rights to *The Fallen Leaves* for £100 as well as *The Black Robe* and *Heart and Science*. Collins apparently left *unpublished notes for a 'drama or novel—or both' called 'The Case of Rosalind Druse' which he intended Leslie to use in March 1887.

IELM, 667.

Fraser's Magazine (1830–82). Literary journal founded by William Maginn and John Fraser. Its authors included Ainsworth, Carlyle, *Coleridge, Ruskin and *Thackeray. Collins contributed one story, *'Mad Monkton', Nov.–Dec. 1855. This had been rejected by *Dickens for *Household Words because it dealt with hereditary insanity. *Fraser's* had published a favourable review of *Mr Wray's Cash-Box* in 1852.

French literature: its influence on Collins Collins very early acquired a lasting enthusiasm for French culture, from literature to *food, and his first holidays abroad without his parents were to *France. On his trips to *Paris he made the rounds of picture galleries and visited the theatre almost nightly, admiring the sophistication of French stagecraft. He learned to read French with ease and spoke it fluently, if not always correctly. On one of his visits he acquired from a Paris bookstall Méjan's *Recueil des causes célèbres* from which he took the plot of *The Woman in White*. Collins's library contained hundreds of volumes in French, the majority fiction and plays, but also the complete works of Diderot and Voltaire.

At a time when French novels and plays were considered immoral and depraved by English readers, their influence on Collins was striking. In his youth he read French popular fiction, from Le Sage to Pigault-Lebrun and Dumas, and learnt the importance of story-telling. The sensational novels of Eugène Sue such as *Les Mystères de Paris* (1842–3) and the risqué fiction of Paul de Kock also had their effect. But it was the novels of Honoré de *Balzac that influenced his work most significantly. Following Balzac's example, Collins took the melodrama of Sue's work and transformed it for serious social purposes. Balzac's character Vautrin, the

France

'The dignity which a Frenchman can always command in the serious emergencies of his life…' (*The Fallen Leaves*)

Collins was a frequent visitor to France. William *Collins took his family to *Boulogne in the summer of 1829 when Collins was a child of 5. In September 1836, on their way to *Italy, they travelled to Boulogne and *Paris, then continued south by carriage and canal-boat to Marseilles, Toulon, Cannes and Nice. Collins next visited France with Charles *Ward in 1844, again in 1847 and 1849, and trav-

elled on his own to Paris in 1845. From the 1850s he made frequent trips with *Dickens. Their return route from Italy in December 1853 passed through Marseilles, Lyons, Paris and Calais.

Collins became fluent in the language, was strongly influenced by *French literature and admired the civilized culture of France.

Frank Leslie's Illustrated Newspaper

New York periodical with literary section. Collins fell out with *Harpers in

criminal who is a master of disguise (based on François Vidocq, the criminal who joined the Paris police and headed the Sureté before becoming a private investigator), is a precursor of a number of Collins's shady characters. Collins wrote a review of Vidocq's *Memoirs* in *All the Year Round* ('Vidocq, French Detective', 14–21 July 1860).

In two further articles in *All the Year Round* ('Portrait of an Author Painted by his Publisher') Collins paid tribute to Balzac, whom he described as virtually unknown in England because of his subject-matter and the difficulties of translating his 'strong, harsh, solidly vigorous language'. Collins's articles form an extended review of a biography of Balzac by Edmond Werdet, the publisher he ruined. They discuss the work as well as the life, pointing out the discrepancies between the often deplorable behaviour of the man towards his long-suffering publisher and other friends, and the genius of his works.

Collins's account of Balzac's methods can be related to his own work. He emphasizes Balzac's subtle and profound understanding of women, which certainly influenced the creation of his own female characters. He also appreciated Balzac's bleak realism: 'a writer who sternly insists on presenting the dreary aspects of human life'. He picked out for especial praise *Eugénie Grandet*, *Le Recherche de l'Absolu*, and above all *Le Père Goriot* (which George Eliot considered 'a hateful book'). He also appreciated the shorter stories. One of the latter, 'Pierre Grassou', is a possible source for the character of the conscientious but untalented painter Valentine Blyth in *Hide and Seek*. Collins's comments on *La Physiologie du mariage* have a particularly close relevance to his own writing.

In England, this book would have been universally condemned as an unpardonable exposure of the most sacred secrets of domestic life. It unveils the whole social side of Marriage in its innermost recesses, and exhibits it alternately in its bright and dark aspects with a marvellous minuteness of observation, a profound knowledge of human nature.

Collins's description of Balzac's working methods are also close to those he himself developed, and resemble his accounts of his own preliminary work on *The Woman in White*, the novel he was writing at the same time as the Balzac ar-

(*top*) William Frith, the painter, aged 30, by Augustus EGG
(*above*) The overture to *The Frozen Deep* by Francesco BERGER

ticles. Both Balzac and Collins thought out their novels in detail before beginning to write, and both obsessively rewrote and altered manuscripts and proofs in the later stages of composition.

'Portrait of an Author, Painted by his Publisher', *All the Year Round*, 18 and 25 June 1859; reprinted in *My Miscellanies* (1863).

Prendergast, C., *Balzac: Fiction and Melodrama*, London 1978.

Puttick & Simpson, *Catalogue of the Library of the Late Wilkie Collins Esq.*, 20 Jan. 1890.

Taylor, A. C., 'Non-French Admirers and Imitators of Balzac', Inaugural Lecture, Birkbeck College, 1950.

Frith, William Powell, R.A.

(1819–1909). Popular Victorian narrative painter, best known for *Derby Day* and *Ramsgate Sands*. Long-standing friend of Collins and Edward *Ward; fellow student of Charles *Collins. Frith participated in *amateur theatricals, including Collins's 1849 production of Goldsmith's *Good Natur'd Man* which inspired the painting *Mr Honeywood Introduces the Bailiffs*. Frith was also a regular visitor to *Dickens, attending The *Frozen Deep at *Tavistock House and playing bagatelle with Collins at *Gad's Hill. Collins travelled to Italy with Frith and his family in 1875. Frith records how one of his guests at a dinner party attempted to insult Collins, remarking that his works were read in every back-kitchen in England. Far from being offended, Collins apparently accepted the comment without a sign of irritation.

Frith, W. P., *My Autobiography and Reminiscences* (3 vols), London 1887-8.

Ward, E. M., *Memories of Ninety Years* (edited by Isabel G. McAllister), London 1924, 52.

Frizinghall

In *The Moonstone*, the nearest town to the Verinder house which is 'high up on the Yorkshire coast and close to the sea'. The location of the house is possibly based on Mulgrave Castle close to Runswick Bay north of *Whitby. The Maharajah Duleep Singh, original owner of the Koh-i-Noor diamond, rented the castle between 1859 and 1864. Collins stayed in nearby Whitby during August 1861.

Mead, H., 'On the Trail of Yorkshire's *Moonstone*', *Yorkshire Journal*, 7 (Autumn 1994), 26–31.

Frozen Deep, The (play).

Play written by Collins during 1856, although con-

Playbill for the production of *The Frozen Deep*, staged at Tavistock House in January 1857

ceived, cast and revised by *Dickens. *The Frozen Deep* was based on the ill-fated 1845 Franklin expedition to discover the North-West Passage. Dickens had published several articles in *Household Words rebutting the charge of cannibalism (later proved to be true) made by John Rae in 1854. The role of Richard *Wardour was acknowledged by Dickens as an influence on the self-sacrificing Sydney Carton of *A Tale of Two Cities* (1859).

The play was first performed at *Tavistock House on 6 January 1857 with subsequent performances on 8, 12 and 14 January. Collins played the part of Frank *Aldersley and Dickens that of Wardour. The scenery was designed and painted by Clarkson *Stanfield and William Telbin, with music composed by Francesco *Berger. There were further performances at the Gallery of Illustration, Regent Street, in July 1857, including a Royal Command performance on the 4th. The play was performed at the Manchester Free Trade Hall on 21, 22 and 24 August as part of the fund-raising for Douglas *Jerrold's widow. The amateur actresses were replaced by professionals and the cast included Ellen Ternan, her mother and sister. In 1866 Collins made revisions for a professional production at the Royal *Olympic Theatre with Henry *Neville as Richard Wardour. The play opened on 27 October and, although receiving fairly good reviews, did not prove a financial success.

The Frozen Deep: A Drama in Three Acts (1866) was 'printed but not published' (48 pp, buff paper wrappers). In 1874, it was adapted for Collins's reading tour of *America and subsequently republished in book form.

Brannan, R. L., *Under the Management of Mr. Charles Dickens: His Production of 'The Frozen Deep'*, Ithaca, NY, 1966.

'Frozen Deep, The' (story).

'He has won the greatest of all conquests— the conquest of himself.'

Story adapted for reading from the 1857 stage play of the same name during the

Boston part of Collins's 1874 tour of *America. Further extended for book publication in The *Frozen Deep and Other Stories* (1874). Serialized in *Temple Bar*, Aug.–Sept. 1874.

➡ Frank *Aldersley becomes engaged to Clara Burnham at a celebration ball the night before he joins an expedition to find the North-West Passage. Clara is an orphan, staying with her best friend, Lucy Crayford, whose husband is a lieutenant on the voyage. The same evening Clara rejects the advances of Richard *Wardour, another admirer. Wardour in bitter despair joins the expedition at the last minute, vowing revenge on his rival with-

out knowing that he is part of the crew.

Two years later, their ships, *The Sea-Mew* and *The Wanderer*, are trapped in the Arctic ice with most of the expedition weak or dying. Wardour has just realized the identity of his rival and is still set on vengeance. The officers cast lots to decide the composition of a search party to bring help from the nearest settlement and chance selects both Aldersley and Wardour. When they become separated from the main group, Wardour wrestles with his conscience over leaving his now weakened opponent to die on the ice.

News meanwhile reaches England that some of the crew have been rescued. Aldersley and Wardour are listed only as missing but Clara, with second sight, sees a vision of her fiancé dying by his rival's hand. Lucy sails to Canada to meet her

rescued husband and is accompanied by the distraught Clara. While they are waiting in a boat-house on the Newfoundland shore, the lone figure of the starving Wardour suddenly appears. Delirious, he fails to understand accusations about Aldersley's safety. Wardour leaves the hut only to reappear carrying his still living companion in his arms. The dying Wardour has nobly resisted the temptation of murder and instead has sacrificed his own life for Clara's happiness.

Frozen Deep, The: and Other Stories (Readings and Writings in America).

Combined 1874 publication in book form of 'The *Frozen Deep: A Dramatic Story, in Five Scenes'; 'The *Dream Woman: A Mystery in Four Narratives'; and '*John Jago's Ghost; or, The Dead Alive: An American Story'. The first two stories were used by Collins for readings in *America; the third was written during his tour. On his return to England, Collins further adapted them for book publication. The dedication is to Oliver Wendell Holmes whom he met in Boston.

'The Frozen Deep' is derived from the 1856 stage play. 'The Dream Woman' is based on the 1855 short story republished in The *Queen of Hearts (1859) with the principal characters renamed Francis Raven and Alicia *Warlock. This version is set within a narrative framework in which the ostler is finally killed by his wife.

Serialization. See individual stories.

Book publication

1st edn. 2 vols, Richard *Bentley, London 1874. Blue cloth, bevelled edges, front covers blocked and lettered in black, spines lettered in gilt, cream endpapers. Half-title in each vol. Published 2 Nov. 1874. Copies in brown cloth with yellow endpapers and *Chapman & Hall advertisements, and without half-titles, are of later issue.

Vol I viii + 248 pp.

Vol II viii (numbered vi) + 284 pp. Publisher's advertisements occupy pp (283–4).

1-vol edns. *Chatto & Windus, 1875–1915 (frontispiece by G. *du Maurier and 8 illustrations by M. F. Mahoney).

Canadian edn. *Hunter, Rose, Toronto 1874 ('The Frozen Deep' and 'The Dream Woman').

1st US edn. Gill, Boston, 1875 ('The Frozen Deep' and 'The Traveller's Story of A *Terribly Strange Bed').

Translation. Russian, St Petersburg 1874; Holland, The Hague 1876; French, Paris 1879.

Front cover to the US edition of *The Frozen Deep* published by William Gill in Boston, 1875

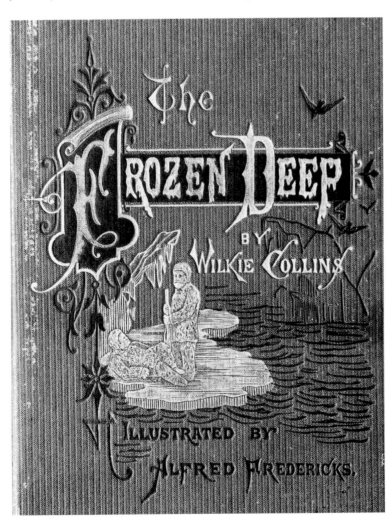

funeral of Collins

'We live, on condition that we die.' (*Blind Love*)

Collins's funeral took place on 27 September 1889, four days after his death. *The Daily Telegraph* of 28 September 1889 recorded how a few friends assembled at the deceased's house in *Wimpole Street. The chief mourners consisted of Caroline *Graves with Harriet and Henry *Bartley, Squire *Bancroft, Frank *Beard, Hall *Caine, Andrew *Chatto, Edward *Pigott, Sebastian *Schlesinger and A. P. *Watt. The coffin of plain oak lay, covered with wreaths, in a small room on the ground floor and bore the inscription 'Wilkie Collins, Born Jan. 8, 1824. Died Sept. 23, 1889.'

A small and respectful group had gathered outside the house from which the hearse left at 11.30. At Kensal Green a much larger, less dignified throng (estimated by the *Pall Mall Gazette* of 3 October as at least one hundred) had assembled by the church steps and round the grave. Many of them had brought with them their favourite volumes of Collins's works.

At the church, the hearse and carriages were joined by the many other mourners. These included Ada *Cavendish, Charles Dickens Junior, Edmund Gosse, Holman *Hunt, Arthur *Pinero, George Redford and Edmund *Yates. Martha *Rudd and her children did not attend the funeral but were represented by a large cross of white chrysanthemums in the name of Dawson. Floral tributes had completely engulfed the hearse. Mamie Dickens sent scarlet geraniums, her father's favourite flower, 'in memory of Charles Dickens'; Blanche Roosevelt, roses and lilies; and the Baroness De Stern, tiger lilies. Other wreaths came from Mary *Braddon, the Comte de Paris, Carlotta Leclercq, Kate Perugini [*Dickens] and the *Society of Authors.

Collins's funeral: his grave in Kensal Green Cemetery

The ceremony was conducted by Dr Edward Ker Gray who also conducted a memorial service two days later at St George's Chapel, Albermarle Street. Collins's *will had specified a modest funeral at Kensal Green with expenses not exceeding £25. He also requested a plain stone cross and the simple inscription 'Author of *The Woman in White* and other works of fiction.' When in June 1895 Caroline Graves was buried in the same grave, located behind the church, no further words were added. (Grave number/Square/Row 31754/141/1.)

G

'Gabriel's Marriage' Short story originally published in *Household Words* 16–23 Apr. 1853. Later included in **After Dark* (1856) as 'The Nun's Story of Gabriel's Marriage'. The plot was rewritten as the basis for *The *Lighthouse* in 1855. ➻ The scene is Brittany at the time of the French Revolution. Gabriel Sarzeau becomes estranged from his fisherman father when he discovers that he committed a murder. Before his marriage, Gabriel confesses his knowledge to Fr. Paul, a fugitive priest. Fr. Paul reveals that he was the victim but survived his wounds. He performs the marriage ceremony, forgives his attacker, and reconciles father and son.

Gad's Hill Place *Dickens's home from 1857, located on the Old Dover Road near Rochester. Dickens realized a childhood dream when he purchased the house in 1856 for £1,700. He wrote most of his later works at Gad's Hill, including *collaborations with Collins: *No Thoroughfare* (1867) was written in the Swiss chalet given to Dickens by *Fechter in 1865.

Collins was a frequent visitor to Gad's Hill. He attended the house-warming party on 19 May 1857 and the following month met there Hans Christian *Andersen. Charles *Collins married Dickens's daughter Kate on 17 July 1860 at the local church in Higham, and the wedding breakfast was held at the house. In September 1860, Dickens made his famous bonfire of letters in the field at Gad's Hill. This destroyed all his letters from literary friends including those from Collins.

Watts, A. S., *Dickens at Gad's Hill*, Reading 1989.

Garrick, Club London theatrical club founded in 1831 in Covent Garden to facilitate the meeting of actors and men of letters. The President was the Duke of Devonshire and members included *Dickens, *Egg, *Fechter, *Reade, *Stanfield and *Thackeray. Collins joined in the early to mid-1850s but resigned in 1858 over 'The Garrick Club Affair', a quarrel between Edmund *Yates, whose father had been a founder member, and Thackeray. Yates offended Thackeray with an article in *Town Talk*, which included gossip gathered at the Club. After a lengthy correspondence, the affair came before the Garrick committee. Yates's prime defender and adviser was Dickens but Collins also strongly supported his cause. When Yates refused to apologize, he was expelled and both Dickens and Collins resigned in protest. They subsequently rejoined only to resign again in 1865 when *Wills, their candidate for election, was blackballed.

Fitzgerald, P., *The Garrick Club*, London 1904.

Yates, E., *Mr Thackeray, Mr Yates and The Garrick Club: The Correspondence and the Facts*, printed for private circulation, 1859; reprinted 1895.

Geddes, Alexander William (*c.*1763–1843). Wilkie Collins's maternal grandfather, married to Harriet Easton in 1789. After leaving the Army in 1791, he settled near Salisbury in 1798 at Shute End House, on the Earl of Radnor's estate at Alderbury, where he lived for the next forty-five years. Wilkie's mother, Harriet *Collins, was the eldest of their six children. Wilkie and Charles *Collins spent holidays with their grandparents and the kindly, easy-going and improvident Alexander Geddes is probably the model for Zack Thorpe's grandfather in *Hide and Seek*.

See also MARGARET CARPENTER.

Geddes, Harriet, née Easton (1762–1842). Wilkie Collins's maternal grandmother, younger daughter of James Easton (1722–99), a prominent Salisbury coal merchant and Mayor in 1785. Harriet married Alexander *Geddes in 1789.

General Theatrical Fund, Royal Benevolent institution for the theatrical profession, founded in 1845 with Queen Victoria as Patroness. Collins was one of several vice-presidents who also included *Bulwer-Lytton, *Dickens, *Forster and *Lemon. Prevented by illness on two earlier occasions, Collins took the chair for the Twentieth Anniversary Festival at Freemasons Tavern on 12 April 1865 and to deafening applause proposed the main toast of 'Prosperity to the Royal General

Group on the lawn at Gad's Hill, including Wilkie Collins and Charles Dickens

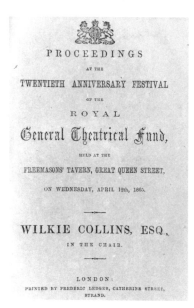

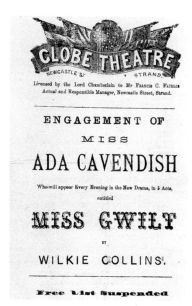

(*above left*) The Royal General Theatrical Fund: proceedings chaired by Wilkie Collins in April 1865
(*above centre*) 'The Ghost's Touch', first serialized in *The Irish Fireside* from September 1885
(*above right*) Programme for the 1876 production of *Miss Gwilt* at the Globe Theatre

Theatrical Fund'. The proceedings were subsequently issued in August 1865 as a 48-page pamphlet which shows that Collins donated ten guineas. His speeches appear on pp 12–14, 17–26, 31–3.

'Ghost in the Cupboard Room, The' See 'BLOW UP WITH THE BRIG!'.

ghost stories See SUPERNATURAL, THE.

'Ghost's Touch, The' *Supernatural short story written especially for Anne (Nannie) *Wynne. Originally published in *The Irish Fireside*, 30 Sept.–14 Oct. 1885; *Harper's Weekly*, 23 Oct. 1885; and in *The Ghost's Touch and Other Stories* (with '*My Lady's Money' and '*Percy and the Prophet', Harper's Handy Series, no. 30, 1885). Reprinted as 'Mrs Zant and the Ghost' in *Little Novels* (1887).
➥ Mr Rayburn, a widower, and his young daughter, Lucy, meet Mrs Zant in Kensington Gardens while she is experiencing a vision of her dead husband. The ghost warns her against his brother, who aims to force her into an illegal marriage. Rayburn rescues Mrs Zant, hoping to marry her himself, while the supernatural force returns to strike her brother-in-law with fatal paralysis.

Gilbert, Sir John, R.A. (1817–97). Illustrator, and painter in oils and watercolours. Regularly contributed drawings to *Punch from 1841. Provided vignette frontispieces for *Sampson Low's collected edition of Collins's works issued between 1861 and 1865: *Antonina, Basil, Hide and Seek, The Dead Secret, The Queen of Hearts*, and *The Woman in White*. The illustrations were reused in later editions by *Smith, Elder and *Chatto & Windus.

'Girl at the Gate, The' Short story originally published in *The *Spirit of the Times*, 6 Dec. 1884; and in the *English Illustrated Magazine*, Jan. 1885. Reprinted in the *Seaside Library (vol 100, no. 2030), 17 Aug. 1885; and as 'Mr Lepel and the Housekeeper' in *Little Novels* (1887).
➥ Lepel and his proud but impecunious friend, Rothsay, witness an Italian play which foreshadows their future lives. Rothsay is in love with a gatekeeper's daughter, Susan Rymer, who is herself in love with Lepel. Lepel falls mysteriously ill and learns from his eminent doctors that he is dying. Intending to help his friend, Lepel agrees to marry Susan so that she can become a rich widow and a suitable wife for Rothsay. Lepel's medicine has been poisoned by his housekeeper, Mrs Mozeen, and when by accident he stops taking it, he immedi-

ately recovers. Lepel now realizes that he is in love with Susan but at the same time has blighted Rothsay's prospects.

Globe Theatre London theatre in Newcastle Street, off the Strand; opened in 1868. Staged *Miss Gwilt* in April 1876. Demolished for road-widening in 1902.

Gloucester Place, 90 (now renumbered 65). Large terraced Georgian house in *Marylebone; Collins's home from September 1867 until February 1888. (He was always careful to designate it 'Portman Square' to avoid confusion with another Gloucester Place off nearby Westbourne Grove.) The house had five

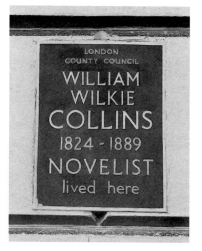

London County Council blue plaque at 90 Gloucester Place (now renumbered 65)

storeys, a large stone staircase and an impressive double drawing-room on the first floor where Collins did most of his writing. The lease included, in the mews to the rear, stables which Collins sublet to subsidize the rent. Caroline *Graves and her daughter, Harriet, lived with Collins for almost all of his time in Gloucester Place. There were three servants and his much-loved dog *Tommie. Collins liked *animals and there was usually a cat in the household as well.

At the end of 1887 the lease on Gloucester Place was running out and Collins complained to Mary *Anderson 'my landlord, the enormously rich Lord [Portman] asked me such exorbitant terms for allowing me to continue to be his tenant that I confronted the horror of moving in my old age'. (In The *Legacy of Cain (1888) Collins called the aristocracy 'A race of people who are rich without earning their money, and noble because their great-grandfathers were noble before them'.) Collins found new accommodation in *Wimpole Street and after twenty years left Gloucester Place in February 1888.

Number 65, as it now is, has a blue plaque denoting Collins's residence, unveiled for the old London County Council by Michael Sadleir on 23 May 1951. The house was damaged during the Second World War and reduced to four storeys. It is currently in a sad state of neglect.

Glyde, Sir Percival Violent-tempered villain of The Woman in White, guided by *Fosco. Marries Laura *Fairlie for her money; prepared to go to any lengths to protect the secret of his illegitimacy and preserve his false title to the estate at *Blackwater Park.

Goldsmid, Lady Louisa Sophia (1819–1908), Wife of Sir Francis Goldsmid (1808–78), first Jewish QC; philanthropist and MP for Reading. Collins advised Lady Goldsmid about *copyright matters in 1861 and in the mid-1860s was invited both to her London home in Regent's Park and to stay at her country house where he met Miss Jekyll. In September 1866 he wrote 'Your kind letter finds me just recovering from one of those severe colds which it is the privilege of "this great country" to confer on the fortunate people who dwell in it.' In Oc-

tober 1866 Collins presented her with a copy of Armadale.
Letters.

Goodchild, Francis Character assumed by the 'laboriously idle' *Dickens in 'The *Lazy Tour of Two Idle Apprentices' (1857).

gout

> 'The torture of the infernal regions.' (Poor Miss Finch)

A metabolic disorder, exacerbated by over-indulgence in *food and alcohol, resulting in a rise in the uric acid content of the blood; characterized by acutely painful attacks of arthritis affecting the joints. In the nineteenth century 'gout' was used as a blanket diagnosis for many illnesses, and although Collins undoubtedly suffered from an acutely painful form of arthritis, the descriptions of his symptoms and those of eyewitnesses do not always suggest that the condition was gout. After Collins's *health began to decline, his eyes seemed to be affected with particular severity. From the ocular manifestations described by himself and others he probably suffered from recurrent attacks of anterior uveitis and associated glaucoma. Hall *Caine remembered Collins saying 'I see that you can't keep your eyes off my eyes, and I ought to say that I've got gout in them, and it is doing its best to blind me.'

Collins told William *Winter that during the writing of The Moonstone 'My suffering was so great . . . that I could not control myself and keep quiet. My cries and groans so deeply distressed my amanuensis, to whom I was dictating, that he could not continue his work, and had to leave me. . . . I was blind with pain, and I lay on the couch writhing and groaning. . . . In that condition and under those circumstances I dictated the greater part of The Moonstone.' In fact only six pages of the manuscript, part of 'The Narrative of Miss Clack', were dictated.

Collins, W., preface to The Moonstone, Smith, Elder 1871 and subsequent editions.
Duke-Elder, S. and A. G. Leigh, System of Ophthalmology, viii: Diseases of the Outer Eye, Part 2, London 1965, 1060.
Peters (1991), 296.

Graphic, The (1869–1932). Illustrated weekly newspaper founded in 1869.

'Miss or Mrs?' in The Graphic Christmas number, 25 December 1871

Collins contributed two stories: 'Miss or Mrs?' in The Graphic Christmas Number, 25 December 1871; and The Law and the Lady, 26 September 1874–13 March 1875.

Collins's association with The Graphic ended in acrimony. His contract stipulated that no changes to the text could be made without his 'consent and approbation'. The editor, however, altered a passage that he regarded as improper. Collins, after the intervention of his lawyers, forced the paper to restore the original wording. The Graphic responded with a public disclaimer 'that the story is not one which we should have voluntarily selected to place before our readers'. Collins enlisted the help of Edmund *Yates, editor of The *World. Yates supported him editorially and published a letter giving Collins's own version of the dispute. (Correspondence reprinted in the Appendix to the 1992 World's Classics edition of The Law and the Lady, edited by Jenny Bourne Taylor).

Graves, (Elizabeth) Caroline (c. 1830–95). The mysterious woman who lived with Wilkie Collins from about 1858 until his death in 1889, except for a two-year period from 1868; dedicatee of The Fallen Leaves (1879). Often described as the original '*woman in white', because of a passage in the biography of *Millais by his son. He described the melodramatic night-time meeting of Millais, Wilkie and Charles *Collins with a distraught woman running away from a man who was keeping her prisoner under mesmeric influence. Though this story was partially corroborated in an account given by Kate *Dickens, it is almost certainly fabricated or greatly exaggerated.

Little about Caroline Graves was as it seemed. She described herself as the daughter of a gentleman named Courtenay, reduced her age by several years, and

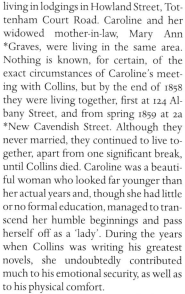

Caroline Graves in the early 1870s

claimed that her late husband, George Robert Graves (1829–52), was 'of independent means'. She was in fact the daughter of a carpenter, John Compton, and his wife, Sarah; born at Toddington in Gloucestershire and christened Elizabeth. She moved to Bath and was married there in 1850 to Graves, a shorthand-writer, the son of a stone-mason. The couple lived in Clerkenwell, London, and a daughter, Harriet Elizabeth (later *Bartley), was born eleven months later. George Graves died in January 1852.

Wilkie Collins probably met Caroline, as she was subsequently known, in the spring of 1856 when he was temporarily

living in lodgings in Howland Street, Tottenham Court Road. Caroline and her widowed mother-in-law, Mary Ann *Graves, were living in the same area. Nothing is known, for certain, of the exact circumstances of Caroline's meeting with Collins, but by the end of 1858 they were living together, first at 124 Albany Street, and from spring 1859 at 2a *New Cavendish Street. Although they never married, they continued to live together, apart from one significant break, until Collins died. Caroline was a beautiful woman who looked far younger than her actual years and, though she had little or no formal education, managed to transcend her humble beginnings and pass herself off as a 'lady'. During the years when Collins was writing his greatest novels, she undoubtedly contributed much to his emotional security, as well as to his physical comfort.

In October 1868, however, the household was suddenly disrupted when Caroline Graves married Joseph *Clow, almost certainly in response to Collins's relationship with Martha *Rudd, and probably after Collins had himself refused to marry Caroline. Her daughter and Collins's doctor, Frank *Beard, were the witnesses and Collins was present at the ceremony at Marylebone parish church. The marriage was clearly a mistake, for by April 1871 Caroline was back at 90 *Gloucester Place, and her relationship with Wilkie was resumed in spite of his continuing commitment to Martha Rudd and his three children by her.

Caroline Graves was known for form's sake as Collins's 'housekeeper' and did not accompany Wilkie on social occasions such as dinner parties; it is also very unlikely that she was ever introduced to Wilkie's mother. Caroline entertained many of his friends who visited them at home, travelled with him on the Continent, went to the theatre with him and sometimes wrote letters on his behalf when he was ill. During Wilkie's last illness she nursed him devotedly and when she died in 1895 was buried in the same grave.

Graves, Harriet Elizabeth ('Carrie')
See BARTLEY, HARRIET ELIZABETH.

Graves, Mary Ann (c.1798–1877). Mother of George Graves, mother-in-law of Caroline *Graves; grandmother of Harriet Elizabeth *Bartley. Stayed at 90 *Gloucester Place during the 1870s. Her death at 21 Molyneux Street, Marylebone, was registered by Sarah Masey, Wilkie Collins's servant.

Guilty River, The

> 'False appearances. As we all know, they lie like the truth.'

Short novel originally published as the 1886 *Arrowsmith's Christmas Annual. Written late in Collins's career, it incorporates two of the themes often featured in his work: the psychological effects of physical handicap, in this case deafness, and the love of a middle-class man for an intelligent and independent woman from a lower social stratum. Collins began writing in September and worked twelve hours a day to enable the story to be published on 15 November.

➡ Gerard Roylake, returned from Germany on the death of his father to take up his inheritance at Trimley Deen, stays with his stepmother, who is keen to introduce him to local society and in particular to the sister of her friend Lady Rachel. On his first evening Gerard walks to the nearby River Loke and recognizes his childhood friend, Cristel Toller, the miller's daughter. He also meets a deaf man living at the mill known only as the Lodger, who has the most beautiful face Gerard has ever seen.

Gerard and Cristel gradually fall in love. The Lodger, who is obsessed with Cristel, becomes insanely jealous. He lends Gerard a manuscript autobiography which describes his fear of inherited evil (from both his father and grandfather) as well as his study of medicine, his illness and subsequent deafness. Pretending friendship, the Lodger invites Gerard to tea, intending to poison him. Despite warnings, the naïve Gerard accepts. Cristel realises the Lodger's deadly intentions and with the help of his servant, Gloody, administers an antidote that

Front cover of *The Guilty River*, Arrowsmith's Christmas Annual for 1886

saves Gerard's life. Gerard proposes marriage, but Cristel refuses him because of their difference in station. She then disappears and although the Lodger is suspected and followed no trace of her is found.

After a year away on a Pacific island, Gerard receives a letter from the now dying and repentant Lodger. He reveals that Cristel, with the aid of her father and Lady Rachel, had been abducted by means of the 'guilty' River Loke. She has been cruising on a yacht with her wealthy uncle, Stephen Toller, whose wife has been improving Cristel's education. On her return to England she marries Gerard.

Book publication

1st edn. 1 vol, J. W. *Arrowsmith, Bristol 1886. Buff paper wrappers, printed in dark blue, black and yellow. No half-title. Arrowsmith's Christmas annual. Published 15 Nov. 1886. Variant binding in maroon cloth.

(viii) + 200 pp. Advertisements occupy pp (i–vi), (viii) and (189–200).

Reissued in Arrowsmith's Bristol Library (no. 19) 1887; 1899, [1911]. Sutton, Stroud 1991.

1st US edn (simultaneous with English). *Harper's Handy Series (no. 105), New York 1886.

Robert Ashley records another story by Collins with the same title, issued in the same year by the same publisher, but with a completely different plot. This was probably what Collins called 'a bogus story' of a dozen pages written and published to preserve the title.

Ashley, R., 'The Wilkie Collins Collection', *The Princeton University Library Chronicle*, 117 (Winter 1956), 81–4.

Wolff, R. L., *Nineteenth-Century Fiction: A Bibliographical Catalogue* (5 vols), New York and London 1981, 259.

Gwilt, Lydia

In *Armadale*, archetypal *sensation-novel female villain with a past. Beautiful, with blue eyes and luxuriant red hair, she conspires with Mrs *Oldershaw to become governess to Miss *Milroy and marry Allan *Armadale for his money. When this fails she sets out to kill him and pass herself off as his widow. The character of Miss Gwilt was described by *The Spectator* (9 June 1866) as 'a woman fouler than the refuse of the streets, who has lived to the ripe age of thirty-five, and through the horrors of forgery, murder, theft, bigamy, gaol, and attempted suicide, without any trace being left on her beauty'.

Gwilt, Miss See *armadale* (PLAY).

Gwilty Governess, The

1876 *parody of Miss Gwilt, the stage version of *Armadale*.

H

Hachette, Librairie & Cie Collins's main French publishers, founded in 1826 and based in Paris. By 1888 they had issued twelve authorized *translations: *Le Secret (The Dead Secret)*; *La Pierre de lune (The Moonstone)*; *Mademoiselle ou Madame? (Miss or Mrs?)*; *La Morte vivante (The New Magdalen)*; *La Piste du crime (The Law and the Lady)*; *Pauvre Lucile! (Poor Miss Finch)*; *Cache-Cache (Hide and Seek)*; *Mari et femme (Man and Wife)*; *La Mer glaciale (The Frozen Deep)*; *Les Deux Destinées (The Two Destinies)*; *L'Hôtel Hanté (The Haunted Hotel)*; *Je dis non ('I Say No').*

Mademoiselle ou Madame? was published by Hachette in 1872 and therefore precedes the first English edition of *Miss or Mrs? The Dead Secret* (1858) was translated by É.-D. *Forgues.

Halcombe, Marian Determined and intelligent heroine of *The Woman in White*. Dark, not conventionally attractive, though possessing a good figure, she is atypical for a Victorian novel. Marian

WILKIE COLLINS

LA

PISTE DU CRIME

TRADUIT DE L'ANGLAIS
AVEC L'AUTORISATION DE L'AUTEUR
PAR
CAMILLE DE CENDREY

TOME PREMIER

1 FR 25 CENT
LE VOLUME

PARIS
LIBRAIRIE HACHETTE ET Cie
79, BOULEVARD SAINT-GERMAIN, 79

French translation of *The Law and the Lady* published by Hachette of Paris in 1875

recognizes Count *Fosco's power for evil at an early stage and engages in a lengthy duel of wits to protect her half-sister, Laura *Fairlie. Marian Halcombe's diary forms one of the main narrative devices of the story.

Hampstead London suburb where Collins lived as a child, when it was still a village separated from the city by fields. His father, William *Collins, painted in Hampstead during the summer months and between 1826 and 1829 the family occupied a cottage on Hampstead Green, Pond Street (now the site of the Royal Free Hospital). In September 1829, they moved to a larger house in Hampstead Square and contemplated living there permanently before ultimately returning to central London. Charles *Collins was born in Hampstead in January 1828.

Although *The Annals of Hampstead* states that Collins lived at 25 Church Row there is no supporting evidence. He was, however, routinely invited by George *Smith, the publisher, who lived at Oak Hill Lodge from 1863 to 1872 and held Friday evening gatherings. Collins was an even more regular visitor to his friends in nearby Highgate, the *Lehmanns. During 1870 he stayed with them at 'Woodlands', Southwood Lane, while writing *Man and Wife* and the opening scene of the novel takes place in Hampstead.

Hampstead also features significantly in several other works. In *The Woman in White*, Anne *Catherick claims that she was born there. It is on the way home from his mother and sisters who live in Hampstead that Walter *Hartright has his first dramatic encounter with her after she escapes from a lunatic asylum: 'I had now arrived at that particular point of my walk where four roads met—the road to Hampstead, along which I had returned, the road to Finchley, the road to West End, and the road back to London.' The likeliest location of this spot would today be at the junction of Finchley Road, Frognal Lane and the top part of West End Lane.

The crossroads meeting with *The Woman in White* on the way from Hampstead, from the one-volume Chatto & Windus edition

In *Armadale*, the Vale of Health is the probable location for Dr Downward's sanatorium, where Lydia *Gwilt attempts to murder Allan *Armadale. Fairweather Vale is 'a new neighbourhood, situated below the high ground of Hampstead on the southern side'. Miss Gwilt lodges at 'Fairweather Vale Villas'. Mr Bruff, the lawyer in *The Moonstone*, lives in Hampstead. It is in his house 'as the clock of Hampstead church struck three' that Rachel *Verinder tells Franklin *Blake that she saw him steal the diamond. In *Blind Love*, the villainous Dr Vimpany lives in a cottage near the Heath at 5 Redburn Place and Lord Harry is found with his throat cut in a lonely spot on the Heath.

Barratt, T. J., *The Annals of Hampstead* (3 vols), London 1912, iii. 18.
Collins, W., *Memoirs*.

Hanover Terrace Nash terrace overlooking London's Regent's Park where Collins lived at number 17 with his mother and brother from August 1850 to

October 1855. The house became a regular meeting place for their literary and artistic friends such as the *Dickens family, the *Wards, *Millais, Holman *Hunt and other members of the *Pre-Raphaelite group. It was later the home of writer Edmund Gosse.

Harley Street Street in London's *Marylebone, renowned for its medical practitioners. Collins lived at 12 Harley Street from 1859 to 1864. He rented rooms from George Gregson, for several years his dental surgeon, who subsequently moved to number 63. George *Critchett, Collins's ophthalmologist, practised at 21 Harley Street.

Harper & Brothers Collins's main publishers in the USA. The firm issued its first book in 1817 under the imprint of J. & J. Harper, becoming Harper & Brothers in 1833. There were four brothers, James (1795–1869), John (1797–1875), Joseph Wesley (1801–70) and Fletcher (1806–77). Harpers recognized both the enormous reading public in the USA and the mass of material available in England. They used *Sampson Low as their London agent. Fletcher Harper was the driving force of the literary department and also realized the need for illustrations. He created the 'theme periodicals' *Harper's Magazine, *Harper's Weekly and *Harper's Bazar. According to Nordhoff (in Exman, The House of Harper), who worked with the firm as reader, adviser and author, Fletcher Harper made few mistakes about his public because he created it.

Harpers first published Collins in 1850, paying £15 for early proofs of Antonina. The Dead Secret appeared anonymously in the Weekly in 1857, although it was not published in book form until 1873. In 1858, Harpers made a five-year agreement for Collins's books in the USA for which they paid royalties of 5 per cent. With his increasing success, they later paid £750 each for The Moonstone (1868) and Man and Wife (1870). Harpers were generally reluctant to issue collections of short stories as they found them unremunerative.

Harpers liberally entertained Collins during his reading tour of North *America, and from 1873 issued a uniform illustrated library edition of his works to commemorate the trip. Relations remained extremely cordial until 1878 when there was a temporary falling out.

17 Hanover Terrace, where Collins lived between 1850 and 1855

Harpers declined to take The Haunted Hotel because of the activities of *pirate publishers and changes in international *copyright which allowed Canadian imprints to be sold in the USA. Relations were restored by 1884 for the publication of 'I Say No'.

Collins was always punctilious in sending advance sheets at the earliest opportunity. For 'I Say No' he let Harpers have the final instalments of the story three months ahead of his English publishers. Harpers were therefore able to issue the book version ahead of the pirates and the US edition preceded first English publication.

Collins's novels and short stories appeared in several of Harper's book series. First book editions of their serializations were printed in double columns, using the same type and illustrations. They were in demy 8vo format and issued simultaneously in cloth and paper wrappers. Titles include: The Woman in White; No Name; Armadale; The Moonstone; Man and Wife; Poor Miss Finch; The New Magdalen; The Law and the Lady; The Two Destinies.

Illustrated Library Edition

The most complete, with seventeen titles between 1873 and 1902. Issued in 12mo green cloth. Contains a facsimile inscription in Collins's handwriting, 'I gratefully dedicate this collected edition of my works, to The American People'. After Dark, and Other Stories; Antonina; Armadale; Basil; Hide and Seek; 'I Say No'; Man and Wife; My Miscellanies; No Name; Poor Miss Finch; The Dead Secret; The Law and the Lady; The Moonstone; The New

(*above*) *Harper's New Monthly Magazine*, which published two chapters from *Rambles Beyond Railways* in April 1851
(*left*) The US publisher Fletcher Harper

Magdalen; *The Queen of Hearts*; *The Two Destinies*; *The Woman in White*.
See illustrations at AMERICA.

Library of Select Novels

Antonina (no. 141)

Harper's Handy Series

The Ghost's Touch and Other Stories (no. 30) 1885; *The Evil Genius* (no. 72) [1886], first book publication; *The Guilty River* (no. 105) 1886.

Harper's Half Hour Series

'Percy and the Prophet' 1877, first separate edition; 'My Lady's Money' 1878, first separate edition.

Franklin Square Library

A cheap series started in 1878 to compete with the pirates. Harpers paid an honorarium to British authors and generally did not use the series for new books. They issued *Man and Wife* in Jan. 1879 (no. 38, 15 cents compared with $1.50 for the Illustrated Library Edition); and '*I Say No*' in July 1884 (no. 385 at 20 cents).

Exman, E., *The Brothers Harper*, New York 1965.
Exman, E., *The House of Harper: One Hundred and Fify Years of Publishing*, New York and London 1967.
Harper (1912).

Harper's Bazar, *A Repository of Fashion and Instruction* (1867–1913). Magazine conceived by Fletcher Harper as a family paper for women. Became the pioneer fashion journal of America but contained important serials, short stories and illustrations. First issued 2 November 1867, it achieved a circulation of 100,000 after six weeks. It serialized *The Two Destinies* by Collins from 25 December 1875 to 9 September 1876.

Harper's New Monthly Magazine
(1850–1900). New York monthly periodical first issued in June 1850. Intended to contain the best of foreign periodical literature, although predominantly from England. The *Magazine* evolved from Harper's book publishing business to which it remained closely allied. It started

with a printing of 7,500 but reached a circulation of 50,000 by the end of 1850. Authors included *Bulwer-Lytton, *Dickens, Lever and *Thackeray.

Collins's titles included:
'The Pilchard Fishery on the Coast of Cornwall' and 'Visit to a Copper-Mine', Apr. 1851, chapters reprinted from *Rambles Beyond Railways*.
'The Siege of the *Black Cottage', Feb. 1857 (wrongly attributed in the index to Mrs Gaskell).
'A Marriage Tragedy', Feb. 1858.
Armadale (Dec. 1864–July 1866). The *Magazine*'s circulation was badly affected after the Civil War and the serialization saved it from closure.
The New Magdalen (Oct. 1872–June 1873)
The *Magazine* also published from September to November 1891 'The Letters of Charles Dickens to Wilkie Collins, edited by Laurence Hutton'; reprinted in book form in 1892.

Harper's Weekly, *A Journal of Civilization* (1857–1916). New York paper first issued 3 January 1857. Created by Fletcher Harper as a high-class weekly for family reading, it achieved a circulation of 120,000. After the outbreak of the Civil War, the Harper brothers became strong War Republicans and gave the *Weekly* a

political dimension. Collins's titles included:

The Dead Secret, 24 Jan.–27 June 1857, published anonymously in vol I.

'The Lazy Tour of Two Idle Apprentices', 31 Oct.–28 Nov. 1857 (attributed solely to *Dickens).

The Woman in White, 26 Nov. 1859–4 Aug. 1860.

No Name, 15 Mar. 1862–24 Jan. 1863.

The Moonstone, 4 Jan.–8 Aug. 1868.

Man and Wife, 11 Dec. 1869–6 Aug. 1870.

Poor Miss Finch, 2 Sept. 1871–24 Feb. 1872.

'Miss or Mrs?', 30 Dec. 1871–13 Jan. 1872.

The Law and the Lady, 10 Oct. 1874–27 Mar. 1875.

'I Say No', 22 Dec. 1883–12 July 1884.

The number for 8 March 1873 contains a portrait of Collins together with a short biographical sketch.

Harte, (Francis) Bret (1836–1902).
American short-story writer, poet and humorist. Harte attended the Lotos Club dinner during Collins's 1873 reading tour of North *America. In his *Condensed Novels*, Harte wrote several *parodies of mainly English novelists. These included 'No Title by W-lk-e C-ll-ns' which features 'the Narrative of Count Moscow'.

Reprinted in Page (1974), 161–7.

Hartright, Walter
Young drawing-master and hero of *The Woman in White*. Hartright's narrative is the key story-telling device of the novel. Engaging in many activities of modern *detective fiction, he restores Laura *Fairlie's identity and ultimately marries her.

The Haunted Hotel: A Mystery of Modern Venice, to which is added My Lady's Money
'Have you ever heard of the fascination of terror?'

Ghost story set in 1860, published in book form with '*My Lady's Money' and dedicated to Mr and Mrs Sebastian *Schlesinger. Apart from supernatural elements, the story contains *detective procedures and an insurance fraud relying on substituted *identity that anticipates the later *Blind Love* (1890). The story is unusually horrific for Collins.

➥ Lord Montbarry breaks off his engagement to Agnes Lockwood to marry the Countess Narona. The couple end a continental tour in Venice where they live

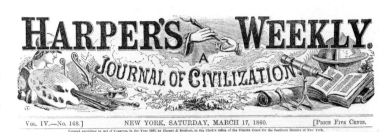

VOL. IV.—No. 168.] NEW YORK, SATURDAY, MARCH 17, 1860. [PRICE FIVE CENTS.

Entered according to Act of Congress, in the Year 1860, by Harper & Brothers, in the Clerk's Office of the District Court for the Southern District of New York.

(above) Harper's Weekly during the serialization of The Woman in White in March 1860

reclusively in a large, decaying palace. They are accompanied by Baron Rivar, brother of the Countess, and by Ferrari, their courier.

Agnes learns from Montbarry's brother, Henry Westwick, that Montbarry, whose life was insured for £10,000 in favour of his wife, has died of bronchitis. The courier has disappeared without trace although Ferrari's wife receives an anonymous note containing £1,000. The insurance companies carefully investigate but find no evidence that Montbarry died other than by natural causes.

The palace is refurbished as a fashionable hotel, and the Westwick family arrange to meet there. Without realizing that they are sleeping in the room where Montbarry died, three of his family separately experience insomnia, nightmares or nauseous smells. Agnes awakes in the night to see a disembodied head descending from the ceiling. A real head is discovered the next day decomposing in a secret compartment in the room above. Henry finds a set of gold false teeth which are later confirmed as Montbarry's by his dentist.

The Countess has also come to Venice, compelled by Destiny. She writes a ghost story in the form of a play which is in effect a confession of Montbarry's murder by herself and the Baron. Ferrari, dying of bronchitis, had agreed to assume the identity of Montbarry to perpetrate an insurance fraud in exchange for the £1,000 sent to his wife. Montbarry's body was disposed of by acid but the head hidden in the secret compartment.

Agnes and Henry return to England and are married privately. They never discuss details of the confession.

Serialization. First published in *Belgravia Magazine*, June–Nov. 1878; and in the *Canadian Monthly*, July–Dec. 1878.

Book publication

1st English edn. 2 vols, *Chatto & Windus,

London 1879 [1878]. Dark brown cloth, front covers blocked in white and lettered in gilt, spines lettered in gilt, black endpapers. Half-title in each vol. Six wood-engravings by Arthur Hopkins, five in vol I and one in vol II. Published in Nov. 1878.

Vol I (xii) + 232 pp. 40pp publisher's catalogue dated Oct. 1878 bound in at end.

Vol II (viii) + 260 pp.

1-vol eds. Chatto & Windus 1879–1915. Sutton, Stroud 1990.

1st US edn. *Seaside Library Pocket Edition, no. 977, New York 1887.

First edition in book form. Rose-Belford, Toronto 1878.

Translations. Russian, St Petersburg 1878; Dutch, The Hague 1879; French, Paris 188?; German, Berlin 1892.

health
'I hope you won't pay the rheumatic penalty of a winter residence in England.' (*The Black Robe*)

Collins's health began to decline from his late twenties. His first attack of serious illness was in May and June 1853. For a time

Illustration by Hopkins to *The Haunted Hotel*

he was reduced to walking with a stick and the symptoms of what he always called 'rheumatic *gout' or 'neuralgia' continued with increasing severity for the rest of his life. Further bouts of illness occurred in 1855 and 1856 when he was in *Paris with *Dickens and was immobilized by rheumatic pain. At this time his eyes began to be affected.

The accident documented in 'The *Lazy Tour of Two Idle Apprentices' (1857) left Collins with a permanently weakened ankle. In addition to problems with walking, the 1860s brought new symptoms of stomach disorders, trembling and fainting. Collins's doctor, Frank *Beard, gave him Colchicum (an extract of meadow-saffron) which was then the standard medication for gout, but it produced side-effects of nausea and vomiting. Beard therefore prescribed combinations of quinine and various other salts, as well as *opium to relieve the pain.

Collins also tried various other remedies. In 1856 he was convinced that sweating was the cure for his rheumatism. In 1863 he visited the spa at *Aix-la-Chapelle, writing to Nina *Lehmann 'So far I can't wear my boots yet, but I can hobble about with my stick much more freely than I could when I left London.' He tried Turkish and electric baths, hypnosis with Dr *Elliotson and in December 1864, with symptoms of giddiness, consulted Dr Radcliffe, an authority on the brain and nerves.

In the late 1860s and 1870s, Wybert *Reeve recalled that Collins had frequent injections of morphia to relieve his 'neuralgia'. Beard referred him to the ophthalmologist George *Critchett and, according to Percy *Fitzgerald's *Memoirs, Charles *Kent once described Collins's eyes as 'literally *enormous bags of blood*'. Beard and his family always knew when 'Wilkie was out of order' with one of his attacks of gout threatening because he became depressed and nervous and started fidgeting.

Collins was often affected by the pressure of work. In February 1883 he wrote to Nina Lehmann 'I finished my story, discovered one day that I was half dead with fatigue and the next day the gout was in my right eye.' The mid-1880s brought more serious symptoms of angina which Collins called 'neuralgia of the chest'. He wrote to Mary *Anderson in March 1885 'My heart has been running down like a clock that is out of repair . . .

but I have been (medically) intoxicated with sal volatile and spirits of chloroform.' He went to *Ramsgate in June to 'oxygenise the blood' and in November 1885 reported to Nannie *Wynne that he was being 'steeped in devilish drugs—arsenic among them'.

In July 1886 he wrote to Reeve 'As for my health, considering that I was 62 years old last birthday—that I have worked hard as a writer—and that gout has tried to blind me first and kill me afterwards, on more than one occasion—I must not complain. Neuralgia, and nervous exhaustion generally, have sent me to the sea to be patched up—and the sea is justifying my confidence in it.' That December he resorted to sniffing glass capsules of amyl nitrate and the following year used hypo-phosphate. In December 1887 another letter to Nannie Wynne records that a 'mingling of spasm suffocation and neuralgia has committed an unprovoked assault on me'. Breathing difficulties due to his heart problems became more common, and he had an attack of bronchitis in January 1889. Collins suffered a stroke on 30 June with a further attack of bronchitis just before his death on 23 September 1889.

According to Frank *Archer, Collins considered that his rheumatic disease was inherited both from his paternal grandfather and from his father whose

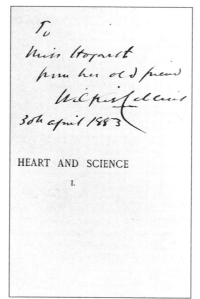

HEART AND SCIENCE
I.

Copy of *Heart and Science* inscribed to Georgina Hogarth in 1883

symptoms of 'violent rheumatic pains' and 'inflammation of the eyes' he had carefully described in the *Memoirs (1848). Collins blamed 'rheumatic gout' for most of his ailments in whatever unlikely part of the body they occurred. His eyes were affected with particular severity. The signs and symptoms described by himself and others, of acute pain, redness and photophobia, suggest he probably suffered from anterior uveitis and glaucoma.

Letters.

Heart and Science: A Story of the Present Time

'Vanity wants nothing but the motive power to develop into absolute wickedness.'

*Didactic novel attacking *vivisection and dedicated to *Sarony. During his research, Collins corresponded with the Surgeon-General C. T. Gordon, writing in July 1882 'I am endeavouring to add my small contribution in aid of the good cause, by such means as Fiction will permit—and I am especially obliged to you for valuable "facts" which I could not have discovered for myself.' In 1884 he wrote to Frances Power Cobbe, discussing cheap reissues and translation of the story, 'What little I have been able to do towards helping this good cause is in a fair way, I hope, of appealing to a large audience.' The assistance of both is acknowledged in the preface where Collins is at pains to point out details of his research. Chapter 32 presents many of the arguments still valid today against what the author calls 'the hateful secrets of Vivisection'. *Heart and Science* received generally favourable reviews although the *Athenaeum* considered it had a weak ending and the *Academy* deemed it an 'anti-vivisection manifesto'. *Swinburne later called it 'a childish and harmless onslaught on scientific research', but thought it the best, after *Man and Wife*, of Collins's didactic tales. He particularly liked the characters of Zo and her father.

➤ Ovid Vere, a brilliant young doctor, is advised to take a long rest to save his health. His formidable mother, Mrs Gallilee, has remarried and he has two half-sisters, the precocious Maria aged 12 and Zoe (called Zo) aged 10, who is hopelessly bad at her lessons. The day before Ovid is due to go away he follows an attractive girl in the street to a concert which his mother also attends. The girl faints and is discovered to be Carmina

Graywell, Mrs Gallilee's niece from Italy, accompanied by her old nurse, Teresa. Carmina's father, Robert, has just died leaving her to be brought up by Mrs Gallilee in London.

Carmina soon recovers and the family solicitor, Mr Mool, reads Robert's will leaving almost his entire estate of £130,000 to Carmina. Mrs Gallilee is appointed her guardian and will receive generous expenses for her trouble. Ovid, already in love, cancels his proposed sailing trip. He takes Carmina, Zo, Maria and their governess Miss Minerva to the Zoo. They encounter Dr Nathan Benjulia, a specialist in diseases of the brain and nervous system. He has an unpleasant reputation as a vivisectionist but maintains a special rapport with young Zo.

Carmina and Ovid become secretly engaged while Miss Minerva, also in love with Ovid, ingratiates herself into Carmina's confidence. Mrs Gallilee had optimistically relied on her brother's will to solve the financial difficulties caused by her extravagance and her numerous scientific committees. If Ovid and Carmina marry, she will lose her guardian's allowance, and the chance that the fortune might revert to Maria and Zo if Carmina remains single. Mrs Gallilee encourages Ovid to go away, ostensibly for the sake of his health but in reality to keep him away from Carmina. Ovid decides on a trip to Canada and visits Benjulia for a letter of recommendation to a medical colleague in Montreal.

Carmina leads an unhappy existence with her guardian and resolves to meet Ovid in Canada. She writes to him explaining her intention to travel with Teresa and complaining of her treatment by Mrs Gallilee. The music master, Mr Le Frank, inadvertently insulted by Carmina, steals her letter in revenge and gives it to Mrs Gallilee.

Mrs Gallilee is also acquainted with Benjulia through her various scientific committees. She hears him tell a slanderous and unsubstantiated story that Carmina is the daughter of an adulterous affair and hopes the will can be invalidated. Mr Mool assures Mrs Gallilee that even if the story were true the terms of the will would still apply. Unhappy with the slur on the family name, he gives Benjulia proof that the story is a lie.

Before Benjulia can explain the truth to Mrs Gallilee she confronts Carmina with the letter to Ovid and taunts her with the

scandal. Teresa ferociously attacks Mrs Gallilee while Carmina collapses in shock and is removed from the house. Mr Gallilee, for once unusually decisive, takes his daughters away and after consulting Mr Mool decides the only means of removing Carmina from his wife's guardianship is to hasten the marriage with Ovid. Carmina is treated by the family physician, Dr Null, while Benjulia in the interests of science passively watches her condition deteriorate. Le Frank meanwhile is caught spying for Mrs Gallilee and loses two of his fingers when they are accidentally trapped in a door by Teresa.

Ovid receives a monosyllabic letter from Zo which brings him back to London. He accuses Benjulia of deliberate neglect and gradually cures Carmina with an unconventional treatment for brain disease suggested by an anti-vivisection manuscript he was given in Montreal. He publishes a book based on the manuscript and Benjulia realizes that his own life's work, relying as it does on vivisection, is a failure. Benjulia releases his captive animals and commits suicide, destroying his laboratory by fire. His will leaves everything to Zo. Ovid and Carmina marry and Mrs Gallilee, recovered from a nervous breakdown, resumes life with her scientific committees.

Serialization. The Manchester Weekly Times Supplement, 22 July 1882–13 Jan. 1883 and several other provincial newspapers; *Belgravia*, Aug. 1882–June 1883.

Book publication

1st English edn. 3 vols, *Chatto & Windus, London 1883. Blue-grey cloth, covers blocked in dark brown, spines lettered in gilt. Green and white floral endpapers. Half-title in each vol. Published in Apr. 1883.

Vol I xvi + 296 pp.

Vol II (iv) + 296 pp.

Vol III (iv) + 304 pp. 32 pp publisher's catalogue dated March 1883 bound in at end.

1-vol edns. Chatto & Windus 1884–1913. Sutton, Stroud 1990; Broadview, Toronto 1996 (critical edition, edited by Steve Farmer).

1st US edn. *Seaside Library (vol 76, no. 1544), New York 1883 (first book publication).

Translations. Dutch, The Hague 1883; Italian, Milan 1884; German, Berlin 1886. At the suggestion of his friend, M. Le Vicomte du Pontavice de Heussey, Collins asked A. P. *Watt to negotiate a French translation in *Le Temps*, an anti-vivisection newspaper.

Page (1974), 212–17.

Letters.

Herncastle, John Character who initiates the action of *The Moonstone*, by looting the diamond at the Siege of Seringapatam in 1799. Ostracized on his return to England, he spends his fortune on experimental chemistry and lives as a recluse surrounded by *animals. Leaves the *Moonstone with its curse to Rachel *Verinder.

Hide and Seek

'He felt . . . that he should mope and pine, like a wild animal in a cage, under confinement in an office.'

Collins's third novel, published in 1854; dedicated to Charles *Dickens 'As a token of admiration and affection'. Dickens wrote to Georgina *Hogarth: 'I think it far away the cleverest novel I have ever seen written by a new hand.' Reviews were enthusiastic but despite praise from the *Athenaeum* and The *Leader* sales were disappointing; Collins believed this was due to the effect of the Crimean War on the book-reading public.

The novel is the first by Collins to explore the positive aspects of physical handicap. It is also one of his least sensational, laying emphasis on domestic affections. The quieter atmosphere may in part be attributed to the influence of Dickens, and also to the use of autobiographical material in the first half of the book. The ebullient and rebellious Zack shares many of Collins's early experiences as well as some of his characteristics. The description of Valentine Blyth's studio was taken from that of William *Collins at Devonshire Terrace, Bayswater.

Collins was already careful to carry out background research; the experiences of the deaf-mute Madonna are closely modelled on examples in Dr John Kitto's 1845 *The Lost Senses*. The character of Mat Marksman was probably influenced by the novels of Fenimore *Cooper.

➡ Valentine Blyth, an artist, and Lavinia, his invalid wife, have an adopted deaf and dumb daughter, Mary, usually called Madonna because of her beautiful eyes and resemblance to a painting by Raphael. There is a mystery about her origins. She was rescued by Blyth from a travelling circus, where she was mistreated by the cruel proprietor after she lost her hearing in an accident. Years before, her dying mother had been helped by the wife of a circus clown, the goodnatured Mrs Peckover, who brought up

Illustration by Mahoney to the Chatto & Windus one-volume edition of *Hide and Seek*

brawl and is rescued by Mat Marksman, an outlandish, nomadic character who was scalped by Indians. Zack arrives home drunk and the following day leaves his father's house to share lodgings with his new-found friend.

Mat, in search of his lost sister, visits his aunt, old Joanna Grice, in the Midlands town of Dibbledean and hears the family scandal which occurred after he went abroad. His sister Mary left home, pregnant with an illegitimate child, and is buried in a pauper's grave in Bangbury. Mat takes a box containing Mary's old love letters as well as a note from Joanna Grice justifying her conduct. The letters identify Mary's lover as Arthur Carr. Carr had written several times but Joanna intercepted his letters. Thinking herself deserted, Mary left home to avoid disgracing the family without realizing that her father had forgiven her.

On his return to London, Mat accompanies Zack to Blyth's studio. He is struck by the resemblance between Madonna and his dead sister and from a comment by Zack guesses that the clue to her origin is locked in Blyth's bureau. Mat gets Blyth drunk, takes an impression of his key and obtains the bracelet. He is resolved to find Arthur Carr and take revenge.

Mat, recognizing that the distinctive brown hair in the bracelet is identical with Zack's, deduces that Zack's father was in reality 'Arthur Carr' and confronts him. Thorpe confesses in a letter to Blyth, while the magnanimous Mat destroys a similar note to Zack and takes him travelling in America. When news comes that Zack's father has died, Mat reveals the whole secret, including the fact that Zack and Madonna are brother and sister. Zack returns home and eventually persuades Mat to leave his solitary life to rejoin his niece and friends in England.

Book publication

1st edn. 3 vols, Richard *Bentley, London 1854. Pale maroon cloth, covers blocked in blind, spines lettered in gilt, pale yellow endpapers. Half-title in each vol. Published 6 June 1854. Variant bindings issued simultaneously in dark brown cloth; and paper boards, half cloth, with white endpapers.

Vol I viii + 300 pp. Publisher's advertisements dated June 1854 occupy pp (299–300).

Vol II (iv) + 324 pp. Publisher's advertisements dated June 1854 occupy pp (323–4).

Vol III (iv) + 332 pp.

1-vol edns. *Sampson Low (sub-titled *The

the orphaned baby as her own. Mrs Peckover agrees to Mary's informal adoption by the Blyths since they can offer her a better life. The only clue to her original identity is a hair-bracelet with the initials MG which Blyth keeps locked in his bureau for fear that Mary's unknown family might one day claim her.

Zachary Thorpe (Zack), closely attached to his gentle mother but at odds with his over-bearing, religious father, is a frequent visitor to the Blyths despite Mr Thorpe's disapproval of Madonna's dubious origins. Madonna falls in love with him, but Zack is too immature to respond. He is a wild 20-year-old who secretly frequents late-night theatres and drinking places against his father's wishes. One night he is involved in a

The *Household Words* office at 16 Wellington Street North

Mystery of Mary Grice, with revised text and a frontispiece by John *Gilbert) 1861–3; *Smith, Elder 1865–72; *Chatto & Windus (with 8 illustrations by M. F. Mahoney) 1875–1921. Dover, New York 1981; World's Classics 1993 (critical edition, edited by Catherine Peters).

1st US edn. Dick & Fitzgerald, New York 1858.

Translations. Russian, St Petersburg 1858; German, Sondershausen 1864; French, Paris 1877.

Hogarth, Georgina (1827–1917). Sister-in-law of Charles *Dickens; housekeeper and confidante after his separation from his wife in 1858. She knew Collins from the early 1850s and played the Shipwrecked Lady in *The *Lighthouse* (1855) and Lucy Crayford in *The *Frozen Deep* (1857). Collins stayed with Dickens at Dover in October 1864 and Georgina Hogarth enthusiastically read the early proofs of *Armadale*.

Despite a lengthy friendship with Collins, Georgina Hogarth was cool about him. She doubted his abilities for a reading tour and once described him as conceited. She was executrix of Dickens's will but failed to give Collins, in contrast to other friends, any of Dickens's personal effects. She was, nevertheless, particularly grateful to Collins for his help during 1879 in editing the *Letters of Charles Dickens* (3 vols, 1880–2). She also compiled *Letters of Charles Dickens to Wilkie Collins, 1851–1870: Selected by Miss Georgina Hogarth*, edited by Laurence Hutton, London 1892.

House to Let, A The extra *Christmas number of *Household Words*, published in December 1858. The narrator is found a new London home by her servant, Trottles, and takes an interest in the house opposite which is 'To Let'. Collins contributed the short story 'Trottles Report' and also collaborated with Dickens on the opening and closing framework narratives, 'Over the Way' and 'Let at Last'.

Household Words (1850–9). Weekly periodical founded and edited by Charles *Dickens. Dickens owned one half in partnership with *Bradbury & Evans (with a quarter share) and W. H. *Wills

and John *Forster (each with an eighth). Bradbury & Evans undertook the printing and publishing but Dickens retained effective control.

Household Words was a family paper for a middle-class audience, fulfilling Dickens's ambition to 'conduct' a journal aimed at the wide readership created by

his novels. Dickens laid great emphasis on the importance of entertainment as well as social purpose in his instructions to contributors. Short stories, novels and verse had a prominent place in the magazine, in addition to items of social concern and informative essays on science, medicine and travel.

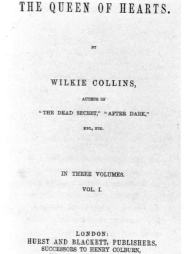

(*left*) Cover of Hunter, Rose Canadian edition of
The Two Destinies in 1876
(*above*) First edition of *The Queen of Hearts*
published in three volumes by Hurst & Blackett in
1859

by '*Gabriel's Marriage' (16 Apr. 1853),
'*Sister Rose' (7–28 Apr. 1855), 'The *Yellow Mask' (7–28 July 1855) and *A *Rogue's
Life* (1–29 Mar. 1856). He joined the permanent staff in October 1856 at a weekly
salary of five guineas on condition that
Household Words would serialize a full-
length novel (*The *Dead Secret*, 3 Jan.–13
June 1857) and advertise his authorship in
advance. Collins wrote altogether more
than fifty short stories and articles, many
of which were republished in *After Dark*
(1856), *The *Queen of Hearts* (1859) and
My Miscellanies (1863). Dickens's letters
frequently mention Collins's industry
and dependability.

Collins contributed to five of the
Christmas numbers, from 1854 to 1858.
He collaborated directly with Dickens on
three of these; also on 'The *Lazy Tour of
Two Idle Apprentices' (3–31 Oct. 1857) and
two lead articles, 'A Clause for the New
Reform Bill' (9 Oct. 1858) and 'Doctor
Dulcerama' (18 Dec. 1858).

Dickens, under the strain of his matrimonial difficulties, fell out with Bradbury
& Evans in 1859. The paper was auc-
tioned and Dickens bought them out for
£3,500. Taking with him both Collins and
Wills, Dickens started a new journal, *All
the Year Round,* 'with which is incorporated *Household Words*'. Bradbury &

Household Words ran for 479 numbers
from 30 March 1850 until 28 May 1859, the
circulation reaching 40,000 per week.
The regular numbers cost 2*d.* each and
usually consisted of twenty-four pages.
They were also available in monthly parts
at 9*d.* and biannual bound volumes at 5*s.*
In addition, there were eight extra
*Christmas numbers of thirty-six pages.

Apart from Dickens and in due course
Collins, staff writers were the sub-editor,
Wills, R. H. Horne and H. Morley. Regular contributors included Mrs Gaskell,
W. B. Jerrold, Grenville Murray and G. A.
*Sala. Occasional authors were *Bulwer-
Lytton, Charles *Collins, Forster, *Kent,
*Lemon, *Townshend and *Yates. All
articles were unsigned so that some of
Dickens's friends such as Douglas *Jerrold declined to write for him. The im-
pact of Dickens's personality on the
paper was so strong that some readers
imagined that the entire magazine was
written by him.

Collins's first contribution was 'A *Terribly Strange Bed' (24 Apr. 1852), followed

Evans launched their own magazine, *Once a Week*.

Lehmann, R. C., *Charles Dickens as Editor*, London 1912.

Lohrli (1973) gives a full listing of Collins's contributions.

'How I Married Him' Short story originally published in The *Spirit of the Times*, 24 Dec. 1881 and *Belgravia*, Jan. 1882. Reprinted as 'Miss Morris and the Stranger' in *Little Novels* (1887).

➥ Nancy Morris, a shopkeeper's daughter from Sandwich, becomes a governess with the help of a benefactor, Sir Gervase Damian. One day she helps a stranger whose advances she gently rebuffs, only to meet him again when she takes a new position in the North. Sir Gervase leaves Nancy £70,000 which she renounces in favour of the only other heir, his nephew. He turns out to be the stranger, Sextus Sax, who refuses the fortune until Nancy, in a leap year, proposes that he should accept both her and the money.

Hunt, (William) Holman (1827–1910). Painter and founder member of the *Pre-Raphaelite Brotherhood. Dedicatee of *The Evil Genius* (1886); close friend of Wilkie and Charles *Collins and their mother, Harriet. Hunt was a frequent visitor with *Millais and other Pre-Raphaelites to the Collins household in Blandford Square and *Hanover Terrace. When Wilkie was too ill to attend his mother's funeral in 1868, Hunt represented him.

Hunt was best man to Charles Collins at his marriage to Kate *Dickens in 1860. He also made a deathbed sketch of him in 1873.

Holman-Hunt, D., *My Grandfather, His Wives and Loves*, London 1969.

Hunt, W. Holman, *Pre-Raphaelitism and the Pre-Raphaelite Brotherhood* (2 vols), London 1905–6; 2nd edition, 1913.

Hunter, Rose Collins's Canadian publishers in Toronto. A partnership between G. Maclean Rose and Hunter (d. 1877); printers and binders of The *Canadian Monthly*. During his reading tour of North *America in 1873–4, Collins was entertained by Rose and his wife.

Hunter, Rose published at Collins's request a book version of *Man and Wife* in June 1870. This experiment in preventing an American periodical *piracy in Canada proved so effective and financially rewarding that Collins found he had created a new market for his books. By 1874 the firm had also published *Poor Miss Finch*, *The New Magdalen*, *Miss or Mrs*, *The Dead Alive*, and *American Readings* which consisted of 'The Frozen Deep' and 'The Dream Woman'.

Other Toronto editions included *The Law and the Lady*, *The Two Destinies*, *The Haunted Hotel* (first edition in book form), *The Fallen Leaves* and *Heart and Science*.

Hurst & Blackett Minor London publishers of fiction, based at 13 Great Malborough Street; successors to Henry Colburn. Published one Collins title, *The Queen of Hearts*, acquiring the three-volume rights for three years from the autumn of 1859. Sadleir speculates that the ambitious Hurst & Blackett, recognizing Collins's potential, were keen to sign him up with a view to the future. They were not prepared to risk a large print run, which accounts for the first edition's current scarcity, and in the event missed out on *The Woman in White* (1860). Henry Blackett approached Collins again in November 1860, wishing to publish his novels in the firm's Standard Library. Collins received an identical offer from *Sampson Low which he preferred to accept in fairness to his existing publishers.

Marston, E., *After Work*, London 1904, 87.

Sadleir (1951), i. 376.

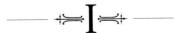

'I Say No'

'The hardest disease to cure that I know of is—worry.'

Mystery story published in 1884 with the heroine turning detective, to reveal the truth about the death of her father. The plot relies heavily on coincidence and, as in *The Law and the Lady*, a supposed murder turns out to have been suicide.

➥ The orphaned Emily Brown and her best friend Cecilia Wyvil attend Miss Ladd's school for young ladies. The date is 1881. On the last day before the summer holidays, Emily and Cecilia are joined by the rich but unattractive Francine de Sor. She has been sent to England by her parents in the West Indies to improve her education. On the same day, a recently employed teacher, Sarah Jethro, is dismissed when her references are discovered to be forged. In saying goodbye, she reveals that she had once known Emily's father but refuses to elaborate. Another teacher at the school is Alban Morris, a drawing master in love with Emily.

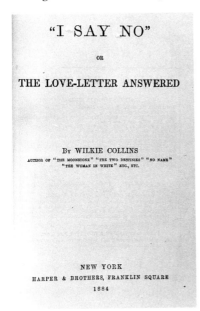

"I SAY NO"

OR

THE LOVE-LETTER ANSWERED

By WILKIE COLLINS

AUTHOR OF "THE MOONSTONE" "THE TWO DESTINIES" "NO NAME"
"THE WOMAN IN WHITE" ETC., ETC.

NEW YORK

HARPER & BROTHERS, FRANKLIN SQUARE

1884

Title-page to the Harpers edition of 'I Say No', published in 1884 three months ahead of the English edition

Emily's only relative is her father's impoverished sister, Letitia, and Emily must therefore earn her own living. With the help of Cecilia she has secured a position in Northumberland as secretary to Sir Jervis Redwood. His staff consist of Mr and Mrs Rook who used to own the Hand-in-Hand Inn in Hampshire until it was forced to close after a gruesome murder. Mrs Rook comes to collect Emily, and is struck silent when she sees that Emily wears her father's locket recording his death on 30 September 1877, the same date as the murder at the inn.

Before Emily can travel north, she is summoned to London because her aunt is dangerously ill. She begins to realize that, in addition to Miss Jethro, all the people she thought she could trust have concealed some aspect of her father's death. They include her dying aunt; Mrs Ellmother, Letitia's faithful old servant; the family doctor; and even Alban Morris. Emily discovers from old newspaper reports that the murder victim had the same name as her father, James Brown. He was robbed of his pocket-book and had his throat cut with a razor while sharing a room at the inn with another man. An old handbill gives a description of this chief suspect who fled the scene of the crime.

Emily stays with Cecilia's family who have returned from the Continent with the charismatic preacher, Miles Mirabel. He falls in love with Emily who becomes the victim of spiteful Francine's jealousy. Emily quarrels with Alban and confronts Mrs Ellmother who admits that aunt Letitia hushed up details of Mr Brown's murder. Miss Jethro is also revealed as Mr Brown's lover.

Emily determines to continue her detective activities to find her father's murderer. She enlists the assistance of Mirabel, not realizing he was the other man at the inn. His sister, Mrs Delvin, lives in Northumberland and Mirabel persuades Emily to stay with her. Mrs Delvin is unsuccessful in preventing Emily from seeing Mrs Rook who has

been hurt in a railway accident. Believing she is dying, Mrs Rook confesses that she stole the bloodstained pocket-book from Emily's already dead father and now returns it to Emily. The pocket-book still has a note from Miss Jethro containing only the words 'I say no.'

Mirabel, knowing he is found out, collapses. Miss Delvin confirms that he was indeed the other man but is innocent of murder. He fled in terror and escaped the police with the help of Miss Jethro. Alban has obtained a letter from her which finally reveals that Mr Brown took his own life with Mirabel's razor when he learned of Miss Jethro's refusal. Emily and Alban are reconciled and marry.

Serialization. First published in several provincial newspapers including the *Glasgow Weekly Herald*, 15 Dec. 1883–12 July 1884; **Harper's Weekly*, 22 Dec. 1883–12 July 1884; and *London Society*, Jan.–Dec. 1884.

Book publication

1st English edn. 3 vols, *Chatto & Windus, London 1884. Light blue cloth, covers blocked in red, spines lettered in gilt. Pale green and white floral endpapers. Half-title in each vol. Published Oct. 1884.

Vol I (viii) + 296 pp. 32 pp publisher's catalogue dated March 1884 bound in at end.

Vol II (viii) + 296 pp.

Vol III (viii) + 324 pp.

1-vol edns. Chatto & Windus 1886–1906. Sutton, Stroud 1995.

US and 1st edn. *Harper, New York 1884 (as 'I Say No': Or the Love-Letter Answered). Published three months ahead of the English edition (see PIRACY).

Translations. Dutch, The Hague 1884; Russian, St Petersburg 1884; German, Berlin 1886; French, Paris 1888.

identity

'I seemed in some strange way to have lost my ordinary identity—to have stepped out of my own character.' (*The Law and the Lady*)

The confusion or substitution of identity is a favourite theme running through many of Collins's stories, beginning with 'The *Twin Sisters' (1851) where Streatfield eventually realizes he has proposed to the wrong identical twin. Identity has obvious relevance to the *sensation novel, but it seems to have had a particular interest for Collins. In real life he assumed a double identity of his own as William *Dawson, in order to observe the proprieties in his relationship with Martha *Rudd.

The use of identity takes several forms. In some cases it is forcibly substituted or stolen, so that Laura *Fairlie is deprived of her identity and made to replace her double, Anne *Catherick, in *The Woman in White* (1860). Nugent Dubourg on the other hand actively supplants his identical twin brother, Oscar, in *Poor Miss Finch* (1872) and Mercy Merrick in *The New Magdalen* (1873) steals the letter that enables her to assume the identity of Grace Roseberry. In *The Haunted Hotel* (1879) and *Blind Love* (1890) the substituted identity of the victim's body forms the basis of the insurance fraud.

In other cases lost identity is rediscovered. Thus Ulpius in *Antonina* (1850) turns out to be Numerian's long-lost brother, and Mat in *Hide and Seek* (1854) finds he is Madonna's uncle. George Vendale discovers by accident that he is the heir to Wilding's fortune in '*No Thoroughfare' (1867) while Simple Sally in *The Fallen Leaves* (1879) turns out to be Mrs Farnaby's stolen daughter. In *The Two Destinies* (1876) George and Mary have altered so much in the intervening years that they recognize each other only by

Old Sharon, the slovenly pipe-smoking detective of 'My Lady's Money', in *The Illustrated London News*, Christmas 1877

means of a childhood memento. The same version of the theme appears in the short stories. In 'The *Dead Hand' (1857) Arthur Holliday's apparently dead companion is later found to be his illegitimate half-brother and Michael Bloomfield in 'A *Shocking Story' (1878) is really the illegitimate son of Mina's aunt.

Other novels depend on a new identity to hide the past. Mannion lives under an assumed name in *Basil* (1852) and Mr Thorpe in *Hide and Seek* had earlier taken the name of Arthur Carr. Sarah Leeson conceals herself as Mrs Jazeph in *The Dead Secret* (1857) while George in *The Two Destinies* must change his name to Germaine in order to secure his stepfather's inheritance. In 'The *Fatal Cradle' (1861) identity is lost for ever because the two babies are mixed up at birth while in *The Legacy of Cain* (1888) Gracedieu deliberately confuses the identities of Helena and Eunice to conceal which has a murderess for her mother.

Most of these aspects of identity appear in *Armadale* (1866) where there are two Allan *Armadales in both the prologue and main story. In the first generation, one Armadale has taken the name of the other. In the second, Allan is innocently unaware of either his background or namesake whereas *Midwinter actively chooses to conceal his true name. Lydia *Gwilt, apart from hiding her true identity, seeks to marry the one Armadale in order to pass herself off as the widow of the other.

Idle, Thomas Character assumed by Collins as a 'born-and-bred idler' in 'The *Lazy Tour of Two Idle Apprentices' (1857).

Illuminated Magazine, The (1843–5). Short-lived monthly periodical intended to appeal to 'the masses'. Edited by Douglas *Jerrold from May 1843 to October 1844. Notable for publishing in August 1843 Collins's first identified work, 'The *Last Stage Coachman', written while working at *Antrobus & Co. Illustrations were by H. C. Hine. Other contributors included Laman Blanchard, Julia Pardoe, Mark *Lemon and Albert Smith. Well-known illustrators were John Leech, Kenny Meadows and Phiz.

Illustrated London News, The Weekly newspaper founded in 1843 to which Collins contributed two stories:

'*My Lady's Money', Christmas 1877; and *Blind Love*, 6 July–28 Dec. 1889. Collins died before completing the novel and it was finished by Walter *Besant from weekly part 19 onwards.

illustrators Most of Collins's English first editions were unillustrated. The exceptions were *Mr Wray's Cash-Box* (1852) with a frontispiece by *Millais; *Rambles Beyond Railways* (1851) with twelve lithographs by Henry *Brandling; *Armadale* (1866) where the engravings by G. H. Thomas were taken from its *Cornhill serialization; *The Haunted Hotel* (1879) with six illustrations by A. Hopkins; *Blind Love* (1890) with sixteen wood engravings taken from its serialization in the *Illustrated London News*; and *The Lazy Tour of Two Idle Apprentices* (1890) with eight photolithographs by Arthur Layard.

Illustrations were generally first introduced to Collins's texts by *Sampson Low with *Gilbert's steel engravings for their *collected edition of 1861–5. Millais drew the frontispiece for *No Name*. *Smith, Elder did not generally add to the existing illustrations for their reprints between 1865 and 1890.

*Chatto & Windus became Collins's main publisher from 1875 and although they illustrated most of his earlier works for the Piccadilly Novels, their superior collected edition, they generally did not

'The Last Stage Coachman' published in *The Illuminated Magazine* of August 1843

use illustrations for new titles. The exceptions were *The Haunted Hotel* and *Blind Love*.

Artists used by Chatto included: A. Concanen (*After Dark, The Queen of Hearts, My Miscellanies*); A. W. Cooper (*No Name*); G. *du Maurier (*The Moonstone, Poor Miss Finch, The New Magdalen, The Frozen Deep*); L. Fildes (*The Law and the Lady, Miss or Mrs?* taken from *The *Graphic*); A. Forestier (*Blind Love*, from *The Illustrated London News*); F. A. Fraser (*The Woman in White, The Moonstone*); S. Hall (*The Law and the Lady*); A. Hopkins (*The Haunted Hotel*); A. B. Houghton (*After Dark*, from the 1862 reprint); E. Hughes (*Poor Miss Finch*); F. W. Lawson (*The Law and the Lady*); M. F. Mahoney (*Basil, Hide and Seek, The Frozen Deep*); C. S. Reinhart (*The New Magdalen*); W. Small (*Man and Wife*).

Collins's main American publishers, Harpers, were much keener on illustrations, using numerous wood engravings in the text. *The Woman in White* and *No Name* were illustrated by John McLenan, *After Dark* by L. Fildes and E. A. Abbey, *Man and Wife* by W. Small and *Armadale* by G. H. Thomas. Engravings for other titles were unattributed.

Nadel, I. B., 'Wilkie Collins and his Illustrators' in *Wilkie Collins to the Forefront: Some Reassessments*, edited by Nelson Smith and R. C. Terry, New York 1995.

International Review, The Bimonthly review with philosophical and religious bias, published by A. S. Barnes & Co of New York. It sold also in England so that its publication of 'A *Shocking Story' (November 1878) upset *Chatto & Windus who issued the same story in the *Belgravia Annual*. *The International Review* also published '*Considerations on the Copyright Question Addressed to an American Friend' (June 1880).

Ioláni; Or, Tahiti as it was; A Romance Collins's first novel, unpublished during his lifetime. *Ioláni* was written during 1844 while he was employed by *Antrobus & Co in the Strand. In 1845 it was submitted to *Longman's who initially considered publishing it on condition that Collins's father would cover the costs. The manuscript was subsequently declined by *Chapman & Hall and other London publishers. Collins later recalled in *Appleton's Journal* (3 Sept. 1870) that his

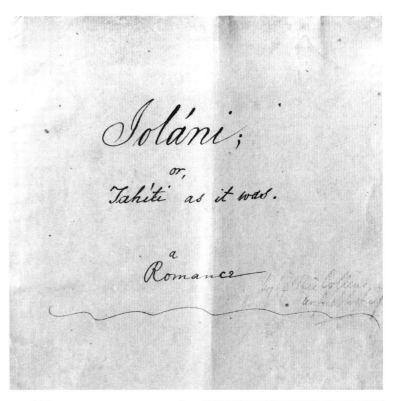

Title-page to the manuscript of *Ioláni* written in Collins's hand

'youthful imagination ran riot among the noble savages, in scenes which caused the respectable British publisher to declare that it was impossible to put his name on the title-page of such a novel.' The manuscript was later given to Augustin *Daly, probably in 1878, and taken to America. In 1900 it was bought at the sale of Daly's library by book-dealer George D. Smith for $23 and resold to Howard T. Goodwin, a Philadelphia collector, for $100. After his death in 1903, *Ioláni* was sold at auction to Joseph M. Fox 'a gentleman and cricketer of note'. It remained with the Fox family until re-emerging in New York during 1991. *Ioláni* is published by Princeton University Press (edited by Ira B. Nadel).

The main source for *Ioláni* was William Ellis's *Polynesian Researches* (second edition, 4 vols, London 1831–2) present in Collins's library. He borrowed the names of the four principal characters, Ioláni, Aimáta, Idía and Mahíné, citing Tahitian pronunciation, marriage customs, scenic descriptions and the practice of infanticide which provides a key issue for the novel. Other possible sources were Mary Russell Mitford's *Christina, The Maid of the South Seas* (1811), Barrow's *Account of

the Mutiny of the Bounty* (1831) and Hall's *Fragments of Voyages and Travels* (1831). The character of *Ioláni* foreshadows the pagan priest, Ulpius, in Collins's next novel, *Antonina* (1850); whereas Aimáta reappears in 'The *Captain's Last Love' (1876).

➼ Ioláni, the evil High Priest of Oro and brother of the king, fathers a child by Idía. To avoid the local custom of putting the first-born to death, Idía flees with the help of her courageous young friend, Aimáta, to another part of the island where they live under the protection of the local chieftain, Mahíné. When war is declared between Mahíné and the king, Ioláni declares Idía as the next human sacrifice. She goes into hiding with Aimáta but they are captured by Ioláni who leaves the child to die in the woods. Idía is saved at the point of sacrifice by Mahíné's warriors and the king is defeated in a bloodthirsty battle. The wounded Ioláni and his brother are exiled to an outlying island while Idía returns to the woods in search of her child. The infant has been saved by an outcast wildman, another

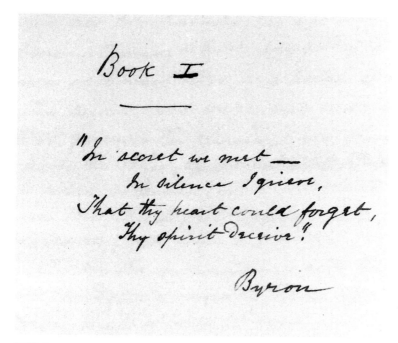

Book I

"In secret we met —
In silence I grieve,
That thy heart could forget,
Thy spirit deceive."

Byron

Quotation from Byron at the start of Book I of
Ioláni

victim of Ioláni's treachery.

Mahíné marries Aimáta and while
blissfully happy neglects his duties as the
new leader. Ioláni escapes from exile and
enlists the aid of Otahára, a sorcerer, who
poisons Idía with herbs. Aimáta and
Mahíné return to Tahiti to find the dying
Idía whose final wish is for Aimáta to
bring up the child. The warriors, tired of
Mahíné's indolence, plan to assassinate
him and bring back the banished king.
Mahíné and Aimáta escape by canoe to
live peacefully in exile while Ioláni eventually kills Otahára in an argument. The
priest is watched by the now totally deranged wildman who takes his own revenge. He forces the tightly bound Ioláni
into a leaking canoe with him and they
sail off into an impending storm to their
certain death at sea.

> Horowitz, G. [Bookseller], *Wilkie Collins:
> Ioláni; or Tahiti as it was; A Romance: The
> Original Autograph Manuscript*, New York
> [1991].

Italy

'The most interesting country in the world.'
(*The Woman in White*)

First visited by Collins with his father
from 1836 to 1838 during the family's
European tour. After three months in
*France they arrived in Genoa on 14 De-
cember 1836, travelling via Pisa to Florence in time for Christmas Eve. They
spent four months in *Rome, left Naples
in a hurry because of cholera and stayed a
month in Ischia during October 1837. Further visits to Naples, Rome and Florence
were followed by a month in *Venice.
They returned to England in August 1838
via Austria, Germany and Holland.

Collins became imbued with Italian art
and culture and learned something of the
language. In 1853 he eagerly took the opportunity to return with Charles *Dickens and Augustus *Egg. They travelled
through *Switzerland, arrived in Milan
on 24 October and proceeded by way of a
thirty-one-hour journey to Genoa (27 October–1 November). They next sailed to
Naples on a dreadfully overcrowded ship.
After a wet night on deck, Dickens teased
the captain into giving him the steward's
cabin; Collins and Egg were relegated to
the ship's store room. Then came Rome
(13–18 November) and Florence (21–23
November) where Dickens introduced
Collins to Sir Walter *Scott's biographer,
J. G. Lockhart. They took over twenty-
four hours to reach Venice (25 November) via Bologna, Ferrara and Padua, and
the travellers returned to England on 11
December by way of *Paris and Calais.

Collins returned to Rome and Italy
with Caroline Graves and her daughter
from December 1863 to March 1864. He
visited Milan and Rome with Edward
*Pigott in October 1866 and made a fur-
ther trip to Italy with *Frith in 1875.

Collins recalled Austrian Italy in 'My
Black Mirror' (reprinted in *My Miscellanies*, 1863) and contributed 'Dead Lock in
Italy' to *All the Year Round* (8 December
1866). In *Armadale* (1866), Lydia *Gwilt
and *Midwinter live in Naples after their
marriage; and most of *The Haunted Hotel*
(1879) is set in Venice.

Collins, W., *Memoirs*.

Lehmann (1908), 47–51.

Page, N., *A Dickens Chronology*, Basingstoke,
1988.

J

Jennings, Ezra In *The Moonstone*, Dr Candy's terminally ill assistant who takes *opium to relieve his symptoms. It could be Collins himself speaking when Jennings suffers 'the vengeance of yesterday's opium, pursuing me through a series of frightful dreams'. Jennings uses *Elliotson's *Human Physiology* to predict Franklin *Blake's behaviour under the influence of a second dose of the drug. The strange character was based on a doctor's assistant Collins and Dickens met during their 1857 walking tour of *Cumberland.

See also 'THE DEAD HAND'.

Jerrold, Douglas William (1803–57). Dramatist, novelist and journalist; early political contributor to **Punch*. Editor of several periodicals including *The *Illuminated Magazine* which published Collins's first recorded work in 1843. The two writers became good friends and appeared together in *amateur theatricals. Collins took over the role of Mr Shadowly Softhead when Jerrold abandoned the 1851 provincial tour of *Not So Bad as We Seem*. Collins later wrote 'Douglas Jerrold was one of the first and dearest friends of my literary life.' His biographical tribute, 'Douglas Jerrold', appeared in **Household Words*, 5 February 1859; reprinted in **My Miscellanies* (1863). Jerrold died suddenly in 1857 and *The Frozen Deep* was revived as one of a series of events to raise funds for his widow, organized by *Dickens.

Jewsbury, Geraldine Endsor (1812–80). Critic for *The Athenaeum*, publisher's reader for *Hurst & Blackett and *Bentley's, minor novelist and contributor to **Household Words*. Wrote generally favourable reviews of *Hide and Seek* (1854) and *The Moonstone* (1868) for *The Athenaeum*.

Gettman, R. A., *A Victorian Publisher: A Study of the Bentley Papers*, Cambridge 1960, 194.
Page (1974), 55–6, 170–1.

Jezebel's Daughter *Sensation novel published in 1880 and dedicated to Alberto *Caccia, Collins's Italian translator. Based on the 1858 play, *The Red Vial*, Collins's attempt to write for 'the masses' resulted in an unduly melodramatic tone. The novel, however, is notable for the way it handles the treatment of lunatics and the mentally retarded; and for the creation of a female character who is effective both in business and as a philanthropist. The plot revolves around the use of poisons and includes forensic details applicable to *detective fiction.

➾ In 1828, the firm of Wagner, Keller and Engelman has offices in London and Frankfurt. After the death of her husband, the progressive Mrs Wagner becomes senior partner, running the London office where she plans to employ women clerks. To prove that lunatics can be cured by kindness, she removes the simple-minded Jack Straw from Bedlam and takes him into her household.

In Frankfurt, Fritz Keller, son of one of the other partners, has fallen in love with Minna Fontaine, daughter of a sinister widow whose husband made a lifetime study of poisons. Keller's father disapproves of Madame Fontaine, who is constantly in debt, and refuses to allow Fritz and Minna to marry. Fritz is sent to London and a young Englishman, David Glenney, who tells the story, goes to Frankfurt in his place. Here he meets Minna and her mother and innocently introduces them to the third partner, Engelman. Madame Fontaine, determined to further her daughter's marriage, uses Engelman, who falls in love with her, to trick her way into Keller's house.

Madame Fontaine possesses a chest of poisons and their antidotes which her husband intended to be destroyed on his death. She doses Keller with a slow-acting poison and to win his goodwill revives him with the antidote. She becomes his nurse and then his housekeeper, having assured him, falsely, that she is no longer in debt. Keller withdraws his objections to the marriage of Fritz and Minna.

Mrs Wagner comes to Frankfurt on business accompanied by Jack Straw, who is much improved by her kindness and devoted to her. He is immediately recognized by Madame Fontaine as 'Hans Grimm', mentally damaged by being accidentally poisoned in her husband's laboratory years before.

Fritz returns to marry Minna. Madame Fontaine has a debt to pay which falls due the day after the wedding, but when the ceremony has to be postponed she steals the key to Mrs Wagner's desk from Jack Straw and embezzles the money she needs from the firm's funds. Mrs Wagner discovers the theft and, unable to pay back the money, Madame Fontaine poisons her with a fast-acting, undetectable poison. Jack Straw unsuccessfully tries to revive his benefactress with the same antidote that had saved Keller and her body is taken to the Deadhouse, where the devoted Jack refuses to leave her. In a lurid scene Madame Fontaine, who has secretly followed them, is accidently poisoned by her own mixtures while Mrs Wagner recovers from a deathlike coma, ringing an alarm bell which alerts the watchman.

Binding of the three-volume Chatto & Windus first English edition of *Jezebel's Daughter* in 1880

Madame Fontaine dies, leaving a self-incriminating diary. Fritz and Minna marry, while Jack remains in the care of Mrs Wagner.

Serialization. First published in the *Bolton Weekly Journal*, 13 Sept. 1879–31 Jan. 1880, and several other *Tillotson syndicated newspapers.

Book publication

1st English edn. 3 vols, *Chatto & Windus, London 1880. White cloth, covers blocked in black, spines lettered in gilt, green and white decorated endpapers. Half-title in each vol. Published in March 1880. Variant binding in tan cloth with later publisher's catalogue dated Apr. 1880.

Vol I viii + 284 pp. 32 pp publisher's catalogue dated Feb. 1880 bound in at end.

Vol II (iv) + 284 pp.

Vol III (iv) + 296 pp.

1-vol edns. Chatto & Windus 1880–1901; Sutton, Stroud 1995.

1st US edn. *Seaside Library (vol 34, no. 696), New York 1880 (first book publication).

Translation. Dutch, The Hague 1880.

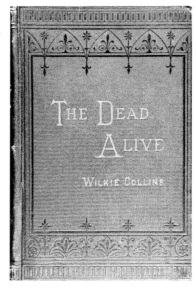

The Dead Alive, the US title for 'John Jago's Ghost' published in 1874

'John Jago's Ghost; Or, The Dead Alive: An American Story' Short story originally published as 'The Dead Alive' in the *Home Journal*, 27 Dec. 1873–4 Feb. 1874; *New York Fireside Companion*, 29 Dec.–19 Jan. 1874; and the *Canadian Monthly*, Jan.–Feb. 1874. Reprinted (as *The Dead Alive*) in book form, Boston 1874 [1873], Toronto 1874, and in *The *Frozen Deep and Other Stories* (London 1874). Written during Collins's reading tour of *America, it is based on the true story of the trial of Jesse and Stephen Boorne of Manchester, Vermont. The missing body in the story also suggests similarities with *The Mystery of Edwin Drood* (1870).

➥ An Englishman, Philip Lefrank, visits his distant relations, the Meadowcrofts, in rural America. The family consists of the father, Isaac, two sons, Ambrose and

Silas, and a middle-aged daughter. Another member of the household is Naomi Colebrook, Isaac's niece, whom Ambrose wants to marry. John Jago, the farm manager, is also in love with Naomi and there is a strong mutual dislike between Jago and the Meadowcroft brothers. When Jago disappears and remains are found in a lime pit, Ambrose and Silas are arrested for murder. Despite the absence of an identifiable body, they are convicted and sentenced to death. Just in time to save the brothers, Jago returns and confesses he disappeared deliberately. The disenchanted Naomi leaves for England to marry Philip.

Ashley, R. P., 'Wilkie Collins and a Vermont Murder Trial', *New England Quarterly*, 21 (Sept. 1948), 368–73.

John Jasper's Secret Sequel to *The Mystery of Edwin Drood* by New York journalist Henry Morford. It was originally published anonymously in parts from October 1871 to May 1872. Morford leaked an announcement mis-attributing authorship to 'Charles Dickens the Younger and Wilkie Collins'. Collins issued an immediate denial but editions by Fenno of New York perpetuated the fraud into the twentieth century. By 1905 the title-page had been corrected but Collins's name and portrait still appeared on the spine of the book.

Walters, J. C., *The Complete Edwin Drood*, London 1912.

journalism Journalism in various *periodicals formed the major part of Collins's early output. Following 'The *Last Stage Coachman' in 1843, his first identified articles appeared in *Bentley's Miscellany* from March 1851 to August 1852 and his first regular employer was Edward *Pigott of The *Leader. Collins made numerous contributions between September 1851 and August 1855 at the same time as writing articles for *Household Words. *Dickens invited him to join the permanent staff in September 1856 and journalism continued to be Collins's main employment and source of income until the success of *The Woman in White* allowed him to resign from *All the Year Round* in January 1861.

Beetz, K. H., 'Wilkie Collins and *The Leader*', *Victorian Periodicals Review*, 15 (Spring 1982), 20–9.

Lohrli (1973).

Oppenlander, E. A., *Dickens' 'All the Year Round': Descriptive Index and Contributors List*, Troy, NY, 1984.

K

Kent, (William) Charles Mark (1823–1902). Friend of Collins, and great admirer of *Dickens about whom he wrote several books and articles. Editor, journalist and contributor to *Household Words*. On Collins's recommendation, unsuccessfully tried *laudanum for insomnia. Described to *Fitzgerald on one occasion that Collins's eyes 'were literally *enormous bags of blood!*'.

Miller, W., *The Dickens Student and Collector*, London 1946.

Kent, Constance, and the Road Murder A notorious murder case used by Collins as source material for *The Moonstone*. In 1860, a 4-year-old boy, Francis Kent, was brutally murdered in his home in the Wiltshire village of Road. Suspicion originally fell on his nurse, Elizabeth Gough. She was twice arrested by the local police officer, Superintendent Foley, but released for lack of evidence. The celebrated Inspector *Whicher of Scotland Yard was called in and arrested the boy's 16-year-old half-sister, Constance Kent. Whicher deduced from the washing-book that one of her nightgowns was missing and had been disposed of because it was bloodstained. Public opinion was sympathetic to Constance Kent and the case against her was dismissed by the local magistrate. Five years later she confessed to having carried out the murder, alone and unaided.

Collins's portrayal of Sergeant *Cuff in *The Moonstone* was based on the character of Inspector Whicher, with some details of his appearance taken from another Scotland Yard officer, Inspector Walker. In *The Moonstone*, as in the Road case, suspicion falls on a servant until a Scotland Yard officer is called in to replace the inept local policeman. Suspicion then falls on the daughter of the house, arousing general indignation. Collins also incorporated the missing nightgown (stained with paint, not blood) and the evidence of the washing-book.

See *The Times*, 21 July 1860, for a report of the arrest and Whicher's questioning of Constance Kent.

L

'Lady of Glenwith Grange, The'

Short story included in *After Dark*, 1856 (no periodical publication).

➤ Ida Welwyn promises her dying mother that she will always look after her younger sister, Rosamond. Against Ida's better instincts, Rosamond marries Baron Franval whom she meets in Paris. A French police agent exposes the Baron as an impostor called Monbrun and he is killed while trying to escape. Rosamond dies of shock leaving her retarded daughter to be brought up by the reclusive Ida at Glenwith Grange.

'Last Stage Coachman, The'

Collins's first identified published work, signed W. Wilkie Collins. Appeared when he was nineteen in Douglas *Jerrold's *Illuminated Magazine*, August 1843. Brief fantasy story, a lament at the passing of the stage coach, displaced by the arrival of the railway. Collins draws on the *supernatural with an imaginary stage coach thundering through the Heavens and 'a railway director strapped fast to each wheel and a stoker between the teeth of each of the four horses. In place of luggage, fragments of broken steam carriages, and red carpet bags filled with other mementos of railway accidents, occupied the roof.'

laudanum Mixture of *opium and alcohol; the name originally used by Paracelsus for his own medical remedies in the early seventeenth century. Laudanum was the form in which opium was generally taken during Collins's time and common brand names of patent medicines included Battley's Sedative Solution, Dalby's Carminative, Godfrey's Cordial and Mother Bailey's Quieting Syrup. Battley's contained calcium hydrate, opium, sherry, alcohol and distilled water.

Booth, M., *Opium: A History*, London 1996.

Hayter, A., *Opium and the Romantic Imagination*, London 1968, 255–70.

law

'But then I am a lawyer, and my business is to make a fuss about trifles.' (*The Law and the Lady*)

Collins entered *Lincoln's Inn as a student in May 1846 but although called to the Bar in November 1851 never actually practised as a barrister. Years later he reflected in *Heart and Science* (1883) 'How I pity the unfortunate men who have to learn the law.' Nevertheless, Collins used his knowledge in several major works, particularly with regard to the marriage settlements and inheritances of his characters. He also consulted his own lawyer, William *Tindell, in writing *Poor Miss Finch* (1872) and for details of the Madeleine Smith trial used in *The Law and the Lady* (1875).

The multiple narratives of *The Woman in White* (1860) present the story as if in a court of law 'by making the persons who have been most closely connected with [the events] at each successive stage, relate their own experience, word for word'. Faithful family solicitors make regular appearances in Collins's novels. Mr Gilmore in *The Woman in White* (1860) is succeeded by Mr Pendril in *No Name*; Mr Darch and Mr Pedgift in *Armadale* (1866); Mr Bruff in *The Moonstone* (1868); Sir Patrick Lundie in *Man and Wife* (1870); Mr Mool in *Heart and Science*; and Mr Sarrazin in *The Evil Genius* (1886).

On the other hand, Collins's cynicism about the law is expressed by Mr Kyrle, also in *The Woman in White*, declaring 'the money question always enters into the law question'; and 'when an English jury has to choose between a plain fact on the surface and a long explanation under the surface, it always takes the fact in preference to the explanation.' Allan *Armadale falls 'headlong into the bottomless abyss of the English Law' while Gabriel *Betteredge in *The Moonstone* observes 'Every human institution (Justice included) will stretch a little, if you only pull it the right way.' More overt attacks on the legal system are reserved for the law on illegitimacy in *No Name*; *marriage laws in *Man and Wife*; the Scottish Not Proven verdict in *The Law and the*

THE LAST STAGE COACHMAN

BY W. WILKIE COLLINS.

HE Last Stage Coachman! It falls upon the ear of every one but a shareholder in railways, with a boding, melancholy sound. In spite of our natural reverence for the wonders of science, our hearts grow heavy at the thought of never again beholding the sweet-smelling nosegay, the un- an old public road—they were now grass-grown and miry, or desecrated by the abominable presence of a "station." I wended my way towards a famous roadside inn : it was desolate and silent, or in other words, "To Let." I looked for "the commercial room:" not a pot of beer adorned the mouldering tables, and not a pipe lay scattered over the wild and beautiful seclusions of its once numerous "boxes." It was deserted and useless ; the voice of the traveller rung no longer round its walls, and the merry horn of the guard

Lady; and the Lunacy Commission in 'A Mad Marriage'.

MacEachen, D. B., 'Wilkie Collins and British Law', *Nineteenth-Century Fiction*, 5 (Sept. 1950), 121–39.

Law and the Lady, The: A Novel

'The actions of human beings are not invariably governed by the laws of pure reason.'

Detective story dedicated to *Régnier, attacking the Scottish Not Proven verdict. Early example of a female sleuth. The heroine is one of Collins's determined and resourceful women characters, who retains the initiative throughout. In the bizarre character of Miserrimus Dexter Collins created one of his most powerful examples of mental disturbance, here combined with physical handicap.

The novel contains several features of modern *detective fiction, including the amateur succeeding where the professionals failed, a court-room cross-examination influenced by the Madeleine Smith trial, the use of an alibi, and the sequential elimination of the various suspects. For details of Collins's dispute with his newspaper publisher during serialization see The *Graphic.

➨ Valeria and Eustace Woodville begin their marriage inauspiciously, when, on honeymoon at Ramsgate, Valeria discovers that her husband's true name is Macallan. As Eustace refuses to explain

Lawson illustration to the one-volume Chatto & Windus edition of *The Law and the Lady*

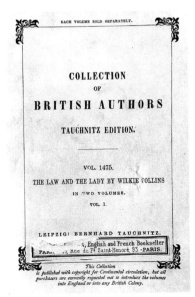

Front cover to the Tauchnitz edition of *The Law and the Lady* published in 1875

she confronts his mother who although sympathetic will also not answer her questions. Valeria becomes 'positively resolved . . . to discover the secret which the mother and son were hiding'.

On returning to London, Valeria establishes that her marriage is legally valid. She also visits Eustace's closest friend, Major Fitz-David. He knows the secret but is on his word of honour not to help its discovery. The Major, a modern Don Juan, is sympathetic to Valeria's position and tacitly allows her to search his rooms. She finds a trial report revealing that Eustace was accused of poisoning his first wife Sarah at Gleninch, his Midlothian house, and is tainted with the Scotch verdict of Not Proven. Valeria is now determined to find the proof of his innocence. Eustace, however, weakly runs away from his wife, going abroad alone.

The medical evidence of poisoning at the trial was conclusive. Eustace admitted buying arsenic but claimed that it was at his wife's request, to improve her complexion. The prosecution alleged the marriage was unhappy and that Eustace was really in love with his cousin, Helena Beauly.

Valeria meets another of Eustace's friends, the eccentric Miserrimus Dexter who gave evidence for him at the trial. Dexter was born without legs and gets around either in a wheelchair or by hopping on his hands. His mood changes violently, from mild and melancholy to the

brink of madness, and he is cared for by his simple-minded but devoted cousin Ariel. When Valeria tells Dexter that she suspects Helena Beauly he immediately agrees, recounting an incriminating conversation he overheard Helena having with her maid. Helena, however, has a perfect alibi. She had attended a somewhat disreputable masked ball while her maid took her place in the house.

Valeria next travels to Edinburgh to meet Mr Playmore, Eustace's lawyer at the trial. Playmore is convinced that Dexter is the villain since he is known to have taken the key to an intercommunicating bedroom door before the night of the poisoning. Valeria revisits Dexter who in a convoluted way begins to tell the story of the fatal events. He mentions a letter torn into pieces but then lapses into permanent madness. He is confined to an asylum, accompanied by Ariel who refuses to leave him.

The torn letter is eventually found in a dust-heap behind the house at Gleninch and painstakingly put together by experts. It is a suicide note to Eustace from Sarah, exonerating all concerned. She had rejected a previous marriage proposal from Dexter who was infatuated with her. When Dexter showed her Eustace's diary, which revealed he had never loved her—he only married her out of gallantry when she compromised herself by visiting him alone at his bachelor lodgings—Sarah took the arsenic. Using the missing key, Dexter stole the letter and once he was sure that Eustace would not be convicted of murder tore it to pieces.

Eustace has meanwhile been injured while heroically fighting for the Brotherhood in Spain. On his recovery, he agrees with Valeria not to read the reconstructed letter which remains sealed in its envelope. It will await the next generation, their newly born son.

*Serialization. The **Graphic*, 26 Sept. 1874–13 Mar. 1875; *Harper's Weekly*, 10 Oct. 1874–27 Mar. 1875.

Book publication

1st English edn. 3 vols, *Chatto & Windus, London 1875. Dark green cloth, covers blocked in blind, spines lettered in gilt, cream endpapers. No half-titles. Published in Feb. 1875.

Vol I (viii) + 248 pp. Advertisement of Collins's previous works occupies p (247). 40 pp publisher's catalogue dated Dec. 1874 bound in at end.

Vol II iv + 272 pp. Advertisement of Collins's previous works occupies p (271).

Vol III iv + 344 pp. Advertisement of Collins's previous works occupies p (343).

1-vol edns. Chatto & Windus 1876–1913 (with 7 illustrations by S. L. Fildes, S. Hall and F. W. Lawson). World's Classics 1992 (critical edition, edited by J. Bourne Taylor).

1st US edn. *Harper, New York 1875.

Translations. Dutch, The Hague 1875; French, Paris 1875; German, Berlin 1875; Russian, Moscow 1875.

Lazy Tour of Two Idle Apprentices, The; No Thoroughfare; The Perils of Certain English Prisoners by Charles

Dickens and Wilkie Collins. Three stories written in *collaboration with *Dickens, and first published in **Household Words* and *All the Year Round*.

1st collected edn. 1 vol, *Chapman & Hall, London 1890. Dark green cloth, covers blocked in black, spine lettered in gilt, black endpapers. Half-title. Eight full-page illustrations by Arthur Layard. viii + 328 pp. Variant binding in red-brown cloth, forms part of the Crown Edition of Dickens works in 17 vols. Later editions in 1895 have the illustrations redrawn.

'Lazy Tour of Two Idle Apprentices, The' (narrative). Humorous ac-

count of Collins's and Dickens's walking tour of *Cumberland during September 1857. Written in *collaboration, it was originally published in **Household Words*, 3–31 Oct. 1857; and *Harper's Weekly*, 31

Illustration to the 1890 Chapman & Hall edition of *The Lazy Tour of Two Idle Apprentices*

Oct.–28 Nov. 1857. Collected in book form in 1890.

Collins assumed the identity of Thomas Idle (a born-and-bred idler) and Dickens that of Francis Goodchild (laboriously idle). Collins wrote three main parts. In the first, he describes his

sprained ankle after a reluctant ascent of *Carrock Fell in the mist. The second, the story of Dr Lorn, was later republished as 'The *Dead Hand'. The remaining section, in which Thomas Idle, stretched out injured on a sofa in *Allonby, reflects that all the great disasters of his life have been caused by being deluded into activity, consists of reminiscences, and is loosely based on Collins's own life. At school, after foolishly winning a prize, he was rejected by the other idle boys as a traitor and by the industrious boys as a dangerous interloper. The only time he played cricket he caught a fever from the unaccustomed perspiration. Mistakenly studying for the Bar, where he was expected to know nothing whatever about the law, he became the target of a persistent legal bore.

Leader, The (1850–1866). Weekly paper founded by George Henry *Lewes and Thornton Hunt to review politics, literature and the arts from a radical standpoint. Edward *Pigott purchased a controlling interest in 1851. *The Leader* gave Collins the opportunity to develop his journalistic skills and his first piece, 'A Plea for the Sunday Reform', appeared on 27 September 1851. His articles were signed 'W. W. C.' until 3 April 1852. Later contributions were either designated 'W.' or remained anonymous, since Collins forbade the use of his name after a disagreement with Pigott over the paper's presentation of controversial religious views. Collins mainly reviewed books, plays and art exhibitions but also contributed to the 'Portfolio' section of the paper. He wrote for *The Leader* until 1855, taking an active interest in its management. It is probable that he carried out editorial duties before joining *Dickens

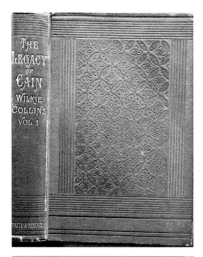

Binding of the Chatto & Windus first edition of *The Legacy of Cain*, 1889

at *Household Words* in 1856. *The Leader* published favourable reviews of *Mr Wray's Cash-Box* (1852), *Basil* (1852), *Hide and Seek* (1854) and *After Dark* (1856).

Beetz, K. H., 'Wilkie Collins and *The Leader*', *Victorian Periodicals Review*, 15 (Spring 1982), 20–9. Gives background to correspondence between Collins and Pigott, particularly on the subject of religion. Identifies contributions by Collins of which twenty-nine are certain and another fifty are possible.

Lecount, Mrs Virginie In *No Name*, French housekeeper of Michael Vanstone and then his son, Noel. Formidable opponent to Captain *Wragge. Unable to prevent Noel's marriage, she thwarts Magdalen *Vanstone's inheritance by persuading Noel to change his will which also leaves her £5,000.

Legacy of Cain, The

'There are inherent emotional forces in humanity to which the inherited influences must submit.'

Novel dedicated to Mrs Henry Powell *Bartley (Carrie Graves) acknowledging her skill and patience in copying manuscripts for the printer. Henry *Bartley was Collins's solicitor and, ironically, embezzled from the estate—the fate suffered by Miss Jillgall in the story. Published in 1888, it was the final novel completed by Collins and the last to be syndicated by *Tillotson. *The Legacy of Cain* explores the theme of hereditary evil, and attacks the idea that 'bad blood' necessarily results in a criminality.

➥ The main story begins in 1875. Helena and Eunice are sisters brought up by their father, the Revd Abel Gracedieu. He has deliberately kept them in ignorance of their true ages because the elder daughter was adopted in 1858, after her natural mother was executed for the brutal murder of her husband. The story's main narrator is the prison governor who always feared the adoption would end badly because of the taint of inherited evil.

The household is joined by the minister's impoverished cousin, Selina Jillgall, to whom Helena takes an immediate dislike. The good-natured Eunice, however, becomes very friendly with Miss Jillgall whose only other ally is a Mrs Tegenbruggen. In 1858 she was Elizabeth Chance, lover of Eunice's murdered father. Mrs Tegenbruggen is determined to discover which daughter is the elder and make trouble.

Eunice, visiting friends in London, meets young Philip Dunboyne. They fall in love but when Philip later sees Helena she captures his affections. Eunice finds out and to compose herself takes some of her ailing father's medicine. Under its influence she sees a ghostly apparition of her executed mother urging her to kill Helena in revenge. Helena incurs the disapproval of both Gracedieu and Philip's father, brother-in-law to the executed woman. The distressed minister asks the governor for advice. Helena, to spite them both, provokes her father and, permanently unhinged, he tries to kill the governor with a razor.

Philip tires of Helena and wishes to marry the now reluctant Eunice. Helena in revenge obtains digitalis with a forged prescription and attempts to poison Philip while pretending to nurse him. She is arrested and sent to prison. Philip fully recovers and finally persuades Eunice to marry him, but only after the governor, to thwart the mischievous Mrs Tegenbruggen, has revealed the truth: it was Eunice who was adopted after her mother's execution. Helena serves a two-year sentence and emigrates to America where she prospers as the leader of a women's religious cult.

Serialization. First published in the *Leigh Journal and Times*, 17 Feb.–29 June 1888, and several other *Tillotson's syndicated newspapers.

Book publication

1st English edn. 3 vols, *Chatto & Windus, London 1889. Dark-blue cloth, front covers blocked in red and black, spines lettered in gilt, grey and white floral endpapers. Half-title in each vol. Published in Nov. 1888.

Vol I viii + 290 pp

Vol II vi + 264 pp

Vol III vi + 282 pp. 32 pp publisher's catalogue dated Oct. 1888 bound in at end.

1-vol edns. Chatto & Windus 1889–1932. Sutton, Stroud 1993.

1st US edns. *Lovell's Library (no. 1176), New York, June or July 1888; *Harpers, New York, 8 July 1888. Both precede English edition.

Translations. Dutch, 1889; Italian, Milan 1890.

Brussel (1935), 64.

Lehmann, Dr Émil German brother of Frederick *Lehmann; translator of Collins, *Dickens, George Eliot and G. H. *Lewes. Lehmann paid £35 in 1869 for the exclusive German-language rights for *The Moonstone*.

Frederick and Nina Lehmann

Lehmann, (Augustus) Frederick

(1819–1905) and **Nina,** née Chambers
(1830–?). Close friends of Collins and ded-
icatees of *Man and Wife* (1870). Frederick
Lehmann, one of seven children of a family originally from Hamburg, settled in
Scotland in the mid-1840s to make a career in commerce. There he met Robert
Chambers, publisher and author of *The
Vestiges of Creation*, and joined his Edinburgh literary circle in 1850–1. He married Chambers's eldest daughter, Nina, in
November 1852.

Nina first met Collins through her
aunt, Janet Chambers (wife of W. H.
*Wills) and they had become friends be-
fore Nina's marriage. The Lehmanns always remained his closest confidants
apart from the *Wards. Collins was a regular visitor to their London homes at 139
Westbourne Terrace and, from the 1870s,
at 15 Berkeley Square. He also visited
them during a trip to Shanklin in 1860 and
stayed with them at *Woodlands*, Highgate, in 1869 and 1870 during the writing
of *Man and Wife*.

The Lehmanns were in turn entertained at *Gloucester Place where Frederick and his brother Rudolf met
Caroline *Graves. Nina, fond as she was
of Collins, never felt it appropriate for
Caroline to accompany Collins to their
artistic gatherings. Frederick was a fine
violinist and many of his friends came

from the world of music. Nina was an
amateur pianist of great talent, playing in
public on at least one occasion when a
professional performer was indisposed.
Collins said that 'after Nina Lehmann
Hallé was the best pianist in England'.

By the mid-1860s any formality had
been dropped and Collins called them
'Fred' and the 'Padrona'. He invited Frederick, together with Holman *Hunt and
Augustus *Egg, to celebrate the publication of *The Woman in White* (1860). Nina,
who suffered from ill-health—her doctors suspected she had consumption—
was for a time forbidden to play the
piano, and stayed for much of 1866 at Pau
in south-west France. In her absence,
Fred Lehmann accompanied Collins to
*Paris in 1866 and on another occasion to
*Switzerland. During 1869 Collins was
temporarily short of money and Frederick immediately offered him a loan.

Throughout their many years of
friendship, Collins maintained a lively
correspondence with both Nina and
Frederick. He wrote in detail about his
travels, his books and frequently about
his other great love, *food. His last letter
to Frederick was dated 3 September 1889.
After Collins's death, Nina called him
'our poor dear genial delightful *matchless*
old Wilkie'.

Lehmann (1908).

Lehmann, J., *Ancestors and Friends*, London
1962.

Lehmann, Rudolf (1819–1905). Older
brother of Frederick *Lehmann and

Drawing of Collins in 1862 by Rudolf Lehmann

noted portrait painter. First visited London in 1850 eventually settling in Campden Hill in the mid-1860s. Married Nina
*Lehmann's sister, Amelia Chambers
(Tuckie), in 1861. Rudolf made two portraits of Collins, a sketch in 1862 reproduced in *Men and Women of the Century*
(London 1896) and an oil painting commissioned by Frederick as a present for
Nina in 1880.

Lehmann, R., *An Artist's Reminiscences*, London 1894.

Lehmann, Rudolph Chambers

(Rudy) (1856–1929). Eldest of *Frederick
and *Nina Lehmann's three children. Author of *Memories of Half a Century* (1908)
and *Charles Dickens as Editor* (1912). Described Collins as 'the kindest and best
friend that boy or man ever had' and
noted that even as children they always
called him Wilkie. His recollections of
Collins include being taken to the pantomime by him with his brother, Freddie;
stories about Tom Sayers, the boxer; and
the help he received with his homework
in translating an ode from Horace;
Collins showed how well it could be done
using a crib.

Leisure Hour Library New York
*pirate imprint, published by F. M. Lup-
ton; claimed to be the 'Cheapest Library
ever issued' with an annual subscription
of thirty-five cents and titles at three or
six cents each. Collins's stories included:
'My Lady's Money' (no. 11); *The Two Destinies* (no. 26); 'Sister Rose' (no. 32); 'The
Yellow Mask' (no. 44); 'The Frozen Deep'
(no. 63); 'Mr Lepel and the Housekeeper'
(17 July 1886); 'The Morwick Farm Mystery' ('John Jago's Ghost') 7 August 1886.

Lemon, Mark (1809–70). Founder and
first editor of *Punch*; journalist and playwright. Took part in *amateur theatricals
with *Dickens and Collins, touring with
Not So Bad as We Seem during 1852. In the
same year Collins played the landlord,
Lithers, in Lemon's *Mr Nightingale's
Diary*, a farce written with Dickens's assistance. After Lemon's performances as
Martin Gurnock in The *Lighthouse (1855)
and Lieutenant Crayford in The *Frozen
Deep* (1857), Collins admired him as a
born actor. Lemon was unsuccessful in
persuading *Webster to produce *The
Lighthouse* at the *Adelphi. Collins and
Lemon met regularly under Dickens's

Mark Lemon, the first editor of *Punch*

(2 vols), English Literary Studies, University of Victoria, 1995.

Beetz, K. H., 'Wilkie Collins and *The Leader*', *Victorian Periodicals Review*, 15 (Spring 1982), 20–9.

The George Eliot Letters, edited by G. S. Haight (9 vols), New Haven, Yale University Press, 1954–5, 1978.

Lighthouse, The Melodrama loosely based on '*Gabriel's Marriage*', but set in the Eddystone Lighthouse of December 1748. In May 1855, Collins sent the finished play to Dickens who enthusiastically took over the production. He played Aaron Gurnock, the head lightkeeper, and arranged for Clarkson *Stanfield to paint the backdrop. Other parts were taken by Collins, Augustus *Egg, Mark *Lemon, Mary Dickens and Georgina *Hogarth.

The production ran for four nights at *Tavistock House, from 16 June 1855, followed by a single performance on 10 July at Campden House, Kensington. It was staged at the Royal *Olympic from 10 August to 17 October 1857, Collins's first professional production. *Robson played Aaron Gurnock and George *Vining read the Prologue. An American version opened at the New Theatre, New York, on 21 January 1858. There was a further amateur production with Palgrave *Simpson on 3 May 1865 at the Royal Bijou Theatre (Lambeth School of Art). *The Lighthouse* was translated into French by Émile *Forgues.

Lincoln's Inn One of the Inns-of-Court which Collins attended as a law student for five years from May 1846. He confessed to engaging in 'little or no serious study' but on 21 November 1851 went through 'the affecting national ceremony' of being called to the Bar'. Collins never actually practised as a barrister but used his knowledge of the *law in several novels.

For a detailed contemporary description of Inns-of-Court and dinners, see Timbs, J., *London and Westminster* (2 vols), London 1868.

Linnell, John (1792–1882). Landscape and portrait painter who had a long-standing but variable friendship with William *Collins. The Linnell and Collins families were neighbours in both *Hampstead and Bayswater. Linnell

roof at *Tavistock House as well as at *Boulogne in 1853 and Folkestone in 1855.

Adrian, A. A., *Mark Lemon: First Editor of Punch*, London 1966.

Lewes, G(eorge) H(enry) (1817–78). Writer, journalist and editor. Friend of *Pigott and the *Lehmanns. Met George Eliot in 1851 and lived as her husband, encouraging her writing.

With Thornton Hunt, Lewes founded *The *Leader* in 1849–50 and was originally its editor for literary matters. Some of Collins's earliest contributions to *The Leader* consisted of a series of six letters addressed to G. H. Lewes with the title 'Magnetic Evenings at Home' (17 Jan.–13 Mar. 1852). They were all on some aspect of the paranormal to which the rationalist Lewes replied with 'The Fallacy of Clairvoyance' (27 Mar. 1852). Collins, in turn, responded with a further letter, 'The Incredible not always Impossible' (3 Apr. 1852).

In the late 1850s and early 1860s, Collins received frequent invitations from the Leweses and attended their Saturday evenings. There was a cooling-off later but both Collins and Lewes retained close links with Pigott. Lewes considered that *No Name* became 'rather dreary'.

Baker, W., *The Letters of George Henry Lewes*

SCENE FROM "THE LIGHTHOUSE," AT CAMPDEN HOUSE, 1855. CHARLES
DICKENS AS GURNOCK.

(above) Scene from *The Lighthouse* in 1855
(far left) William Collins from a painting by John Linnell
(left) Binding of the first three-volume edition of *Little Novels*
in 1887

ROYAL

LYCEUM THEATRE.

Licensed by the Lord Chamberlain to **MRS. BATEMAN,**
Actual and Responsible Manager.

THIS AND EVERY EVENING UNTIL FURTHER NOTICE,

Will be presented,

A NEW PLAY,

Adapted, by the Author's express permission, from the Popular Novel of

WILKIE COLLINS',

ENTITLED, **THE**

DEAD SECRET,

IN WHICH

MISS BATEMAN

(MRS. CROWE,)

WILL APPEAR.

Produced under the Personal **Superintendence** of

MR. HENRY IRVING.

Programme for the 1877 Lyceum production of *The Dead Secret*

painted the pictures of William and Harriet *Collins which were bought by Horace *Pym at the 1890 *auction of Collins's paintings. The frontispiece portrait to *Memoirs of The Life of William Collins, Esq., R.A.* (1848) was provided by Linnell who also advised Wilkie Collins and Henry *Brandling on the illustra-

tions for *Rambles Beyond Railways* (1851). In *The Black Robe* (1881), one of Linnell's pictures hangs in Lord Loring's art gallery.

Story, A. T., *The Life of John Linnell*, London 1892.

Little Novels Collection of fourteen *short stories published, after revision, in 1887. All had previously been issued with different titles in various American or English *periodicals. Unlike Collins's earlier collections, *After Dark* (1856) and *The Queen of Hearts* (1859), there is no connecting narrative but most of the stories revolve around the theme of love and marriage, frequently across the social barriers of class and money. Some also include *supernatural or *detective elements. For further details, see original titles in parentheses.

'Mrs Zant and the Ghost' ('The Ghost's Touch').

'Miss Morris and the Stranger' ('How I Married Him').

'Mr Cosway and the Landlady' ('Your Money or Your Life').

'Mr Medhurst and the Princess' ('Royal Love').

'Mr Lismore and the Widow' ('She Loves and Lies').

'Miss Jéromette and the Clergyman' ('The Clergyman's Confession').

'Miss Mina and the Groom' ('A Shocking Story').

'Mr Lepel and the Housekeeper' ('The Girl at the Gate').

'Mr Captain and the Nymph' ('The Captain's Last Love').

'Mr Marmaduke and the Minister' ('The Mystery of Marmaduke').

'Mr Percy and the Prophet' ('Percy and the Prophet').

'Miss Bertha and the Yankee' ('The Duel in Herne Wood').

'Miss Dulane and My Lord' ('An Old Maid's Husband').

'Mr Policeman and the Cook' ('Who Killed Zebedee?').

Serialization. See individual stories.

Book publication

1st edn. 3 vols, *Chatto & Windus, London 1887. Blue cloth, covers blocked in red, spines blocked in red and lettered in gilt, grey and white floral endpapers. Half-title in each vol. Published in May 1887.

Vol I (vi) + 320 pp.

Vol II (vi) + 332 pp.

Vol III (viii) + 304 pp. 32 pp publisher's catalogue dated Apr. 1887 bound in at end.

1-vol Chatto & Windus editions 1887–1902.
No US edn in this format although some stories were published individually.
Australia, Melbourne 1887.

Liverpool Visited by Collins during a very successful *amateur theatrical tour in 1852. In November 1867 Collins travelled there with his brother and several members of the Dickens family for a farewell party prior to *Dickens's departure for America. Collins left from Liverpool for his own *American reading tour on 13 September 1873, returning there on 18 March 1874. The Alexandra Theatre staged the first performance of *Miss Gwilt*, 9 December 1875.

Longman, Brown, Green & Longman Publishers in November 1848 of Collins's first book, *Memoirs of the Life of William Collins, Esq., R.A.* Collins arranged for the printing and binding while the publishers distributed the book on a commission basis. By 12 January 1849 more than half the edition of 750 copies had been sold, recouping Collins's own expenses. He had disposed of 200 copies, Longmans 300. The rest were remaindered in 1852.

Longman's Magazine (1882–1905). Successor to *Fraser's Magazine*, publishing short stories, serials and poetry. Authors included Hardy, Kipling and Mrs *Oliphant. Collins contributed '*Royal Love', Christmas 1884.

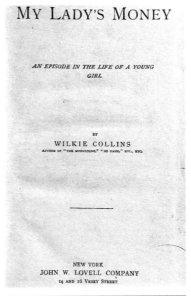

MY LADY'S MONEY

AN EPISODE IN THE LIFE OF A YOUNG GIRL.

BY

WILKIE COLLINS

AUTHOR OF "THE MOONSTONE," "NO NAME," ETC., ETC.

NEW YORK
JOHN W. LOVELL COMPANY
14 AND 16 VESEY STREET.

Title-page of Lovell's US edition of 'My Lady's Money'

'Love's Random Shot' Short story published in the *Seaside Library (vol 87, no. 1770) January 1884; and in the Seaside Library Pocket Edition (no. 175). Reissued in *Love's Random Shot and Other Stories* (with '*The Dream Woman') Munro, New York 1894. Not published in England during Collins's lifetime.

Collins wrote of this and '*Fie! Fie! Or the Fair Physician' 'These stories have served their purpose in periodicals, but are not worthy of republication in book form. They were written in a hurry, and the sooner they are drowned in the waters of oblivion the better. I desire that they shall not be republished after my death.'
Brussel (1935), 59–60.

Lovell's Library New York publisher of cheap *pirated reprints, mainly at ten or twenty cents. Set up by John W. Lovell in Vesey Street. Published a number of Collins's novels although, apparently, not *The Woman in White*. Lovell purchased advanced sheets of *The Legacy of Cain* from *Tillotson in February 1888 and offered Collins a proportion of the profit. Other titles included: *The Moonstone* (1882, 2 vols, nos. 8, 9); *The New Magdalen* ([1882], no. 24); *Heart and Science* ([1883], no. 87); 'I Say No' ([1884], no. 418); *Tales of Two Idle Apprentices* (no. 437); *The Ghost's Touch* (no. 683); *My Lady's Money* (no. 686); *The Evil Genius* ([1886], no. 722); *The Guilty River* ([1887], no. 839); *The Dead Secret* (1887, no. 957); *The Queen of Hearts* ([1887], no. 996); *The Legacy of Cain* (1888, no. 1176, precedes English edition).

Lyceum Theatre, Royal London theatre in Wellington Street off The Strand, managed by Charles *Fechter from 1863 to 1867. *The Dead Secret* was staged during Miss Bateman's season from 29 August 1877. Mary *Anderson appeared there for three tours in the 1880s and Augustin *Daly's company in 1888 and 1890.

'Mad Marriage, A' Short story reprinted in the 1875 edition of *Miss or Mrs? and Other Stories in Outline*. First published as 'A Fatal Marriage' in *All the Year Round*, 17–24 Oct. 1874. Reprinted with the original title in *Lotos Leaves*, London and Boston 1875; and as 'A Sane Madman' in *Alicia Warlock*, Boston 1875.

Overt attack on the Lunacy Commission and the Court of Chancery ('the most despotic authority on the face of the earth'), whereby the next-of-kin, if assisted by a dishonest doctor, could lawfully imprison a person for life.

➥ Mary Brading secretly marries Roland Cameron and helps him to escape from a lunatic asylum where he has been confined by his relatives to prevent him from inheriting his father's estate. The married couple sail for America where they live free and happy, though without Roland's fortune.

'Mad Monkton' Short story with *supernatural overtones first published as 'The Monktons of Wincot Abbey' in *Fraser's Magazine*, Nov.–Dec. 1855; subsequently included in The *Queen of Hearts* (1859) as 'Brother Griffith's Story of Mad Monkton'. The story was originally offered to *Household Words* in 1853 but declined by *Dickens who thought the theme of hereditary madness unsuitable for a family magazine.

➥ The Monktons are a reclusive, ancient family afflicted by hereditary insanity. The young Alfred Monkton is obsessed by a family curse and haunted by the ghost of his uncle, killed in a duel. Alfred delays his marriage in order to travel to Naples to search for the body, convinced that he will be the last of the line if his uncle is not buried in the family vault.

The decomposing corpse is eventually discovered outside a Capuchin convent. Sealed in a lead coffin, it is taken by sea for burial in England but a violent storm sinks the ship and the coffin is irretrievably lost. Monkton dies of brain fever and, last of the line, is buried in the family vault where one niche remains empty, that intended for his uncle.

Man and Wife: A Novel

'It is the nature of Truth to struggle to the light.'

Novel published in 1870, dedicated to Frederick and Nina *Lehmann with whom Collins stayed during much of its composition. Their surname, thinly disguised, and their musical abilities on the violin and piano appear in the characters of Julius Delamayn and his wife. Often cited as Collins's first *didactic work, *Man and Wife* attacks both Irish and Scottish *marriage laws as well as arguing the case for a Married Woman's Property Act. The book also campaigns against the cult of athleticism, as leading to moral and physical corruption, personified in the villain, Geoffrey Delamayn. Contemporary reviewers generally praised the excitement and cleverness of the plot but did not appreciate Collins's higher motives. The *Saturday Review* (9 July 1870) considered 'If one moral is generally too much, two morals are surely unjustifiable. Mr Collins might be content with assaulting running and boat-racing without breaking a lance at the same moment against all our marriage laws.' The story of Hester Dethridge, as well as strengthening the novel's attack on the marriage laws by illustrating the helplessness of working-class married women, also represents a contribution by Collins to the *detective genre by creating an early example of a 'locked-room' murder. The story was originally conceived as a play and the book is divided into fifteen Scenes.

➥ In 1855, a clever young lawyer called Delamayn finds a loophole in the Irish marriage laws which enables John Vanborough to annul the marriage that stands in the way of his parliamentary ambitions. The abandoned wife, Anne Silvester, lives with her old friend, Blanche, married to Sir Thomas Lundie, together with their respective daughters, also called Anne and Blanche.

Twelve years later Vanborough and Anne and Blanche senior are all dead. Sir Thomas has remarried but dies shortly

Illustration by Small for the one-volume Chatto & Windus edition of *Man and Wife*

after, when the title and estate pass to his likeable brother, Sir Patrick Lundie, a retired lawyer in his seventies. Sir Thomas is survived by his second wife, the overbearing Lady Lundie, now responsible for the two daughters. The lawyer, Delamayn, has succeeded in life and become Lord Holchester with two sons, Geoffrey and Julius.

The main action of the story begins in 1868 at Windygates, the Perthshire home of Lady Lundie. Blanche is now 18 and Anne, acting as her governess, 25. Visiting them are Sir Patrick; Arnold Brinkworth, engaged to Blanche; and Geoffrey Delamayn, the school friend who once saved Arnold's life. Geoffrey has promised to marry Anne but is now trying to break the secret engagement because he will be cut out of his father's will. Anne persuades him to accept a secret marriage and knowing a little of the Scottish law arranges to go to a lonely inn at Craig Fernie where she will announce that she is waiting for her husband. If Geoffrey arrives and openly asks for his wife, the presence of witnesses will validate the marriage according to Scottish law.

Geoffrey receives a telegram that his father is dangerously ill and must go to London with his brother. He therefore asks Arnold to deliver a message to Anne at the inn, carefully telling him not to use his own name but merely to ask for his 'wife'. Arnold reluctantly agrees but makes Geoffrey put the message in writing. The note, stating Geoffrey's intention to marry, is written on the back of a letter from Anne signed 'your loving wife'. Arnold arrives at Craig Fernie and to preserve Anne's reputation pretends to be her husband in front of the landlady and the head waiter, Bishopriggs. Anne reads the letter which is subsequently stolen by Bishopriggs while Arnold innocently continues the deception, sleeping on the sofa and leaving early the next morning.

Lord Holchester recovers but on his sick-bed remembers he was responsible for the infamous treatment of Anne's mother and asks Julius to help her if she should ever need assistance. At the same time Lord Holchester will accept Geoffrey back into the family only if he makes a respectable marriage. Julius and his mother have in mind the young widow, Mrs Glenarm, whom Geoffrey will meet on his return to Scotland.

Anne is worried about her marital status and, without disclosing Arnold's name, has Blanche consult Sir Patrick. Geoffrey overhears the opinion that the marriage is ambiguous, but that two people are legally bound in Scotland if they pretend to be married. He therefore adopts the view that Anne is technically married to Arnold and he is free to marry Mrs Glenarm. By this time Geoffrey has agreed to represent the South in the great foot-race, a national athletic event against the North, although a medical guest in the house, Mr Speedwell, warns that the exertion would endanger his health.

Anne visits Blanche at Windygates and meets Geoffrey who declares he cannot now marry her as she is already married to Arnold. In a state of shock, she deliberately leaves her friends and hides in Glasgow where she consults two different lawyers. They give conflicting opinions as to whether she is married and she collapses under the strain, miscarrying Geoffrey's child.

Ignorant of Anne and Arnold's position, Sir Patrick brings forward Blanche's wedding to Arnold. The couple are recalled from their honeymoon in Switzerland when Sir Patrick hears from Anne, who reveals Arnold's predicament and the conflicting legal opinions. Anne meanwhile recovers the stolen letter from Bishopriggs and tries to convince Mrs Glenarm of Geoffrey's prior marriage. Lady Lundie deduces that Arnold was the man at Craig Fernie and mischievously persuades Blanche to leave Arnold for her house in London where Mrs Glenarm is also staying. Sir Patrick must prove the Craig Fernie marriage is invalid to safeguard Arnold's position with Blanche, whereas Mrs Glenarm wants it confirmed so that Geoffrey is free to marry her.

Geoffrey has rented a secluded house in Fulham, left to Lady Lundie's former cook Hester Dethridge, an elderly woman who is mute after a traumatic marriage to a drunken husband and communicates only in writing. Against medical advice Geoffrey completes his intensive training for the foot-race. On the last lap of the four-mile course he collapses, unable to continue. He is abandoned by his friends because they lost money on the race and is taken home by his trainer, Perry.

Two days after the race, all parties attend a family conference with their lawyers. Geoffrey refuses to accept Anne as his wife and Blanche will not return to Arnold until the ambiguity of the Craig Fernie marriage is resolved. Anne, despite knowing she will have to return to Fulham, bravely produces her letter which according to the Scottish law of consent confirms her marriage to Geoffrey.

Following the death of Lord Holchester, Julius has inherited the family title and visits Geoffrey to propose a separation. In return Julius will honour an unsigned codicil to their father's will, leaving Geoffrey a secure income. Geoffrey, however, having no grounds for divorce, intends to kill his wife. Pretending he will be a good husband he refuses his brother's offer and keeps Anne prisoner in the house.

Geoffrey has always been unnerved by the silent and withdrawn Hester Dethridge. The secret of her own terror of him is revealed in a written confession of murder. Years before, when she complained to the police that her husband ill-treated her and stole her money, they were unable to help because the law gave a married woman no right to her own earnings. She determined to kill him as the only way to end her misery. While her husband lay in a drunken stupor, she suffocated him through the partition wall of his locked bedroom after carefully removing and replacing the lath and plaster. Hester was not suspected of the crime but now sees visions of a second self urging her to kill again.

Geoffrey blackmails Hester into helping him murder Anne by the same means but at the last moment she sees her recurrent apparition and attacks Geoffrey. In the same instant he suffers a fatal stroke. Hester is confined in an asylum while Anne, free of Geoffrey at last, supplants Lady Lundie by marrying Sir Patrick and becoming the new female head of the family.

Serialization. *Cassell's Magazine*, 20 Nov. 1869–30 July 1870; *Harper's Weekly*, 11 Dec. 1869–6 Aug. 1870.

Book publication

1st English edn. 3 vols, F. S. *Ellis, 1870. Dark red cloth, covers blocked in blind, spines lettered in gilt, black or dark green endpapers. Half-title in each vol. Published in June 1870.

Vol I xiv + 356 pp. 8 pp publisher's advertisements bound in at end.

Vol II vi + 360 pp.

Vol III vi + 348 pp.

2nd and 3rd editions, 3 vols, 1870.

1-vol edns. *Smith, Elder 1871 (with a new preface noting a change in the law); *Chatto & Windus 1875–1932 (with 12 illustrations by W. Small); Dover 1983; Sutton, Stroud 1990; World's Classics 1995 (critical edition, edited by N. Page).

1st US edn. *Harper, New York 1870.

Translations. Dutch, The Hague (*Belinfante Brothers) 1870; Russian, St Petersburg 1870; French, Paris (by C. Bernard-Derosne), 2 vols, 1872; German, Leipzig 1872; Italian, Milan, 2 vols, 1877.

Despite the disagreement with Collins over the second edition of *The Moonstone*, *Tinsley tried to negotiate for *Man and Wife*. In the end they were unable to agree terms and the book was published by F. S. Ellis on 10 per cent commission although Collins frequently expressed doubts about Ellis's abilities. Sadleir suggests that the current scarcity of the title is because Ellis was 'ill-equipped to distribute a commercial product like a three volume novel'. Nevertheless the first edition of 1,000 copies sold well and a corrected second edition of 500 appeared by the end of June. A third edition, also of 500, was printed in July but at least part of this was remaindered in April 1875.

Gasson (1980), 68–71.

Sadleir (1951), i. 376.

Man and Wife (play). Dramatic version of the book, which had originally been conceived for the stage. The play opened under the direction of the *Bancrofts at the *Prince of Wales Theatre on 22 Feb-

ruary 1873. The first night was eagerly awaited, with speculators selling tickets for up to five guineas, and proved 'an extraordinary success'. The play ran for 136 performances, until August 1873, and was seen several times by members of the royal family. The London run was followed by a successful provincial tour. *Man and Wife* was revived at the Haymarket in 1887.

In England, *Man and Wife: A Dramatic Story in Four Acts* was 'published by the author' in 1870 (1 vol, 152 pp, tan paper wrappers). An American pirated version by H. A. Webber was issued as no. 4 in Ames' Series of Standard and Minor Drama, Clyde, Ohio, 1873. Collins was probably unaware of the play's first production at the Green Bay Opera House, Wisconsin, on 8 January 1870. At New York's Fifth Avenue Theatre, Augustin *Daly staged his own version which ran for ten weeks from 13 September 1870.

Parrish (1940), 81–3, 160.

Man, Isle of Visited by Collins, with Caroline *Graves and her daughter, in August 1863 while researching scenes for *Armadale* (1866). Collins called the island 'the one inaccessible place left in the world' and found it primitive and uncomfortable, but the scenery in the south, near the Calf of Man, was 'wild and frightful, just what I wanted . . . for my occult literary purposes'. The Manx novelist Hall *Caine claimed that Collins wrote letters to *The Times* protesting at the poor treatment of lunatics on the is-

land and so provoked the intervention of the Home Office, but there is no evidence of this.

Caine, H., *My Story*, London 1908, 19.

manuscripts The majority of Collins's manuscripts for novels, short stories and plays were sold at *auction after his death in 1889, and have survived in some form of draft. In Britain, the main holdings are in the British Library; King's School, Canterbury; Mitchell Library, Glasgow; University of Durham; and the Victoria & Albert Museum. The majority of manuscripts, however, are now located in various institutions in the United States, with significant holdings in the following collections: Berg, New York; Houghton, Harvard; Henry E. Huntington, California; Pierpoint Morgan, New York; Morris L. Parrish, Princeton; Harry Ransome Humanities Research Centre, Austin, Texas. These collections also hold a large number of Collins's letters although many remain in private hands. A collected edition of Collins's letters is currently in preparation.

See Appendix I and illustrations to *Iolani* and 'She Loves and Lies' for examples of Collins's manuscripts.

See also UNPUBLISHED DRAFTS.

IELM.

marriage laws

'After thirty years' practice as a lawyer, I don't know what is *not* a marriage in Scotland.' (*Man and Wife*)

Man and Wife (1870), inspired by *The Report of The Royal Commissioners on The Laws of Marriage* (London 1868), was Collins's main vehicle for exposing injustice in the prevailing marriage laws. The novel's prologue attacked an old statute whereby a marriage was invalid if performed in Ireland by a Catholic priest between a Catholic and a former Protestant convert of less than twelve months. The law, which in the book unfairly releases John Vanborough from his wife, was repealed in 1870.

A second target was the Scotch Irregular Marriage, or Marriage by Consent, which first binds Anne Silvester to Arnold Brinkworth because they unwittingly spend the night under the same roof and then confirms her as previously married to Geoffrey Delamayn because there had

After which, will be played,

MAN AND WIFE

A DRAMATIC STORY, IN FOUR ACTS,

WRITTEN BY

WILKIE COLLINS;

Rehearsed under the Author's Direction.

Act I.   *The Summer-House at Windygates.*

Act II.   *The Inn at Craig Fernie.*

Act III. *The Library.*

Act IV.   *The Picture Gallery.*

Painted by Mr. GEORGE GORDON & Mr. HARFORD.

PERIOD—The Present Time.   SCENE—Scotland.

CHARACTERS.

Sir Patrick Lundie	-	Mr. HARE
Geoffrey Delamayn	-	Mr. COGHLAN
Arnold Brinkworth	-	Mr. HERBERT
Mr. Speedwell	-	Mr. BANCROFT
Mr. Moy	-	Mr. DENISON
Bishopriggs	-	Mr. F. DEWAR
Duncan	-	Mr. FRANKS
Lady Lundie	-	Mrs. LEIGH MURRAY
Blanche Lundie	-	Miss MARIE WILTON (Mrs. BANCROFT.)
Anne Silvester	-	Miss LYDIA FOOTE
Mistress Inchbare	-	Miss LEE

THE BAND WILL PLAY THE FOLLOWING SELECTIONS—

Conductor, Mr. J. MEREDITH BALL.

Galop	..	" Rosy Morn"	..	LEE
Selection	..	.." Scotch Melodies"	J. MEREDITH BALL
Polka	..	"L'Artiste"	..	W. H. WESTON
Waltz Galop	..	"Craig Fernie"	..	J. MEREDITH BALL
	Published by Horwood & Crew, 42 New Bond Street.			
Valse	..	" Lily of the Valley"	..

Programme for the 1873 production of *Man and Wife* at the Prince of Wales Theatre

been letters of intent. The Scottish law on Irregular Marriages was not changed until July 1939.

The first Married Women's Property Act of August 1870 which established 'the right of a married woman, in England, to possess her own property, and keep her own earnings' partially answered Collins's other grievance. The novel shows the ill-used Hester Dethridge robbed by her drunkard husband, with the police, according to the law of the time, unable to take action.

Collins, W., preface and appendix B to *Man and Wife*.

MacEachen, D. B., 'Wilkie Collins and British Law', *Nineteenth-Century Fiction*, 5 (Sept. 1950), 121–39.

Marylebone Central London district approximately bounded by Oxford Street in the south and Regent's Park to the north, and including parts of St John's Wood. The area where Collins was born and lived for most of his life. Except for intermittent periods away from home, he remained with his family until the winter of 1858. After this time, Wilkie lived with Caroline *Graves, with one period of separation of approximately two years, until his death in 1889. Also in Marylebone, Collins first installed Martha *Rudd, at 33 Bolsover Street, moving her to 55 Marylebone Road and finally to 10 Taunton Place where she remained from 1874 to 1890. Harriet *Collins's last address in London was 2 Clarence Terrace which Wilkie used, possibly only for correspondence, between December 1858 and February 1859. Several of Collins's friends, doctors and associates lived in the Marylebone area, including Frank *Beard at 44 Welbeck Street, George *Bentley in Regent's Park, George *Critchett at 21 Harley Street and Edward *Ward at 33 Harewood Place.

Collins's Marylebone addresses

11 *New Cavendish Street: 1824, born, 8 January; 38 Blandford Square: 1848–50; 17 *Hanover Terrace: 1850–6; Howland Street: 1856, short-term lodgings; 2 (renumbered 11) Harley Place (not the present street with this name): 1856–8; 124 Albany Street: 1859, first lived with Caroline Graves; 2A New Cavendish Street: 1859; 12 Harley Street: 1859–64; 9 Melcombe Place: 1864–7; 90 *Gloucester Place: 1867–88; 82 *Wimpole Street: 1888–9, died 23 September.

THE MOONSTONE AND MOONSHINE.

PROLOGUE.

THE FALL OF KAFOOZLEM (1799).

I.

[Y cousin John Horncastle and myself were fellow-officers in the 103rd Belochee Bunns, and we were attacking the stronghold of ozlem, the celebrated oriental monarch who ssed the Moonstone.

he Moonstone was the largest diamond ever , and it was called the Moonstone because is subjected to the influences of the moon.

ran through the body; the third seized the sacred banjo and fled, pursued by John.

He had just reached the grand staircase, when my cousin, overtaking him, with one blow severed his head from his body. The head went bounding down the 360 stairs. My cousin seized the banjo, and followed the head. The lowest stair had been reached, and my cousin was escaping with his prize, when the head opened its eyes, turned them full upon John, and exclaimed, in a voice of thunder—

"I'LL HAVE YOUR DIAMOND!"

Parody of *The Moonstone* in *The Mask* of August 1868

Clarke, W. M., *Wilkie Collins: Where He Lived*, WCS, 1994.

Mackenzie, G., *Marylebone: Great City North of Oxford Street*, London 1972 (for a general history of the area).

Peters (1991).

Mask, The (Florence). Illustrated literary journal published in Italy and distributed in Europe and the USA. In October 1924, it reprinted Collins's essay 'The *Air and the Audience' as 'The Use of Gas in Theatres' with a foreword by John Balance.

Mask, The: A Humorous and Fantastic Review of the Month (London). Humorous periodical, written, edited and illustrated by Alfred Thompson and Leopold Lewis from 1868. Volume 1 contains two *parodies of Collins: 'No Thoroughfare: The Book in Eight Acts', Feb. 1868, 14–18; and 'The Moonstone and Moonshine', Aug. 1868, 205–13.

Méjan, Maurice See *recueil des causes célèbres*.

Memoirs of the Life of William Collins, Esq., R.A.: With Selections from his Journals and Correspondence Collins's first published book, a biography of his father published in 1848. Dedicated to Sir Robert Peel, valued patron of William* Collins.

William Collins had always intended his biography to be written by his son. The journal for 1 January 1844 records 'As I think it quite possible that my dear son, William Wilkie Collins, may be tempted . . . to furnish the world with a memoir of my life, I purpose occasionally noting down some circumstances as leading points, which may be useful.'

The 23-year-old Collins was at work on *Antonina* the evening his father died on 16 February 1847. He put the novel to one side, noting on the manuscript: 'Thus far have I written during my father's lifetime—This portion of Chapter 3rd was composed on the last evening when he was alive.' As a mark of respect he left the remainder of the page blank, resuming the story on 25 July 1848. In the interval, Collins wrote the *Memoirs* in chronological fashion reaching 1815 by May 1847 and completing the book a year later. The biography draws on William Collins's journals, correspondence and notes. Collins's introduction acknowledges also the help of his father's friends and the literary advice of Alaric A. Watts. The book gives some insight into Wilkie's formative years while describing William Collins's early struggles, his artistic career, his family and friends, and his travels in England, Scotland and Europe. There are also detailed descriptions of his paintings.

The *Memoirs* received generally good notices from the *Observer*, the *Athenaeum*, *Westminster Review* and *Blackwood's Magazine*. Maria Edgeworth praised the clear and unaffected style, and the absence of eulogy. Walter de la Mare later called it 'a remarkable book . . . for its endearing loyalty and affection, its modesty, insight, judgement, dignity, and quiet and sedate style'.

For Wilkie Collins's correspondence with the American writer R. H. Dana and the painter George Richmond, see Parrish (1940).

Book publication. 2 vols, *Longman, Brown, Green, and Longman, London 1848. Purple-brown cloth, covers blocked in blind, spines lettered in gilt, cream endpapers. No half-titles. Vol I has an engraved portrait after *Linnell and illustrated title with vignette of *The Shrimper's Return*; vol II has

Vol I. page 69.

"The Reluctant Departure" (1815). The Descriptions of pictures Exhibited before 1823, are taken from my mother's recollections of them on the Royal Academy walls. In this case, I have evidently mistaken what she told me — and perhaps, her memory may also have been a little at fault. On, and after 1823, my mother spoke (and I wrote) of what she had seen in progress in my father's studio. Her memory — in these cases (tested by old friends of my father who lived to read my life of him) was declared to be wonderful.

27 Nov 1884

illustrated title with vignette of *Visiting the Puppy*. Variant in grey-blue cloth with different blocking and lettering and the illustrated titles in vols I and II reversed. Published in Nov. 1848.

Vol I xii + 348 pp. 32 pp publisher's catalogue dated 29 Apr. 1848 bound in at end.

Vol II vi + 354 pp.

The only other edition is a facsimile by E. P. Publishing, 1 vol, Wakefield 1978: useful for its added index of names and places.

Memorial to Collins A few days after Collins's death on 23 September 1889, Harry *Quilter set up a committee to establish 'some permanent mark of honour from the English public'. The appeal appeared in various papers under Quilter's name and the committee included Meredith, Hardy, *Beard, *Besant and *Caine. *Pigott declined to be associated with the idea, writing to *Yates on 5 October 1889 that Wilkie's work 'was the only monument he cared for; and he was the last of men to claim the honour of a medallion in a crypt'. A *Daily Telegraph* leader of the same date also strongly opposed the idea. The Dean and Chapter of St Paul's objected on moral grounds, taking 'other considerations than Mr

Paris, November 3d 1889

The Wilkie Collins Memorial Fund.

To the Manager,

LONDON JOINT STOCK BANK (Pall Mall Branch).

SIR,

Be so good as to enter my name as a Subscriber to THE WILKIE COLLINS MEMORIAL FUND to the amount of £ 5 s. 5 d. 0

Yours, etc.,

Name *Henry James*

Address 34 De Vere Gardens Kensington. W.

DICKS' STANDARD PLAYS.

Number 459. COMPLETE.

A MESSAGE FROM THE SEA.

BY JOHN BROUGHAM.

ORIGINAL COMPLETE EDITION.—PRICE ONE PENNY.

*** THIS PLAY CAN BE PERFORMED WITHOUT RISK OF INFRINGING ANY RIGHTS.

LONDON: JOHN DICKS, . STRAND.

(*top*) Annotation by Collins to a copy of *The Memoirs of the Life of William Collins, Esq. R. A.* given to A. P. Watt in 1884

(*above left*) Contribution of £5-5-0 by Henry James to the Wilkie Collins Memorial Fund in November 1889

(*above right*) *A Message from the Sea* issued in Dicks's Standard Plays

Collins' literary excellence into account' and the plan for a major memorial never came to fruition. Quilter nevertheless managed to raise a few hundred pounds. He used the fund to establish the 'Wilkie Collins Memorial Library of Fiction', consisting of about 1,100 novels, at the People's Palace (later Queen Mary's College) in London's East End.

The Author, 4 (1893–4), 336.

Message from the Sea, A Collaboration by Collins and *Dickens for the extra *Christmas number of *All the Year Round*, Dec. 1860. Researched during their trip to the West Country in October 1860, the story is set in Devon and Cornwall. The village of Steepways is based on Clovelly. The plot concerns a message found sealed in a bottle at sea and the rightful ownership of the Raybrock family's £500. Collins contributed Chapter IV, 'The Seafaring Man'; and parts of Chapter II, 'The Money', and Chapter V, 'The Restitution'. Dickens wrote most of the remainder with minor contributions from Charles *Collins, H. F. *Chorley, Amelia Edwards and Harriett Parr.

Message from the Sea, A: A Drama in Three Acts Version by *Dickens and Collins to establish the dramatic *copyright of their December 1860 Christmas story. A pirated production was staged at the Britannia Theatre, 7 January 1861. Dickens and Collins visited Counsel's chambers the same day and threatened legal action against the manager, Mr Lane. Dickens put the authors' case in a letter to *The Times*.

A Message from the Sea: A Drama in Three Acts was published by G. Halsworth at the office of *All the Year Round*, 1861. (1 vol, 68 pp, buff paper wrappers). A version in four acts by John Brougham was issued in Dicks' Standard Plays, no. 459 [ND].

'Midnight Mass, The' Translation with possible assistance by Collins of *Balzac's short story, 'Épisode sous la Terreur'. Set, like '*Nine o'Clock', in the French Revolution and published in *Bentley's Miscellany*, June 1852.

Davis, N. P., *The Life of Wilkie Collins*, Urbana, Ill., 1956, 115.

Midwinter, Ozias The dark hero of

Millais's first book illustration, to *Mr Wray's Cash-Box* published in 1852

Armadale (1866). His real name is Allan Armadale but he has taken an alias from the gypsy vagabond who brought him up. Recipient of his father's deathbed confession of murder from nineteen years earlier. Friend and third cousin to the other Allan *Armadale, resolved to protect and keep him in ignorance of their family connection. Marries Lydia *Gwilt under his real name. His depressed and fatalistic approach to life convinces him that Allan's dream is prophetic and that he is destined to bring him harm.

Millais, Sir John Everett, Bt., P.R.A. (1829–96). Painter and founder member of the *Pre-Raphaelite Brotherhood; a close friend of Wilkie and Charles *Collins. Millais took part in *amateur theatricals at Blandford Square and stayed at *Hanover Terrace for two months during *1854. *Dickens, who disliked the Pre-Raphaelites, violently attacked Millais's painting in *Household Words* ('Old Lamps for New Ones', 15 June 1850). Wilkie's mother, Harriet *Collins, invited them both to dinner and successfully made peace between them.

They eventually became good friends.

Millais married John Ruskin's estranged wife Effie in July 1855. His fears that he, like Ruskin, would be unable to consummate the marriage were sympathized with by Charles Collins but ribaldly dismissed by Wilkie who wrote, 'I can't resist *Priapian* jesting on the marriage of my friends.'

Millais painted his classic portrait of Collins in 1850 and also sketched him conversing at a dancing party with Richard Doyle, the artist. *Mr Wray's Cash-Box* (1852) featured his first-ever book illustration. He drew the frontispiece for the 1864 edition of *No Name* but was unable to illustrate *Armadale* because of other commitments. He drew a deathbed sketch of Dickens in 1870. Millais was elected a full member of the Royal Academy in 1863 and ultimately became President in 1896. In 1889 he was instrumental in setting up the National Portrait Gallery which now holds his painting of Collins.

Millais was with Wilkie and Charles Collins at the reputed first meeting of Caroline *Graves during the early 1850s. Millais's son records how:

One night in the fifties Millais was returning home to Gower Street from one of the many parties held under Mrs. Collins' hospitable roof in Hanover Terrace [when] . . . they were suddenly arrested by a piercing scream coming from the garden of a villa close at hand. It was evidently the cry of a woman in distress; and while pausing to consider what they should do, the iron gate leading to the garden was dashed open, and from it came the figure of a young and very beautiful woman dressed in flowing white robes that shone in the moonlight. She seemed to float rather than to run in their direction, and, on coming up to the three young men, she paused for a moment in an attitude of supplication and terror. Then, seeming to recollect herself, she suddenly moved on and vanished in the shadows cast upon the road.

'What a lovely woman!' was all Millais could say. 'I must see who she is and what's the matter,' said Wilkie Collins as, without another word, he dashed off after her. His two companions waited in vain for his return, and next day, when they met again, he seemed indisposed to talk of his adventure. They gathered from him, however, that he had come up with the lovely fugitive and had heard from her own lips the history of her life and the cause of her sudden flight. She was a young lady of good birth and position, who had accidentally fallen into the hands of a man living in a villa in Regent's Park. There for many months he kept her prisoner under threats and mesmeric in-

Illustration by Fildes to *Miss or Mrs?*

fluence of so alarming a character that she dared not attempt to escape, until, in sheer desperation, she fled from the brute, who, with a poker in his hand, threatened to dash her brains out. Her subsequent history, interesting as it is, is not for these pages.

> Millais, J. G., *The life and Letters of Sir John Everett Millais* (2 vols), London 1899, i. 278–82.
> Sotheby's, *English Drawings and Watercolours*, 18 Mar. 1971, Lot 147.

Milroy, Miss Eleanor (Neelie). In *Armadale* (1866), the daughter of Major David Milroy, who spends all his time constructing a mechanical clock, and his bedridden, jealous wife, Anne. Miss Milroy is in love with and eventually marries Allan *Armadale.

'Miss Bertha and the Yankee' Title used for 'The *Duel in Herne Wood' in *Little Novels* (1887).

'Miss Dulane and My Lord' Title used for 'An *Old Maid's Husband' in *Little Novels* (1887).

Miss Gwilt See *armadale* (PLAY).

'Miss Jéromette and the Clergyman' Title used for 'The *Clergyman's Confession' in *Little Novels* (1887).

'Miss Mina and the Groom' Title used for 'A *Shocking Story' in *Little Novels* (1887).

'Miss Morris and the Stranger' Title used for '*How I Married Him' in *Little Novels* (1887).

'Miss or Mrs?' Novella originally published as 'Miss or Mrs? a Christmas Story in Twelve Scenes' in The *Graphic Christmas number, 25 December 1871; 200,000 copies were sold. Republished in *Miss or Mrs? and Other Stories in Outline* (1873). The story of an emancipated girl of 15 was considered somewhat shocking when it first appeared. The theme of a secret marriage to a minor and the danger of a charge of abduction was taken from the real-life experience of Collins's close friend, Edward *Ward.

➥ Natalie Graybrook is engaged to the much older Richard Turlington whom she detests but who needs her fortune of £40,000 to avoid bankruptcy. She is, however, in love with her cousin Launcelot Linzie. They marry secretly, though Natalie remains with her father Sir Joseph, to avoid a charge of abduction against Launcelot. Turlington, who is sole executor of Sir Joseph's will, learns of the secret marriage and arranges to have Sir Joseph murdered by an accomplice, Wildfang. The plot fails and Turlington is himself killed when his own revolver misfires.

Miss or Mrs? and Other Stories in Outline

Collection of short stories published in 1873 and dedicated to Baron Von *Tauchnitz. Includes '*Miss or Mrs?', '*Blow up with the Brig!'; and 'The *Fatal Cradle'. The second edition (*Chatto & Windus 1875) includes also 'A *Mad Marriage' and six illustrations.

Serialization. See individual stories.

Book publication

1st edn. 1 vol, Richard *Bentley, London 1873. Reddish-brown cloth covers, blocked and lettered in black, spine lettered in gilt, cream endpapers. No half-title. Published 17 Jan. 1873. Variant binding in green cloth, front cover blocked in black and lettered in gilt; no definite priority. viii + 328 pp. Publisher's advertisement occupies p (327).

Later *Chatto & Windus edns. 1875–1925; Sutton, Stroud 1993.

Both the Tauchnitz edn (1872, first issue without dedication) and continental translations precede the first English edition.

Translations. French, Paris 1872; Dutch, The Hague 1872; German, Leipzig 1872.

Moonstone, The: A Romance

'Do you feel an uncomfortable heat at the pit of your stomach . . . and a nasty thumping at the top of your head? . . . I call it the detective-fever.'

Published in 1868, one of the two books (with *The Woman in White*) for which Collins is most famous. *The Moonstone* was described by T. S. Eliot as 'the first and greatest of English detective novels' although priority is now usually given to *The *Notting Hill Mystery*. *The Moonstone* has several archetypal features of modern *detective fiction and created many of the ground rules for the genre. Several incidents in the story are taken from the real life Constance *Kent Road case and the plot is Collins at his intricate best.

Elwin quotes a contemporary critic that 'not a window is opened, a door shut, or a nose blown, but, depend upon it, the act will have something to do with the end of the book'. Geraldine *Jewsbury didn't care for the 'sordid detective element' but admired the 'wonderful construction of the story' and 'the skill with which the secret is kept to the last'. *The Moonstone* was immensely successful as a serial in *All the Year Round* and *Dickens originally liked the story. At a low point in his relationship with Collins, however, he

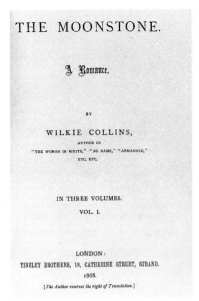

THE MOONSTONE.

A Romance.

BY

WILKIE COLLINS,

AUTHOR OF
"THE WOMAN IN WHITE," "NO NAME," "ARMADALE,"
ETC. ETC.

IN THREE VOLUMES.
VOL. I.

LONDON:
TINSLEY BROTHERS, 18, CATHERINE STREET, STRAND.
1868.

[*The Author reserves the right of Translation.*]

wrote to *Wills 'The construction is wearisome beyond endurance, and there is a vein of obstinate conceit in it that makes enemies of readers.'

In addition to its success as a detective story, *The Moonstone* is notable for its enlightened social attitudes. Collins's respectful handling of the Indians and the religious motivation of their quest for the *Moonstone is in marked contrast to the hatred and contempt exhibited by most English writers (including Dickens) for 'lesser breeds' after the Indian Mutiny. Collins is also ahead of his time in his sympathetic and serious characterization of the reformed thief and servant Rosanna *Spearman.

Much of *The Moonstone* was written while Collins was taking large quantities of *opium to alleviate the agonies of *gout. His own experiences of the drug are portrayed in the character of Ezra *Jennings, the incurably ill addict who suffers relief from pain at the expense of hideous nightmares. Like *The Woman in White*, *The Moonstone* is told in the form of multiple narratives. The chief exponent is the house-steward, Gabriel *Betteredge, who confirms 'I am forbidden to tell more in this narrative than I knew myself at the time. Or, to put it plainer, I am to keep strictly within the limits of my own experience.'

➥ The Moonstone is a magnificent yellow diamond 'large as a plover's egg' which had originally adorned the fore-

(above left) Title-page to the first edition of *The Moonstone* published in three volumes by Tinsley *(above right)* Sergeant Cuff illustrated by Fraser in the 1875 Chatto & Windus edition of *The Moonstone*

head of the Hindu moon-god. It was subsequently looted at the siege of Seringapatam in southern India in 1799 by Colonel John *Herncastle. On his return to England he was ostracized by his family and society, and in revenge for a slight by his sister, Lady Julia Verinder, he leaves the diamond, said to carry a curse, to his niece Rachel *Verinder. Rachel's cousin, Franklin *Blake, is to deliver the diamond to the Verinder house near *Frizinghall on the Yorkshire coast.

The Moonstone is presented to Rachel at a dinner-party for her eighteenth birthday. The guests include Godfrey *Ablewhite, another cousin; Mr Candy, the family doctor; Mr Murthwaite, a celebrated traveller in India; and Drusilla Clack, an interfering evangelist. The party goes badly. Rachel and Franklin Blake have become fond of each other while decorating her sitting-room door and Rachel had earlier refused a marriage proposal from Ablewhite. In addition, Blake quarrels with Mr Candy about the competence of doctors.

Blake had been followed in London and Murthwaite identifies three Indians seen near the house as high-caste Brahmins. Rachel places the diamond in her bedroom cabinet but the next morning it is missing.

The local police superintendent, Seegrave, is a bungling incompetent so Blake calls in the celebrated Sergeant *Cuff of the detective police. He rules out the suspicious Indians but realizes the importance of smeared paint on Rachel's sitting-room door. The smear has been made by an article of dress, whose owner is almost certainly the thief. Rachel behaves inexplicably, obstructing the investigation and refusing to have anything more to do with Franklin Blake. Cuff concludes that she has stolen her own diamond assisted by Rosanna Spearman, a deformed housemaid fascinated by the local quicksand. Rosanna is a reformed thief who is acquainted with a dubious London moneylender, Septimus Luker. She is also in love with Franklin Blake and after acting strangely drowns herself in the Shivering Sand. Cuff is dismissed from the case by Lady Verinder but correctly predicts future developments.

In London, both Ablewhite and Luker are attacked and searched, Luker losing a receipt for a great valuable. Lady Verinder dies of a heart condition and Rachel reluctantly agrees to marry Ablewhite whose father has become her guardian. They move to Brighton where they are visited by Mr Bruff, the family solicitor. The engagement is broken off when he reveals that Ablewhite is in debt and is marrying Rachel for her money.

Blake returns from travels abroad but Rachel refuses to see him. Determined to restore her good opinion, he revisits Yorkshire where Rosanna Spearman's only friend, Limping Lucy, gives him a letter from the dead housemaid. This leads him to the Shivering Sand where Rosanna has hidden his nightgown, smeared with paint, with a confession that she concealed the nightgown and killed herself out of love. The confused Blake returns to London and contrives a meeting with Rachel at Mr Bruff's house in *Hampstead. There she tells him that she knows he had financial problems and with her own eyes saw him take the diamond. Her own actions have been to protect his reputation.

Blake meets Mr Candy's assistant, Ezra Jennings, who saved Candy's life from a fever caught after the birthday dinner. Jennings had recorded Candy's delirium which revealed that Candy had secretly given Blake opium to prove his point in their argument. Blake therefore unknow-

ingly 'stole' the diamond under the influence of the drug, in order to keep it safe. Jennings explains to Blake that if he takes opium again under similar conditions he may repeat his actions of the previous year and reveal where he placed the diamond. Blake agrees and the experiment is conducted with Mr Bruff as an observer. Blake takes a substitute gem but fails to reveal the Moonstone's hiding place. Rachel, really in love with him, is also present and has already forgiven him.

Bruff in the mean time has Luker's bank watched. The moneylender is observed passing the diamond to a sailor who is followed to a dockside inn. Later the same night he is murdered. Cuff, brought out of retirement by Blake, discovers that the sailor is Godfrey Ablewhite in disguise. He was the real thief and stole the gem to save himself from financial ruin. He has been killed by the Indians who have now recovered the diamond. In a religious ceremony witnessed in India by Murthwaite, the Brahmins return the diamond to the god of the moon.

Serialization. *All the Year Round, 4 Jan.–8 Aug. 1868; and in *Harper's Weekly, 4 Jan.–8 Aug. 1868.

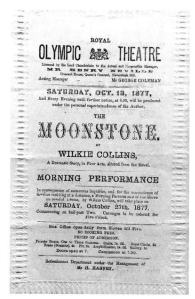

Programme for *The Moonstone* in October 1877

Book publication

1st edn. 3 vols, *Tinsley Brothers, 1868. Violet cloth, covers blocked in blind, spines lettered in gilt, cream endpapers. Half-title in each vol. Published in July 1868 in an edition of 1,500 copies.

Vol I viii + 316 pp.

Vol II (vi) + 298 pp. Single leaf of publisher's advertisements usually inserted before half-title, but sometimes forms pp [299–300].

Vol III (iv) + 312 pp. Publisher's advertisements occupy pp [311–12] but sometimes inserted before half-title.

A 2nd edn. of 500 copies in 3 vols was published from the same type. It is distinguished from the first by 'second edition' on the title-page and 'Tinsley Brothers' in italic on the spine. Both editions contain the misprint 'treachesrously' on p 129 of vol. II.

1-vol edns. *Smith, Elder 1871 (revised text with new preface); *Chatto & Windus 1875–1907 (with 9 illustrations by George *du Maurier and F. A. Fraser).

Critical edns. World's Classics 1928 (introduced by T. S. Eliot); Everyman Library 1944 (introduced by D. L. *Sayers); Penguin 1966 (edited by J. I. M. Stewart); Pan 1967 (introduced by A. Burgess); World's Classics 1982 (edited by A. Trodd); Everyman Library 1992 (introduced by C. Peters).

1st US edn. *Harper, New York 1868; reissued till 1900.

Translations. German (by Émil *Lehmann), Berlin 1868; Russian, Moscow 1868; Italian, Milan 1870; French, Paris 1872; Irish language, Dublin 1933.

The diamond illustrated in the first American edition of *The Moonstone* in 1868, published by HARPERS

Eliot, T. S., introduction to the 1928 World's Classics edition, based on 'Wilkie Collins and Dickens' in *Selected Essays 1917–1932*, London 1932.

Elwin, M., *Victorian Wallflowers*, London 1937, 225

Gasson (1980), 65–7.

Page (1974), 168–81.

Moonstone, The (the diamond).

'Carbon, Betteredge! Mere carbon.'

The fabulous diamond which carries a curse. Collins researched several diamonds similarly cursed, including the Orloff diamond, the Pitt diamond and the Koh-i-Noor. Charles *Reade claimed that it was based on a moonstone which his brother brought back from India. The appearance of this stone, however, was altogether different from Collins's description, in which the yellow colour is taken from the King of Portugal's gem: 'As large, or nearly, as a plover's egg! The light that streamed from it was like the light of the harvest moon. When you looked down into the stone, you looked into a yellow deep that drew your eyes into it so that you saw nothing else. It seemed . . . unfathomable as the heavens themselves . . . and it shone awfully out of the depths of its own brightness, with a moony gleam, in the dark.'

De la Mare (1932), 76–7.

Peters, C., introduction to *The Moonstone*, Everyman's Library, London 1992.

Moonstone, The (play). Stage version of the novel in four acts, performed at the Royal *Olympic Theatre from 17 September to 17 November 1877. Collins oversimplified the adaptation, omitting Rosanna *Spearman, Ezra *Jennings and the Indians. He restricted the action to a twenty-four-hour period at Rachel *Verinder's countryhouse in Kent. The production was not well received and both Henry *Neville (Franklin *Blake) and Laura Seymour (Miss Clack) left the cast before the end of the run. It was the last part played by Mrs Seymour before her death in 1879.

The Moonstone: A Dramatic Story in Three Acts, Altered from the Novel for Performance on the Stage was never published but 'privately printed for the convenience of the author' (1 vol, 176 pp, paper wrappers (variants in blue or white) printed in black).

Morford, Henry See JOHN JASPER'S SECRET.

'Mr Captain and the Nymph' Title used for 'The *Captain's Last Love' in *Little Novels* (1887).

'Mr Cosway and the Landlady' Title used for '*Your Money or Your Life' in *Little Novels* (1887).

'Mr Lepel and the Housekeeper' Title used for 'The *Girl at the Gate' in *Little Novels* (1887).

'Mr Lismore and the Widow' Title used for '*She Loves and Lies' in *Little Novels* (1887).

'Mr Marmaduke and the Minister' Title used for 'The *Mystery of Marmaduke' in *Little Novels* (1887).

'Mr Medhurst and the Princess' Title used for '*Royal Love' in *Little Novels* (1887).

'Mr Percy and the Prophet' Title used for '*Percy and the Prophet' in *Little Novels* (1887).

'Mr Policeman and the Cook' Title used for '*Who Killed Zebedee?' in *Little Novels* (1887).

Mr Wray's Cash-Box; or The Mask and the Mystery: A Christmas Sketch Sentimental story heavily influenced by *Dickens's Christmas books and published in a similar format; Collins's only attempt to exploit the genre. The idea of taking a cast from a statue is repeated in 'The *Yellow Mask' (1853). Notable for the frontispiece by *Millais, his first book illustration. Collins had hoped to include further illustrations by his brother, Charles, and Holman *Hunt. In the original preface, Collins explains that the tale is based on fact and reveals the mystery of the cashbox. The second edition eliminates most of the introduction and provides a good example of the young novelist learning the craft of suspense.

➧ Reuben Wray, a retired actor of little note, once worked with the illustrious John Kemble at Drury Lane. He now earns a precarious living teaching elocution. He arrives in Tidbury-on-the-Marsh, accompanied by his grand-daughter Annie and Martin Blunt, his clumsy but good-natured assistant. They had all left Stratford-upon-Avon in a hurry because Mr Wray had made a mask of Shakespeare, his lifelong hero, and believes the authorities are pursuing him.

The local Tidbury villains, Benjamin Grimes and Chummy Dick, see the old cash-box in which the mask is concealed and set out to steal it. When they discover there is no money they destroy the plaster cast and escape, leaving Mr Wray demented at the loss of his prized possession. The local squire, Matthew Colebatch, in whose failed play Mr Wray had once acted, befriends him but, despite the squire's attentions, he recovers only when Annie and Martin retrieve the original mould which had been left at Stratford and make another mask. They encourage his delusion that the robbery was all a bad dream. The squire obtains a legal opinion confirming no crime was committed in taking the mask and suggests Mr Wray should manufacture them for a living. Squire Colebatch invites himself for Christmas dinner at which he persuades Mr Wray to allow Annie and Martin to marry.

Book publication

1st edn. 1 vol, Richard *Bentley, London 1852 [1851]. Blue cloth, front cover blocked in blind and lettered in gilt, spine blocked in blind, cream endpapers. Half-title. Preface dated December 1851. Frontispiece by J. E. Millais, *Mr Wray's Cash-Box*. Variant binding in blue-grey cloth. Published 17 Dec. 1851.

ADVERTISEMENT.

THE main incident on which the following story turns, is founded on a fact which many readers of these pages will probably recognise as having formed a subject of conversation, a few years back, among persons interested in Literature and Art. I have endeavoured, in writing my little book, to keep the spirit of its title-page motto in view, and tell my "honest tale" as "plainly" as I could— or, in other words, as plainly as if I were only relating it to an audience of friends at my own fireside.

W. W. C.

HANOVER TERRACE, REGENT'S PARK.
January, 1852.

Shortened preface to the second edition of *Mr Wray's Cash-Box*, dated January 1852

viii + 176 pp. Publisher's advertisements occupy pp (173–6).

2nd edn, 1852, now subtitled 'A Modern Story', shortened preface dated Jan. 1852, and frontispiece retitled *The New Neckcloth*.

In *Crime for Christmas*, edited by Richard Dalby, London 1991; Stroud 1996.

US edn. Philadelphia [1862], as *The Stolen Mask: or the Mysterious Cash-Box*.

'Mrs Zant and the Ghost' Title used for 'The *Ghost's Touch' in *Little Novels* (1887).

Mudie's Lending Library The largest of the *circulating libraries, founded in 1842 by Charles Edward Mudie (1818–90) and at its most powerful between 1860 and 1890. Originally in Southampton Row, moved to New Oxford Street in 1852 and then to Museum Street, with branches in the City, Birmingham and Manchester. Mudie's subscription of one guinea a year significantly undercut the existing libraries and allowed the firm to expand rapidly while absorbing failed competitors. They added 960,000 volumes between 1853 and 1862, nearly half of them fiction, and by the end of the century housed over seven million books. The library became a limited company in 1864 with half the capital owned by Mudie and the remainder by publishers, principally John Murray and Richard *Bentley. Mudie's succeeded on the back of a booming book trade and the *three-decker, a system it largely perpetuated until 1894. The library declined with the end of high-priced fiction and eventually closed in the 1930s.

Mudie was a profound influence on the fiction published in the second half of the nineteenth century. Even more than W. H. *Smith, his moralistic approach to books could dictate the subject-matter, title and even the colour and style of binding. Collins dubbed them both 'the twin tyrants of literature'. Mudie asked Bentley to retitle *The New Magdalen* (1873), invoking Collins's indignant response 'Nothing will induce me to modify the title. . . . But the serious side of this affair is that this ignorant fanatic holds my circulation in his pious hands.' The previous year Mudie had forced Bentley to accept only £48 19*s*. for 484 copies of *Poor Miss Finch* and the library altogether refused *The Fallen Leaves* (1879).

Charles Edward Mudie

Gettman, R. A., *A Victorian Publisher*, Cambridge 1960.

Griest, G. L., *Mudie's Circulating Library and the Victorian Novel*, Bloomington, Ind., and Newton Abbot 1970.

music

'One *must* like music.' (*Heart and Science*) Collins enjoyed music and frequently attended evenings given by his friends Frederick and Nina *Lehmann, both fine musicians. He liked Italian composers and heard their works at the Paris Opera as early as 1845. He admired Verdi and in the late 1880s inspired a *dedication in Blanche Roosevelt's *Verdi, Milan and Othello*.

*Fosco in *The Woman in White* (1860) considers Rossini's *Moses in Egypt* a 'divine oratorio', and the overture to *Guillaume Tell* a 'symphony under another name'. During the performance of *Lucrezia Borgia*, before he recognizes Pesca and flees in terror, 'not a note of Donizetti's delicious music was lost on him'.

Mozart held the highest place in Collins's estimation. Uncle Joseph in *The Dead Secret* (1857) constantly plays Mozart on his music-box, claiming 'there is always comfort in Mozart' and calling him 'the King of all the music-composers that ever lived'. In *The Frozen Deep*, Clara Burnham's favourite piece is the ninth variation of Mozart's *Air in A, with Variations*, 'the music that harmonises so subtly with the tender beauties of night'.

Collins considered the violin as

'music's most expressive instrument' ('*I Say No*' 1884) but the violoncello the 'big and dreary member of the family of fiddles' (*Heart and Science* 1883). His particular dislike, however, was modern German music which he called in *The Fallen Leaves* (1879) 'the pretentious instrumental noises which were impudently offered to them as a substitute for melody'. In *Heart and Science* Carmina 'in common with Mozart and Rossini' held the opinion that 'music without melody is not music at all'.

Although Lydia *Gwilt in *Armadale* declares Beethoven 'the only man I care two straws about', Collins disliked the Kreutzer Sonata. But most of all he detested the works of Schumann, thinly disguised in '*Miss or Mrs?' as 'The great Bootmann playing the Nightmare Sonata'. In February 1869 he attended a recital with Mrs *Benzon and subsequently wrote to her: 'I hope you were

not the worse for this concert. As for *me*, Herr Schumann's music, Madame Schumann's playing, *and* the atmosphere of St James's Hall, are three such afflictions as I never desire to feel again. I think of sending a card to Erards:- "Mr Collins's compliments, and he would be glad to know how the poor piano is?" '
Letters.

musical dedications Collins, in common with other nineteenth-century figures, had his works commemorated by pieces of popular music. Several related to the highly successful *Woman in White* (which also had publicity in the form of cloaks, bonnets, perfumes and toilet requisites).

The Fosco Galop, by G. Richardson, 4s.

The Woman in White, words by J. E. Carpenter, music by C. W. Glover, 2s. 6d.

The Woman in White Waltz, by C. H. R. Marriott, 4s.

Collins also agreed to be mentioned in connection with an 1861 poem called 'Laura's Song', written and adapted for

music by E. Soundy.

No Thoroughfare Galop, by Charles Coote Junior, 3s. Coote's Quadrille Band was mentioned in *The Black Robe* (1881).

Joey Ladle, Words by Harry Hunter, music by G. W. Hunt. Sung by Mr Robert Fraser by express permission of Messrs Wilkie Collins and Charles Dickens.

Ellis (1931), 29–30.

'My Lady's Money: An Episode in the Life of a Young Lady'

'Suspect, in this case, the very last person on whom suspicion could possibly fall.'

Romantic novella originally published in the 1877 Christmas number of *The *Illustrated London News*; reprinted with *The *Haunted Hotel* (1879). First book publication by *Tauchnitz (1877) and *Harpers (New York 1878). Although most of the story is concerned with the eventual marriage of the heroine, it adds to Collins's contributions to *detective fiction. The 'Exhaustive System of Reasoning' and Old Sharon, the pipe-smoking detective

Musical dedications: (*below left*) *The Woman in White Waltz*
(*below right*) *The Woman in White*

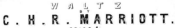

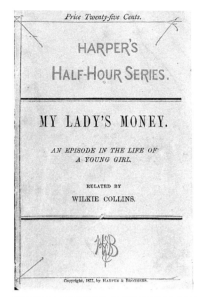

'My Lady's Money' published in Harper's Half-Hour Series in 1877

who works out the problem by deduction, are both possible influences on Conan *Doyle's Sherlock Holmes.

➧ A £500 bank note is stolen from Lady Lydiard. Present in the household are Isabel Miller, her adopted daughter; Felix Sweetsir, her nephew; Robert Moody, the steward; and Alfred Hardyman who has come to advise about *Tommie, the ailing Scotch terrier. Suspicion rests on Isabel who goes to stay with her aunt until her name is cleared. Moody, in love with Isabel, engages the slovenly detective Old Sharon to find the real thief. In the country at South Mordern, Isabel once again meets Hardyman who proposes marriage. She accepts on condition that Hardyman's family and friends will accept her. On the day of a celebratory luncheon they cancel because Felix, the real thief, has leaked the news that Isabel is suspected. In fact Felix stole the bank note to repay a gambling debt to Hardyman. The note is in Hardyman's missing pocket-book, discovered by the gallant Tommie playing canine detective. Felix makes a lame excuse to Lady Lydiard before escaping to the Continent. Isabel agrees to marry the faithful Moody.

My Miscellanies Collection of twenty-four essays and stories, dedicated to Henry *Bullar. Consisting of light-hearted pieces, serious social comment

and historical narratives, all had previously been published in *Household Words* (HW) or *All the Year Round* (ATYR).
Vol I

'Talk Stoppers' (HW, 25 Oct. 1856). Humorous essay about enemies to the art of conversation.

'A Journey in Search of Nothing' (HW, 5 Sept. 1857). Reflections on the difficulty of enforced idleness.

'A Queen's Revenge' (HW, 15 Aug. 1857). Reprinted in *Alicia Warlock, Boston 1875. Historical account of the murder at Fontainebleau in 1657 of the Marquis Monaldeschi at the instigation of the Swedish Queen Christina.

'A Petition to the Novel-Writers' (HW, 6 Dec. 1856). Lament at the dullness and unoriginality of contemporary fiction.

'Laid up in Lodgings' (HW, 7–14 June 1856). Accounts of lodging-houses and their landladies in *Paris and London, based on Collins's own experiences of being laid up. Notable for his sympathetic attitude towards domestic servants.

'A Shockingly Rude Article' (HW, 28 Aug. 1858). More enemies to conversation in the shape of 'Lady-Bores'.

'The Great (Forgotten) Invasion' (HW, 12 Mar. 1859). Historical account of the landing in February 1797 by 1,400 Frenchmen on the coast of Wales.

'The *Unknown Public' (HW, 21 Aug. 1858). The estimated three million readers of penny novel-journals who should be taught to appreciate better-quality fiction.

'Give Us Room!' (HW, 13 Feb. 1858). The dangers of crinoline and overcrowding at parties given in private houses.

'Portrait of an Author, Painted by his Publisher' (ATYR, 18–25 June 1859). Review of a colourful biographical sketch of *Balzac.

'My Black Mirror' (HW, 6 Sept. 1856). Reprinted in *Alicia Warlock, Boston 1875. Reminiscences on continental travel in Austrian *Italy and *Switzerland.

'Mrs Badgery' (HW, 26 Sept. 1857). Reprinted in vol 6 of *Novels and Tales from Household Words*, *Tauchnitz vol 416, 1857; and in *Alicia Warlock, Boston 1875. Story of how a bachelor, on moving into his new house, is persecuted by the constant presence of the widow of its former occupant.
Vol II

'Memoirs of an Adopted Son' (ATYR, 20 Apr. 1861). Reprinted in *Alicia Warlock,

Boston 1875. Narrative taken from records of the French police about the daring eighteenth-century robber Poulailler and the legend of his supernatural birth and death.

'The Bachelor Bedroom' (ATYR, 6 Aug. 1859). Bachelor types, including a parody of Hans Christian *Andersen as Herr von Muffe.

'A Remarkable Revolution' (HW, 1 Aug. 1857). Account of the quiet revolution of 1741 which placed on the throne of Russia Princess Elizabeth, daughter of Peter the Great, masterminded by the French Marquis de la Chétardie and the German surgeon Lestoc.

'Douglas *Jerrold' (HW, 5 Feb. 1859). Reprinted in vol 11 of *Novels and Tales from Household Words*, Tauchnitz vol 481, 1859. Biographical sketch partly based on W. B. Jerrold's *The Life and Remains of Douglas Jerrold*.

'Pray Employ Major Namby!' (ATYR, 4 June 1859). Account of the narrator's noisy military neighbour who conducts his domestic affairs from his front garden; brief reappearance of Lady Malkinshaw from *A *Rogue's Life* (1856).

'The Poisoned Meal' (HW, 18 Sept.–2 Oct. 1858). Reprinted in vol 10 of *Novels and Tales from Household Words*, Tauchnitz vol 475, 1859. True story of the trial, imprisonment and eventual release of Marie-Françoise Victoire Salmon, falsely accused of murder in 1781.

'My Spinsters' (HW, 23 Aug. 1856). Discourse on the different personalities of marriageable young ladies.

'Dramatic Grub Street' (HW, 6 Mar. 1858). Lament in the form of a letter at the low remuneration paid to dramatic writers, explaining the poor quality of plays on the contemporary English stage in comparison with the French.

'To Think, or Be Thought for?' (HW, 13 Sept. 1856). Suggestion that we should form our own opinions on art and not be governed by the cant of established criticism.

'Save Me from My Friends' (HW, 16 Jan. 1858). Wry look at the disruptive influence on a writer of too many well-meaning friends.

'The Cauldron of Oil' (ATYR, 11 May 1861). In 1700 the three sons of the murdered Saturnin Siadoux, by forcing the local priest to betray the confidence of the confessional, incur the death penalty for all of them as well as the murderer.

Illustration by Concanen to 'A Remarkable Revolution' in the Chatto & Windus edition of *My Miscellanies*

'Bold Words by a Bachelor' (*HW*, 13 Dec. 1856). On the loss of true friendship between a bachelor and his male friends after their marriage.

'Mrs Bullwinkle' (*HW*, 17 Apr. 1858). Story of a nurse who 'eats little and often' but consumes enough food almost to bankrupt her employer.

Serialization. See individual articles.

Book publication

1st edn. 2 vols, *Sampson Low, London 1863. Green cloth, covers blocked in blind, spines lettered in gilt, green-ochre endpapers. No half-titles. Published in Nov. 1863. Copies in brown cloth, with yellow endpapers with *Chapman & Hall advertisements are of later issue (1873–4).

Vol I (viii) + 292 pp.

Vol II (iv) + 300 pp.

16 pp publisher's catalogue dated Nov. 1863 bound in at the end of each vol.

1-vol edns. *Chatto & Windus 1875–99 (with frontispiece portrait by Halpin and 8 illustrations by Alfred Concanen; stories rearranged omitting 'Dramatic Grub Street' and an addition to original preface).

1st US edn. *Harper, New York 1874.

'Mystery of Marmaduke, The'
Satirical short story originally published in The *Spirit of the Times*, 28 December 1878; and in *Temple Bar*, January 1879.

Reprinted as 'Mr Marmaduke and the Minister' in *Little Novels* (1887).

•❖ Marmaduke Falmer falls in love with Felicity, a minister's daughter, while sheltering from a storm in the Scottish town of Cauldkirk. The minister visits the married couple in London because Felicity is worried about her husband's mysterious disappearance each evening. All is explained when Marmaduke confesses to being Barrymore, the actor, famous in a profession of which the minister wholly disapproves.

N

Neville, (Thomas) Henry (Gartside) (1837–1910). Romantic actor; lessee and manager of the *Olympic from 1873 to 1879. Neville was the first professional to play Richard *Wardour in *The Frozen Deep*, at the Olympic from 27 October 1866. He also played Franklin *Blake in *The Moonstone* from 17 September 1877. Neville took the part of George Vendale in the successful run of *No Thoroughfare* at the *Adelphi from December 1868 and at the Olympic in November 1876.

New Cavendish Street Street in *Marylebone where Collins was born, at number 11. He returned to live at number 2A with Caroline *Graves from April to December 1859.

New Magdalen, The: A Novel Novel published in 1873, dedicated to the memory of Charles Allston *Collins who died during its composition. One of the most *didactic of Wilkie Collins's 'novels with a purpose', treating the then fashionable theme of the 'fallen woman' who attempts to put her past behind her but is repeatedly thwarted by the prejudices of respectable English society. The heroine is not only, conventionally, 'rescued' by a clergyman but, unconventionally, finally married to him.

•◆ Mercy Merrick has been tricked into the tragic life of a woman of the streets, after a childhood with strolling players and gypsies. She struggles to rehabilitate herself, inspired by a sermon given by a young clergyman, Julian Gray, in the refuge where she was living. Working as a volunteer nurse in the Franco-German war of 1870, she meets Grace Roseberry, a penniless but well-connected and respectable young woman. When Grace is apparently killed by a German shell, Mercy assumes her identity. Armed with a letter of introduction to Grace's relation by marriage, Lady Janet Roy, she is helped to reach England by Horace Holmcroft, a war correspondent and acquaintance of Lady Roy. Mercy is warmly welcomed and becomes her companion

and adopted daughter. With Lady Roy's approval, she becomes engaged to Horace.

Grace is not dead, however, since her life has been saved by a German brain surgeon. She returns to England and is introduced to Lady Roy by Julian Gray but, lacking the evidence to back up her claim, is rejected as an impostor. Mercy is prepared to confess until antagonized by Grace's vengeful, unforgiving nature. Grace is deemed insane and is about to be confined in an asylum when Mercy once more comes under the influence of Julian Gray, who falls in love with her, and she finally admits her deception. Horace breaks off their engagement while Grace accepts £500 as a bribe for her silence and leaves for Canada. Lady Roy, genuinely fond of Mercy, tries unsuccessfully to persuade her to remain as companion. At first Mercy refuses to marry Julian, in order not to ruin his career and social position. However, he becomes seriously ill and on his recovery she finally agrees to marry him. Rejected by society, they sail to the New World to start life afresh.

Binding of the two-volume Richard BENTLEY edition of *The New Magdalen* in 1873

Serialization. *Temple Bar*, Oct. 1872–July 1873; *Harper's New Monthly Magazine*, Oct. 1872–June 1873.

Book publication

1st edn. 2 vols, Richard *Bentley, London 1873. Red-brown cloth, covers blocked in black, spines lettered in red-brown on gilt, cream endpapers. No half-titles. Published 17 May 1873. 2 vols in 1, green cloth with pale yellow endpapers and *Chapman & Hall advertisements 1873.

Vol I vi + 298 pp.

Vol II iv + 300 pp. Publisher's advertisement occupies p 299.

1-vol edns. Bentley 1874; *Chatto & Windus 1875–1925 (with 7 illustrations by George *du Maurier and C. S. Reinhart); Sutton, Stroud 1993.

1st US edn. *Harper, New York 1873.

Translations. Dutch, The Hague 1873; French, Paris 1873; Russian, St Petersburg 1873.

New Magdalen, The (play). Stage version written at the same time as the novel. First produced on 19 May 1873 at the *Olympic Theatre by Ada *Cavendish who played the part of Mercy Merrick opposite Frank *Archer as Julian Gray. The play was a great success, running for four months prior to a provincial tour. On the Continent it was performed in *Paris, *Rome, Berlin and Vienna; and in *America Collins was present for the opening of Augustin *Daly's production at New York's Broadway Theatre (10 November 1873). There were numerous revivals: at the Charing Cross, subsequently moving to the National Standard Theatre (Bishopsgate), 1875; the Novelty, 1884; the Margate Theatre Royal, 1885; the Oldham Colosseum, 1887; and the Marlborough (Holloway Road), 1906.

The New Magdalen: A Dramatic Story in a Prologue and Three Acts was 'Published by the Author' in 1873 (1 vol, 158 pp, buff paper wrappers). There was also a version by A. D. Ames (no. 112), Clyde, Ohio 1882.

Parrish (1940), 91–3.

'Nine O'Clock!' Short story published in *Bentley's Miscellany*, August 1852.

Reprinted for the first time in *Wilkie Collins: The Complete Shorter Fiction*, edited by Julian Thompson, 1995.
➥ Set in the French Revolution of 1793, one of Collins's earliest tales of the *supernatural. On the eve of his execution, the Girondin deputy, Duprat, narrates how his brother and father before him both had visions that predicted their precise hour of death. True to his destiny, Duprat is then guillotined at exactly nine o'clock.

No Name (book). Published in 1862 at the peak of Collins's career, one of his four major novels. Dedicated to Francis Carr *Beard. Following the success of *The Woman in White*, *Sampson Low paid Collins £3,000 for *No Name* and published a large first edition of 4,000 copies. All but 400 sold by the afternoon of the first day. An early *didactic novel, it addresses the theme of illegitimacy. In spite of its popular success many of the critics were scathing about the topic and disapproved of the heroine's near-criminal career. H. L. Mansel of *The Quarterly Review* wrote, 'We have often heard an illegal connexion and its result euphemistically designated a "misfortune"; but this is the first time as far as we are aware in which a lawful marriage has been denominated an "accident".' The novel features one of

Collins's most dynamic heroines and one of his most engaging rogues, Captain *Wragge.
➥ Magdalen *Vanstone is a headstrong girl of 18, with a gift for amateur dramatics. She lives a prosperous and respectable life in the country with her parents, her quieter older sister Norah and their governess and friend Miss Garth. Magdalen falls in love with a weak young man, Francis Clare, the son of an acerbic neighbour. They become engaged, though neither Magdalen's parents nor Clare's father are in favour of the match. Clare is sent first to London and then to China to make his fortune.

The middle-aged Andrew Vanstone and his wife are dismayed when they discover that Mrs Vanstone is pregnant once more. Worse is to follow. Mr Vanstone, on his way to see his lawyer in London, is killed in a railway accident and Mrs Vanstone goes into premature labour on hearing the news; both she and the child die. The family lawyer Mr Pendril breaks the news to Magdalen and Norah that they are illegitimate—they have 'no name'. Their father and mother had only recently been able to marry after the death of Mr Vanstone's first wife in Canada. They are also penniless, since their father had been on his way to sign a new will, essential after his recent mar-

riage. Now the estate will go to his estranged brother Michael Vanstone who vindictively refuses to give his nieces any fair share of their father's fortune.

Norah stays with Miss Garth, their staunch friend, and becomes a governess. Magdalen, resolved to earn her living on the stage, runs away to York. Here she encounters a disreputable cousin by marriage, Captain Wragge, an amiable villain who persuades Magdalen he can help her. She lives with Wragge and his simpleminded wife, and prepares a one-woman stage show playing various 'characters'. Her career, managed by Wragge, is a great success.

When Michael Vanstone dies, leaving no will, Magdalen appeals to his physically and mentally feeble son Noel. She receives a dismissive reply from his formidable housekeeper Mrs *Lecount. Determined on revenge, she visits Noel in London, disguised as Miss Garth. Her request for half the fortune is rejected. Mrs Lecount sees through her disguise and snips a piece of cloth from her dress as evidence.

Magdalen now decides to retrieve her inheritance by marrying her cousin Noel—her engagement to Francis Clare has been broken off. With Wragge's help, she follows Noel to *Aldborough and is introduced as Wragge's niece, Susan Bygrave. Mrs Lecount is again suspicious but Wragge lures her away to her family in Zurich with a forged letter. Noel is fascinated by Magdalen and proposes. Mag-

(below left) Printed version of *The New Magdalen* play in 1873
(below right) Serialization of *No Name* in *All The Year Round*, beginning on 15 March 1862

THE

NEW MAGDALEN:

A Dramatic Story,

IN A PROLOGUE AND THREE ACTS.

BY

WILKIE COLLINS.

(Represented for the first time in London at the Olympic Theatre, May 19th, 1873.)

LONDON:
PUBLISHED BY THE AUTHOR,
90, GLOUCESTER PLACE, PORTMAN SQUARE.
1873.

W. CLOWES & SONS.   ENTERED AT STATIONERS' HALL.   [STAMFORD STREET.

"THE STORY OF OUR LIVES FROM YEAR TO YEAR."—Shakespeare.

ALL THE YEAR ROUND.

A WEEKLY JOURNAL.

CONDUCTED BY CHARLES DICKENS.

WITH WHICH IS INCORPORATED HOUSEHOLD WORDS.

Nᵒ. 151.]   SATURDAY, MARCH 15, 1862.   [Price 2*d.*

NO NAME.

BY THE AUTHOR OF "THE WOMAN IN WHITE," &c.

THE FIRST SCENE.
COMBE-RAVEN, SOMERSETSHIRE.
CHAPTER I.

THE hands on the hall-clock pointed to half-past six in the morning. The house was a country residence in West Somersetshire, called Combe-Raven. The day was the fourth of March, and the year was eighteen hundred and

the state of the spring temperature written redly on her nose. The lady's-maid followed—young, smart, plump, and sleepy. The kitchen-maid came next—afflicted with the face-ache, and making no secret of her sufferings. Last of all, the footman appeared, yawning disconsolately; the living picture of a man who felt that he had been defrauded of his fair night's rest.

The conversation of the servants, when they assembled before the slowly-lighting kitchen fire, referred to a recent family event, and turned at starting on this question: Had Thomas, the

dalen, horrified at the prospect of marriage to a man she loathes, buys a lethal dose of *laudanum and contemplates suicide, but finally goes through with the match.

Mrs Lecount returns and convinces Noel that he has been deceived into marrying his cousin. Finding Magdalen's bottle of laudanum, she also persuades him that Magdalen planned to poison him. Noel alters his will, leaving the fortune to a cousin, Admiral Bartram, with a secret trust passing the inheritance to the Admiral's son George Bartram, on condition he marries within six months. Noel, who has a weak heart, collapses and dies.

Magdalen, convinced that the legacy to Admiral Bartram conceals a secret intention, disguises herself as a maid, and takes a position in the Admiral's house. She narrowly fails in an audacious attempt to find the concealed letter and escapes to London. Penniless and desperately ill, she is nursed back to health by Captain Kirke, whom she first met at Aldborough. They fall in love and marry. Meanwhile Norah, without knowing anything of the will, has met and married George Bartram.

Serialization. *All the Year Round, 15 Mar. 1862–17 Jan.1863; and *Harper's Weekly, 15 Mar. 1862–24 Jan. 1863.

Book publication

1st edn. 3 vols, *Sampson Low, London 1862. Scarlet embossed cloth, covers blocked in blind, spines lettered in scarlet on gilt, pale yellow endpapers. Half-titles in vols I and II. Published between 14 and 31 Dec. 1862.

Vol I x + 340 pp.

Vol II (iv) + 364 pp.

Vol III ii + 408 pp.

New edn., 3 vols 1863.

1-vol edns. Sampson Low 1864 (with frontispiece by *Millais); *Smith, Elder 1865–86; *Chatto & Windus 1890–1932. Dover, New York 1978; World's Classics 1986 (critical edition, edited by V. Blain).

1st US edns. *Harper, New York 1863; Gardner Fuller (2 vols), Boston 1863 (Parrish gives priority to this edition); West & Johnson, Richmond, V., 1863.

Translations. Russian, St Petersburg 1862; German, Leipzig 1862–3; Dutch, Amsterdam 1863; French, Paris 1863 (by É.-D. *Forgues).

No Name (play). *No Name* was never produced as a play in England although there were two different adaptations. The first version, *No Name: A Drama in Five Acts* (60 pp, pink paper wrappers), was written by W. B. Bernard in 1863: Collins hoped this

Millais's illustration to the 1864 one-volume Sampson Low edition of *No Name*

would be produced at the *Olympic Theatre. The second, *No Name: A Drama in Four Acts* (160 pp, buff paper wrappers), was written and published by Collins himself in 1870. In New York, this version was altered by Wybert *Reeve and produced by Augustin *Daly at the Fifth Avenue Theatre, with the first night on 7 June 1871. Reeve eventually took his dramatization to *Australia. The 1863 text was also published in De Witt's Acting Plays (no. 104), New York [nd].

'No Thoroughfare' (story). Mystery story written by Collins in *collaboration with *Dickens. Originally published in the extra *Christmas number of *All the

Year Round, 12 Dec. 1867 and in *Every Saturday, Boston, Dec. 1867. Written with a stage adaptation in mind, the story is divided into an 'Overture' and three 'Acts'. The dramatization followed publication almost immediately, opening at the *Adelphi Theatre on 26 December 1867. The story was later republished in *The* *Lazy Tour of Two Idle Apprentices* (1890); it was translated into Dutch (1868), Norwegian (1868) Russian (1868) and Spanish [1890]. The route in Act III (Strasbourg, Lausanne, Geneva and the Simplon Pass to Milan) follows that of Collins, Dickens and Augustus *Egg during their European tour in October 1853. (For authorship of the various parts see

(left) Programme for *No Thoroughfare* at the Olympic Theatre
(above) No Thoroughfare issued in Dicks's Standard Plays

the same name. He determines to find the rightful owner of his fortune. All his investigations end in 'no thoroughfare' and he dies shortly after.

Vendale now learns that a remittance to Defresniers has been stolen and he must deliver personally a forged receipt so that the criminal's handwriting can be identified. The thief is Obenreizer who volunteers to travel to Switzerland with Vendale, hoping that he can recover the evidence. While they attempt to cross the Simplon Pass in a blizzard, Obenreizer confesses his guilt. He has drugged Vendale and intends to leave him to die on the mountain. Marguerite, however, has followed with Joey Ladle, the head cellarman, and rescues Vendale from the edge of a precipice. They later confront Obenreizer who maliciously reveals that Vendale is illegitimate. He is, in fact, the true heir to Wilding's fortune. Vendale marries Marguerite and Obenreizer perishes in an avalanche.

See also MUSICAL DEDICATIONS.

No Thoroughfare (play) Stage adaptation by Collins of the story 'No Thoroughfare' written in collaboration with *Dickens. Written and produced in 1867 during Dickens's absence in America.

No Thoroughfare was first performed on 26 December 1867 and successfully ran

Oppenlander's *Dickens's 'All the Year Round'*, New York 1984.)
•➔ The 'Overture' is set in the London Foundling Hospital. In 1835 a woman who has left her child there begs to know the new name he has been given, and is told it is Walter Wilding. In 1847 she returns to adopt the boy called Walter Wilding, whom she believes to be her son.

Wilding grows up to be a successful wine merchant and in 1861 takes a new partner, George Vendale. On his first day Vendale visits Jules Obenreizer, the English agent for the firm's Swiss champagne supplier Defresniers. He meets Obenreizer's niece, Marguerite, and they fall in love despite Obenreizer's attempts to prevent their relationship. Wilding, meanwhile, learns from his new housekeeper, once a nurse in the Foundling Hospital, that he is not his supposed mother's son. That boy had been adopted and taken abroad, and a second boy given

The North Foreland Lighthouse at Broadstairs which inspired the naming of *The Woman in White*

for 200 performances at the *Adelphi Theatre. The play starred Charles *Fechter as Obenreizer, Benjamin *Webster as head cellarman Joey Ladle and Carlotta Leclercq as Marguerite. Henry *Neville played Vendale, repeating the part in a later production at the *Olympic in November 1876. Fechter and Dickens wrote a different version in French called *L'Abime*, first produced at the Vaudeville in *Paris on 2 June 1868. There were various pirated versions in the USA including one at the Park Theatre, Brooklyn, 6 January 1868.

No Thoroughfare: A Drama in Five Acts was published at the Office of *All the Year Round* in 1867 (90 pp, buff paper wrappers). There were three other editions: De Witt's Acting Plays (no. 14), New York [nd]; and two by Louis Lequel, *Identity: or No Thoroughfare*, French's Standard Drama (no. 348), New York and London 1867; and *No Thoroughfare: A Drama in Four Acts*, Dicks Standard Plays (no. 1052), London [nd].

North Foreland Lighthouse Lighthouse on the clifftops just outside *Broadstairs which provided the inspiration for naming *The Woman in White*. Collins had great difficulty in finding a title for the novel. He left London for Broadstairs and in desperation walked for hours on the cliffs between the *Fort House and Kingsgate. Exhausted, he threw himself on the grass admonishing the lighthouse: 'You are ugly and stiff and awkward; you know you are: as stiff and as weird as my white woman. White woman!—woman in white! The title, by Jove.'

This story was originally published in 'Celebrities at Home. No. 81. Mr Wilkie Collins in Gloucester Place', *The *World* (26 Dec. 1877), 5; repeated almost word for word in Hall *Caine's *My Story* (1908).

Notting Hill Mystery, The (1865). Sometimes cited as the first full-length detective novel; written by Charles Felix and serialized in *Once a Week* from November 1862. The story does not have the enduring quality of *The Moonstone* (1868) and the detective, Ralph Henderson, is an insurance investigator who plays a minor role.

obituaries Collins maintained his popularity as a public figure right up to the time of his death on 23 September 1889. During his last illness *The Times* had issued frequent bulletins, recording on 15 July 'The Queen has made special enquiries as to his health.' In America, *The New York Times* of 3 July featured a front-page headline 'Wilkie Collins Stricken.' On the day of his death *The Echo* recorded that 'The interest felt in the state of his health was well nigh universal.'

Generally favourable obituary notices appeared in the major newspapers the following day, 24 September: 'A master of plot and a master of dramatic situations', *The Times*; 'His is a name of the Victorian age, which posterity will not readily let die', *The Daily Telegraph*; 'We lose, unquestionably, one of the representative men of our time', *The Globe*. *The Daily News*, however, still remained highly critical of **Basil* (published thirty-seven years earlier) but conceded that Collins

'continued from time to time to furnish entertainment to numberless readers by successive instalments of his well-known fictions'.

Further notices appeared in the weeklies of 28 September: 'The greatest writer of sensation fiction that England has produced', *Saturday Review*; 'The peculiar talent of Wilkie Collins, as a novelist, was that of devising and conducting a plot in which some concealed action of wicked intrigue or conspiracy was gradually developed, presenting a complex problem of circumstantial evidence, so as to excite the curiosity of his readers', *The *Illustrated London News*. More personal tributes were written by Harry **Quilter, Hall **Caine and Edmund **Yates. Quilter in the **Universal Review* of October 1889 defended the notion that 'it *is* a little thing to have written stories so well that the whole world listened to them gladly for forty years'. Caine contributed his 'Personal Recollections' for *The Globe* of 4 Oc-

tober and various provincial newspapers, while Yates wrote in *The *World* of 25 September: 'I am robbed of a friend with whom . . . I had ever maintained a warm and pleasant intimacy . . . Of that little coterie which used to meet at Mrs Collins's house in Hanover Terrace forty years ago . . . "All, all are gone, the old familiar faces." Dear good staunch Wilkie, who has now gone to rejoin them.'

'Old Maid's Husband, An' Short story originally published in *The *Spirit of the Times*, 25 Dec. 1886; and in **Belgravia*, Jan. 1887. Reprinted as 'Miss Dulane and My Lord' in **Little Novels* (1887).
➡ The elderly Miss Dulane makes a marriage of convenience with the impecunious Lord Howel Beaucourt. The marriage is happy but she discovers that her newly engaged companion, Mrs Evelin, had been in love with Beaucourt under the assumed name of Vincent. Mrs Evelin had declined his proposal, wrongly thinking that her own late husband had disgraced her with a bigamous marriage. She leaves for New Zealand and on returning finds both that her marriage was in fact legal and that Lady Beaucourt has died. The couple are free to marry and somewhat reluctantly accept a legacy from Lady Beaucourt's will.

Oldershaw, Mrs Maria (Mother Oldershaw). In *Armadale* (1866), encourages and finances Lydia **Gwilt in her attempts to marry Allan **Armadale for his money. Brought up Lydia Gwilt as a child before she became maid to Jane Blanchard. Originally peddling quack medicines, Mrs Oldershaw graduated to the 'Ladies' Toilette Repository' of Diana Street, Pimlico, selling wigs and beauty treatments. The character of Mrs Oldershaw was based on the infamous Madame Rachel Leverson who had a shop at 47A

Obituaries: memorandum to YATES at *The World* by C. Thomas in October 1889, complaining there has been 'too much W.C.' (Yates replies 'Yes, but it is a necessary evil!')

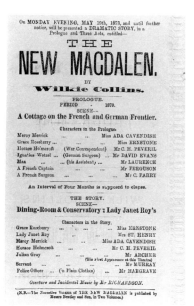

On MONDAY EVENING, MAY 19th, 1873, and until further notice, will be presented a DRAMATIC STORY, in a Prologue and Three Acts, entitled—

THE NEW MAGDALEN.

BY
Wilkie Collins.

PROLOGUE.
PERIOD - 1870.
SCENE—
A Cottage on the French and German Frontier.

Characters in the Prologue.

Mercy Merrick ...	...	Miss ADA CAVENDISH
Grace Roseberry ...	...	Miss ERNSTONE
Horace Holmcroft	(War Correspondent)	Mr C. H. PEVERIL
Ignatius Wetzel ...	(German Surgeon)	Mr DAVID EVANS
Max ...	(his Assistant) ...	Mr LAURENCE
A French Captain	...	Mr FERGUSON
A French Surgeon	...	Mr C. PARRY

An Interval of Four Months is supposed to elapse.

THE STORY.
SCENE—
Dining-Room & Conservatory : Lady Janet Roy's

Characters in the Story.

Grace Roseberry ...	...	Miss ERNSTONE
Lady Janet Roy	...	Mrs ST. HENRY
Mercy Merrick ...	...	Miss ADA CAVENDISH
Horace Holmcroft	...	Mr C. H. PEVERIL
Julian Gray ...	...	Mr ARCHER
	(His first Appearance at this Theatre)	
Servant ...	...	Mr MURRAY
Police Officer ...	('n Plain Clothes)	Mr HARGRAVE

Overture and Incidental Music by Mr RICHARDSON.

(N.B.—The Narrative Version of THE NEW MAGDALEN is published by Messrs Bentley and Son, in Two Volumes.)

Programme for the first night of *The New Magdalen* at the Olympic Theatre, 19 May 1873

New Bond Street and was eventually sentenced to five years penal servitude in 1868 after the case of Mrs Borradaile and Lord Ranelagh.

Ellis (1931), 37.

Oliphant, Mrs Margaret, née Wilson (1828–97). Prolific novelist, regular contributor and critic for *Blackwood's Magazine*. Admired Collins's technical skill in *The Woman in White*, acknowledging his superiority in the field of the *sensation novel. She regarded *Man and Wife* as reviving his reputation, but had earlier attacked *No Name*, considered *The Dead Secret* 'a dreary web' and *Basil* 'a revolting story'.

Page (1974).

Olympic Theatre (later Royal Olympic). Located in Wych Street, Strand (where the Aldwych now is), it acquired the reputation for well-acted melodrama. Its managers included Horace Wigan, W. H. Liston, Ada *Cavendish and Henry *Neville. Demolished in 1904. The Olympic staged the following dramatizations of Collins's works: *The Lighthouse* (10 Aug.–17 Oct. 1857); *The Red Vial* (opened 11 Oct. 1858);

The Frozen Deep (opened 27 Oct. 1866); *The Woman in White* (9 Oct. 1871–24 Feb. 1872); *The New Magdalen* (19 May–27 Sept. 1873); *No Thoroughfare* (opened 27 Nov. 1876); *The Moonstone* (17 Sept.–17 Nov. 1877).

opium

'That all-potent and all-merciful drug.' (*The Moonstone*)

Taken by Collins from the early 1860s in the form of *laudanum to alleviate the symptoms of *gout and rheumatic pain. There were no legal restrictions on the use of opium until 1868 and it was the chief ingredient of many patent medicines. Collins recorded in the *Memoirs of the Life of William Collins Esq., R.A.* (1848) that his father took 'Battley's Drops' to relieve pain during 1846.

Opium was regularly prescribed for medical reasons by Collins's doctor, Frank *Beard, as a pain-killer and sedative—never for mere gratification. Despite various attempts to give up the habit, using hypnosis by *Elliotson in 1863 and morphia by injection in 1869, Collins took increasingly large doses 'by the tablespoon' until in later life he became totally dependent. The *Bancrofts related Collins's difficulty in obtaining opium in *Switzerland and also told the story of a dinner-party with the ophthalmologist George *Critchett where the famous surgeon Sir William Fergusson agreed that Collins's normal dose was sufficient to kill every man seated at the table. Edmund *Yates in his 1889 obituary recorded that Collins 'was in the habit of taking daily . . . more laudanum than would have sufficed to kill a ship's crew or company of soldiers'.

Hall *Caine claimed he saw Collins drink laudanum by the wineglass 'to stimulate the brain and steady the nerves' and told the unsubstantiated and probably untrue story that Collins's manservant killed himself by drinking just half a glass. William *Winter recalled Collins saying 'opium sometimes hurts . . . but, also, *sometimes*, it helps'. Despite an enormous tolerance to the drug, Collins admitted to both Mary *Anderson and Percy *Fitzgerald that he experienced hallucinations. He began to be disturbed by the movement of shadows in his gas-

Letter from Collins to Mrs BENZON about giving up opium (laudanum)

lit study, and phantoms would follow him upstairs to bed where a green woman with tusks would wait for him.

The nightmares caused by opium are vividly described by Ezra *Jennings in *The Moonstone* where the drug forms an integral part of the plot. Collins described to both William Winter and Mary Anderson how he wrote much of the book under the effects of opium and when finished hardly recognized the work as his own. Magdalen *Vanstone contemplates suicide with laudanum in *No Name* (1862), whereas Lydia *Gwilt in *Armadale* (1866) writes in her diary 'Who was the man who invented laudanum? I thank him from the bottom of my heart.' Although opium features prominently in these novels of the 1860s, it is merely mentioned in later works. When Turlington visits Wildfang in '*Miss or Mrs?' (1871) 'The smell of opium was in the room'; and the 'composing medicine' appropriated by Eunice in *The Legacy of Cain* (1888) stimulates a typically laudanum-induced apparition.

Bancroft, S. and M., *The Bancrofts: Recollections of Sixty Years*, London 1909, 174.

Booth, M., *Opium: A History*, London 1996.

Hayter, A., *Opium and the Romantic Imagination*, London 1968, 255–70.

Pall Mall Gazette, The Literary evening paper, founded in 1865 by George Smith and Frederick Greenwood; the title was taken from Thackeray's *Pendennis*. The paper's editor was Dutton Cook and contributors included Matthew Arnold and Anthony *Trollope. It published unfavourable reviews of *The Moonstone* (17 July 1868) and of Collins reading 'A Terribly Strange Bed' at a charity performance which he used as a rehearsal for his *American reading tour (30 June 1873). The paper also published:

'Books Necessary for a Liberal Education' (by Collins), 11 Feb. 1886. See also REMINISCENCES.

'Wilkie Collins about Charles Dickens, from a Marked Copy of Forster's "Dickens" ', 20 Jan. 1890 (coincided with the *auction of Collins's books). Excerpts reprinted in Robinson (1951), 258–9.

Paris Collins's favourite city, first visited as a boy with his family for two weeks in September 1836. He developed a lifelong taste for French art, theatre and food, and chose Paris for his first independent trip abroad with Charles *Ward in August 1844, returning with him in August 1847. Collins had stayed there on his own at the Hôtel des Tuileries during September 1845 and had to write home for money.

In February 1855 *Dickens invited Collins to accompany him to the Hôtel Meurice, writing to *Régnier 'I want . . . to throw myself *en garçon* on the festive *diableries de Paris.*' Collins suffered one of his early attacks of illness and while Dickens walked all over the city 'the invalid sits by the fire or is deposited in a café'. This did not prevent their dining 'in a different restaurant every day, and at seven or so we go to the theatre'. Dickens and his family were in Paris the following winter and Collins visited them for six weeks from late February. Despite rheumatic pains he did the rounds of art galleries and theatres, finished *A Rogue's Life* and planned *The Dead Secret*. It was during this trip in 1856 that he found Méjan's *Recueil des causes célèbres*.

Collins returned to Paris with Caroline *Graves in October 1860 when the success of *The Woman in White* allowed him to travel in comfort. He was there again with Frederick *Lehmann in February 1865 and April 1866, and made several short visits during early 1867 to discuss with Régnier a theatrical version of *Armadale*. Collins continued to visit Paris during the mid-1870s.

PELCD.

parodies and imitation Collins's works were the subject of several parodies, listed below. In addition, the title of *The Woman in White* was imitated by others such as H. J. Byron in *La Sonnambula* (1865) 'being a passage in the Life of a famous Woman in White'; and by Watts Phillips in *The Woman in Mauve: A Sensation Drama in Three Acts* (1864) which actually quotes the crossroads meeting from Collins's novel. E. C. Bentley's classic detective story, *Trent's Last Case* (1913), was called in America *The Woman in Black* and Susan Hill used the same title for her 1983 ghost story. There have been numerous

NO TITLE.

BY W—LK—E C—LL—NS.

——

PROLOGUE.

THE following advertisement appeared in the "Times" of the 17th of June, 1845:—

WANTED. — A few young men for a light genteel employment. Address J. W., P. O.

In the same paper, of same date, in another column :—

TO LET. — That commodious and elegant family mansion, No. 27 Limehouse Road, Pultneyville, will be rented low to a respectable tenant if applied for immediately, the family being about to remove to the continent.

Under the local intelligence, in another column :—

MISSING. — An unknown elderly gentleman a week ago left his lodgings in the Kent Road, since which nothing has been heard of him. He left no trace of his identity except a portmanteau containing a couple of shirts marked "209, WARD."

To find the connection between the mysterious disappearance of the elderly gentleman and the anonymous communication, the relevancy of both

'No Title', a parody by Bret Harte

other 'Women' in Black, Grey, Mauve and Red.

Parodies

'Tom Tiddler's Ground.' The Committee of Concoction. Cartoon and parodies of *Dickens's *Christmas numbers, including Collins's *sensational style.

'Slow Thoroughfare' by Warles Chickens and Chilky Dollins. *Banter*, 23 Dec. 1867.

'No Thoroughfare; the Book in Eight Acts', *The *Mask*, vol 1, Feb. 1868.

Parodies of Collins's titles in *Punch 7–14 Mar. 1868, republished in *Mokeanna!* by F. C. Burnand, 1873.

'The Moonstone and Moonshine', *The Mask*, vol 1, Aug. 1868.

'No Thoroughfare' by C-s D-s, Boston 1868, Bellamy Brownjohn & Domby.

'No Title' by W-lk-e C-ll-ns, by Bret *Harte, in *Condensed Novels*, Boston 1871.

'The Gwilty Governess and The Downy Doctor; or, Another Good Lady Help Gone Wrong! A New Sensation Drama, in One Prologue and Two Compartments', by G. M. Layton. Theatre Royal, and Opera House, Brighton, 31

Parody of *No Thoroughfare* in *The Mask* of February 1868

July 1876. Directed by John Hollingshead.

'Wilkie Collins', parody of diary narrative in *The Bird o' Freedom*, edited by John Corlett, 13 Aug. 1879.

'The Woman in Tights by Wilkie Collins', by W. E. Rose, *Weekly Dispatch*, 25 Feb. 1883 (300-word parody competition).

  Hamilton, W., *Parodies of the Works of English and American Authors*, vol 6, London 1889.

'Parson's Scruple, The' Short story originally published as 'A New Mind' in *Household Words*, 1 Jan. 1859; reprinted in *The *Queen of Hearts* (1859) as 'Brother Owen's Story of The Parson's Scruple'.
➽ The puritanical Revd Alfred Carling marries privately Mrs Emily Dunbar. Several years later he learns that she is divorced and that he has unwittingly violated his own religious principals. Despairing but still in love, he leaves the country for missionary work in the South Seas only to die shortly after at sea.

A slight story but containing the germ of future novels. The divorce element echoes the experiences of Collins's friend, Frances *Dickinson, and reappears in *The Evil Genius* (1886) where Captain Bennydeck declines to marry Catherine Linley for religious reasons. The confusion between Scottish and English *marriage laws is more fully attacked in *Man and Wife* (1870).

'Passage in the Life of Mr Perugino Potts, A' Humorous short story published in *Bentley's Miscellany*, February 1852. Reprinted for the first time in *Wilkie Collins: The Complete Shorter Fiction*, edited by Julian Thompson, 1995.
➽ Perugino Potts is an incompetent but enthusiastic and permanently optimistic painter, who keeps a journal in which he chronicles his attempts to hit the public taste with pictures in every conceivable style, always without success. He moves to Italy where he suffers further misadventures, fleeing from a Roman thief who wants to kill him and a gargantuan Marchesina who wants to marry him. Satirizes British painting, the Italian police and miracle cures. The character of Potts is a preliminary sketch for Valentine Blyth in *Hide and Seek*.

Payn, James (1830–98). Prolific novelist and regular contributor to *Household

James Payn, from a drawing in 1888

Words. Editor of *Chambers's Journal* and *The *Cornhill*, reader and literary adviser to *Smith, Elder. Friend and admirer of Collins, *Dickens and *Reade. Collins enjoyed the mystery of Payn's *Lost Sir Massingberd* (1864) and advised him on literary matters. Payn, in turn, *dedicated *Gwendoline's Harvest* to Collins in 1870.

  Lehmann (1908).

  Payn, J., *Some Literary Recollections*, London 1884, 242–3.

Pedgift, Augustus Senior In *Armadale* (1866) Allan *Armadale's lawyer at *Thorpe Ambrose, taking over from the old family solicitor, Mr Darch. Pedgift resigns when Allan refuses to take his advice over Lydia *Gwilt. His son, Augustus Junior (Gustus), is also a lawyer and strikes up a friendship with Allan, using detective skills to connect Miss Gwilt with Mrs *Oldershaw.

'Percy and the Prophet' Short story with *supernatural overtones, originally published as the extra Summer number of *All the Year Round* (2 July 1877) under the editorship of Charles Dickens Junior. Reprinted in book form with other stories by *Tauchnitz, 1877; *Harpers, 1877 and 1885; and as 'Mr Percy and the Prophet' in *Little Novels* (1887).
➽ The action takes place in 1817. The mysterious Dr Lagarde, an émigré Frenchman scratching a living in London by fortune-telling, predicts in a hypnotic trance that Percy Linwood and Captain Arthur Bervie will fight a duel over Char-

lotte Bowmore. Everything occurs exactly as foretold but the two men are reconciled and become friends. Percy, now engaged to Charlotte, is involved with her father's ineffectual political intrigues. Bervie warns Percy and Mr Bowmore that warrants have been issued for their arrest but when they refuse to flee the country he tricks them into leaving England by pretending to elope with Charlotte. After they have arrived safely in Paris, Percy and Charlotte are married, while Bervie fulfils his own destiny thirteen years later in finding Dr Lagarde dead in the streets of Paris, shot in the French revolution of 1830.

'Perils of Certain English Prisoners, The: And their Treasure in Women, Children, and Silver and Jewels' Story written in *collaboration with *Dickens, originally published as the extra *Christmas number of *Household Words*, December 1857. Reprinted in *The Lazy Tour of Two Idle Apprentices and Other Stories* (1890).

Dickens wanted a story of heroism by civilians, relevant to the Indian Mutiny. Collins, asked to provide a suitable setting and the outline of the plot, came up with a South American island called Silver-Store where, in 1744, a small colony of English is betrayed to local pirates in search of treasure. The English bravely

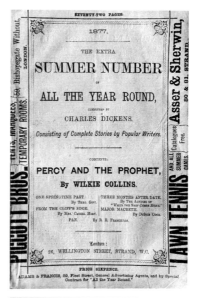

'Percy and the Prophet', the extra Summer number of *All the Year Round* for 1877

escape from imprisonment in a Mayan temple, the pirates are captured at sea and the silver recovered. Collins wrote the whole of the second, longest chapter, 'The Prison in the Woods', which describes the march through the jungle and an escape by raft.

periodicals

'The all influencing periodical literature of the present day.' ('The Lady of Glenwith Grange')

Collins contributed to weekly and monthly periodicals throughout his writing career. His first published work, 'The *Last Stage Coachman', appeared in The *Illuminated Magazine of August 1843. This was followed in the 1850s by *journalism and *short stories, mainly in *Bentley's Miscellany, The *Leader, *Household Words and *All the Year Round. At the peak of his career in the 1860s most of his writing took the form of full-length novels which began as *serializations in the popular literary journals of the time. These included *Harpers' magazines in the USA. Collins gradually returned to writing short stories in the late 1870s. Most of these first appeared in US periodicals with subsequent publication in a wide range of English magazines. Three of Collins's later novels were syndicated in *Tillotson's periodicals and his last work, Blind Love, was being serialized in The *Illustrated London News at the time of his death in 1889.

The majority of Collins's output appeared in the following periodicals (all of which have individual entries).

English journals: All the Year Round; Belgravia; Bentley's Miscellany; Boy's Own Paper; Cassell's Magazine; Cornhill Magazine; English Illustrated Magazine; Fraser's Magazine; The Graphic; Household Words; Illuminated Magazine; Illustrated London News; The Leader; Longmans Magazine; Pall Mall Gazette; Temple Bar; Universal Review; The World.

North American journals: Atlantic Monthly; Canadian Monthly; Every Saturday; Frank Leslie's Illustrated Newspaper; Harper's Bazar; Harper's New Monthly; Harper's Weekly; International Review; Leisure Hour Library; Spirit of the Times; Youth's Companion.

Perugini, Kate See DICKENS, KATHERINE.

Peterson, T. B. & Brothers Philadel-

phia publishers, issuing various unauthorized editions of Collins's works. They began in 1855 with *Sister Rose, published in paper wrappers and mis-attributed to Dickens. For Basil, Peterson preferred the title The *Crossed Path [1860], more expensively produced in cloth.

*Harpers had co-operated with Peterson's in publishing Dickens, but in 1873 accused them of a direct violation of trade courtesy for reprinting Mad Monkton and Other Stories and Miss or Mrs? They also noted an assurance from Collins that 'nothing which Messrs. Peterson publish under his name was authorized by him'. Harper's nevertheless offered $100 for Peterson's plates for The Dead Secret and Basil which they intended to melt. Peterson's had also issued several other stories including 'The Ghost in the Cupboard Room' [1861], Hide and Seek (1862), After Dark [1863], and Rambles Beyond Railways as Sights-A-Foot [1871].

Brussel (1935), 46.
Harper (1912), 347–8.

photographers Collins regarded photography with cynicism, describing it to *Sarony and Frank *Archer and in The Moonstone as 'Justice without mercy' (an expression he admitted borrowing from George Richmond, the portrait painter). Collins often regarded photographic sittings as a necessary interruption to his work but nevertheless had carte de visite portraits made by several distinguished

Photograph of Collins by John and Charles Watkins

photographers during his career:

Cundall, Downes & Co of New Bond Street. Produced a portrait frontispiece for the one-volume *Sampson Low edition of The Woman in White (1861–5).

Herbert Watkins of Regent Street in 1864. Other subjects included *Dickens and *Millais.

John & Charles Watkins of Parliament Street. Other subjects included Queen Victoria, Lady Millais and E. M. *Ward.

Elliott & Fry of Baker Street in 1871. Other subjects included John *Linnell and Holman Hunt's wife.

Lock and Whitfield. Photographed Collins in 1881 for the fifth series of Men of Mark.

In America, Collins sat for Sarony of Broadway, New York, and Warren of Washington Street, Boston.

Pigott, Edward Frederick Smyth (1824–95). Proprietor and editor of the socialist paper The *Leader. A fellow student at Lincoln's Inn, Pigott was a lifelong friend of Collins and dedicatee of The Dead Secret (1857). The two were regular *sailing companions and their trip to the Scilly Isles in September 1855 was described in 'The *Cruise of the Tomtit' where they featured as Mr Jollins and Mr Migott. They enjoyed later trips to Cherbourg in 1856, from Broadstairs with Henry *Bullar in 1862, and from Great Yarmouth with Charles *Ward in 1864. Collins was accompanied by Pigott on his trip to *Italy in October 1866. Pigott also had an interest in the theatre, playing Captain Ebsworth in The Frozen Deep (1857). He became the Examiner of Plays in the Lord Chamberlain's Office in 1874.

Pinero, Sir Arthur Wing (1855–1934). Actor and author of many plays including The Second Mrs Tanqueray (1893) and The Magistrate (1885). His first London role was Mr Darch in *Miss Gwilt, the dramatic version of Armadale which opened at the *Globe Theatre on 15 August 1876. Pinero had earlier played the same part at the Alexandra Theatre *Liverpool and later recalled Collins's kindness towards him during rehearsals. 'His goodness to me, so flattering from an eminent man to a mere youth, was ever in my mind, and to this day I feel grateful to him.' Pinero also played Shrowl in the 1877 stage version of The Dead Secret. He was standing with Collins at the back of the *Adelphi dress

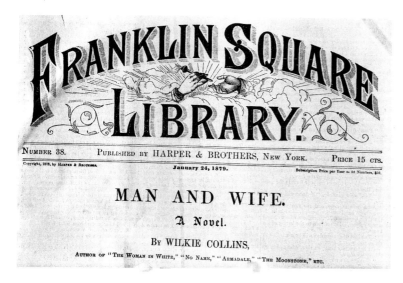

Man and Wife published in the Franklin Square Library, a cheap edition put out by Harpers to compete with the pirates

circle during the first performance of the ill-fated *Rank and Riches* on 9 June 1883.
de la Mare (1932), 68 note 1.

piracy, literary In the second half of the nineteenth century it was accepted practice in *America, as well as Europe, for publishers to reprint large editions of foreign authors without permission or payment.

Collins was only one of many English authors plagued by this practice which in the USA was more or less encouraged by the prevailing copyright legislation. There were several legitimate objections to pirates. Not only did they make no copyright payments, competing on unfair terms with existing publishers; they printed unrevised texts over which the author had no control, and they revived early works or juvenilia that authors did not wish resurrected. There was certainly no protection to those 'not a citizen of the United States'. The lack of international *copyright, the high price of English books and the absence of *circulating libraries provided the ideal environment in which American pirates could flourish.

The success of pirated books depended on cheap production and volume sales at low price by mail order. Titles were usually produced on subscription in paper wrappers, as part of a dated and numbered series, so qualifying for the cheapest possible postal rates. Even an established and always legitimate firm such as *Harpers felt threatened. In 1878, they

set up their Franklin Square Library to compete and felt forced to produce cheap books at a loss.

Between the 1860s and 1880s, numerous firms produced unauthorized editions at 10c instead of the ususal $1.50, and 20c instead of $4.00. Publishers included the *Seaside, *Lovell's, *Leisure Hour, Fireside and Dime Libraries in New York; Donnelley's Lakeside Library in Chicago; and *Peterson in Philadelphia. Typical annual subscription rates were $30 for Lovell's and $50 for the Seaside Library. It was estimated that some five hundred novels a year were required to satisfy the various series, with an inevitable deterioration in quality by the 1880s.

There was particularly fierce competition among the US publishers for English authors and they would resort to almost any lengths to obtain texts. They bribed compositors at London printers to obtain early proofs; one of Collins's serials in *Harper's Weekly* was copied part by part in a Philadelphia paper; and shorthand writers transcribed plays at first-night performances. Printers were even employed to set up copy on board ships making the transatlantic crossing.

Combating piracy significantly influenced the way legitimate books were produced in the USA and explains why many English titles were first published in America. Conscientious authors sent sheets in advance to give their authorized publishers a head start. They would often stipulate the day of publication to be the

same as that in England, but this request was often ignored.

Collins was particularly vociferous in his opposition to piracy and bluntly called it literary theft. His views were set out in *Considerations on the Copyright Question Addressed to an American Friend* (1880). He was always at pains to send Harper's proof sheets at the earliest possible date. With the publication of 'I Say No' (1884), Collins suggested that he should send them the concluding parts in manuscript form and the book was therefore published three months ahead of the English edition. *The Woman in White* and *Armadale* are both highly illustrated. The illustrations, however, stop short two or three chapters before the end because of the speed required to publish ahead of the opposition.

Collins had many similar difficulties with continental publishers. He frequently requested *Chatto & Windus to provide multiple copies of advance proof sheets for authorized translation into various European languages. In the case of the *Belinfante Brothers in Holland, Collins considered he had won a major victory when they agreed to pay, albeit a trifling sum, for *Man and Wife*.
Brussel (1935) introduction by G. Pollard, 3–31.

plays Drama was always one of Collins's main interests, an enthusiasm shared with *Dickens and *Reade. He participated in *amateur theatricals from the 1840s and was an eager theatre-goer both in London and when travelling abroad. He regarded fiction and drama as inextricably linked, as he explained early in his career in the introduction to *Basil* (1852)

Believing that the Novel and the Play are twin-sisters in the family of Fiction; that the one is a drama narrated, as the other is a drama acted; and that all the strong and deep emotions which the Play-writer is privileged to excite, the Novel-writer is privileged to excite also, I have not thought it either politic or necessary, while adhering to realities, to adhere to common-place, everyday realities.

This belief is manifested in the dramatic structure of many of Collins's novels. Some such as *No Name* (1862) and *The Black Robe* (1881) are laid out in 'Scenes'.

The New Magdalen (1873) was written simultaneously as a book and a play: the descriptions in the book of Lady Roy's house and the movement of characters through the various rooms apply equally well as stage directions. *The Evil Genius* (1886) was also written simultaneously as novel and play, though it was never produced on the stage. *Man and Wife* (1870) was conceived as a play but appeared first in book form, while the novel *Jezebel's Daughter* (1880) took its origin from the play *The Red Vial* (1858).

Despite his enthusiasm, Collins was never wholly successful as a dramatist and for some plays (e.g. *No Name*) he had difficulty in securing a theatre. As a playwright he is now best remembered for *The Frozen Deep* (1857) written for Dickens's amateur company. In the professional theatre, his greatest successes were *The New Magdalen*, *Man and Wife* and *No Thoroughfare*. Other plays such as *The Red Vial* and *Rank and Riches* were outright failures.

For further details of Collins's original plays and dramatic adaptations see the following separate entries:

'Plot in Private Life, A' Short story originally published as 'A Marriage Tragedy' in *Harper's New Monthly Magazine*, Feb. 1858. Reprinted in *The *Queen of Hearts* (1859) as 'Brother Griffith's Story of A Plot in Private Life'. Also the title for

the *Tauchnitz edition containing five stories from *The Queen of Hearts*.

➥ William, the narrator and faithful servant to rich widow Mrs Norcross, tells the story of her unhappy second marriage to James Smith. A detective lawyer's clerk, Mr Dark, both confirms Smith's bigamous remarriage and, following his disappearance, proves Mrs Norcross and William innocent of murder. Dark also recovers jewellery stolen by the maidservant and establishes her guilt. William's amiable relationship with the experienced detective foreshadows that between *Betteredge and *Cuff in *The Moonstone* (1868).

Poe, Edgar Allan (1809–49). American short-story writer and poet, celebrated for his *Tales of Mystery and Imagination*. Poe is often cited as an influence on Collins who possessed the Baudelaire edition in his library. There are obvious similarities between 'A *Stolen Letter' and 'The Purloined Letter'. 'A *Terribly Strange Bed' and 'The Pit and the Pendulum' both have the instrument of death descending from the ceiling. The cypher in *Jezebel's Daughter*, as in 'The Gold-Bug', is decoded according to letter frequency while 'William Wilson' and 'A Tale of the Ragged Mountains' both anticipate Collins's favourite theme of *identity. Poe's tales tend to rely on pure horror whereas Collins is prepared to introduce a *supernatural element.

Poe can claim priority in the field of *detective fiction, although he wrote only short stories such as 'Murders in the Rue Morgue'. Collins, in addition to his

short pieces, wrote the full-length works for which he is best known. Collins's detectives are unique to a particular story whereas Poe's Dupin is used three times. Both writers, however, constructed plots in which the mystery is solved by logical means and which conform to the modern ideal of 'fair play'.

'Poetry Did It, The: An Event in the Life of Major Evergreen' Humorous short story published in *The *Spirit of the Times*, 26 Dec. 1885, and in *The *English Illustrated Magazine*, Jan. 1886. Reprinted for the first time in *Wilkie Collins: The Complete Shorter Fiction*, edited by Julian Thompson, 1995.

Sir John Bosworth and young Cyril Corydon compete for the hand of Major Evergreen's niece, Mabel. She eventually chooses Cyril after finding Sir John has plagiarized one of the Major's inveterately bad poems.

Poor Miss Finch: A Novel

'You *will* persist in thinking that my happiness depends on my sight.'

Published in 1872 and dedicated to Mrs Elliot (Frances *Dickinson). Collins returns to the theme of 'bodily infirmity' with the story of a young girl's temporary recovery of sight 'exhibiting blindness as it really is'. Collins did a considerable amount of research into recovered sight for the book and the descriptions of Lucilla's 'learning to see' ring remarkably true. They also anticipate several later clinical studies. Initial elation is frustrated by the difficulties of experiencing the real world through sight without the aid of

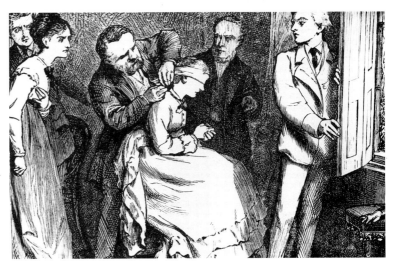

Ilustration by Hughes to the one-volume Chatto & Windus edition of *Poor Miss Finch*

touch. Depression follows, ending in rejection of the newly acquired sense. More unlikely are the clinical premisses for Lucilla's infant cataracts and the extent to which she recovers lost vision after twenty years, without even the need for spectacles to write her journal. The reading public, however, were convinced and Collins after several requests for the address of the German oculist, Herr Grosse, was obliged to add a note to the second edition that he had 'no (individual) living prototype' and was 'a caricature instead of a character'. In order to create the hero's 'blue' appearance, horrifying to Lucilla after she regains her sight, Collins was forced to rely on a rare and already outmoded type of treatment for epilepsy.

Other details of the novel seem genuinely autobiographical. Collins stayed in Lewes during March 1870; little Jicks and Mrs Finch's latest child were the same age as Collins's daughters, Marian and Harriet *Dawson.

➥ Madame Pratolungo, the narrator, is a Frenchwoman, widow of a South American republican. She takes the position of companion to Lucilla Finch who is now 21 and has been blind with cataracts since she was a year old. Lucilla lives in a wing of her father's house in the Sussex village of Dimchurch, near Lewes. Finch, a pompous clergyman, fell out with his first wife's family, the Batchfords. However, he has fourteen children from his second marriage and, perpetually short of money, is delighted to accept an over-generous allowance from Lucilla's personal inheritance.

Lucilla falls in love with their close neighbour, the reclusive Oscar Dubourg, whose main interest is making objects from precious metals in his work-room. Oscar is totally devoted to his identical twin brother, Nugent, who narrowly saved him from hanging by discovering crucial evidence proving him innocent of a murder.

Oscar is savagely attacked and robbed of his gold and silver plate, and sends a message for help written in blood on the frock of Lucilla's wandering three-year-old half-sister, Selina (called Jicks). Oscar appears to recover from a blow to the head but begins to suffer from increasingly bad epilepsy. He is offered a cure: prolonged treatment with silver nitrate which has the side-effect of permanently

staining the skin dark blue, almost black. The marriage is postponed and, against the advice of Madame Pratolungo, Oscar misleads Lucilla into thinking that it is Nugent who has been undergoing the treatment.

Nugent, identical to Oscar except for his skin colour, has returned from America where he squandered his half of the family fortune. The only way Lucilla can tell the brothers apart is by her sense of touch which produces a 'tingle' with Oscar. Knowing of Lucilla's blindness, Nugent brings with him the eccentric and exuberant Herr Grosse, a noted German oculist who examines Lucilla in collaboration with the staid English doctor Mr Sebright. Their opinions differ but Lucilla, eager to take any chance of actually seeing her beloved Oscar, follows the advice of Grosse and has an operation.

Nugent is also in love with Lucilla and knowing her peculiar prejudice against dark colours is happy to perpetuate the confusion of identity. When the bandages are removed he contrives to be the first person seen by Lucilla and as intended is mistaken for his brother. The real Oscar, an object of pity and horror, leaves Dimchurch to go abroad, prepared to sacrifice his own happiness for that of Lucilla and the brother who saved his life. Grosse reluctantly consents to the deception because the shock of the truth may hinder his patient's recovery. He recommends Lucilla to take the air at Ramsgate and in the absence of Madame Pratolungo, in France to nurse her incorrigibly gallant old father, Lucilla is accompanied by her aunt, Miss Batchford.

Nugent writes to Lucilla pretending to be Oscar and then impersonates him at Ramsgate. He tries to press Lucilla into an immediate marriage before either Finch or Madame Pratolungo can uncover the deception. Lucilla's old sense of touch tells her that something is wrong and the stress causes her sight to deteriorate. Nugent, in desperation, tries to convince her that Madame Pratolungo is her enemy. He tricks Lucilla into leaving for London where she stays with his married relative while a marriage licence is obtained in the name of Oscar.

Madame Pratolungo has traced Oscar and they return to England to prevent the fraudulent marriage. Lucilla has once more lost her sight and immediately recognizes her true love by touch. Nugent

repents and gives Oscar the marriage licence permitting the wedding two days later. Nugent, asking them to name their future son after him, joins an unsuccessful Arctic expedition and is eventually found frozen to death clutching a lock of Lucilla's hair.

Serialization. *Harper's Weekly*, 2 Sept. 1871–24 Feb. 1872; *Cassell's Magazine*, 2 Sept. 1871–24 Feb. 1872.

Book publication

1st edn. 3 vols, Richard *Bentley, London 1872. Brown cloth, covers blocked in black, spines lettered in black, cream endpapers. No half-titles. Published 26 Jan. 1872. Copies in bright blue cloth, spines lettered in gilt with no publisher's imprint are of later issue.

Vol I (xii) + 316 pp. Publisher's advertisements occupy p (315).

Vol II iv + 316 pp.

Vol III iv + 320 pp.

1-vol edns. Bentley 1873 (with additional 'note to this edition'); *Chatto & Windus 1875–1913 (with 12 illustrations, by G. *du Maurier and E. Hughes); Sutton, Stroud 1994; World's Classics 1995 (critical edition, edited by C. Peters).

1st US edn. Harper, New York 1872.

Translations. Russian, St Petersburg 1873, 1875; German, Leipzig 1874; French, Paris 1876.

Cheselden, W., *Philosophical Transactions of the Royal Society*, 25, London 1728.

Gregory, R. L. and Wallace, J. G., 'Recovery from Early Blindness: A Case Study', *Exp Psychol Soc*, 2, London 1963.

Sacks, O., 'To See and not See', in *An Anthropologist on Mars*, New York and London 1995.

von Senden, M., *Space and Sight*, London 1960.

Watson, T., *Lectures on the Principles and Practice of Physic*, 4th edn, London 1857.

Pre-Raphaelite Brotherhood

Founded in 1848 by a group of anti-establishment English artists which included D. G. Rossetti, J. E. *Millais and Holman *Hunt, and soon expanded to include T. Woolner and W. M. Rossetti. Many of them were Collins's close friends and he discussed their work in 'The Exhibition of the Royal Academy' for *Bentley's Miscellany* (June 1851). Charles *Collins enthusiastically associated with the group but was never admitted to full membership.

The distinctive Pre-Raphaelite style emphasized stylized figures in allegorical situations represented in rich voluptuous colours. Literary allusions and references often supplemented their natural approach which united the sensual with the spiritual.

Prince of Wales Theatre Run by the *Bancrofts until they moved to the Haymarket Theatre in 1880; staged *Man and Wife* in May 1873. Originally the slightly disreputable Queen's Theatre, Tottenham Street. To fulfil her ambition to play comedy, Mrs Bancroft (as Marie Wilton) had taken over the theatre, borrowed £1,000 for renovations in 1865 and obtained permission to rename it.

publishers Collins used several publishers throughout his career. Once established as a writer, his relations were a mixture of hard bargaining and cordiality. Collins was a tough negotiator paying careful attention to details in his contracts. He was prepared to enforce their conditions and was direct in asking for payment if not received by the due date. When necessary, however, he could be both fair and generous. For reprints, he favoured *Sampson Low out of loyalty over *Hurst & Blackett and he offered *Bentley a refund when the lending libraries undermined the commercial viability of *Poor Miss Finch*. Collins remained on friendly terms with most of his publishers, being entertained by George Bentley, Andrew *Chatto and Fletcher *Harper.

Collins's first book, *Memoirs of the Life of William Collins, Esq., R.A.* (1848), was produced by *Longman on a commission basis. He then turned to Richard Bentley who published various short pieces in his *Miscellany* and five books, *Antonina* (1850), *Rambles Beyond Railways* (1851), *Mr Wray's Cash-Box* (1852), *Basil* (1852) and *Hide and Seek* (1854). During the late 1850s Collins was trying to find the right publishing niche while the publishers began to appreciate his future potential. He used *Smith, Elder for *After Dark* (1856), *Bradbury & Evans for *The Dead Secret* (1857) and Hurst & Blackett for *The Queen of Hearts* (1859).

The Woman in White (1860), *No Name* (1862) and *My Miscellanies* (1863) went to Sampson Low who also produced a collected edition up to 1865. Smith, Elder then outbid all others for *Armadale* (1866) as well as taking over Collins's cheap reprints until the mid-1870s. Collins used

PUNCH'S FANCY PORTRAITS.—No. 66.

WILKIE COLLINS,

AS THE MAN IN WHITE DOING INK-AND-PENANCE FOR HAVING WRITTEN THE *BLACK ROBE*.

*Tinsley for *The Moonstone* (1868) and F. S. *Ellis for *Man and Wife* (1870) before returning to Bentley. They published *Poor Miss Finch* (1872), *Miss or Mrs?* (1873), *The New Magdalen* (1873) and *The Frozen Deep* (1874). From *The Law and the Lady* (1875) onwards, *Chatto & Windus became Collins's main publishers for the rest of his life. They issued all his remaining titles except *A Rogue's Life* (Bentley, 1879), *The Guilty River* (*Arrowsmith, 1886) and *The Lazy Tour of Two Idle Apprentices* (*Chapman & Hall, 1890). Chatto & Win-

Cartoon in *Punch* of 14 January 1882 with Collins 'As the Man in White doing Ink-and-Penance for having written the *Black Robe*'

dus also took over most of Collins's copyrights and published their own cheap reprints in various formats.

In the USA, Harpers were Collins's main publisher for many years. There were temporary difficulties over *copyright between 1878 and 1884 and he switched his allegiance to other publishers such as *Appleton and Leslie. Collins

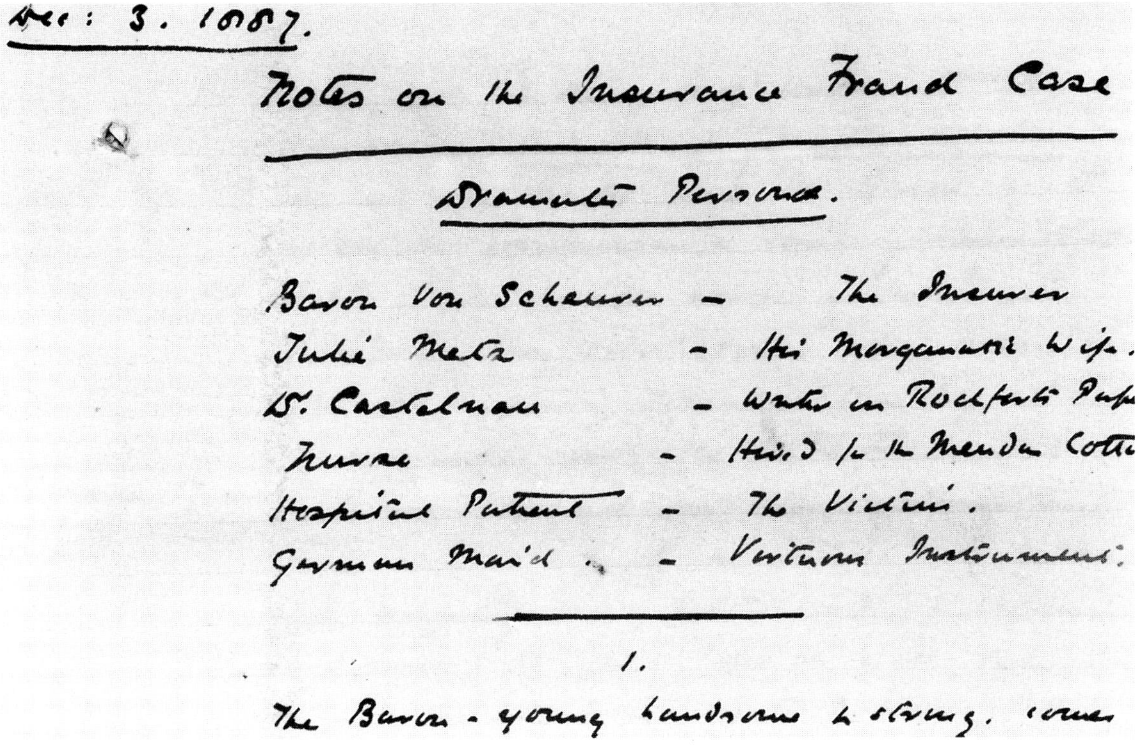

Dec: 3. 1887.

Notes on the Insurance Fraud Case

Dramatis Personæ.

Baron Von Scheurer — The Insurer
Julie Metz — His Morganatic Wife.
Dr. Castelnau — Writer in Rochfort Papers
Nurse — Hired for the Meudon Cottage
Hospital Patient — The Victim.
German Maid — Virtuous Instrument.

1.

The Baron - young handsome & strong, comes

Notes prepared for Collins by Horace Pym about the Von Scheurer fraud

was also published against his wishes by numerous American *pirates such as the Lakeside, *Lovell's and *Seaside Libraries. In Canada, he used *Hunter, Rose of Toronto.

On the Continent, *Tauchnitz published English-language editions throughout Collins's career. There were also pirated *translations in Europe although *Hachette were Collins's authorized publishers in France as ultimately were the *Belinfante Brothers in Holland.

See also JOURNALISM, PERIODICALS, SERIALIZATION.

Punch, or The London Charivari
Illustrated humorous weekly, jointly founded and edited by Mark *Lemon and Joseph Stirling Coyne. Staff included *Burnand, *du Maurier, *Jerrold, Leech, Tenniel and *Thackeray. Collins was mentioned on three occasions:

6 April 1861. Cartoon by John Leech: AWFUL APPARITION! Mrs T. (To Mr T., who has been reading the popular novel). "Pray, Mr Tomkins, are you Never coming Up-stairs? How much longer are you going to Sit up with that 'Woman in White?' "

7–14 March 1868. Parodies by F. C. Burnand of, among others, Collins's titles 'by the Sensation Novel Company (Limited)' (e.g. 'The Woman with No Name').

14 January 1882. Punch's Fancy Portraits—no. 66. Wilkie Collins as 'The Man in White doing Ink-and-Penance for having written *The Black Robe*', drawn by Linley Sambourne.

Pym, Horatio Noble (Horace)
(1844–96). Friend of Collins, the *Lehmanns and Georgina *Hogarth. Provided details of the *Von Scheurer insurance fraud for the plot of *Blind Love*. Owner, after Wilkie Collins's death, of the Collins family portraits painted by *William Collins, John *Linnell and Andrew *Geddes. In his *A Tour Round My Book-Shelves* (1891), Pym records correspondence by Collins and Dickens.

Sotheby's, *The Library of Horace N. Pym*, 23 Apr. 1996.

Q

Queen of Hearts, The Collection of ten short stories set within the connecting narrative of 'The Queen of Hearts'. Dedicated to Émile *Forgues. 'The Queen of Hearts' is the school nickname of Jessie Yelverton who arranges to stay for six weeks with her elderly guardian, Griffith, a retired lawyer. Griffith lives with his two brothers, Owen the clergyman and Morgan the doctor, in an isolated house in south Wales. Griffith's son, George, is in love with Jessie and the three brothers set out to delay her departure for ten days so that George can propose on his return from the Crimean war. In a kind of Arabian Nights story-telling, the three brothers draw on their professional experiences to entertain their young guest with a different story each evening:

Brother Owen's Story of The *Black Cottage.

Brother Griffith's Story of The *Family Secret.

Brother Morgan's Story of The *Dream Woman.

Brother Griffith's Story of *Mad Monkton.

Brother Morgan's Story of The *Dead Hand.

Brother Griffith's Story of The *Biter Bit.

Brother Owen's Story of The *Parson's Scruple.

Brother Griffith's Story of A *Plot in Private Life.

A PLOT IN PRIVATE LIFE

AND OTHER TALES,

BY

WILKIE COLLINS,

AUTHOR OF "AFTER DARK," "HIDE AND SEEK," &c.

COPYRIGHT EDITION.

LEIPZIG

BERNHARD TAUCHNITZ

1859.

The Right of Translation is reserved.

A Plot in Private Life, the 1859 Tauchnitz edition of five stories from *The Queen of Hearts*

Brother Morgan's Story of *Fauntleroy.

Brother Owen's Story of *Anne Rodway.

Serialization. **See individual stories.**

Book publication

1st edn. 3 vols, *Hurst & Blackett, London 1859. Grey-green cloth, covers blocked in blind, spines lettered in gilt, pale yellow endpapers. No half-titles. Published in Oct. 1859.

Vol I (vi) [paged (iv)] + 314 pp. 16 pp publisher's catalogue, undated, bound in at end.

Vol II (ii) + 360 pp.

Vol III (ii) + 308 pp.

1-vol edns. *Sampson Low 1862 (with a frontispiece by J. *Gilbert); *Smith, Elder 1865–74; *Chatto & Windus 1875–1911 (with 8 illustrations by A. Concanen).

1st US edn. *Harper, New York 1859.

Quilter, Harry (1851–1907). Art critic, journalist and practising artist. Wrote for *The Spectator* and *The Times* and maintained a running quarrel with Whistler. Quilter was a great admirer of Collins and wrote 'A Living Story-teller' for the *Contemporary Review* of April 1888. He described Collins as the author who 'has told stories better than they have ever been told in the world before'.

Quilter started the *Universal Review in 1888 and persuaded Collins to contribute one of his rare autobiographical pieces. 'Reminiscences of a Story Teller' appeared in the second number of June 1888. The issue for October 1889 carried Quilter's sympathetic *obituary of Collins, 'In Memoriam Amici' (reprinted in Quilter's *Preferences in Art, Life, and Literature*, London 1892). Quilter also formed a committee that attempted to arrange a suitable public *memorial to Collins.

radio adaptations (BBC)

'A Terribly Strange Bed' (Mar. 1946); schools programme.

Armadale (from Apr. 1948); sixteen-part adaptation.

No Name (15 June–29 Aug. 1952); twelve-part adaptation by Howard Agg, produced by David H. Godfrey.

Poor Miss Finch (1952); Woman's Hour.

A Book at Bedtime: 'The Dream Woman' (July 1954); 'Mr Lepel and the Housekeeper' (19–23 July 1954); 'Miss Bertha and the Yankee' (26–30 July 1954).

'Blow Up with the Brig!' (Sept. 1957); schools programme.

The Dead Secret (1957); Woman's Hour.

The Dead Secret (May 1977); Storytime.

A Rogue's Life (July 1979); Storytime.

The Moonstone (14 Oct.–18 Nov. 1979); six-part adaptation by Brian Gear, produced by Brian Miller. (Other adaptations from the mid-1940s.)

'Mrs Zant and the Ghost' (Aug. 1982).

Basil (1983).

Most other radio productions took place during 1989, the centenary of Collins's death.

No Name (22 Sept. 1989–27 Oct. 1989, repeated 1995); six-part adaptation by Ray Jenkins with Sophie Thompson as Magdalen Vanstone, Jack May as Captain Wragge and Eleanor Bron as Mrs Lecount.

Short stories, adapted by Michael Bakewell:

'The Dream Woman'(3 Nov. 1989), read by David Suchet.

'The Biter Bit' (10 Nov. 1989), read by John Rowe.

'A Terribly Strange Bed' (17 Nov. 1989), read by Paul Daneman.

'The Stolen Letter' (24 Nov. 1989), read by Garard Green.

'The Dead Hand' (1 Dec. 1989), read by Peter Marinker.

Rambles Beyond Railways: Or Notes in Cornwall Taken a-foot

'An unexplored region offered to the curiosity of the tourist.'

Illustrated travel book narrating Collins's 1850 walking tour of *Cornwall with his artist friend, Henry *Brandling. Published in 1851 and dedicated to the Duke of Northumberland. In those days 'even the railway stops short at Plymouth' and the travellers had to sail to their first destination at St Germains.

Collins found the locals hospitable, though inquisitive, and *Rambles* became an amiable mixture of travelogue, vivid descriptive writing, Cornish history and legend, and social observation. The route of 234 miles took them along the south

RAMBLES BEYOND RAILWAYS;

OR,

Notes in Cornwall taken A-foot.

BY WILKIE COLLINS,

AUTHOR OF

"ANTONINA," "THE WOMAN IN WHITE," ETC.

The Land's End, Cornwall.

NEW EDITION.

LONDON:

RICHARD BENTLEY: NEW BURLINGTON STREET.

Publisher in Ordinary to Her Majesty.

1861.

Title-page to Bentley's new edition of *Rambles Beyond Railways* in 1861

Ramsgate from the sea, showing the crescent which Collins visited

coast to the Lizard and Penzance, returning through northern Cornwall to Tintagel and Launceston. An appendix gives precise details of the itinerary, the miles walked and the inns at which they stayed. Some of these, such as the Ship at Looe, still exist.

Collins's notebook was filled with stories about the wreckers; the plague of rats in Looe, solved by eating the rodents cooked with onions; royalist supporters of Charles I at St Michael's Mount; the destruction and re-assembly of the Loggan stone; and the graves of fishermen either drowned or frozen to death. The legend of a supernatural storm sinking a ship in an instant re-appears in '*Mad Monkton' (1855). At Kynance Cove, Collins was exhilarated by the Devil's Throat which inspired the description of Mannion's death in *Basil (1852). Inland, he saw the prehistoric remains known as the Cheese-Wring and the Hurlers. A highlight of the book is a long description of a visit to the Botallack copper mine, where the workings extended beneath the sea and the ghostly sound of the surf could be heard as 'a long, low, mysterious moaning'.

Collins also collected numerous statistics. He noted that the population was 341,269 at the last census, that nearly 5 per cent of those in the Penzance area emigrated to Australia or New Zealand in 1849, and that St Ives exported an average of 22,000 hogsheads of pilchards, each containing up to 3,000 fish.

Rambles sold well and a second edition was published the following year. Collins added an 'advertisement', noting 'Since this work first appeared, the all-conquering Railway has invaded Cornwall; and the title of my book has become a misnomer already.'

Serialization. Chapters 8 and 11 were published as 'The Pilchard Fishery on the Coast of Cornwall' and 'A Visit to a Copper-Mine' in *Harper's New Monthly Magazine,* Apr. 1851.

Book publication

1st edn. 1 vol, Richard *Bentley, London 1851. Beige cloth, covers blocked in blind, spine lettered in gilt, yellow endpapers printed with publisher's advertisements. No half-title. Twelve full-page tinted lithographs by Henry Brandling, printed separately. Published 30 Jan. 1851.

(viii) + 304 pp.

2nd edn. published 9 Jan. 1852. As the first except for minor differences in blocking of covers, cream endpapers and darker illustrations.

New edn. 1861 and 1863. Now dedicated to Henry C. Brandling. Omits two chapters and has only two black-and-white illustrations. Also contains 'The *Cruise of the Tomtit'. Modern reprints 1948; 1982, Anthony Mott, London, The Cornish Library

Series, no. 5.

US edn. (as *Sights-A-Foot*) Peterson, Philadelphia [1871].

Ramsgate Seaside resort in Kent which Collins regularly visited with Caroline *Graves from the early 1870s. Both Collins and his doctor, Frank *Beard, were convinced that the sea breezes were good for his health and gave relief from the oppressive London heat in summer. He reputedly joined the local yacht club with Edward *Pigott who confided to Beard he thought Collins's destiny was to live in Ramsgate. As a child, Wilkie had first stayed there with his father and family in 1833 and Ramsgate became the setting for scenes in later works including *Poor Miss Finch* (1872), *The Law and the Lady* (1875) and *The Fallen Leaves* (1879).

Collins routinely stayed at 14 Nelson Crescent under the care of landlady Rebecca Shrive. When his morganatic family was old enough, he was joined by Martha *Rudd and his children. To observe the proprieties, they stayed in the equally impressive terrace at 27 Wellington Crescent where Collins discreetly visited them as Mr William *Dawson.

Blaker, C., *Strange Doings at the Seaside or: Wilkie Collins (1824–1889) and Ramsgate. Ramsgate Remembered,* 13 (1997).

New Year card sent by Collins to Wybert Reeve in December 1883

Rank and Riches: A Play in Four Acts and Five Tableaux Unsuccessful

play begun in 1880 and produced by Edgar Bruce at the *Adelphi Theatre, 9 June 1883. The strong cast was led by George Alexander and Alice Lingood, supported by George Anson playing an Italian 'bird-doctor' and Charles Hawtrey. The plot was supremely complicated with the Lady Calista in love with a lawyer's clerk accused of embezzlement, a consumptive secretary of a Communist club, and peers of the realm revealed as illegitimate offspring of a bigamous marriage. It proved too much for the audience and, despite a direct appeal from Anson, was hooted off the stage. Dutton *Cook deftly described how the play 'by no means contented the audience' and 'on such occasions there are always wilder spirits present who stay to ridicule what they came to enjoy'. The play was never published but the manuscript exists as well as that of an earlier draft headed ' "the Bird-Doctor" ... being a re-written version of "Lady Calista" '.

'Rank and Riches' in The *World, 13 June 1883, 9.
de la Mare (1932), 69, note.
IELM

Reade, Charles (1814–84). Dramatist, novelist and journalist, author of The

Cloister and the Hearth. Friend of Collins, *Dickens, *Archer and the *Lehmanns. Reade lived with actress Laura Seymour as his housekeeper from 1854 till her death in 1879. Apart from this unofficial liaison, and an illegitimate son (known as his nephew) from an earlier relationship, Reade had much else in common with Collins. He studied law, loved the theatre, carried out careful research for his plots, and wrote *sensation novels. These were frequently attacked for immorality although their *didactic nature influenced Collins's later writing. Collins advised Reade on publication with *Harpers and *Hunter, Rose and helped to arrange French translations by *Forgues. Both writers shared strong opinions on international *copyright although Reade was considered a plagiarist, borrowing plots from other novelists for several of his stage plays.

At his last meeting with James *Payn, Reade described Collins as a great artist. He regarded *The Woman in White* as a great book but was critical of *No Name*. *The Frozen Deep* he considered poorly acted with too much narrative although original and interesting with a great and pathetic closing scene. Collins, in turn, dedicated *The Two Destinies* (1876) to Reade as 'my old friend and brother in the art' and after his death wrote 'We have lately lost one of the "last of the Romans"—my dear old friend Charles Reade.'

Marston, E., *After Work*, London 1904, 97.
Reade, C. L. and Reade, C. *Charles Reade: A Memoir* (2 vols), London 1887.

reading tour See AMERICA.

Recueil des causes célèbres (2nd edn, 26 vols, Paris 1808).

'A book of trials published in the French language.' (*The Guilty River*)
Records of French legal cases by Maurice Méjan. Purchased, along with Richer's *Causes célèbres et intéressantes*, when Collins was in *Paris in 1856. He described them to Wybert *Reeve as 'a sort of French *Newgate Calendar* and as the source of some of his best plots. The eighteenth-century Douhault case notably provided the idea for *The Woman in White*.

Hyder, C. K., 'Wilkie Collins and *The Woman in White*, PMLA 54 March (1939), 297–303. Douhault case summarized; sub-

stantially quoted by Robinson (1951), 137–8.
Reeve (1906).

Red Vial, The: A Drama in Three Acts Unpublished play produced at the

Royal *Olympic Theatre from 11 October 1858; starred Frederick *Robson as Hans Grimm, the lunatic cured by kindness, and Mrs Stirling as Madame Bergmann. Described as 'the most brilliant failure of the day'. The plot was later adapted as the basis for *Jezebel's Daughter* (1880).

Ellis (1931), 24.
Pascoe, C. E., *The Dramatic List: Actors and Actresses of the British Stage*, London 1879.

Reeve, Wybert (1831–1906). Actor and friend of Collins. He originally played

Walter *Hartright in *The Woman in White* from its opening on 9 October 1871. When George *Vining fell ill, Reeve took over the role of *Fosco from 11 January 1872 and subsequently took the production on tour in England for over a year. He joined Collins on his reading tour of North *America and played Fosco at the Broadway Theatre, New York. During an eight-year period, Reeve played the role over 1,500 times in England, Canada and the USA.

Reeve also dramatized works for the stage including, at Collins's request, *No Name*. Although never staged in England, it was performed in both New York and, with the new title *Great Temptation*, in Melbourne during 1879. Reeve spent much of his theatrical life touring in the USA and *Australia. In December 1883, Collins sent him a New Year card of English oaks adding the note 'a little bit of English landscape, my Dear Reeve, to remind you of this old country and this old friend'.

Reeve (1906) has several anecdotes concerning Collins. These include how Reeve had arranged to dine with Wilkie and be his guest at a performance of *Man and Wife* on 9 April 1873, the night that Charles *Collins died; Wilkie's opinion of *Forster's *Life of Dickens*; and the reading tour of America.

Régnier de la Brièrre, François Joseph Philocles (1807–85). Lead-

ing French actor comedian of the Théatre Français. Dedicatee of *The Law and the Lady* (1875). First met by Collins during his trip to Paris with *Dickens in 1855.

reminiscences and autobiographical works

'Reminiscences of a story-teller' in *The Universal Review*, June 1888

ning, keeps the story always advancing, and decides on the end.

'Reminiscences of a Story-Teller', *Universal Review*, June 1888; reprinted WCS, Oct. 1991. Personal recollections, including the school bully who started Collins on his story-telling career by forcing him to tell stories before going to sleep; and encounters with various readers both in person and by letter.

The Art of Authorship, edited by George Bainton, London 1890. Collins, in common with several other authors, was tricked into supplying reminiscences without realizing they would be published (in Collins's case posthumously). Brief notes of his writing methods and how his proofs pass through four revisions for periodicals, followed by a fifth correction for book publication.

See also *memoirs of the life of william collins esq., r.a.*

Collins collaborated with Régnier for the French dramatic versions of *Armadale*, *The Woman in White* and *The New Magdalen*.

reminiscences and autobiographical works Collins wrote very few personal articles or reminiscences. In January 1889, when pressed for his memoirs by the Dutch-American syndicate publisher Edward Bok (1863–1930), he declined by saying ' . . . we have had (to my mind) more "Reminiscences" latterly published in England than are really wanted. It will soon become a distinction *not* to have written one's autobiography.' The following are the few personal pieces written by Collins or the results of interviews by contemporary journalists:

'Memorandum, Relating to the Life and Writings of Wilkie Collins', 21 Mar. 1862; reprinted in Parrish (1940), 4–5. Brief résumé of his works to date for an unidentified French correspondent.

'Wilkie Collins', *Appleton's Journal*, 3 Sept. 1870. Recollections of his early years including the unsuccessful attempts to find a publisher for *Ioláni*.

'Celebrities at Home, Number 81, Mr Wilkie Collins in Gloucester Place', *The *World*, 26 Dec. 1877. Describes the four steps in the 'Méthode Collins' used in writing *The Woman in White*—of finding the central idea, finding the characters, letting the incidents bring themselves about from the nature of the characters, and to begin at the beginning.

'Wilkie Collins's Recollections of Charles *Fechter' in *Charles Albert Fechter*, Kate Field, Boston 1882 (154–73). Contains a few personal notes associated with their meetings.

'Books Necessary for a Liberal Education', *Pall Mall Gazette*, 11 Feb. 1886. Following a recent selection by the scientific author Sir John Lubbock, Collins's own recommendations include Sterne's *Sentimental Journey*, Byron's *Childe Harold*, Moore's *Life of Byron* and Lockhart's *Life of Scott*. For fiction he suggests *Balzac, *Dickens, *Cooper, Dumas, Marryatt, *Reade and *Scott. (The contents of Collins's library are recorded in Puttick & Simpson's *auction catalogue for 20 Jan. 1890).

'How I Write My Books: Related in a Letter to a Friend', *The Globe*, 26 Nov. 1887; reprinted as appendix c to the Riverside Edition of *The Woman in White*, Boston 1969; and appendix D to the World's Classics edition, 1980. Uses *The Woman in White* as an example to show how Collins obtains the central idea and the chief characters, begins at the begin-

Revue Britannique (1825–1902). French periodical specializing in translations from English, edited by Amadée Pichot. In 1856 published a translation of '*Mad Monkton'. Pichot told Collins that the story was much admired by the dramatist Eugène Scribe.

Revue des deux mondes, La French review of arts, literature and philosophy. Founded in 1829 and acquired in 1831 by François Buloz who made it into a leading European periodical. Authors included *Balzac, Dumas *père*, Hugo and *Forgues who contributed 'William Wilkie Collins' to the series 'Études sur le roman anglais' (Nov. 1855).

Robson, Frederick (Thomas Robson Brownhill) (d. 1864 aged 43). Celebrated actor famed for his ability to combine the comic and the macabre; regularly appeared at the *Olympic Theatre from 1850. 'Great little Robson' played the parts of Aaron Gurnock in the professional production of *The Lighthouse* (1857) and Hans Grimm in *The Red Vial* (1858).

Fitz-Gerald, S. J. A., *Dickens and the Drama*, London 1910, 44, 51.

Graham, P., *West Norwood Cemetery: The Dickens Connection*, London 1995, 14.

Rogue's Life, A: From his Birth to his Marriage

'Man is the sport of circumstances.'

Short novel originally published in *Household Words* during 1856. Republished in book form in 1879 after an invitation from George *Bentley 'to take a place in his new series of pretty volumes in red'. Collins made minor changes to the text and noted in some 'Introductory Words' that it was written 'at a very happy time in my past life . . . at Paris, when I had Charles Dickens for a near neighbour and a daily companion'. He also revealed that he had intended, but never written, a further series of the Rogue's adventures in *Australia. The theme of picture forgery and the character of Frank Softly were probably inspired by *Memoirs of a Picture*, written by Collins's grandfather, William *Collins Senior. The Scotch marriage of Frank and Alicia anticipates Collins's later attack on marriage laws in *Man and Wife* (1870).

⇥ Frank Softly is a poor young gentleman whose snobbish father sends him to boarding school to make useful connections, but without success. He tries a variety of professions to earn his living but by the time he is 25 has failed at medicine, caricaturing, portrait painting, forging Old Masters and administering a scientific institution.

Frank then falls in love with Dr Dulcifer's daughter, Alicia, but discovers that her father is a counterfeit-coin maker. Our likeable hero is unwillingly recruited into forging to compromise him as a felon. At this point the doctor considers him unsuitable as a son-in-law and sends Alicia away to Wales. The counterfeiters are betrayed to the Bow Street Runners but Frank escapes, finds Alicia and elopes with her to Scotland. Immediately after their wedding, Frank is arrested, tried and transported to Australia. As a model prisoner he becomes servant to his own wife who has travelled to the New World in the person of a widow. By the time Frank is officially released, their speculations have proved so successful that he is a rich man and a rogue no longer.

Serialization. *Household Words* 1–29 Mar. 1856, as 'A Rogue's Life: Written by Himself'.

Book publication

1st edn. 1 vol, Richard *Bentley, London 1879. Red flexible cloth, covers blocked in black, spine lettered in gilt, black endpapers. No

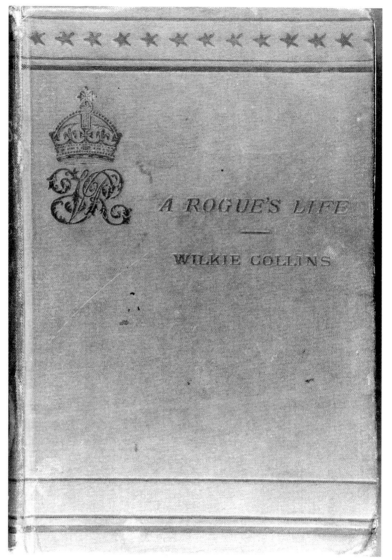

Binding of the one-volume first edition of *A Rogue's Life* in 1879

half-title. Published 7 Apr. 1879. Number 7 in Bentley's Empire Library, a half-crown series with a mixture of fiction and non-fiction.

iv + 188 pp.

1-vol edns. *Chatto & Windus 1889–1903. Sutton, Stroud 1984.

1st US edn. *Appleton's New Handy-Volume Series, New York 1879.

Translation. Spanish, New York 1892, 1897.

Rome One of Collins's favourite cities, first visited as a boy with his father during the family's tour of *France and *Italy.

They were in Rome between January and April 1837 and from February to April 1838, staying near the Pincian Hill which became one of the settings for *Antonina* (1850). Collins revisited the city 13–18 November 1853 on his European trip with Charles *Dickens and Augustus *Egg. He later took Caroline *Graves and her daughter there for three months from December 1863, staying once again in the Hôtel des Iles Britanniques, hiring a cook and their own carriage. While they were in Rome, their German courier Niedecker died of 'gastric fever'; his brother later wrote to express his gratitude for Collins's care of him. Collins returned there in November 1866 with Edward *Pigott.

Routledge, George (1812–88). London publisher and pioneer of popular cheap fiction. Originally a bookseller, began publishing from Soho Square about 1844. On the Continent, Routledge provided the only serious competition to *Tauchnitz for cheap reprints. Edmund Routledge (1843–99), second son of George, was in correspondence with Collins during 1867 but the firm did not publish any of his titles until 1897–1904. It then issued *Antonina*, *Basil*, *Hide and Seek* and *The Woman in White* in the Railway Library, Handy Novels and Caxton Novels.

> Topp, C. W., *Victorian Yellowbacks and Paperbacks, 1849–1905*, i (George Routledge), Denver, Colo., 1993.

Royal Academy of Arts Society founded in 1768 for the purposes of culti-

vating and improving the arts of painting, sculpture and architecture. Collins was well acquainted with the Royal Academy. His father, William *Collins, was elected an associate in November 1814, an Academician in February 1820 and appointed Librarian in July 1840. Charles *Collins attended the Royal Academy Schools but was never elected.

Several of Collins's friends were Academicians, including Augustus *Egg, William *Frith, Rudolf *Lehmann, Edward *Ward and Thomas Woolner. In his twenties, Collins dabbled in painting for his own amusement and succeeded in showing *The Smuggler's Retreat* at the 1849 Summer Exhibition. He also reviewed the 1851 Exhibition for *Bentley's Miscellany* (1 June 1851) and in the same journal gently satirized the Academy in 'A *Passage in the Life of Mr Perugino Potts' (Feb. 1852). In April 1864, the Academy invited Collins to their Grand Dinner.

For original sketches by Collins, see Robert Lee Wolff, 'Contemporary Collectors 42: Nineteenth-Century Fiction I', *The Book Collector*, 14 (Autumn 1965), 335–47; and Peters (1991), illustration 6.

> Collins, W., *Memoirs*.
> Parrish, (1940), 9.

'Royal Love' Short story originally published in *Longman's Magazine*, Christmas 1884. Reprinted as 'Mr Medhurst and the Princess' in *Little Novels* (1887).

➡ Ernest Medhurst is unwittingly caught up in a minor political intrigue while second secretary to a small German Court. The Princess falls in love with him and to avoid the possibility of scandal affecting her forthcoming marriage her father ensures that Medhurst is duped into leaving the country. This ultimately works to Medhurst's advantage as he then marries Jeanne, the daughter of his old singing master.

Rudd, Martha (1845–1919). The younger of the two women with whom Collins had long-term relationships; mother of his three children in what he described to the *Lehmanns as his 'morganatic family'. Martha Rudd was born on 10 January 1845 in the Norfolk village of Martham. She subsequently lived in nearby Winterton, on the coast close to Great Yarmouth. Her parents were James Rudd (d. 1893), a shepherd, and Mary (née Andrews) (1808–88). Martha had four

Part of William Collins's Royal Academy Certificate on his election in February 1820

GEORGE THE FOVRTH BY THE GRACE OF GOD KING OF GREAT-BRITAIN, FRANCE, AND IRELAND, DEFENDER OF THE FAITH, &c. TO OVR TRVSTY AND WELL-BELOVED WILLIAM COLLINS ESQVIRE, GREETING.

WHEREAS WE HAVE THOVGHT FIT TO ESTABLISH, IN THIS OVR CITY OF LONDON, A SOCIETY FOR THE PVRPOSES OF CVLTIVATING AND IMPROVING THE ARTS OF PAINTING, SCVLPTVRE, AND ARCHITECTVRE, VNDER THE NAME AND TITLE OF "THE ROYAL ACADEMY OF ARTS", AND VNDER OVR OWN IMMEDIATE PATRONAGE AND PROTECTION: AND WHEREAS WE HAVE RESOLVED TO ENTRVST THE SOLE MANAGEMENT AND DIRECTION OF THE SAID SOCIETY, VNDER VS, VNTO FORTY ACADEMICIANS, THE MOST ABLE AND RESPECTABLE ARTISTS RESIDENT IN GREAT-BRITAIN: WE, THEREFORE, IN CONSIDERATION OF YOVR GREAT SKILL IN THE ART OF PAINTING, DO, BY THESE PRESENTS, CONSTITVTE AND APPOINT YOV TO BE ONE OF THE FORTY ACADEMICIANS OF OVR SAID ROYAL ACADEMY; HEREBY GRANTING VNTO YOV ALL THE HONORS, PRIVILEGES, AND EMOLVMENTS, THEREOF, ACCORDING TO THE TENOR OF THE INSTITVTION. GIVEN VNDER OVR ROYAL SIGN MANVAL, VPON THE TENTH DAY OF DECEMBER, ONE THOVSAND SEVEN HVNDRED AND SIXTY EIGHT, AND IN THE NINTH YEAR OF OVR REIGN. AND WE ARE THE MORE READILY INDVCED TO CONFER VPON YOV THIS HONORABLE DISTINCTION AS WE ARE FIRMLY PERSVADED THAT YOV WILL, VPON EVERY OCCASION, EXERT YOVRSELF IN SVPPORT OF THE HONOR, INTEREST, AND DIGNITY, OF THE SAID ESTABLISHMENT; AND THAT YOV WILL FAITHFVLLY AND ASSIDVOVSLY DISCHARGE THE DVTIES OF THE SEVERAL OFFICES TO WHICH YOV SHALL BE NOMINATED. IN CONSEQVENCE OF THIS OVR GRACIOVS RESOLVTION, IT IS OVR PLEASVRE THAT YOVR NAME BE FORTHWITH INSERTED IN THE ROLL OF THE ACADEMICIANS, AND THAT YOV DO SVBSCRIBE THE OBLIGATION IN THE FORM AND MANNER PRESCRIBED. GIVEN AT OVR ROYAL PALACE OF SAINT IAMES'S, THE FIFTEENTH DAY OF NOVEMBER, IN THE FIRST YEAR OF OVR REIGN.

Martha Rudd

a degree of respectability, assumed the identities of Mr and Mrs William *Dawson, the name given to their three children. Their first child, Marian, was born at Bolsover Street in July 1869 followed by Harriet in May 1871. In January 1874, during his *American reading tour, Collins learned that the landlord wished to sell the house. On his return, he moved Martha briefly to 55 Marylebone Road and then to a cottage at 10 Taunton Place, at the top of Gloucester Place and close to *Hanover Terrace where Wilkie had lived in the 1850s. Martha remained here, listed in the Post Office Directory, for the next sixteen years. Their youngest child, William Charles Collins *Dawson ('Charley'), was born in Taunton Place on Christmas day 1874. His birth was officially registered, as was by then required by law. The births of the two girls do not appear to have been registered.

Although the children were regular visitors to Gloucester Place, there is no evidence of Martha visiting the house. The two households also maintained their separate identities during Collins's regular summer visits to *Ramsgate, though Charley stayed there with Wilkie and Caroline in 1885. Martha received a generous monthly allowance, but never took part in any of Collins's social activities. Perhaps surprisingly, she claimed that she could have married Wilkie any time she wanted. When Collins died in 1889, Martha and the children did not attend the *funeral and were represented only by a wreath. Collins's *will explicitly recognized his children, and intended them to be well provided for. In 1890, when Taunton Place was redeveloped, Martha moved to Brondesbury and subsequently to Southend where she died. She is buried in the Sutton Road Cemetery (grave no. 2702, plot D). Martha tended Wilkie's grave after Caroline's death in June 1895.

Clarke (1988).

Peters (1991).

brothers and three sisters. In 1861 she and her elder sister, Alice, were working as servants for an innkeeper, John Bartram, who lived at 15 New Toll Gate, Runham (then a suburb of Great Yarmouth) and kept an inn at 16 Vauxhall Gardens, near the railway terminus.

Collins almost certainly met Martha during the summer of 1864 when she was 19 and he had turned 40. He stayed at the Victoria Hotel in Great Yarmouth while researching locations for *Armadale*. The exact date when Martha came to London is uncertain but she was installed by Collins at 33 Bolsover Street by 1868. This is likely to have been connected with Caroline *Graves's temporary departure from *Gloucester Place during her brief marriage to Joseph *Clow.

Wilkie and Martha, to give their liaison

sailing

'He had a thoroughly English love of the sea
and of all that belongs to it.' (*Armadale*)

Collins's main outdoor recreation. His
regular sailing companions were Edward
*Pigott, Henry *Bullar and Charles
*Ward. Both Collins and his doctor,
Frank *Beard, were convinced that the
sea breezes were good for his health.
Collins's first major trips were with
Pigott to the Scilly Isles in 1855 and
Cherbourg in 1856. He sailed from
*Broadstairs in 1858 and the early 1860s,
and from Great Yarmouth in 1864. In his
later years, he sailed off *Ramsgate from
the 1870s.

Collins was himself a good sailor although he has the inebriated Zack in *Hide
and Seek* (1854) produce 'sounds nauti-
cally and lamentably associated with
white basins, whirling waves, and misery
of mortal stomachs wailing in emetic despair'. Sailing featured in several other
stories, including 'The *Cruise of the
Tomtit' (1855), 'A *Plot in Private Life'
(1858), *Armadale* (1866) and '*Miss or
Mrs?' (1871).

Sala, George Augustus (Henry)

(1828–95). Journalist, illustrator and nov-
elist. Friend of Collins and *Dickens.
Regular contributor to *Household Words*
and *All the Year Round*. Co-founder of
*The *Train* and editor of *Temple Bar*.
Published his reminiscences in 1894,
Things I have Seen and People I have Known.

Sampson Low

London publisher of
general literature. Sampson Low
(1797–1886) originally worked at Longman and then in 1819 set up a bookshop,
circulating library and reading-room in
Lambs Conduit Street. He sold the library in 1849 and established in Fleet
Street a partnership with his eldest son,
Sampson Low Junior (1822–72). They
moved to larger premises in Ludgate Hill
in 1852 and the partnership was joined by
Edward Marston in 1856. Apart from
Collins, the firm published *Bulwer-
Lytton, Charles *Collins, Elizabeth

Gaskell, James *Payn and Charles
*Reade.

From 1837, Low issued the *Publishers
Circular* which continued as the *English
Catalogue of Books*. He also became the
English literary agent for *Harpers. Low
was a noted philanthropist and instrumental in establishing the forerunner of
the London Fire Brigade. He was also a
fierce opponent of underselling books.

The firm altogether issued eight titles
by Collins. Starting in January 1860, they
outbid *Smith, Elder for the immensely
successful publication of *The Woman in
White*. They secured his next novel, *No
Name* (1862), against strong competition,
paying Collins £3,000. They were accused
by Charles Reade of forcing large quantities on the *circulating libraries to recoup
their expenses. The following year, 1863,
they published *My Miscellanies*.

In November 1860, Collins favoured
Sampson Low over *Hurst & Blackett
who had offered an identical sum to publish a cheap edition of his novels. Sampson Low issued *Antonina*, *Hide and Seek*,
The Dead Secret and *The Woman in White*
in 1861; *Basil* and *The Queen of Hearts* in
1862. They were advertised as 'The Novels and Romances of Wilkie Collins (Revised with New Prefaces by the Author).
Cheap and Uniform Edition; hand-
somely bound in cloth, with Vignette Il-

(*top right*) Sampson Low Junior
(*right*) Sampson Low Senior
(*below*) Sampson Low's Cheap and Uniform
Edition, 1861–4

lustrations.' The steel engravings were by John *Gilbert and all but *Basil* are the first editions in one volume. They were subsequently included in 'Low's Favourite Library of Popular Books', together with *No Name* in 1864.

Marston, E., *After Work*, London 1904, 87.

Sarony, Napoleon (1821–96). Celebrated New York photographer, dedicatee of *Heart and Science* (1883). During his reading tour of *America, Collins sat for Sarony in his studio at 680 Broadway and they afterwards became good friends. Collins wrote to him: 'You have taken just the sort of photograph I like. Those taken of me over here are perfect libels, but I feel like giving all your pictures to my friends.' Most of the series taken by Sarony show Collins wearing a coat with a large astrakhan collar. In 1887 Saroney forwarded a parcel of photographs including nude studies which sent Collins into raptures of appreciation.

Sayers, Dorothy Leigh (1893–1957). Author of an unfinished biography of Collins. Best known for her detective fiction and her character Lord Peter Wimsey. Sayers had an interest in Collins extending over many years. There is correspondence as early as 1921 about her intended 'Life'; followed by an insertion in *The Times Literary Supplement* of 21 June 1929 with a request for documents; and in July 1957, a few months before her death, she wrote that she still hoped to finish the biography. During this period she accumulated an extensive Collins collection (now at Austin, Texas) which included 37 of his works, 24 manuscripts and proof copies and 152 autograph letters. Both Kenneth Robinson and Robert Ashley were apparently denied access to her material for their own biographies.

Sayers completed only five chapters and these were eventually published as *Wilkie Collins: A Critical and Biographical Study*, edited by E. R. Gregory, Toledo, Ohio, 1977. She did, however, mention Collins in several essays and introductions, compiled the entry for the 1940 *Cambridge Bibliography of English Literature*, wrote the introduction to the 1944 Everyman Library edition of *The Moonstone*, and edited various collections of short stories which contained '*The Biter Bit' and '*Mad Monkton'.

Sayers greatly admired Collins who

Photograph taken by Sarony in New York during Collins's reading tour of America in 1873–4

strongly influenced her works. She followed his example in taking great pains to ensure the accuracy of her plots. *The Documents in the Case* (1930) is written in the narrative style of *The Moonstone*. Lady Mary in *Clouds of Witness* (1926) behaves like Rachel *Verinder, trying to protect Gerald, Duke of Denver, whom she incorrectly assumes is guilty of the crime, and in 'Other People's Detectives' (1939) she cites *Cuff when writing that for a detective to be truly great he must have presence.

Gilbert, C. B., *A Bibliography of the Works of Dorothy L. Sayers*, London 1978.

Schlesinger, Sebastian Benzon Executor of Collins's *will and dedicatee (with his wife) of *The Haunted Hotel* (1879). Boston associate of Ernst *Benzon of Naylor Vickers, employing for a while Wilkie's godson Frank *Ward.

Collins first met Schlesinger during his reading tour of *America and was frequently entertained by him. Collins described him to Frederick *Lehmann as 'the brightest, nicest, kindest, little fellow I have met with for many a long day . . . He also makes the best cocktail in America. Vive Sebastian!'

Schlesinger assisted Collins with business matters, including the arrangement of life insurance. They didn't meet for many years after the American trip but Schlesinger confided in Collins about his

'domestic calamities', and continued a warm correspondence up to the September of Collins's death. During the late 1880s, Schlesinger lived in London at 45 Albert Gate, Knightsbridge.

Lehmann (1908), 67.

Scilly Isles See 'CRUISE OF THE TOMTIT, THE'.

Scott, Sir Walter (1771–1832). Historical novelist, poet and dramatist. Collins admired him as one of his three 'Kings of Fiction', along with *Balzac and Fenimore *Cooper. Collins urged Frank *Archer to study Scott as 'the greatest novelist that has ever written' and described him to William *Winter as 'the Prince, the King, the Emperor, the God Almighty of novelists'. Amelius Goldenheart in The *Fallen Leaves* turns to Scott as 'the one supreme genius who soars above all other novelists'.

There are several references to Scott in Collins's *Memoirs of his father. William *Collins illustrated *The Pirate* (1821) and met Scott during his trip to Edinburgh in 1822. In common with Wilkie Collins, Scott was called to the Bar and, in great pain while writing *The Bride of Lammermoor* (1819), took *opium, later claiming he did not recognize the ending of the novel as his own.

Archer, F., *An Actor's Notebooks*, London 1912, 281.

Winter, W., *Old Friends*, New York 1909, 219.

Seaside Library One of the most successful New York publishers of cheap *pirated reprints. Run by George Munro who sent Collins payment for some stories; in 1886 Collins considered offering him *The Guilty River*. The Seaside Library was usually issued three times a week, mainly at ten or twenty cents. There also followed a later series, the Seaside Library Pocket Edition.

Collins titles included: *The Woman in White* (no. 10); *The Dead Secret* (1877, no. 14); *Man and Wife* (1877, no. 22); *The Queen of Hearts* (1877, no. 32); *Hide and Seek* (1877, no. 42); *The New Magdalen* (1877, no. 76); *The Law and the Lady* (1877, no. 94); *Armadale* (no. 180); *My Lady's Money* (no. 191); *The Two Destinies* (1879, no. 225); *No Thoroughfare* (Dickens and Collins, no. 239); *No Name* (no. 250); *After Dark* (no. 286); *The Lazy Tour of Two Idle Apprentices* (no. 372, by 'Dickens'); *The Haunted Hotel*

The Sensation Novel Company (Limited) in *Punch*, 7 March 1868

(no. 409); *A Rogue's Life* (1879, no. 487); *The Yellow Mask* (1879, no. 551); *Poor Miss Finch* (1879, no. 634); *Jezebel's Daughter* (1880, no. 696, first book edition); *Basil* (1880, no. 721); *The Captain's Last Love* (1880, no. 713); *The Magic Spectacles* (1880, no. 745); *The Duel in Herne Wood* (1880, no. 905); *Who Killed Zebedee?* (1881, no. 928); *The Black Robe* (1881); *The Frozen Deep* (1881, no. 971); *Your Money or Your Life* (1881, no. 1164); *Heart and Science* (1883, no. 1544); *Fie! Fie! or the Fair Physician* (1883, no. 1587); *'I Say No'* (1884, no. 1856); *The Girl at the Gate* (1885, no. 2030); *The Evil Genius* (1886, no. 2069).

Munro was notoriously unreliable in allocating numbers but most of those titles traced follow a logical sequence according to the date of publication.

Seaside Library Pocket Edition:

Heart and Science (1883, no. 167); *The Queen of Hearts* (1885, no. 591); *My Lady's Money* (1885, no. 623); *The Evil Genius* ([1886], no. 764); *The Guilty River* (1886, no. 896); *The Haunted Hotel* (1887, no. 977); *The Legacy of Cain* (1888, no. 1095); *A Rogue's Life* ([1890], no. 1347).

Brussel (1935).

Seaver, Colonel William A. (d.

1883). Famous New York *raconteur*; from 1868 conductor of the 'Editor's Drawer' of *Harper's Magazine*. Collins had a letter of introduction from Edmund *Yates and met Seaver during the 1873 reading tour of *America. They became good friends

and Seaver entertained him liberally including, on 22 October, a magnificent breakfast banquet for twenty-four distinguished guests at the Union Club of New York. Seaver was in turn entertained by Collins and Caroline *Graves during a vist to London in the summer of 1880.

Harper (1912), 522.

sensation novel A style of fiction which flourished from the 1860s, closely allied to melodrama on the stage. Plots typically included murder, bigamy, false *identity, lunatic asylums, guilty secrets and premonitions. Sensation novels were frequently written by women and often featured a female protagonist. They empowered women with the resources, often violent, to challenge the dominance of the masculine world. The novels coincided with the rise of literacy and became the bestsellers of the day with contemporary stories, frequently at odds with conventional Victorian morality. Within a short while parodies such as the 'Sensation Novel Company' appeared in *Punch.

Collins, who excelled in plot and incident, is often regarded as the prime exponent of the genre. Many of the themes in his earlier fiction culminated in *The Woman in White* (1860) which is considered the archetypal sensation novel. He had many imitators, including Mary *Braddon, Charles *Reade, Mrs Henry Wood and numerous others now lost in obscurity. It was usually the sensational

rather than the detective elements of his fiction that were copied so that the genre later developed into the pure thriller.

Hughes, W., *The Maniac in the Cellar: Sensation Novels of the 1860s*, Princeton 1980, 137–65.

Phillips, W. C., *Dickens, Reade and Collins: Sensation Novelists*, New York 1919.

Rance, N., *Wilkie Collins and Other Sensation Novelists*, London 1991.

serialization The majority of Collins's novels and longer short stories were serialized in the popular *periodicals of the time. The main exceptions were his early books between 1848 (*Memoirs of the Life of William Collins, Esq., R.A.*) and 1854 (*Hide and Seek*). The first story long enough to require serialization was 'Gabriel's Marriage' in *Household Words* (two parts, 16–23 Apr. 1853). The same journal published 'Sister Rose' (four parts, 7–28 Apr. 1855), 'The Yellow Mask' (four parts, 7–28 July 1855), 'The Diary of Anne Rodway' (two parts, 19–26 July 1856) and *A Rogue's Life* (five parts, 1–29 Mar. 1856).

Collins's full-length novels from 1857 were serialized in the following English journals (see separate entries):

The Dead Secret, Household Words (3 Jan.–13 June 1857).

The Woman in White, All the Year Round (26 Nov. 1859–25 Aug. 1860).

No Name, All the Year Round (15 Mar. 1862–17 Jan. 1863).

Armadale, The Cornhill (Nov. 1864–June 1866).

The Moonstone, All the Year Round (4 Jan.–8 Aug. 1868).

Man and Wife, Cassell's Magazine (20 Nov. 1869–30 July 1870).

Poor Miss Finch, Cassell's Magazine (2 Sept. 1871–24 Feb. 1872).

The New Magdalen, Temple Bar (Oct. 1872–July 1873).

The Frozen Deep, Temple Bar (Aug.–Oct. 1874).

The Law and the Lady, The Graphic (26 Sept. 1874–13 Mar. 1875).

The Two Destinies, Temple Bar (Jan.–Sept. 1876).

The Haunted Hotel, Belgravia (June–Nov. 1878).

The Fallen Leaves, The World (1 Jan.–23 July 1879).

Jezebel's Daughter, *Tillotson papers (Sept. 1879–Jan. 1880).

The Black Robe, Sheffield & Rotherham Independent (2 Oct. 1880–26 Mar. 1881).

Heart and Science, Belgravia (Aug.

1882–June 1883).

'*I Say No*', *London Society* (Jan.–Dec. 1884).

The Evil Genius, *Leigh Journal & Times* (11 Dec. 1885–30 Apr. 1886).

The Legacy of Cain, Tillotson papers (Feb.–July 1888).

(The above six novels were also syndicated in several provincial newspapers.)

Blind Love, *Illustrated London News* (6 July–28 Dec. 1889).

Collins's main publishers in the USA were *Harpers who first published his novels in their *Weekly* or *Monthly* magazines. In the UK, several of the later *short stories were collected after serialization in *Miss or Mrs? and Other Stories in Outline* (1873), *The Frozen Deep and Other Stories* (1874) and *Little Novels* (1887).

Sette of Odd Volumes, The Literary dining club founded in 1878 and still in existence. Papers presented at meetings are sometimes published as Privately Printed Opuscula. *Wilkie Collins: An Odd Volume* (Cambridge 1968) is no. 107 in the series, originally read before the 666th meeting on 11 April 1967 by Arthur Brown, Bookmaker to the Sette. The text of about 4,000 words consists of a brief biographical sketch, remarks about Collins's approach to fiction, his attention to accuracy, and a résumé of his main works.

'She Loves and Lies' Short story originally published in *The *Spirit of the Times*, 22 December 1883; and in *Tales from Many Sources*, vol 4, 1885. Reprinted as 'Mr Lismore and the Widow' in *Little Novels* (1887). Collins presented the manuscript of the story to A. P. *Watt in January 1884.
➡ Ernest Lismore is in financial difficulties. In return for a token marriage, he is offered help by the elderly Mrs Callender whom years before he saved from a fire. Lismore eventually agrees and they live abroad as mother and son until he meets

an attractive girl in an art gallery. Forced to decide between the girl and his wife, he chooses the older woman only to find they are one and the same person. The artifice was to ascertain that Lismore loves her rather than her money.

'Shocking Story, A' Short story originally published in Barnes's *International Review*, 2 Nov. 1878, and in the *Belgravia Annual*, Christmas 1878. Reprinted in book form by A. S. Barnes, New York 1878; and as 'Miss Mina and the Groom' in *Little Novels* (1887).
➡ Mina shocks society by falling in love and marrying Michael Bloomfield, a groom in the household of her aunt and uncle with whom she lives. Discovering that her aunt has recognized the orphaned Bloomfield as her illegitimate son, Mina promises to conceal his true identity.

short stories

'People who read stories are said to have excitable brains.' (*Heart and Science*)

The majority of Collins's short stories were written either at the beginning or towards the end of his career. The early tales were mainly published in *Household Words* and *All the Year Round*, subsequently collected in *After Dark* (1856), *The Queen of Hearts* (1859) and *My Miscellanies* (1863). Most of Collins's output at the peak of his fame consisted of full-length novels but some short pieces were included in *Miss or Mrs? and other Stories in Outline* (1873). Later stories were published in a wide range of English and American *periodicals and fourteen were reissued with new titles in *Little Novels* (1887). Collins's uncollected stories are now available in *Wilkie Collins: The Complete Shorter Fiction*, edited by Julian Thompson, 1995.

See also DETECTIVE FICTION; SUPERNATURAL, THE.

Simpson, John Palgrave (1807–87). Dramatist, novelist and distinguished amateur actor. Secretary of the Dramatic Authors' Society and friend of Collins and the *Bancrofts. Played Aaron Gurnock in the 1865 production of *The *Lighthouse* at the Royal Bijou Theatre.

'Sister Rose' Long short story originally published in *Household Words*, 7–28 Apr. 1855. With an added Prologue, later

Privately Printed Opuscula
Issued to Members of the Sette of Odd Volumes
NO. CVII

WILKIE COLLINS

An Odd Volume

BY

ARTHUR BROWN

Bookmaker to the Sette

A Paper read before the 666th Meeting of

𝕿𝖍𝖊 𝕾𝖊𝖙𝖙𝖊 𝖔𝖋 𝕺𝖉𝖉 𝖁𝖔𝖑𝖚𝖒𝖊𝖘

on 11th April, 1967
at Corpus Christi College, Oxford

CAMBRIDGE
Imprynted by R. I. Severs Ltd, King's Hedges Road
MCMLXVIII

(*left*) Title-page to *Wilkie Collins: an Odd Volume* a privately printed Opusculum of the Sette of Odd Volumes
(*below*) Collins's inscription on the manuscript of the short story, 'She Loves and Lies', presented to A. P. Watt in January 1884

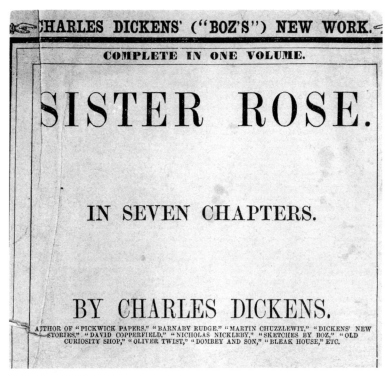

(*left*) The 1855 Peterson edition of Collins's story of the French Revolution, 'Sister Rose', wrongly attributed to Dickens
(*above*) George Smith II

included in *After Dark* (1856) as 'The French Governess's story of Sister Rose'. First separate edition by *Peterson, Philadelphia 1855, wrongly attributed to Dickens.

➡ Set against the background of the French Revolution, the story concerns Louis Trudaine; his sister, Rose, who contracts an unhappy marriage to the aristocratic Charles Danville; and Danville's land-steward, Lomaque, who is indebted to Trudaine's father. Trudaine fulfils a deathbed promise to his mother to protect Rose and arouses Danville's animosity. Danville denounces Trudaine to the revolutionary authorities, implicating Rose. Through his lies at their trial, both brother and sister are condemned to the guillotine. Lomaque, who has become a police agent, saves their lives by removing their names from the death list with a chemical formula. Freed by the downfall of Robespierre, the brother and sister confront Danville three years later as he is about to remarry. He is rejected by his mother and killed in a duel. The Trudaines and Lomaque return to the tranquillity of the family home in Rouen.

The story is a likely influence on *Dickens's *A Tale of Two Cities* (1859), set in revolutionary France and featuring an escape from prison through substitution.

Smith, Elder (1816–1916). London publishing firm noted for its association with many of the foremost writers of the day, including the Brontës, Ruskin and *Thackeray. Founded by George Smith (1789–1846) and Alexander Elder (*c.* 1790–1876), the firm began as booksellers and stationers in Fenchurch Street, moving to 65 Cornhill in 1824. It was also involved in agency and banking with a strong Indian connection. In 1833, Smith, Elder started The Library of Romance, original works in one volume at 6*s.*, the first of a number of attempts by publishers to reduce the price of fiction, already dictated by the *circulating libraries.

George Smith II (1824–1901) became sole head of the firm in 1846, moving to Waterloo Place in 1869. He was renowned as an honourable, hard-working and astute businessman, backing his judgement by offering authors generous payments. Smith founded The *Cornhill* in 1860 and the **Pall Mall Gazette* in 1865, and launched the *Dictionary of National Biography* in 1882. The firm was absorbed by John Murray in 1916.

Collins was first introduced to Smith by Ruskin, with a view to publishing *Antonina*. Smith declined, not wanting a classical novel, but issued *After Dark* in 1856. Smith always regretted missing *The Woman in White*. After a few instalments of the serial, in January 1860, Collins received an offer from Sampson Low. He had promised Smith the opportunity of bidding for the book and wrote to him accordingly. Smith asked his clerks but none of them was familiar with the serial. He therefore dictated a hasty note offering a modest £500 and rushed off to a dinner-party where he learned that everyone was raving about *The Woman in White*. He subsequently claimed that had he known this he would have multiplied his offer fivefold.

Smith was also unsuccessful in obtaining *No Name*, succeeding only in pushing up the price paid by *Sampson Low to £3,000. Still determined to publish Collins, he secured *Armadale* for *The Cornhill* with an offer of £5,000, the largest sum at that time paid to any novelist except *Dickens. Smith, Elder also published for Collins the dramatic version of *Armadale* (1866) in an edition of twenty-five copies.

From 1865 Smith, Elder added to *After Dark* the seven copyrights previously held by Sampson Low. Until the mid 1870s

Smith, Elder issued various one-volume editions which included *Armadale* and, from 1871, *The Moonstone*. Smith at this time declined Collins's proposal for cheap reissues. In 1875, therefore, the copyright to most of his earlier works was transferred to *Chatto & Windus. There was some period of overlap since Smith, Elder *yellowbacks dated 1876 continued to advertise their editions although Chatto & Windus had already issued thirteen titles by July 1875. Smith, Elder retained *Armadale*, *After Dark* and *No Name* and continued to issue them throughout the 1880s. They were not published by Chatto & Windus until 1890.

Huxley, L., *The House of Smith, Elder*, privately printed, London 1923, 92, 152–4.
Lee, Sir Sidney, 'Memoir of George Smith' in *Dictionary of National Biography*, Oxford.

Smith, W. H. & Son Firm of newsagents, booksellers and stationers; founded in 1792 and becoming the second largest *circulating library. They expanded rapidly under William Henry Smith II (1825–91) during the railway boom of the 1850s. Smiths increased their railway bookstalls from thirty in 1850 to more than five hundred by 1870. At the same time, they improved bookstall respectability and sold vast quantities of 'railway fiction' or *yellowbacks. They also acquired the copyrights of a number of novelists and for over twenty years published cheap editions in discreet collaboration with *Chapman & Hall.

In 1860 Smiths set up their own circulating library in opposition to *Mudie who had declined to co-operate the previous year. By 1862 Smiths had 185 branches around the country. They preferred single-volume books since they were more easily carried by passengers but Smiths were more than happy to take advantage of the *three-decker system while it remained profitable.

During the time at which Collins was writing Smiths exerted a significant influence on the distribution of fiction. In 1872 they refused *Bentley's three-volume edition of *Poor Miss Finch*, instead buying 400 copies of the bound-up *Cassells Magazine*.

Wilson, W., *First with the News: The History of W. H. Smith 1792–1972*, London 1985.

Society of Authors Established in 1884 for 'the maintenance, definition and defence of Literary Property', following a meeting held on 28 September 1883. Tennyson was elected President and Walter *Besant became Chairman of the Committee of Management. Collins was an enthusiastic founder-member and honorary vice-president, along with *Reade, *Sala and Margaret *Oliphant. The Society was launched at a Lord Mayor's Banquet on 18 October 1884, at which 150 members were present. The Society's first objective was to obtain copyright for English authors in the United States while other aims included the promotion of a Bill for the Registration of Titles.

Collins attended the Society's annual dinners when he was well enough. His last appearance was as a steward at a dinner held on 15 July 1888 at the Criterion Restaurant, to honour visiting American authors. The Society was presented by Besant with a large collection of Collins's papers relating to international *copyright. In 1890 it republished in its journal *Considerations on the Copyright Question Addressed to an American Friend* under the title 'Thou Shalt Not Steal' (*The Author*, 1 (June 1890), 31–5).

Bonham-Carter, V., *Authors by Profession*, London 1978.

Spearman, Rosanna Tragic figure in *The Moonstone*, wrongly suspected of stealing the diamond. A reformed thief who becomes a housemaid to the Verinder family, keeping herself apart from the other servants. Hopelessly in

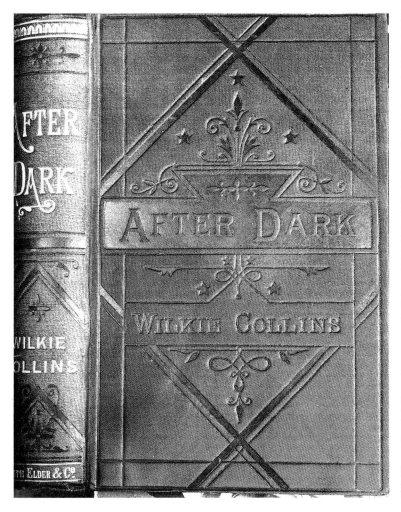

Binding of the one-volume Smith, Elder illustrated edition of *After Dark* in 1888. Bright red cloth blocked and lettered in black; spine lettered in gilt

love with Franklin *Blake, she hides his paint-smeared nightgown to conceal his responsibility for the theft and drowns herself in the Shivering Sand.

Spirit of the Times, The New York periodical to which Collins contributed Christmas stories between 1876 and 1887. Most were republished in a wide variety of English magazines and, with different titles, in *Little Novels* (1887).

'The Captain's Last Love' ('Mr Captain and the Nymph'), 23 Dec. 1876.

'The Duel in Herne Wood' ('Miss Bertha and the Yankee'), 22 Dec. 1877.

'The Mystery of Marmaduke' ('Mr Marmaduke and the Minister'), 28 Dec. 1878.

'The Devil's Spectacles', 20 Dec. 1879.

'Who Killed Zebedee?' ('Mr Policeman and the Cook'), 25 Dec. 1880.

'How I Married Him' ('Miss Morris and the Stranger'), 24 Dec. 1881.

'Fie! Fie! Or the Fair Physician', 23 Dec. 1882.

'She Loves and Lies' ('Mr Lismore and the Widow'), 22 Dec. 1883.

'The Girl at the Gate' ('Mr Lepel and the Housekeeper'), 6 Dec. 1884.

'The Poetry Did It: An Event in the Life of Major Evergreen', 26 Dec. 1885.

'An Old Maid's Husband' ('Miss Dulane and My Lord'), 25 Dec. 1886.

'The First Officer's Confession', 24 Dec. 1887.

Stanfield, (William) Clarkson, R.A. (1793–1867). Artist well known for his seascapes, originally working as a scenery painter in London and Edinburgh. Friend of *Dickens and recruited to design and paint the sets for *The Lighthouse* (1855) and, with William Telbin, *The Frozen Deep* (1857).

'Stolen Letter, A' Early story of detection, probably influenced by Edgar Allan *Poe's 'The Purloined Letter'. Originally published with the title 'The Fourth Poor Traveller' in 'The Seven Poor Travellers', the extra *Christmas number of *Household Words* for December 1854; subsequently included in *After Dark* (1856) as 'The Lawyer's Story of a Stolen Letter'. ➥ The narrator is a lawyer who contrives, in a series of ingenious moves, to steal back an incriminating letter from a blackmailer. The letter contains a confession to an attempted forgery by the dead

Supernatural: 'The Ghost's Touch' issued as the first of 'Mason's Popular Stories'

father of a poor young governess, Miss Smith. The lawyer's success enables her marriage to a rich young man, Frank Gatliffe, to take place without the threat of scandal.

Strand, The London thoroughfare where Collins had his first employment at *Antrobus & Co. Also the location of his bankers, *Coutts at 440, and several publishing offices such as The *Illustrated London News*, *Punch*, *Chapman & Hall, and The *Illuminated Magazine*. Home of the *Adelphi, *Globe, *Lyceum and *Olympic theatres, and close to *Lincoln's Inn and the law courts.

supernatural
'I have given up, long since, all idea of ever discovering a man who has himself seen a ghost, as distinguished from that other inevitable man who has a bosom friend who has unquestionably seen one.' ('The Unknown Public')

Collins's contributions to the true ghost story are fairly limited. He seems to have acquired his reputation as a writer of ghost stories mainly by association with various anthologies such as *The Supernatural Omnibus* (edited by Montague Summers, London 1933) and *Tales of Terror and the Supernatural* (edited by Herbert van Thal, New York 1972).

His main contributions to the genre are *The *Haunted Hotel* (1879) in which Agnes Lockwood sees the bloodstained

head of Lord Montbarry descend from the ceiling; and 'The *Ghost's Touch' (1885) where a supernatural force protects Mrs Zant from her brother-in-law. '*John Jago's Ghost' on the other hand is not a ghost story despite the title and 'The Ghost in the Cupboard Room' (renamed '*Blow up with the Brig!') represents Collins's most unlikely haunting in the form of a bedroom candlestick. In 'The *Yellow Mask' although Fabio truly believes he sees his dead wife at the masked ball, the explanation is entirely natural. 'Memoirs of an Adopted Son' (reprinted in *My Miscellanies*) gives an historical account of the daring eighteenth-century robber, Poulailler, and the legend of his supernatural birth and death.

Collins nevertheless made extensive use of the supernatural throughout his career but in the much more ambiguous form of visions, dreams and Fate. His first identified work, 'The *Last Stage Coachman' (1843), presents a vision in the heavens and '*Nine O'Clock' (1852) has both an out-of-body experience and a premonition of death. The narrator of 'The *Dream Woman' (1855) asks whether it is 'the creature of a dream, or that other creature from the unknown world called among men by the name of ghost?' and in '*Mad Monkton' (1855) the reader must decide whether Alfred has really seen his dead uncle or if his mind is suffering from obsessional madness.

In the appendix to *Armadale* (1866), Collins notes that he deliberately leaves his readers 'in the position which they would occupy in the case of a dream in real life—they are free to interpret it by the natural or supernatural theory, as the bent of their own minds may incline them'. The lengthy dream sequence forms an important part of the plot by predicting the future for Allan *Armadale and Ozias *Midwinter. Other visions are almost telepathic, providing the means of communication between George and Mary in *The Two Destinies* (1876), while the narrator of 'The *Clergyman's Confession' (1875) sees an apparition of Miss Jéromette at the precise moment of her death. In *The Legacy of Cain* (1888), the dreaming Eunice is urged by the ghost of her executed mother to murder Helena; and Hester Dethridge in *Man and Wife* (1870) sees the apparition of a second self impelling her to kill again.

During his later years, Collins admitted suffering from his own hallucinations caused by *opium and in March 1885 wrote to Mary *Anderson that the effects of sal volatile and chloroform had given him the idea for a new ghost story.

Swinburne, Algernon Charles (1837–1909). Poet and influential critic, associate of the *Pre-Raphaelites. Wrote a well-balanced critique of Collins in which he described *The Moonstone* as a masterpiece and *Armadale* as astonishingly ingenious and inventive. Swinburne appreciated *Man and Wife* as the first and best of the *didactic novels but considered others such as *Heart and Science* a good way behind. He summed up Collins's later works with the well-known couplet, parodying Pope:

What brought good Wilkie's genius nigh perdition?
Some demon whispered—'Wilkie! have a mission.'

Nevertheless Swinburne correctly predicted Collins's recognition by future generations.

'Wilkie Collins', *Fortnightly Review* (1 Nov. 1889); reprinted in *Studies in Prose and Poetry*, London 1894.

Switzerland Visited by Collins with Charles *Dickens and Augustus *Egg during their trip to *Italy in October 1853. On 13 October they stayed at the Hôtel de Paris in Strasbourg. Their subsequent route through Lausanne, where they stayed with C. H. *Townshend in his beautiful lakeside villa, Geneva, Chamonix, Martigny and across the Simplon Pass to Milan was later used in *No Thoroughfare* (1867). Collins was shocked at the cases of mental retardation and goitre then common in the country.

Some of Collins's early recollections of travel in Switzerland were given in 'My Black Mirror' (reprinted in *My Miscellanies*, 1863). The *Bancrofts related another story of Collins's holiday with Frederick *Lehmann. They had been in St Moritz and when they reached Coire on the homeward journey Collins discovered he had run out of *opium. As local regulations limited the amount that could be bought, Lehmann, a German-speaker, visited all six chemists in the town to obtain a sufficient quantity.

Bancroft, S. B., *The Bancrofts: Recollections of Sixty Years*, London 1909, 174.

syndication See SERIALIZATION and TILLOTSON.

Tauchnitz, Bernhard

'She looked into a place filled with Tauchnitz editions.' (*Blind Love*)

Leipzig publishers founded in 1837 by (Christian) Bernhard Tauchnitz, first Baron (1816–95). Anglophile, long-standing friend of Collins and dedicatee of *Miss or Mrs? and Other Stories in Outline*. The firm began with cheap reissues and in 1841 started The Collection of British Authors, published in English for a continental audience. Tauchnitz approached English writers personally and from 1843, despite the absence of international *copyright, invariably offered suitable payment. These 'sanctioned' or 'copyright' volumes were prohibited in England or any British colony but Tauchnitz sold thousands in America, publishing complete sets of particular authors. The Collection reached no. 500 by 1860 and the special Volume 2000 in 1881. The firm continued well into the twentieth century until the premises were destroyed in 1943.

Tauchnitz first approached Collins in June 1856 for the publication of *After Dark*. Collins accepted 'the remuneration offered' and subsequently complimented Tauchnitz on 'the neat and elegant appearance which my book presents in your form of publication'. Their relationship continued until *Blind Love* in 1890 although Tauchnitz's son wrote to A. P. *Watt in October 1889 that 'sales of his later novels remained extraordinarily behind that of his former ones and it was chiefly out of regard for our long personal friendly relations that we did not propose to lessen the price'.

Tauchnitz altogether published twenty-eight titles under Collins's name in exactly fifty volumes, plus two collaborations with Dickens. The volumes were frequently reprinted but invariably retain the date of first publication on the title-page.

After Dark (1856, vol 367); *Hide and Seek* (1856, vols 370, 371); *The Dead Secret* (1857, vols 386, 409); *A Plot in Private Life and Other Tales* (1859, vol 493) (stories from *The Queen of Hearts*); *The Woman in White* (1860, vols 525, 526); *Basil* (1862, vol 620); *No Name* (1863, vols 631, 632, 633); *Antonina* (1863, vols 678, 679); *Armadale* (1866, vols 838, 839, 840); *The Moonstone* (1868, vols 972, 973, 974); *Man and Wife* (1870, vols 1103, 1104, 1105); *Poor Miss Finch* (1872, vols 1200, 1201); *Miss or Mrs?* (1872, vol 1233) (precedes first English edition, and dedicated to Baron Tauchnitz); *The New Magdalen* (1873, vols 1325, 1326); *The Frozen Deep: and Other Stories* (1874, vol 1455); *The Law and the Lady* (1875, vols 1475, 1476) (possibly simultaneous with or precedes first English edition); *My Lady's Money and Percy and the Prophet* (1877, vol 1706); *The Haunted Hotel* (1878, vol 1785); *The Fallen Leaves* (1879, vols 1833, 1834); *Jezebel's Daughter* (1880, vols 1895, 1896); *The Black Robe* (1881, vols 1979, 1980); *Heart and Science* (1883, vols 2137, 2138); *'I Say No'* (1884, vols 2298, 2299); *The Evil Genius* (1886, vols 2421, 2422); *The Guilty River and The Ghost's Touch* (1887, vol 2439) (first book publication of the second story); *The Legacy of Cain* (1888, vols 2554, 2555); *Blind Love* (1890, vols 2629, 2630).

By Dickens and Collins: *Christmas Stories* (1862, vol 609); *No Thoroughfare* (1868, vol 961).

Bernhard von Tauchnitz

In addition, several of Collins's short stories had their first book publication in *Novels and Tales Reprinted from Household Words* (1856–9).

'A Rogue's Life' in vol I, 1856 [376] (first book publication); 'The Diary of Anne Rodway', vol II, 1856 [377]; 'The Wreck of the Golden Mary', vol III, 1857 [383]; 'A Queen's Revenge', vol V, 1857 [409]; 'The Lazy Tour of Two Idle Apprentices' and 'Mrs Badgery', vol VI, 1857 [416]; 'The Perils of Certain English Prisoners' and 'The Little Huguenot', vol VII, 1858 [427]; 'The Poisoned Meal', 'Over the Way', 'Trottles Report' and 'Let at Last', vol X, 1859 [475]; 'A New Mind' and 'Douglas Jerrold', vol XI, 1859 [481].

Peters (1991), 433.

Todd, W. B. and Bowden, A., *Tauchnitz International Editions in English 1841–1955: A Bibliographical History*, New York 1988.

Der Verlag Bernhard Tauchnitz 1837–1912, Leipzig 1912, 75–9.

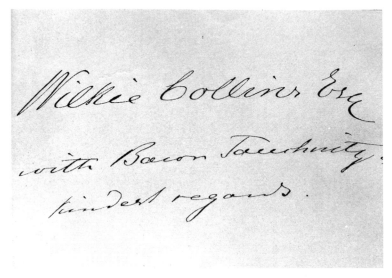

(*above*) Inscription from Baron Tauchnitz to Wilkie Collins on the special edition of the Collection of British Authors, Volume 2000, in 1881
(*right*) Tavistock House, Dickens's home from 1851 and the setting for his amateur theatricals

Tavistock House *Dickens's home in London's Tavistock Square from November 1851. It was finally sold in the summer of 1860 after he had moved to *Gad's Hill. The large schoolroom was converted into 'the smallest theatre in the world' for *amateur theatricals. These included productions of *The Lighthouse* (1855) and *The Frozen Deep* (1857).

television adaptations
The Moonstone (BBC, 23 Aug.–2 Oct. 1959); seven-part adaptation by A. R. Rawlinson, produced by Shaun Sutton; with Patrick Cargill as *Cuff and James Hayter as *Betteredge.

The Moonstone (BBC, 16 Jan.–13 Feb. 1972); five-part adaptation by Hugh Leonard, directed by Paddy Russell; with John Welsh as Cuff and Basil Dignam as Betteredge.

The Moonstone (BBC, 29–30 Dec. 1996); two-part film adaptation by Kevin Elyot, directed by Robert Bierman; with Greg Wise as Franklin Blake, Antony Sher as Cuff and Peter Vaughan as Betteredge.

The Woman in White (BBC, 2 Oct.–6 Nov. 1966); six-part adaptation by Michael Voysey, directed by Brandon Acton-Bond; with Francis de Wolff as *Fosco, Jennifer Hilary as Laura *Fairlie, Nicholas Pennell as Walter *Hartright, and Alethea Charlton as Marian *Halcombe.

The Woman in White (BBC, 14 Apr.–12 May 1982); five-part adaptation by Ray Jenkins, directed by John Bruce; with Alan Badel (his last role) as Count Fosco, Jenny Seagrove as Laura Fairlie, Daniel Gerroll as Walter Hartright, and Diana Quick as Marian Halcombe.

There have also been German television films of *The Woman in White*, *The Moonstone* and *Armadale*.

See also FILM VERSIONS, RADIO ADAPTATIONS

Temple Bar (1860–1906). Literary magazine founded in December 1860 by the publisher J. Maxwell. Its first editor was G. A. *Sala who was succeeded in 1866 by his assistant editor Edmund *Yates. George *Bentley bought *Temple Bar* in January 1866 for £2,750 and became its editor from 1867 until his death in 1895. Collins contributed: *The New Magdalen*, Oct. 1872–July 1873; *The Frozen Deep*, Aug.–Oct. 1874; *The Two Destinies*, Jan.–Sept. 1876; 'The Mystery of Marmaduke', Jan. 1879.

Two articles about Collins appeared: 'The Novels of Wilkie Collins', by Edmund Yates, Aug. 1890, 528–32; and 'Wilkie Collins', by Lewis Melville, Sept. 1903, 360–8.

TAVISTOCK HOUSE.

'Terribly Strange Bed, A' Short story originally published 24 April 1852 as Collins's first contribution to *Household Words. Later included in *After Dark* (1856) as 'The Traveller's Story of a Terribly Strange Bed'.

➤ Faulkner, the narrator, tells how as a young man he visited a low-class gambling house in Paris. After breaking the bank, he accepts accommodation rather than risk taking his large winnings home late at night. The canopy of the four-poster bed is attached to a screw by which

it can be lowered from the room above to suffocate unsuspecting victims. Unable to sleep, Faulkner discovers the danger, escaping to return with the police.

The same plot was used for 'The Inn of the Two Witches' (1913), a tale by Joseph Conrad who claimed never to have read Collins's story.

Thackeray, William Makepeace

(1811–63). Novelist and journalist, contributor to *Fraser's Magazine* and *Punch, first editor of The *Cornhill. Collins met him at *Gad's Hill and Folkestone, and in 1855 attended a dinner given before Thackeray's departure to America. In 1857 Thackeray, *Dickens and *Lemon were Collins's guests at the *Olympic for the first night of The *Lighthouse. The following year, however, Collins and Dickens both resigned from the *Garrick Club over Thackeray's disagreement with *Yates.

Thackeray liked *The Woman in White* and sat up all night reading it. He also congratulated Collins on the £5,000 negotiated for *Armadale*. After Thackeray's sudden death in 1863, Collins reflected that he 'never became intimate with him—but we always met on friendly and pleasant terms. He has left a great name, most worthily won.' Thackeray was a neighbour and close friend of Charles and Kate *Collins in his last years, and it

(above left) Jenny Seagrove as Laura Fairlie and Daniel Gerroll as Walter Hartright in the 1982 BBC television production of *The Woman in White*
(above right) *Temple Bar* for March 1876 during the serialization of *The Two Destinies*
(right) Programme for *The New Magdalen* at the National Standard Theatre, May 1875

was to them that his daughters turned first when he died unexpectedly.

The Cornhill, 6 (August 1862), 285.
Ray, G. N., *Letters and Private Papers of W. M. Thackeray,* vol 4, London 1945.
Robinson (1951), 185.

theatres In addition to *amateur theatricals, Collins's *plays were professionally produced at several London theatres: *Globe (*Miss Gwilt*); National Standard (*The New Magdalen*); Novelty (*The New Magdalen*); *Prince of Wales (*Man and Wife*); Royal *Olympic (*The Frozen Deep, The Moonstone, The New Magdalen, No Thoroughfare, The Red Vial, The Woman in White*); Royal *Lyceum (*The Dead Secret*); Surrey Theatre (unauthorized production of *The Woman in White*); Theatre Royal *Adelphi (*Black and White, No Thoroughfare, Rank and Riches*); Theatre Royal Haymarket (*Man and Wife*); Vaudeville (*The Evil Genius*).

Collins's plays also appeared in provincial theatres such as: Alexandra Theatre, *Liverpool (*Miss Gwilt*); Colosseum, Oldham (*The New Magdalen*); Margate The-

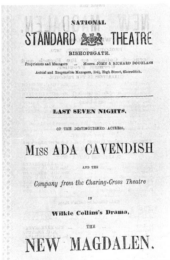

atre Royal (*Man and Wife*); Theatre Royal Guernsey (*Man and Wife*); Theatre Royal Leicester (*The Woman in White*).

American theatres included: Boston Museum (*No Thoroughfare*); Broadway, New York (*The New Magdalen, The Woman in White*); Fifth Avenue, New York (*Man and Wife, No Name*); Globe, Boston (*Black and White*); Park, Brooklyn (unauthorized production of *Identity; or No Thoroughfare*); Wallack's, New York (*Miss Gwilt*).

Parrish (1940).

theatrical productions See AMATEUR THEATRICALS; PLAYS; THEATRES.

Thomas, Charles Worked with the printers Robson & Sons during the 1879 serialization of *The *Fallen Leaves*; congratulated by Collins on 'the admirably correct manner in which the proofs have been read'. Thomas subsequently assisted editorially on *The *World*, writing a memo to Edmund *Yates complaining of 'a little too much W.C.'

Thorpe Ambrose In *Armadale* (1866), Allan *Armadale's Norfolk country house. Also the name of the nearby town which according to S. M. Ellis was based on either Aylsham or Thorpe, a suburb of Norwich. Collins had personally investigated the Norfolk Broads, staying in Great Yarmouth during August 1864. Hurle Mere where *Midwinter first meets Lydia *Gwilt is based on Horsey Mere.

Ellis (1931), 36.

three-deckers Victorian novels issued in three volumes. The name derived from the three-decked ships of the eighteenth century when most early novels had been issued in two to seven volumes. From the time of Scott's death in 1832 and for the next sixty years, the format for the majority of fiction was standardized at three volumes with a price of 10s. 6d. each, or 31s. 6d. for the complete novel.

The system of high-priced fiction ideally suited the *circulating libraries such as *Mudie's and *Smiths. Most people were unable to afford 31s. 6d. and subscribed to the libraries which, by buying large quantities, could negotiate huge discounts. Three separate volumes meant books could be lent simultaneously to three different subscribers to increase profits further. When a title was no longer required for loan, it was sold second-hand for a price which often recouped much of the original cost. Typically, the book version of a novel was published a few weeks before serialization finished which further encouraged borrowing. Publishers were also keen on the system. They operated on large profit margins, even though the discounted price gradually dropped from 20s. to 15s. between 1850 and 1870, and they were also able to achieve guaranteed sales in advance to the libraries.

Most authors were happy to publish in three volumes because it gave them respectability and once they achieved library sales their reputations became established. The format therefore dictated the way in which a story was written. Volumes I and II would typically end at a point of suspense and the beginning of the next volume would incorporate a summary in case its predecessor was not to hand. In *The Woman in White* Volume I ends with Laura Fairlie's doomed marriage to Glyde; and Volume II concludes with Laura standing beside her own gravestone. Marian Halcombe and Walter Hartright give summaries at the beginning of the second and third volumes respectively.

To fill three volumes authors padded out stories while publishers used large type, wide margins, generous line spacing and heavy paper. Collins accused the 'vicious circulating library system' of encouraging 'interminable descriptions, dull moralisings, or tedious conversations'. Of his own books, nineteen were first issued in three volumes, nine in two volumes and only six in one volume.

The fortunes of authors and publishers were inextricably linked with the three-volume format. Sadleir described how in 1894, when the circulating libraries no longer found them profitable, 'In an orgy of magniloquence . . . the three decker plunged to extinction.' The demise was assisted by the falling quality of many novels and the increasingly early publication of cheap one-volume editions.

Griest, G. L., *Mudie's Circulating Library and the Victorian Novel*, Bloomington, Ind., and Newton Abbot 1970.
Sadleir, M., *The Evolution of Publishers' Binding Styles 1770–1900*, London 1930, 73.

Tillotson,   William   Frederic (1844–89). Northern newspaper proprietor who owned the *Bolton Weekly Journal* and several other Lancashire papers. In 1873 Tillotson set up the 'Fiction Bureau'. This paid popular authors a fixed fee for the rights to serialize their works in his syndicate of English newspapers without conflicting with book publication rights. This appealed to Collins as a way of reaching a far wider audience and his works appeared in provincial papers such as the *Eccles and Patricroft Journal*, *Farnworth Journal and Observer*, *Leigh Journal and Times* and *Tyldesley Weekly Journal and Atherton News*. Other authors included Mary *Braddon, Charles *Reade and Anthony *Trollope.

Collins's dealings with Tillotson began in 1879 with the syndication of *Jezebel's Daughter* in the *Bolton Weekly Journal* (13 Sept. 1879–31 Jan. 1880) and several other Northern newspapers. The relationship, however, was fraught with difficulties and Collins subsequently used A. P.

Three-deckers (and two-deckers), the predominant publishing format for fiction during the nineteenth century

*Watt to arrange the serialization of *The Evil Genius* (Dec. 1885–May 1886) and *The Legacy of Cain* (Feb.–July 1888). Both Collins and Tillotson complained through Watt of each other's behaviour throughout their association. Tillotson also acquired the American rights to *The Legacy of Cain* and sold advance sheets to *Lovell's Library.

Law, G., 'The Serial Publication in Britain of the Novels of Wilkie Collins', *Humanitas*, 33 (20 Feb. 1995), Waseda University Law Society.

Law, G., 'Wilkie in the Weeklies: The Serialization and Syndication of Collins's Late Novels' in *Victorian Periodicals Review*, 30 Autumn 1997

Peters, C. (1991), 416–17.

Singleton, F. *Tillotsons, 1850–1950: Centenary of a Family Business*, Bolton and London 1950.

Tindell, William Collins's friend and confidant; his solicitor from the 1860s until succeeded by Henry *Bartley in 1877. Apart from relying heavily on Tindell for personal and *copyright matters, Collins frequently asked his advice on legal points for his novels. Tindell's firm Benham and Tindell was located in Essex Street off the *Strand. They drew up the 'regular corker' of a contract with *Tinsley for the publication of *The Moonstone*. Correspondence between Collins and Tindell is located in The Mitchell Library, Glasgow.

Tinsley, William (1831–1902). London publisher at 8 Catherine Street, Strand; originally in partnership with his younger brother, Edward (d. 1866). The firm was noted for its novels and light literature. William Tinsley has been portrayed as stupid and uneducated, 'quite witless and quite h-less.' Nevertheless his impressive list of authors reads like a roll-call of nineteenth-century fiction. Apart from Collins, it included Mary *Braddon, Rhoda Broughton, Thomas Hardy, Ouida, G. A. *Sala, Anthony *Trollope, Mrs Henry Wood and Edmund *Yates. In 1864, Tinsley suffered from the closure of his biggest customer, the Library Company, and ultimately the firm failed in 1878, due mainly to extravagant living and financial naïvety.

Tinsley was introduced to Collins through *Dickens and published *The Moonstone* in 1868. Edward Downey, Tinsley's employee, recorded of the contract that 'Wilkie's solicitors sent in a draft which was a regular corker; it would pretty well cover the gable of an ordinary-sized house'. Tinsley felt that sales of three-volume novels were falling off and was prepared to print only a relatively small first edition of 1,500 copies. Despite *Mudie's disappointing order for only 500, the edition easily sold out. Tinsley, obviously short of money, paid Collins cash for only £300 of the £1,400 total. The remainder was in bills of hand or postponed until receipts were in. Collins was keen for a second edition of 500 copies, and asked for advance payment of a flat sum in proportion to the first printing. According to Tinsley, he considered this too risky and proposed payment according to actual sales. Shortly after, he intervened with his printer to stop another publisher from using the standing type. Prompted by a favourable review in *The Times*, Collins finally accepted Tinsley's terms, which the publisher reduced by £50 for his trouble. Despite their disagreement, Tinsley in 1870 wanted to publish both *Man and Wife* and a cheap edition of *The Moonstone*.

Downey, E., *Twenty Years Ago*, London 1905, 23–6.

Sutherland, J. A., *Victorian Novelists and Publishers*, London 1976, 46–7.

Tinsley, W., *Random Recollections of an Old Publisher* (2 vols), London 1900, i. 114–17.

William Tinsley, the publisher of *The Moonstone* in 1868

Tommie Collins's Scotch terrier. Immortalized in *My Lady's Money* as possibly the first canine detective, of whom at the end of the story 'he was too fond to say good-bye'.

See also ANIMALS AND PETS.

Townshend, Revd Chauncy Hare (1798–1868). Wealthy and eccentric friend of *Dickens, *Bulwer-Lytton, Baroness Burdett-Coutts and *Millais. Poet, author and contributor to *Household Words*; amateur painter, musician and geologist. Also a collector of coins and gems, and one of the first connoisseurs and collectors of early photography. Townshend was interested in clairvoyance and mesmerism and met Dickens in 1840 through Dr *Elliotson. He was a witness at Charles *Collins's wedding to Kate *Dickens in July 1860. Dickens dedicated *Great Expectations* (1861) to Townshend who in turn made Dickens his literary executor.

Collins met Townshend at *Tavistock House and later in *Boulogne and Lausanne, where Townshend spent most of his later life. It is very likely that Limmeridge House in *The Woman in White* is based on Townshend's house in Norfolk Street and that Townshend, himself a renowned hypochondriac with a servant called Henri Foosters, forms the model for Mr Fairlie with his jewels and valet Louis. Collins describes in the novel '. . . a large, lofty room with a magnificently carved ceiling . . . little stands in buhl and marquetterie, loaded with figures in Dresden China, with rare vases, ivory ornaments, and toys and curiosities that sparkled at all points with gold, silver and precious stones.' Mr Fairlie in the novel arranges to have his collection photographed.

*Fitzgerald considered the eccentric Cousin Feenix in *Dombey and Son* was also based on Townshend. His collection of jewels is now in the Wisbech Museum. This also houses the original manuscript of *Great Expectations* as well as an 1850s' letter from Collins discussing a 'bell-pulling ghost'.

Haworth-Booth, M. (editor), *The Golden Age of British Photography 1839–1900*, London and New York 1984, 15, 21.

PELCD, vol 8

Train, The (1856–8). Illustrated literary periodical founded by Edmund *Yates as

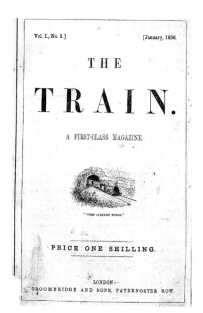

The first issue in 1856 of Edmund Yates's magazine *The Train*

a co-operative venture with G. A. *Sala, Frank Smedley and others. Later contributors were Lewis Carroll, John Hollingshead and Palgrave *Simpson. In June 1857, Collins was the second in the 'Men of Mark' series. Yates described him as the most conscientious novelist of the day and a story-teller without equal. He placed Collins fourth in rank among the British writers of the time, behind *Dickens, *Thackeray and Charlotte Brontë.

translations Collins's works were routinely translated into French, German, Italian, Russian and Spanish and to some extent into Polish (*Miss or Mrs?*, 1873 and *After Dark*, 1877); Swedish (*No Thoroughfare*, 1868 and *Jezebel's Daughter*, 1880) and Hungarian (*The Legacy of Cain*). In 1883 Collins even learned that beginning with *The Woman in White* his works were about to be translated into Bengali. *Pirated translations were common and amounts paid for authorized publication were generally small. The German translation rights of *The Moonstone* earned £35; *The Law and the Lady* in Italian 200 francs (£8); *Man and Wife* in Dutch 100 guilders (£8–£9); and *The Moonstone* in French received an offer of £20–£40.

Beginning in 1858 with *The Dead Secret*, Collins's main authorized French publishers were *Hachette, although *The Woman in White* and *No Name* were issued in Paris by J. Hetzel. Translators included É.-D. *Forgues, Camille de Cendrey and C. Bernard-Derosne against whom Collins took legal action in 1878 to stop the use of his and *Dickens's name for *La Crime de Jasper*.

Italian translators included Alberto *Caccia, Lida Cerracchini and A. M. Lessona. Authorized publishers in Milan were Fratelli Treves (*The Moonstone*, 1870) and Edoardo Sonzogno (*Heart and Science*, 1884), but Collins complained of pirate newspapers stealing *The Law and the Lady* in 1875 and *The Fallen Leaves* in 1879.

By 1888 Collins recalled that virtually all of his books had appeared in German where his main translator was Émil *Lehmann. In Holland, *Belinfante Brothers of The Hague originally produced pirated editions, in common with other firms from Amsterdam that issued *The Dead Secret* in 1858, *The Woman in White* in 1861 and *Basil* in 1864. After a lengthy battle over payment for *Man and Wife* (1870), however, Belinfante became Collins's authorized Dutch publishers and by 1885 had issued twenty-five titles.

In Russia, Collins was always extremely popular and almost all of his works were translated. The publication dates of both serializations and book editions were remarkably early with the *Delo Journal*, for example, issuing *The Frozen Deep* (July–Aug. 1874) and *The Law and the Lady* (Nov. 1874–May 1875). In Moscow he was issued by the University Press while the most frequent book publishers in St Petersburg were I. N. Glazunov (*The Myrtle Room* [*The Dead Secret*] 1857, *The Woman in White* 1860, *No Name* 1862, *The Moonstone* 1868); and E. N. Akhmatova (*Poor Miss Finch* 1873, *The Queen of Hearts* 1875, *The Black Robe* 1881). Short stories included 'Mad Monkton' (1866), 'John

---

(*below*) A modern Russian edition of *Armadale*
(*bottom left*) An Italian edition of *Man and Wife* in 1877
(*bottom right*) A Swedish edition of *No Thoroughfare* in 1868

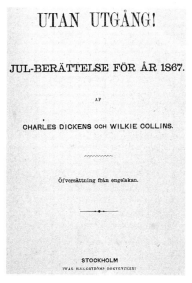

Jago's Ghost' (1875) and 'She Loves and Lies' (1884). *The Woman in White* and *The Moonstone* have constantly been republished and modern editions have printings of several hundred thousand copies.

> Gesamtverzeichnis des deutschsprachigen Schrifttums (GV) 1700–1910 (complete index of German Language Literature 1700–1910).
>
> 'Saltykov Schedrin' (catalogue of the St Petersburg Public Library).

Trollope, Anthony (1815–82). Prolific novelist best known for his Barsetshire and Palliser series. Highly regarded by Collins for his energetic but consistently workmanlike production of fiction. He wrote to Horace *Pym in 1887: 'By comparison with my late "colleague", Anthony Trollope, with his watch on the table, and his capacity for writing a page in every quarter of an hour, I am the slowest coach now on the literary road.'

Though Trollope, who confessed to being uninterested in plot, thought that a good novel might be both 'realistic' and 'sensational', Collins's fiction received a rather guarded assessment in Trollope's 1883 *Autobiography*. 'Of Wilkie Collins it is impossible for a true critic not to speak with admiration, because he has excelled all his contemporaries in a certain most difficult branch of his art.' Trollope continues, however, 'The construction is most minute and most wonderful. But I can never lose the taste of the construction . . .. One is constrained by mysteries and hemmed in by difficulties, knowing, however, that the mysteries will be made clear, and the difficulties overcome at the end of the third volume. Such work gives me no pleasure.'

Nevertheless, *The Eustace Diamonds* (1873) borrows more than a little from *The Moonstone* (1868) and in 1873 Collins was in correspondence with *Harpers on Trollope's behalf concerning US publication.

> Harper (1912), 346–7.
>
> Milley, H. J. W., 'The Eustace Diamonds and The Moonstone', *Studies in Philology*, 36 (Oct. 1939), 651–63.
>
> Pym, H. N., *A Tour Round My Book-Shelves*, privately printed, 1891, 41.

'Twin Sisters, The' Short story originally published in *Bentley's Miscellany*, March 1851. Collins's earliest attempt at fiction with a contemporary setting. It introduces the themes of love at first

Caricature of Anthony Trollope in *Once a Week*, 1 June 1872

sight which re-appears in *Basil* (1852) and *identity which features in much of his subsequent work. In 1859, Collins unsuccessfully submitted an adaptation of 'The Twin Sisters' as a farce for the *Olympic Theatre.

⦿ Mr Streatfield falls in love at first sight with a girl he sees on a balcony. He effects an introduction to Jane Langley, proposes and is accepted. But on the eve of their wedding he meets her twin sister, Clara, and realizes he has proposed to the wrong girl. Jane nobly sacrifices her own happiness by retiring to a life of seclusion. Streatfield marries Clara, but the girls' aunt knows he will come to regret his choice.

> Ashley, R. P., 'Wilkie Collins' First Short Story', *More Books*, 23 (Mar. 1948), 105–6.
>
> Wolff, R. L., *Nineteenth-Century Fiction: A Bibliographical Catalogue* (5 vols), New York and London, 1981.

Two Destinies, The: A Romance

'The only happy marriages are those in which the two destined spirits have succeeded in meeting one another in this sphere of life.'

Illustration to Harpers US edition of *The Two Destinies* in 1876; first serialized in *Harper's Bazar*

Novel published in 1876 and dedicated to Charles *Reade. Collins explores the themes of 'destined spirits' and *supernatural visions. He acknowledges taking the second idea from a case reported in Robert Dale Owen's *Footfalls on the Boundary of another World*. This describes how a ship's captain is convinced to change course after seeing an apparition and saves the passengers of a wrecked ship, including the person in the vision.
•❖ George and Mary are childhood sweethearts in Suffolk's Greenwater Broad. Despite a prediction from Mary's grandmother, old Mrs Dermody, that their two destinies are inextricably linked, George's father disapproves. He separates them by taking his family to America where he subsequently dies. George and his mother return to England where she marries Mr Germaine, a rich suitor she had known before her first marriage.

George has no way of tracing Mary and leads a dissolute existence which prematurely ages his appearance. He reforms, trains to become a surgeon, and takes up an appointment in India. After being wounded in the shoulder, George returns to England where he inherits his step-father's fortune and estate in Perthshire. There is a condition that he must change his name to Germaine.

Mary meanwhile has suffered a serious illness which has totally changed her looks. She has married a Dutchman called Van Brandt and is also living in the same part of Scotland. When Mary dis-covers that her marriage is bigamous, she throws herself into the river but is saved by George.

They fail to recognize each other but develop an almost telepathic attraction. George sees an apparition of Mary calling him to Edinburgh. They meet and he learns that Mary had dreamed of him at exactly the same time. She declines his help and he next sees her in London, still in company with Van Brandt. George proposes marriage but Mary, who has a baby daughter, refuses, for fear of spoiling his life.

George goes away to the Shetlands to forget but injures his wounded shoulder. He is nursed back to health by the mysteriously disfigured Miss Dunross to whom he confides his story. On his recovery, he sees another apparition which leads him to Mary and her child, starving in lodgings near St Paul's. Van Brandt is in a debtors' prison and George helps by paying off the debts. He again proposes but Mary goes abroad with Van Brandt.

George's mother dies shortly after. Alone and in despair, he returns to Suffolk where he contemplates suicide. He is saved by a third apparition which takes him to the ghost town of Enkhuizen on the coast of Holland. Van Brandt has embezzled money from his old company and abandoned Mary and her child. When she refuses marriage for a third time, George resolves to drown himself and take Mary with him. At the last moment she sees a childhood memento which she once made for him. They finally recognize each other and their two destinies are reunited. Newly married, they are ostracized from society because of malicious scandal. They leave England to start a new life in Naples.

Serialization. *Harper's Bazar*, 25 Dec. 1875–9 Sept. 1876; *Temple Bar*, Jan.–Sept. 1876.
Book publication
1st edn. 2 vols, *Chatto & Windus, London 1876. Reddish-brown cloth, front covers blocked in black, spines lettered in gilt, cream endpapers. Half-title in vol I. Published between 16 and 31 Aug. 1876. Variant binding in green cloth.
Vol I (viii) + 312 pp.
Vol II iv + 304 pp. 32 pp publisher's catalogue dated Sept. 1876 bound in at end.
1-vol edns. Chatto & Windus 1878–1906. Sutton, Stroud 1995.
1st US edn. *Harper, New York 1876.
Translations. Russian, St Petersburg 1876, 1878; Dutch, The Hague 1877; Italian, Milan 1884; French, Paris 188?.

Universal Review, The (1888–90). Elaborately illustrated literary journal, founded and edited by Harry *Quilter from May 1888. Authors included William Archer, Alphonse Daudet and Victor Hugo; artists, W. Crane, W. P. *Frith, F. Leighton and D. G. Rossetti. It published Collins's '*Reminiscences of a Story-Teller' in June 1888 and 'In Memoriam Amici (Wilkie Collins)' by Harry Quilter in October 1889.

'Unknown Public, The' Essay written for *Household Words (21 Aug. 1858) and reprinted in *My Miscellanies (1863). Collins discovers the penny novel-journals and an estimated 'monster audience of at least three million!' who accept through ignorance dull, conventional fiction of the poorest quality. The article recognizes that 'The future of English fiction may rest with this Unknown Public, which is now waiting to be taught the difference between a good book and a bad.'

Throughout his career Collins was keen to be published in cheap editions to achieve the widest possible readership. He consistently aspired to gain 'The readers who rank by millions . . . who give the widest reputations, who return the richest rewards, and who will therefore command the service of the best writers of their time.' In January 1867 Collins seriously considered writing for the penny journals and William *Frith later recalled that Collins refused to be insulted when accused of being read in 'every back-kitchen in England'.

unpublished drafts At his death Collins left a miscellany of notes, fragments and drafts of unpublished material.

'The Case of Rosalind Druse': notes for a 'drama or novel—or both', originally intended for *Frank Leslie's Illustrated Newspaper of 5 Mar. 1887.

'A Little Fable': one-page story about the meeting between two old friends, a mathematician and a lawyer, probably written at the same time as Heart and Science, bearing a strong similarity to the opening lines of Chapter 2. (Published by the WCS, July 1996; and see below.)

'Love and Liberty': outline for a story.

'The Marriage in Cana': draft essay on the history of art.

'Miss Warrener's Wedding': twenty-three-page draft of a plot for a locked-room murder.

'Monotonous Lives of the Middle Class': notes for a possible novel.

'The Story of the Mad Woman who was no Mad Woman': annotated draft dated 20 Dec. 1860, told to Collins by a Mr Lutwych.

'The Widowed Wives': notes for a comedy.

Index of English Literary Manuscripts, Rosenbaum, B. and P. White, iv: (1800–1900), London and New York 1982, 663–79.

'A Little Fable'

The other day, two good friends—a lawyer and a mathematician—happened to meet in a remote part of London, in front of a cheap bookshop. The stall outside the shop presented a row of novels, offered at half price.

Having exchanged the customary expressions of pleasure and surprise, and having made the necessary enquiries on the subject of wives and children, the two gentlemen relapsed into a momentary silence. Perceiving in his friend signs of mental pre-occupation, the lawyer asked what he was thinking of. The mathematician answered, 'I was looking back along the procession of small circumstances, which has led me from the starting-point of my own door to this unexpected meeting in the street.'

Hearing this, it occurred to the lawyer to look back, on his side. He also discovered that a procession of small circumstances had carried him, by devious ways, to the morsel of pavement on which he then stood. 'Well,' he said, 'and what do you make of it?'

'I have led a serious life,' the mathematician announced, 'for forty years.'

'So have I,' the lawyer said.

'And I have just discovered,' the other continued, 'that a man in the midst of reality is also, in this strange life of ours, a man in the midst of romance.'

The lawyer pondered a little on that reply. 'And what does your discovery amount to?' he asked.

'Only to this. I have been to school; I have been to college; I am sixty years old—and my education is not complete. Good morning.'

They parted. As soon as the lawyer's back was turned, the mathematician retraced his steps to the book-shop—and bought a novel.

The lawyer looked round at that moment. A strong impression was produced on him. He walked back to his friend. 'When you have done with that book,' he said, 'lend it to me.'

USA See AMERICA.

Vanity Fair (1868–1928). Society paper noted for its colourful cartoons and biographical sketches, founded in 1868 by Thomas Gibson Bowles (1842–1922).

Artists included Spy (Leslie *Ward), Ape (Carlo Pellegrini) and Adriano Cecioni who drew Collins as 'The Novelist Who Invented Sensation' for the issue of 3 Feb.

No. 170. **MEN OF THE DAY, No. 39.**
" The Novelist who invented Sensation."

1872. The text was by Bowles, using the pseudonym Jehu Junior: 'His best work is perhaps *Armadale*, and his special merit is that he treats a labyrinthine story in an apparently simple manner.'

Vanstone, Magdalen Eighteen-year-old heroine of *No Name*, an example of one of Collins's determined female characters. Disinherited on the death of her parents, she sets out to earn her living on the stage as a character actress. Attempts to recover the family fortune by marrying her wealthy cousin, Noel Vanstone, under the assumed name of Susan Bygrave, but is finally thwarted by Mrs *Lecount.

Venice Visited by Collins with his father in May and June 1838, and with Charles *Dickens and Augustus *Egg in November 1853. Used as the setting for *The Haunted Hotel* (1879).

Verinder, Rachel In *The Moonstone*, niece of John *Herncastle and recipient of the legacy of the *Moonstone. After the diamond is stolen, Rachel behaves in a way which is inexplicable to the other characters. In his preface, Collins states that the object of the novel is 'to trace the influence of character on circumstances. The conduct pursued, under a sudden emergency, by a young girl, supplies the foundation on which I have built this book.'

verse Collins wrote verse as a young man. A comic example exists in an 1844 letter to his parents, and for his *amateur theatricals he composed a verse prologue for *The Good-Natur'd Man*. The only published examples identified are in *Antonina* (1850) and a few lines in 'The *Poetry Did It' (1885). Other verses are given in R. C. *Lehmann's *Memories of Half a Century*, light-hearted pieces sent to Nina *Lehmann. Also included is Collins's

'The Novelist Who Invented Sensation', cartoon of Collins in *Vanity Fair*, 3 February 1872

translation of an ode by Horace from Latin to English, done from an English prose version, to help Rudy Lehmann with his homework.

'Victims of Circumstances Discovered in Records of Old Trials'

Collins narrates the story of two miscarriages of justice. The unfortunate victims are wrongly convicted on circumstantial evidence and executed for crimes they did not commit.

First published in the *Youth's Companion*, Boston, 19 August 1886. Republished in the English *Boy's Own Paper* where Part I, 'A Sad Death and Brave Life' appeared on 23 Oct. 1886; Part II, 'Farmer Fairweather', on 26 Sept. 1887. Reprinted by the WCS, Nov. 1992; and in *Wilkie Collins: The Complete Shorter Fiction*, edited by Julian Thompson, 1995.

Vining, George J. (1824–75). Actor

playing Count *Fosco in *The Woman in White*. With Collins he co-directed the first authorized production at the *Olympic Theatre from 9 October 1871 to 24 February 1872. Wybert *Reeve, who recalled Vining's indecision resulting in tiresome and argumentative rehearsals, replaced him because of illness from 11 January 1872. Reeve took the play on its successful provincial tour following Collins's disagreement with Vining over alterations to the play.

Reeve (1906).

vivisection Issue covered in Collins's *didactic novel *Heart and Science* (1883). Chapter 32 presents many of the arguments still valid today against what the author calls 'the hateful secrets of Vivisection'. Collins had a great liking for *animals and in *The Moonstone* (1868) *Betteredge protests against the way gentlefolks 'catch newts, and beetles, and spiders, and frogs, and . . . cut them up, without a pang of remorse, into little pieces'.

Von Scheurer fraud Insurance fraud in 1883–4 that formed the basis of *Blind Love* (1890). The details were told to Collins by Horace *Pym over lunch at Frederick *Lehmann's, 1 December 1887. Collins was so excited by the case that he immediately wanted to jot down the details for future use. Two days later Pym sent him the complete history of the fraud but Collins was unable to use it until he had completed the serialization of *The Legacy of Cain* (1888).

Baron Von Scheurer insured his life for some £15,000 in favour of his morganatic wife, Juliana Metz. In Paris, they recruited Dr Henri Castelnau, 'a man of the vilest character'; found a dying consumptive patient called Carl Glockner with a strong resemblance to Von Scheurer; and passed him off as the dead baron. The suspicious insurance companies reluctantly paid up but the truth was

Collins's notes for the Von Scheurer fraud, from details given to him by Horace Pym in 1888

discovered in 1887 via one of the servants. Juliana Metz, Castelnau and two accomplices eventually received long prison sentences; Von Scheurer committed suicide and the companies recovered £11,000.

Pym, H. N., *A Tour Round My Bookshelves*, privately printed 1891.

The Times, 25–7 Apr. and 1 May 1888.

Walker, Frederick, A.R.A. (1840–75). Influential painter in oils and water-colours; illustrator for *Thackeray and *The *Cornhill*. Friend of *Millais, Wilkie Collins and his brother Charles *Collins, at whose house Walker made the original sketch for his striking theatre poster of *The Woman in White*.

See illustrations on p. 146.

Ward, Charles James (1814–83). Elder brother of Edward *Ward and ded-icatee of *Basil* (1852). Followed his father, also Charles Ward, into *Coutts & Co and in addition to his lifelong friendship became financial adviser to Collins. He married Jane Carpenter, Wilkie's favourite cousin, in February 1845 and they had eleven children over a period of fourteen and a half years.

Ward travelled with Collins to *France in 1844, 1847 and 1849, and to Belgium in 1846. The 1847 Normandy trip appeared as 'A Pictorial Tour to St George Bosherville' in *Bentley's Miscellany*, May 1851; reprinted WCS, 1996. Ward was a fre-quent dinner guest of the Collins house-holds in *Harley Street and *Gloucester

Place. He sailed with Collins and *Pigott off *Broadstairs in 1862 while Wilkie was writing *No Name*, and from Great Yarmouth in 1864 during research for *Ar-madale*. Collins also used Ward for other research such as the time taken for a letter to reach Zurich (in *No Name*). He became executor to Collins's last *will in 1882, being replaced after his early death from cancer by H. P. *Bartley.

Smith, R. J., 'Margaret Carpenter (1793–1872): A Salisbury Artist Restored', *Hatcher Review*, 4 (Autumn 1993), 2–32.

Ward, Charles James (Senior) (1781–1858). Father of *Charles and *Ed-ward Ward. Friend of Wilkie's father, William *Collins, and manager for *Coutts & Co. Married to Mary Ford.

Ward, Edward Matthew, R.A. (Ned) (1816–79). Brother of *Charles Ward and long-standing friend of Collins. Associate of the *Royal Academy in 1846 and a full member in 1855, he typically painted scenes from English history of the seven-teenth century. These included Collins posing as a courtier in *The Disgrace of*

Clarendon. Another subject was Henrietta *Ward (no relation) whom he secretly married in 1848. Collins verified the legal situation, masterminded the elopement and later made use of the theme of secret marriage in *Basil* (1852), 'The *Biter Bit' (1858) and '*Miss or Mrs?' (1871). Ward de-signed costumes and enjoyed *amateur theatricals with Collins such as Sheridan's *The Rivals*, which appears in *No Name*. He also designed the admission ticket for *Dickens's production of *Not So Bad as We Seem* at Devonshire House in 1851. Ward went through periods of depres-sion and committed suicide by cutting his throat in January 1879.

Ellis (1931), 49–50.

Ward, Francis (Frank) (b. 1850). Son of *Charles and *Jane Ward; godson of Collins. Employed for a while by Sebast-ian *Schlesinger in the USA and acted as Collins's secretary for part of his reading tour to North *America in 1873.

Ward, Henrietta Ada Mary, née Ward (1832–1924). Wife of Edward *Ward and historical artist in her own right. Sat for Ward's *South Sea Bubble* which was ex-hibited at the *Royal Academy in 1847. They became engaged when she was fourteen and a half and, in the face of parental opposition to such a young mar-riage, they eloped on 4 May 1848. They had six children: Alice (b. 1849 and Wilkie's goddaughter), Eva, Flora, *Leslie, Wriothesley and Stanhope. Collins considered Henrietta's best pic-ture *Palissy the Potter* in 1866.

Maas, J., *The Victorian Art World in Pho-tographs*, London 1984, 55.

Ward, H. M., *Mrs E. M. Ward's Reminis-cences*, edited by Elliott O'Donnell, Lon-don 1911.

Ward, H. M., *Memories of Ninety Years*, edited by Isabel G. McAllister, London 1924.

RICHARD WILSON   DANIEL DEFOE

E. M. Ward's ticket design for Dickens's production of *Not So Bad as We Seem* for the Guild of Literature and Art in 1851

Ward, Jane, née Carpenter (1826–91). Collins's favourite cousin, daughter of his aunt Margaret *Carpenter. Married Charles *Ward in February 1845. Died in Ilfracombe aged 65.

Ward, Sir Leslie (Spy) (1851–1922). Second child of *Edward and *Henrietta Ward. Always a favourite of Wilkie, of whom he made a pencil sketch when he was only 11. Artist best known for his cartoons and character portraits in *Vanity Fair* from 1873 onwards. Knighted in 1918.

Wardour, Richard Self-sacrificing character in *The Frozen Deep* (1857). Played by Charles *Dickens to such effect that, according to Dickens, Collins as Frank *Aldersley 'shook like a mound of jelly'.

Watt,   Alexander   Pollock (1834–1914). Generally regarded as the first professional literary agent. Following a career with the publisher, Alexander Strahan, Watt set up as an agent in the mid- to late 1870s and dominated the field for some twenty-five years. Collins first approached him on 5 December 1881 and they signed a formal agreement five days later. Watt negotiated the 1882 newspaper serialization of *Heart and Science* and their association continued for many years. Other clients included Conan *Doyle, Bret *Harte, Mrs *Oliphant and James *Payn.

Collins had always been very successful in negotiating with publishers and established a reputation as a fair but hard bargainer. By 1880, there were some twenty books in print for which he had constantly to review contracts and ensure payment for revised English, American, Colonial and translated editions. In addition, Collins did not like dealing with some publishers such as *Tillotson and he needed to place new novels and several short stories. Employing Watt was therefore a logical step to avoid the constant drain on his time which could be better spent in writing books. The two became good friends and Collins presented Watt with the manuscript of '*She Loves and Lies' in January 1884 and an annotated copy of the *Memoirs of the Life of William Collins, Esq., R.A.* in April 1885. Watt also arranged at Collins's suggestion that Walter *Besant should complete *Blind Love*.

In a memorandum attached to his will,

Collins wrote: 'I desire that my friend and literary representative, Mr A. P. Watt, of 2 Paternoster Square, may act as my Literary Executor, and that his advice may be accepted as representing my literary interests and wishes in regard to the copyrights of my books which may remain to be sold after my death by my other executors.' This statement was reprinted with other testimonial letters in the firm's 1893 publicity booklet.

   Hepburn, J., *The Author's Empty Purse*, London 1968, 51–5.

Webster,   Benjamin (1797–1882). Character actor, proprietor and manager of the Theatre Royal *Adelphi during the 1860s. Webster declined *The Lighthouse* in 1855 but later staged the successful *No Thoroughfare* in 1867, himself playing the part of Joey Ladle.

Whicher, Jonathan (d. 1871).
> 'Even in the detective police, a man may have a reputation to lose.' (*The Moonstone*)

The detective inspector on whom Sergeant *Cuff of *The Moonstone* is partly based. Whicher joined the police force in 1840 and the newly formed detective police in 1842. He featured prominently in the 1860 Constance *Kent Road case but his reputation as the 'Prince of Detectives' suffered after Constance Kent was acquitted and he wrongly arrested an innocent man during a subsequent murder

(right) Wilkie Collins drawn by Leslie Ward in 1862, when the artist was 11 years old
(below) Statement by Collins used by A. P. Watt in a book of testimonials

case in 1861. Whicher was also the model for Dickens's 'Sergeant Witchem' in his *Household Words* articles on the detective police: 'A Detective Police Party' (27 July and 10 Aug. 1850); and 'The Artful Touch' in 'Three "Detective" Anecdotes' (14 Sept. 1850).

Whitby North Yorkshire coastal town which Collins visited with Caroline *Graves during August 1861. He stayed at the Royal Hotel, on the West Cliff overlooking the harbour. *Reed's Illustrated Guide to Whitby* (1854) described it as a splendid establishment where every attention was paid to the comfort and requirements of the visitor. Collins began work on *No Name* (1862) but was so disturbed by the noise of children playing and a brass band hired by the proprietor that he returned to London via York and

The Late WILKIE COLLINS, Esq.

To the intense regret of all lovers of fiction, Mr. Wilkie Collins *died on the 23rd of September* 1889. *Attached to his Will was the following memorandum in his own handwriting:—*

> 90 Gloucester Place, Portman Square, W.,
> *January* 1, 1887.

I desire that my friend and literary representative, Mr. A. P. Watt, of 2 Paternoster Square, may act as my Literary Executor, and that his advice may be accepted as representing my literary interests and wishes in regard to the copyrights of my books which may remain to be sold after my death by my other executors.

WILKIE COLLINS.

*Aldeburgh. Collins was in Whitby at the same time as the extravagantly eccentric Maharajah Duleep Singh, original owner of the Koh-i-Noor diamond. The town would have been close to the fictional *Frizinghall in The Moonstone (1868).

Borish, E., *Literary Lodgings*, London 1984.

'Who is the Thief?' See 'BITER BIT, THE'

'Who Killed Zebedee?' Short story of revenge, murder and *detection; originally published in The *Spirit of the Times, 25 Dec. 1880. Reprinted in the *Seaside Library (vol 45, no. 928), 26 Jan. 1880; and as 'Mr Policeman and the Cook' in *Little Novels (1887).

➡ The narrator's deathbed confession describes a murder case in which he was personally involved as a young policeman. John Zebedee was found stabbed in his bed and although his wife, a known sleepwalker, confessed she was guilty, the case against her was dropped. The narrator, trying to make a name for himself, continued the investigation and discovered from the partially engraved murder weapon that the cook, Priscilla Thurlby, was the murderer, taking revenge on Zebedee for jilting her. The policeman admits he was in love with Priscilla and suppressed the evidence to save her from being hanged.

Wilkie, Sir David, R.A. (1785–1841). Popular Scottish painter and Wilkie Collins's godfather after whom he was named. Collins describes in the *Memoirs of the Life of William Collins, Esq., R.A.* (1848) how at the christening Sir David 'whose studies of human nature extended to everything but *infant* human nature . . . after looking intently into the child's eyes . . . exclaimed to the father with serious astonishment and satisfaction, "He *sees!*" '. Collins also recollects 'The writer of this biography remembers being often taken upon his knee, giving him a pencil and paper, and watching him, while he drew at his request, cats, dogs, and horses with a readiness and zeal which spoke eloquently for his warmth of heart and gentleness of disposition.' Sir David encouraged William *Collins to take his family to *Italy in 1836. The two artists were close friends and lengthy extracts of their correspondence are included in the *Memoirs*.

will of Wilkie Collins

'Always distrust a man's last wishes on his deathbed—unless they are communicated to his lawyer, and expressed in his will.' (*Jezebel's Daughter*)

Collins's final will was drawn up by his solicitor, Henry *Bartley, and dated 22 March 1882. The executors were Sebastian *Schlesinger, Frank *Beard and Henry Bartley. The estate was valued at £10,831 to which could be added proceeds from the *auction sales of manuscripts (£1,310), pictures (£415) and books (£200). Further sales of copyrights were made and in November 1892 the executors sold the dramatic version of *The Woman in White* for £100.

Apart from *funeral details and small bequests to servants, friends and relatives, the will formally acknowledged Collins's three children by Martha *Rudd and made provision for both her and Caroline *Graves. Martha received his gold watch and chain, £200 and half of the income from the estate for life. Caroline received his gold studs and cuff-links, items of furniture, £200 and the remaining half of the income from his estate for life. Harriet Bartley, her daughter, would inherit the same lifetime interest but after her death the income would revert to Martha's children so that they became the ultimate beneficiaries. Despite Collins's careful arrangements, Henry Bartley diverted the money from its intended recipients.

Clarke (1988), 3–8.

Wills, William Henry (1810–80). Subeditor, contributor, general manager and joint proprietor of *Household Words and *All the Year Round. Married Janet Chambers, daughter of publisher Robert Chambers; brother-in-law of Nina *Lehmann and uncle of R. C. *Lehmann. Described by *Tinsley as 'one of the best known men of his time in the London literary world'.

Wills was on the original staff of *Punch and assistant editor of *Chambers's Edinburgh Journal* (1842–5). He became *Dickens's secretary in 1845 during the establishment of the *Daily News* and subsequently worked on its staff. *Forster suggested Wills for *Household Words* and he worked with Dickens until a riding accident in 1869.

Collins first met Dickens in 1851 when Wills, who participated in the *amateur theatricals, declined to play the valet in

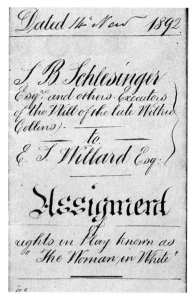

Assignment of *The Woman in White* play to E. S. Willard in Collins's will in 1892

Not So Bad as We Seem. Collins was recruited for the part by *Egg. Wills was later prompter for *The Frozen Deep* while his wife played the part of the nurse gifted with second sight. Wills acted as intermediary for most of Dickens's negotiations with Collins, including his original appointment to *Household Words* in 1856. Dickens and Collins proposed Wills to the *Garrick Club in September 1864. When Wills was blackballed the following year, both Dickens and Collins resigned, together with *Fechter.

Although Dickens considered Wills without genius and commonplace in literary matters, he valued their friendship and long association. He wrote to Wills in January 1862 'we doubt whether any two men can have gone on more happily and smoothly, or with greater trust and confidence in one another'.

Lehmann, R. C., *Charles Dickens as Editor*, London 1912.

Wimpole Street, 82 House in *Marylebone where Collins lived for the last eighteen months of his life. He wrote to Mrs *Wynne in December 1887 'The deed is done, in the matter of my future living place . . . and having solemnly vowed never to take another house—I have taken refuge in the upper floors of 82 Wimpole Street, having the whole place to myself excepting only the dining

rooms. I *may* move next month. I *must* move in February.' Wimpole Street was still convenient for his family and surviving friends, and close to his doctors in Harley Street. Collins died there on 23 September 1889.

    Letters.

Winter, William (1836–1917).

Influential dramatic critic of *The New York Tribune* from 1865 to 1909. American friend of Collins, introducing him to Mary *Anderson on her first London tour. In his personal recollections and theatrical sketches, Winter quotes correspondence and gives a comprehensively sympathetic account of Collins. 'He was a great writer: as a story-teller, specifically, he stands alone,—transcendent and incomparable: but his personality was even more interesting than his authorship. To be in his company was to be charmed, delighted stimulated and refreshed.'

    Winter, W., *Old Friends*, New York 1909.
    Winter, W., *The Wallet of Time* (2 vols), New York 1913.

Woman in White, The (book).

    'This is the story of what a Woman's patience can endure and what a Man's resolution can achieve.'

Published in 1860, one of the two novels (with *The Moonstone*) for which Collins is most famous. It firmly established his reputation with the reading public and helped raise the circulation of *All the Year Round*. As *Smith, Elder found to their cost, 'everyone was raving about it'.

S. M. Ellis described how *The Woman in White* was so popular that 'every possible commodity was labelled "Woman in White". There were "Woman in White" cloaks and bonnets, "Woman in White" perfumes and all manner of toilet requisites, "Woman in White" Waltzes and Quadrilles.' It was *parodied in *Punch and even such a critical reviewer as Mrs *Oliphant was unusually favourable. Edward Fitzgerald read it several times and considered naming a sailing boat after the determined Marian *Halcombe. Prince Albert read the book and approved. *Thackeray was engrossed from morning to sunset, and Gladstone found the story so absorbing that he missed a visit to the theatre. *The Woman in White* has never been out of print since its first publication. In the twentieth century there have been theatre, film and television adaptations and even a comic-strip version.

    The Woman in White is generally regarded as the first *sensation novel and inspired numerous imitations, most notably from Mary *Braddon. The story is in part based on an eighteenth-century case of abduction and wrongful imprisonment, taken from Méjan's *Recueil des causes célèbres*. It uses the theme of substituted *identity, a favourite with Collins, and also attacks the misuse of lunatic asylums. The story can be considered an early example of *detective fiction with the hero, Walter *Hartright, employing many of the sleuthing techniques of later

private detectives. The use of multiple narratives draws on Collins's legal training and as he points out in his Preamble: 'the story here presented will be told by more than one pen, as the story of an offence against the laws is told in Court by more than one witness'. Collins described his method of writing *The Woman in White* in 'Mr Wilkie Collins in Gloucester Place', no. 81 in 'Celebrities at Home', *The *World*, 26 Dec. 1877; and 'How I Write my Books', *The Globe*, 26 Nov. 1887. See also MUSICAL DEDICATIONS.

•◦ Walter Hartright, a young drawing-master, has secured a position in Cumberland on the recommendation of his old friend Professor Pesca, a political refugee from Italy. While walking home from *Hampstead on his last evening in London, Hartright meets a mysterious woman dressed in white, apparently in deep distress. He helps her on her way but later learns that she has escaped from an asylum. The next day he travels north to Limmeridge House. The household comprises Mr Frederick *Fairlie, a reclusive valetudinarian; Laura *Fairlie, his niece; and Marian Halcombe, her devoted half-sister. Hartright finds that Laura bears an astonishing resemblance to the woman in white, called Anne *Catherick. The simple-minded Anne

(*above left*) William Winter
(*above centre*) Letter written by Collins to Holman Hunt from 82 Wimpole Street in June 1888
(*above right*) W. H. Wills, Dickens's sub-editor on *Household Words* and *All the Year Round*

had lived for a time in Cumberland as a child and was devoted to Laura's mother, who first dressed her in white.

Hartright and Laura fall in love. Laura, however, has promised her late father that she will marry Sir Percival *Glyde, and Marian advises Walter to leave Limmeridge. Anne Catherick, after sending a letter to Laura warning her against Glyde, meets Hartright who is convinced that Glyde was responsible for shutting her in the asylum. Laura and Glyde marry in December 1849 and travel to Italy. Hartright also leaves England, joining an expedition to Honduras.

After their honeymoon, Sir Percival and Lady Glyde return the following June to his family estate in Hampshire, *Blackwater Park. They are accompanied by Glyde's friend, Count *Fosco, who married Laura's aunt, Eleanor Fairlie. Marian Halcombe is also living at Blackwater and learns that Glyde is in financial difficulties. Sir Percival unsuccessfully attempts to bully Laura into signing a document which would allow him to use her marriage settlement of £20,000. Marian now realizes that Fosco is the true villain and is plotting something more sinister, especially as Anne has reappeared, promising to reveal to Laura a secret which will ruin Glyde. Marian eavesdrops on Fosco and Glyde but is caught in the rain. She collapses with a fever which turns to typhus.

While she is ill Laura is tricked into travelling to London. Her identity and that of Anne Catherick are then switched. Anne Catherick dies of a heart condition and is buried in Cumberland as Laura, while Laura is drugged and placed in the asylum as Anne Catherick. When Marian recovers and visits the asylum hoping to learn something from Anne Catherick, she finds Laura, supposedly suffering from the delusion that she is Lady Glyde.

Marian bribes the attendant and Laura escapes. Hartright has safely returned and the three live together in obscure poverty, determined to restore Laura's identity. Exposing the conspiracy depends on proving that Laura's journey to London took place after the date on the death certificate. While looking for evidence, Hartright discovers Glyde's secret. Several years earlier, Glyde had forged the marriage register at Old Welmingham Church to conceal his illegitimacy. Glyde attempts to destroy the register entry, but the church vestry catches fire and he perishes in the flames. Hartright then discovers that Anne was the illegitimate child of Laura's father, which accounts for their resemblance.

Hartright hopes that Pesca can identify Fosco but to his surprise finds that the Count is terrified when he recognizes Pesca as a fellow member of a secret society. Hartright now has the power to force a written confession from Fosco and Laura's identity is restored. Hartright and Laura have married and, on the death of Frederick Fairlie, their son becomes the Heir of Limmeridge.

Serialization. *All the Year Round, 26 Nov. 1859–25 Aug. 1860; and *Harper's Weekly, 26 Nov. 1859–4 Aug. 1860.

Book publication
1st English edn. 3 vols, *Sampson Low, London 1860. Purple embossed cloth, covers blocked in blind, spines lettered in purple on gilt, pale yellow endpapers. No half-titles. Published 15–16 Aug. 1860.
Vol I viii + 316 pp.
Vol II (ii) + 360 pp.
Vol III (ii) + 368 pp. 16 pp publisher's catalogue dated 1 Aug. 1860 bound in at end.

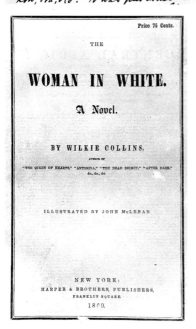

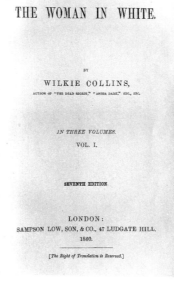

(*top*) Memorandum attached by Collins to the manuscript of *The Woman in White*, sold at AUCTION by Sotheby in June 1890
(*far left*) Cover of the first American edition of *The Woman in White*, published by Harpers in August 1860 (very unusual in paper wrappers)
(*left*) Title-page to the English three-volume seventh edition of *The Woman in White* published in 1860

NB Copies of both the 1st and 2nd 3-volume editions exist with advertisements dated May 1860. Other copies have advertisements dated Nov. 1860.

Other 3-vol edns. Between August and November 1860 there were altogether eight 3-vol editions. The 'second' to 'seventh' were designated as such on the title-page, followed by a 'new edition' on 1 November. These editions might more correctly be referred to as impressions but analysis of the text and errata shows that small differences exist between the various issues.

The complex story revolves around certain key dates and in the interests of accuracy Collins was obliged to make progressive alterations to the chronology of the plot. A review in *The Times* of 30 October 1860 by E. S. Dallas proved that the date of Laura's journey to London was impossible. Collins wrote to Edward Marston of *Sampson Low on 31 October 'If any fresh impression of "The Woman in White" is likely to be wanted, stop the press till I come back. The critic in The "Times" is (between ourselves) right about the mistake in time. Shakespeare has made worse mistakes—that is one comfort, and readers are not critics who test an emotional book by the base rules of arithmetic, which is a second consolation. Nevertheless we will set it right the first opportunity. . . .' The mistake, however, was not rectified until the first one-volume edition in 1861.

1-vol edns. Sampson Low 1860–3, with a new preface and illustrated title by J. *Gilbert; *Smith, Elder 1865–72; *Chatto & Windus 1875–1932 (with 8 illustrations by F. A. Fraser); *Routledge 1904.

Critical edns. Riverside, Boston 1969 (edited by A. Trodd and introduced by K. Tillotson); World's Classics 1980 (edited by H. P. Sucksmith), 1996 (edited by J. Sutherland); Penguin 1974 (edited by J. Symons); Everyman Library 1991 (introduced by N. Rance).

1st US edn. 1 vol, *Harper, New York, Aug. 1860.

Issued in paper wrappers and various coloured cloths (commonly black or brown), covers blocked in blind, spine lettered in gilt and illustrated with the silver figure of a woman. The advertisements form part of the collation and there are three states:

1. p (261) has 'Muloch' for 'Mulock' and lists nine titles; p (262) advertises *The Mill on the Floss*.
2. 'Mulock' is correctly spelled on p (261), eleven titles are listed and p (262) advertises *The Mill on the Floss*.
3. 'Mulock' is correctly spelled with eleven titles listed, but p (262) advertises nine titles by *Thackeray.

Further Harper's editions 1861–1902.

Translations. Russian, St Petersburg 1860; French (in *Le Temps*), Paris 1861, 2 vols, Paris 1862; Dutch, Amsterdam 1861, 1866; German, Stuttgart 1862, Vienna 1902.

Publication Dates

The Woman in White was published in England in mid-August 1860. The exact date, however, remains uncertain. Sampson Low consistently advertised publication on 15 August although Collins noted it as 16 August. The title-page of the manuscript contains a note in Collins's hand, signed and dated 4 October 1860:

I began this story on 15 August 1859, at Broadstairs, and finished it on the 26th July 1860 at 12 Harley Street, London. It was first published, in weekly parts, in 'All the Year Round', beginning in the number for November 23rd 1859, and ending with the number for August 22nd 1860. During the same period, it was periodically published at New York, US (by special arrangement with me) in 'Harper's Weekly.' The story was reprinted for the first time, by Mess Sampson Low, Son, & Co. It was published in three volumes post 8vo, on the 16th of August 1860. In the United States, in Canada, and in Germany it was also reprinted, about the same time; and, shortly afterwards, a translation of it into German appeared at Leipzig. A French translation followed, published at Brussells [sic] and Paris. The first chapters (forming the first weekly part, and the opening of the second) were rewritten, after they had been set up in type. The printed fragments inserted, here and there, at the beginning of the Mss comprise those portions of the first proofs which it was not found necessary to alter, and which were not attached to the written text to save the trouble of transcription. The whole of the rest of the Mss was written for the press, once, and once only—exactly as it is here preserved. In all cases, where there is any important difference between the printed copy and the original manuscript, the additions and alterations (Miss Halcombe's *Dream*, for example, among the number) were made, on the spur of the moment, upon the proofs—which I have not preserved.

Wilkie Collins, October 4th, 1860'

A later addition to the note states:

'After the sale in three volumes had come to an end (in February 1861) an edition in one volume, with a photographic portrait of the author, was published in April 1861.' Collins's own dates for *All the Year Round* are incorrect, so there may be some doubt about 16 August.

In the USA, it is generally accepted that *The Woman in White* was also published during August and the date is often given as the 15th (Brussel merely states 'during August 1860'). Collins was punctilious in his dealings with publishers. The likeliest conclusion is that he intended simultaneous English and US publication and the true dates probably do not differ by more than a day or so.

Cruse, A., *The Victorians and their Books*, London 1935, 322–3.

Ellis, S. M., *Wilkie Collins, Le Fanu, and others*, London 1931, 29–30.

Gasson, A., 'The Woman in White: A Chronological Study', *WCSJ*, 2 (1982), 5–14.

Hüttner, K., *Wilkie Collins's* The Woman in White—*Analysis, Reception and Literary Criticism of a Victorian Bestseller*, Wissenschaftlicher Verlag, Trier 1996.

Marston, E., *After Work*, London 1904, 85.

Mott, H., 'Wilkie Collins (1824–1889). The Woman in White. New York, 1860.', *Bibliographical Society of America*, 26 (3rd quarter 1942), 232.

Sotheby, Wilkinson & Hodge, *Catalogue of the Original Manuscripts, by Charles Dickens and Wilkie Collins*, 18 June 1890.

Sutherland, J., 'The Woman in White' in *Is Heathcliff a Murderer?*, Oxford 1996, 117–22.

Woman in White, The (play). First performed as 'A Drama in Three Acts' at the Surrey Theatre (Blackfriars Road, Lambeth), a short-lived pirated production opening on 3 November 1860; revived at the Theatre Royal, Leicester, 26 August 1870. Collins's own version of *The Woman in White*, extensively rewritten from the novel, ran with great success at the *Olympic Theatre from 9 October 1871 to 24 February 1872. The original cast consisted of Wybert *Reeve as Walter *Hartright, George *Vining as *Fosco, Ada Dyas as Laura *Fairlie and Anne *Catherick, and Mrs Viner as Marian *Halcombe.

Reeve later played Fosco both at the Olympic and on provincial tour, as well as for a two-week run at the Broadway Theatre, New York, from 15 December 1873. Reviews of the London production were published as *Specimens of Criticism Extracted from Notices of "The Woman in White" in the Press* (16 pp, 1871). Fred *Walker designed the arresting poster for the play which was in turn used by F. W. Waddy to caricature Collins in *Once a Week*, 24 February 1872. A German ver-

---

(*opposite*) F. W. Waddy's caricature of Collins with Frederick Walker's striking poster to *The Woman in White*

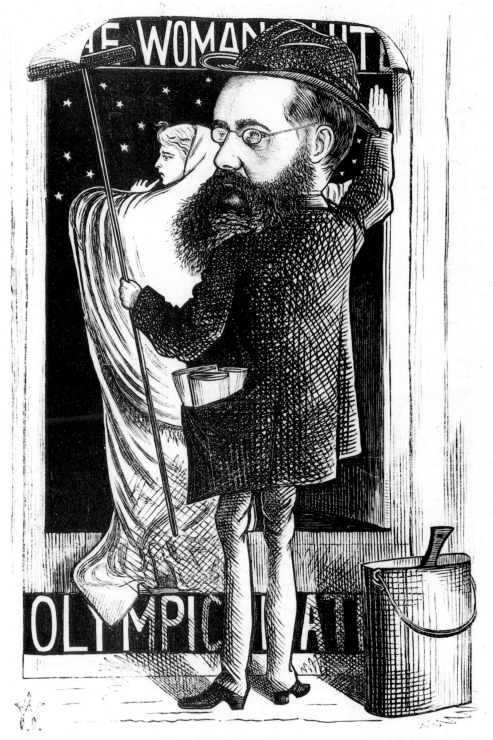

"HE WROTE 'THE WOMAN IN WHITE.'"

sion of the play was a great hit in Berlin during December 1866.

The Woman in White: A Drama in Prologue and Four Acts. (Altered from the novel for performance on the stage) was 'Published by the author' in 1871 (1 vol, 172 pp, buff paper wrappers). There have been at least two versions in the twentieth century: by Dan Sutherland at the 'Q' Theatre, London, 25 May 1954 (*Mystery at Blackwater*, French's Acting Edition, no. 326, London 1955); and by Melissa Murray, Greenwich Theatre, 1 December 1988.

women's rights See MARRIAGE LAWS; *JEZEBEL'S DAUGHTER*.

World, The: A Journal for Men and Women (1874–1922). Weekly paper edited by Edmund *Yates and founded in partnership with Grenville Murray, 8 July 1874. Yates became sole proprietor in early 1875 after disagreements over policy. Collins had known Yates since the 1850s but contributed only two stories: 'The *Clergyman's Confession' (4–18 Aug. 1875); and *The Fallen Leaves* (1 Jan.–23 July 1879). *The World*, however, contains much other Collins material.

17 Mar. 1875, editorial support by Yates for Collins in his dispute with The *Graphic.

24 Mar. 1875, letter from Collins giving his version of the dispute and thanking Yates.

5 Sept. 1877, unfavourable review of Bramwell's stage adaptation of *The Dead Secret*.

26 Dec. 1877, 'Mr. Wilkie Collins in Gloucester-Place', no. 81 in the Celebrities at Home series. Gives a description of Collins; discusses his early works, *The Woman in White* and the *méthode Collins* in writing fiction. Reprinted in *Celebrities at Home* (Third Series) 1879.

6 June 1883, no. 72 in the series of Letters to Eminent Persons by 'Kosmos' [T. H. S. Escott]. Tribute to Collins while lamenting the general decline of fiction.

13 June 1883, unfavourable review by Dutton Cook of *Rank and Riches*.

25 Sept. 1889, obituary by Yates.

2 Oct. 1889, 'One who Knew Him' by Yates, criticizing distortions of the truth in other papers' recollections of Collins; and several paragraphs by 'Atlas' on *Blind Love*, *The Woman in White*, and Collins's aversion to personal reminiscences.

9 and 16 Oct. 1889, further paragraphs by 'Atlas' on *Armadale*, the executors to Collins's *will, Hall *Caine and a protest at *Quilter's proposed memorial to Collins.

Edwards, P. D., 'Wilkie Collins and Edmund Yates: A Postscript', *WCSJ* (in preparation).

Gasson, A., 'Wilkie Collins, Edmund Yates and *The World*', *WCSJ* 4 (1984), 5–17.

Yates, E., *Edmund Yates: His Recollections and Experiences* (2 vols), London 1884.

Wragge, Captain Horatio Key character in *No Name*. A likeable, self-acknowledged rogue who calls himself a moral agriculturist. Collins describes him as having 'a lean, long, sallow face, deeply pitted with small-pox, and characterized, very remarkably, by eyes of two different colours—one bilious green, one bilious brown, both sharply intelligent. Persuasion distilled from his mildly-curling lips; and, shabby as he was, perennial flowers of courtesy bloomed all over him from head to foot.' Launches Magdalen *Vanstone on her stage career and helps her attempts to recover the family inheritance. He engages in a lengthy duel of wits with Mrs *Lecount. Finally prospers by selling patent medicines.

Wreck of the 'Golden Mary', The *Collaboration planned by Collins and *Dickens during the winter of 1855–6. Published as the extra *Christmas number of *Household Words, Dec. 1856. Consists of three main parts:

'The Wreck', the story of a shipwreck, written mainly by Dickens. Collins contributed the concluding section, 'John Steadiman's Account'.

'The Beguilement in the Boats' (nothing by Collins), an ordeal at sea in open boats. Consists of 'The Armourer's Story' (Percy Fitzgerald), 'Poor Dick's Story' (Harriet Parr), 'The Supercargo's Story' (Percy Fitzgerald), 'The Old Seaman's Story' (Adelaide Anne Proctor) and 'The Scotch Boy's Story' (the Revd James White).

'The Deliverance', the story of the rescue. Written entirely by Collins except for the first paragraph.

Stone, H., *The Uncollected Writings of Charles Dickens: Household Words 1850–1859*, Indiana 1968, 563–9.

Wynne, Anne Elizabeth le Poer (Nannie). Daughter of the widowed Mrs

Programme for the 1871 dramatic version of *The Woman in White* at the Olympic Theatre (note the misspelling of 'Fosko' corrected in later issues)

Henry Wynne whom Collins probably met through Frank *Beard, and who was also a friend of Edward *Pigott and Robert Browning. Collins, always fond of children, engaged in a remarkable correspondence with her daughter, Nannie, spanning the period June 1885 to February 1888, when she was aged between 12 and 15. By 5 November 1885 he wrote to her as 'Dear and admirable Mrs Collins' and continued to call her 'wife' or 'Mrs Wilkie'. At the same time he extended their light-hearted charade by sometimes signing himself 'devoted husband'.

The correspondence covers a wide range of topics, from his ill-health, 'if this weather goes on . . . you will be *a widow*'; the pressures of work, 'I get up to write the "weekly part" of *The Evil Genius* . . . and then tumble down again'; medical treatments, 'I have been taking forced holidays with my excellent friends opium and quinine'; to advice on roulette when she was staying at Monaco. Other letters to Mrs Wynne, his 'mother-in-law', are more serious and include the horrors of moving from *Gloucester Place to *Wimpole Street. Collins still refers to Nannie as his wife and on one occasion offers a 'divorce' if she is tiring of him.

THE

Wreck of the Golden Mary,

BEING THE

CAPTAIN'S ACCOUNT OF THE GREAT DELIVERANCE
OF HER PEOPLE IN AN OPEN BOAT AT SEA.

A NEW

CHRISTMAS STORY,

BEING A

CHRISTMAS NUMBER OF HOUSEHOLD WORDS.

CONDUCTED BY

CHARLES DICKENS.

NEW YORK:
DIX, EDWARDS & CO., No. 321 BROADWAY.
1856.

(*above left*) Illustration to *The Woman in White* play
published in *The Illustrated London News*
(*above*) US edition of *The Wreck of the 'Golden
Mary'*, Christmas 1856, a collaboration between
Collins and Dickens
(*left*) One of Collins's letters to Anne (Nannie)
Wynne complaining about his gout

There was no suggestion of impropriety and their meetings for lunch or tea always took place with her mother. 'The *Ghost's Touch' was specially written for his 'wife': 'In return for your flowers, dear Nannie, I have written a ghost-story for you. It wants—what you never want—correction, and then it will be ready for you.' Nannie, presumably the original for Lucy in the story, may also have influenced the character of Kitty Linley in *The Evil Genius* (1886).

Clarke, W. M., 'A Teasing "Marital" Correspondence with a Twelve Year Old' in N. Smith and R. C. Terry (eds.), *Wilkie Collins to the Forefront: Some Reassessments*, New York 1995.
Letters.

Y

Yates, Edmund Hodgson (1831–94). Journalist, editor, minor novelist and playwright; the son of well-known actor-managers. Long-standing friend of Collins.

Yates introduced himself to *Dickens in the summer of 1854 and probably first met Collins during the production of *The Lighthouse* in June 1855. By this time, Yates was writing for several journals including *Bentley's Miscellany* and was founder and editor of The *Train (1856–8), in which he wrote a very favourable critique of Collins's work to date in June 1857. The same year, as part of Dickens's plan to raise money for Douglas *Jerrold's widow, Yates organized charitable performances of *The Frozen Deep*.

Yates had joined the *Garrick Club in 1848 but, despite the public support of both Collins and Dickens, he was expelled in 1858 following his disagreement with *Thackeray. Yates continued his literary career with contributions to *Household Words* and *All the Year Round*. He became editor of *Temple Bar* in 1866 and *Tinsley's Magazine* in 1867. By 1875 he had fulfilled a lifelong ambition to own and edit his own journal, The *World. Collins contributed only two stories, 'The *Clergyman's Confession' (1875) and The *Fallen Leaves (1879).

Yates prided himself on his Celebrities at Home series, and no. 81 (26 December 1877) featured 'Mr Wilkie Collins in Gloucester Place'. Shortly after the publication of *Heart and Science* (1883), Collins appeared as no. 72 in the series Letters to Eminent Persons. This article consisted of nearly two thousand words of adulation and praise for his past and present works.

There were two *obituaries of Collins by Yates, the more comprehensive appearing in *Temple Bar* (August 1890). *The World* of 25 September 1889, two days after Collins's death, published a shorter piece by Yates, followed by several brief tributes in the following three issues. In reply to his assistant's memorandum 'there seemed, I thought, with your own article, a little too much W.C.', Yates replied in his distinctive violet ink 'Yes, but it is a necessary evil!'

Edwards, P. D., 'Wilkie Collins and Edmund Yates: A Postscript', *WCSJ* (in preparation).

Gasson, A., 'Wilkie Collins, Edmund Yates and *The World*', *WCSJ* 4 (1984), 5–17.

Yates, E., *Edmund Yates: His Recollections and Experiences*, London 1884.

Engraved by Joseph Brown.

(*facing*) Edmund Yates, editor of *The World*
(*above*) Yellowback Chatto & Windus edition of *The Law and the Lady*

'Yellow Mask, The' Short story originally published in *Household Words* 7–28 July 1855. Later included in *After Dark* (1856) as 'The Professor's Story of the Yellow Mask'. Uses the idea of making a mask from the cast of a statue, first employed in *Mr Wray's Cash-Box* (1852). A second theme, of recovering money for the Church, reappears in *The Black Robe* (1881).

➡ Count Fabio d'Ascoli is a pupil of the master-sculptor Luca Lomi. Lomi's brother, Fr Rocco of Pisa, believes that part of the young Count's inheritance is money stolen from the Church. In order to recover it, Rocco plans to have Fabio marry Lomi's daughter, Maddalena, over whom he can exert influence. He persuades Fabio's true love, the naïve model Nanina, to leave Pisa. The marriage takes

place but Maddalena dies the following year after the birth of a daughter. Rocco decides to play on Fabio's superstitions to prevent him from remarrying. He employs the mercenary Brigida to impersonate Maddalena at a masked ball by wearing a yellow mask over a cast of Maddalena's face. Fabio is so shocked at the ghost of his dead wife that his mind is temporarily unhinged. Nanina is able to prove that he has been tricked and they are happily married.

yellowbacks (pictorial boards, railway fiction). Cheap editions, usually of fiction, issued from the 1850s to the early twentieth century; generally priced at 2*s*. and sold at railway bookstalls. The binding consisted of strawboard covered with glazed coloured paper, usually yellow, on which appeared an eye-catching illustration.

*Sampson Low used these pictorial boards in 1865 for *Antonina, The Queen of Hearts* and *The Woman in White*. As Collins's copyrights changed hands, *Smith, Elder issued ten titles in this format, *Chatto & Windus twenty-nine and *Routledge (never Collins's publishers during his lifetime) four.

Sadleir, M., *Aspects of Book-Collecting: Collecting Yellowbacks (Victorian Railway Fiction)*, London 1938.

Sadleir (1951).

Topp, C. W., *Victorian Yellowbacks and Paperbacks, 1849–1905*, vol 1 (George Routledge), Denver, Colo., 1993.

'Your Money or Your Life' Short story originally published in the *Belgravia Annual*, Christmas 1881; the *People's Library*, 17 Dec. 1881; and in the *Seaside Library* (vol 57, no. 1164), 1881. Reprinted as 'Mr Cosway and the Landlady' in *Little Novels* (1887). Collins acknowledged that the first part of the story where the landlady forces her young creditor into marriage was taken from

Cover of the Smith, Elder yellowback edition of *Armadale* in 1871

Lockhart's *The Life of Sir Walter Scott* (1825).

➡ When Edwin Cosway hears that the wife he was tricked into marrying has died, he falls in love with Adela Restall. Her father objects and their elopement is foiled by the malicious Miss Benshaw who turns out to be Edwin's wife with her name changed to inherit the family fortune. She is drowned and her will leaves half a million pounds to Adela provided that she does *not* marry Edwin, a condition that Adela happily ignores.

Youth's Companion An American weekly paper for 'Young People and the Family', run by Perry Mason of Washington Street, Boston. First published '*Victims of Circumstances Discovered in Records of Old Trials', 19 August 1886. Other authors included Harriet Beecher Stowe, 'Sophie May' and Mrs Helen C. Weeks.

APPENDIX A

MS OF 'AFTER DARK'

Part of the original manuscript of *After Dark*

⊰═ APPENDIX B ═⊱

CHARACTERS IN THE NOVELS OF WILKIE COLLINS

CHARACTER	BOOK OR STORY	ROLE
Ablewhite, Godfrey	*The Moonstone*	Rachel Verinder's villainous cousin
Aimáta	*Ioláni*	Courageous young friend of Idía
Aldersley, Frank	*The Frozen Deep*	Naval officer engaged to Clara Burnham
Antonina	*Antonina*	Daughter of Numerian, captured by Hermanric
Ariel	*The Law and the Lady*	Miserrimus Dexter's devoted cousin
Armadale, Allan	*Armadale*	Naïve hero, unaware of his ancestry
Bartrum, Admiral	*No Name*	George Bartram's uncle; holder of the secret trust
Bartrum, George	*No Name*	Noel Vanstone's cousin
Bashwood, Felix	*Armadale*	Armadale's steward spying for Miss Gwilt
Basil	*Basil*	Hero who marries a linen-draper's daughter
Benjamin	*The Law and the Lady*	Valeria's faithful friend, her father's former clerk
Benjulia, Dr Nathan	*Heart and Science*	Brain specialist and vivisectionist
Bennydeck, Captain	*The Evil Genius*	Religious friend of Sydney Westerfield's father
Benwell, Father Ambrose	*The Black Robe*	Jesuit priest scheming to recover Vange Abbey
Betteredge, Gabriel	*The Moonstone*	Verinder house-steward and chief narrator
Betteredge, Penelope	*The Moonstone*	Betteredge's daughter; Rachel Verinder's maid
Bishopriggs	*Man and Wife*	Waiter at Craig Fernie inn
Blake, Franklin	*The Moonstone*	Rachel Verinder's cousin
Blanchard, Jane	*Armadale*	Allan Armadale's mother
Blunt, Martin	*Mr Wray's Cash-Box*	Mr Wray's clumsy assistant
Blythe, Mrs Lavinia	*Hide and Seek*	Disabled wife of Valentine Blythe
Blythe, Valentine	*Hide and Seek*	Zack Thorpe's artist friend; Madonna's guardian
Brinkworth, Arnold	*Man and Wife*	Delamayn's friend, engaged to Blanche Lundie
Brock, Revd Decimus	*Armadale*	Allan Armadale's tutor and guardian
Brown, Emily	*'I Say No'*	Orphan investigating her father's death
Bruff, Mr	*The Moonstone*	Verinder family lawyer
Burnham, Clara	*The Frozen Deep*	Fiancée to Frank Aldersley
Buschmann, Uncle Joseph	*The Dead Secret*	Sarah Leeson's Mozart-playing uncle
Candy, Dr	*The Moonstone*	Verinder family doctor
Catherick, Anne	*The Woman in White*	Woman in white, Laura Fairlie's double
Catherick, Mrs	*The Woman in White*	Rigidly respectable mother of Anne Catherick
Chennery, Dr	*The Dead Secret*	Clergyman friend of the Treverton family
Clack, Drusilla	*The Moonstone*	Rachel Verinder's aunt; interfering evangelist
Clara	*Basil*	Basil's devoted sister
Clare, Frank	*No Name*	Good-for-nothing fiancé to Magdalen Vanstone
Colebatch, Matthew	*Mr Wray's Cash-Box*	Squire of Tidbury-on-the-Marsh
Crayford, Lucy	*The Frozen Deep*	Clara Burnham's best friend
Cuff, Sergeant	*The Moonstone*	Celebrated rose-growing detective
Darch, Mr	*Armadale*	Blanchard family lawyer, offended by Armadale
de Sor, Francine	*'I Say No'*	Spiteful school friend of Emily Brown
Delamayn, Geoffrey	*Man and Wife*	Villain reneging on marriage to Anne Silvester
Delamayn, Julius	*Man and Wife*	Geoffrey Delamayn's older brother
Dermody, Mary (Mrs Van Brandt)	*The Two Destinies*	Childhood sweetheart of George Germaine
Dethridge, Hester	*Man and Wife*	Lady Lundie's mute and eccentric cook

Dexter, Miserrimus	*The Law and the Lady*	Legless eccentric, friend of Eustace Macallan
Dingwell, Rufus	*The Fallen Leaves*	Worldly American; befriends Goldenheart
Downward, Dr (Dr le Doux)	*Armadale*	Dubious doctor; accomplice of Mrs Oldershaw
Dubourg, Nugent	*Poor Miss Finch*	Deceitful twin trying to steal Lucilla Finch
Dubourg, Oscar	*Poor Miss Finch*	'Blue' twin in love with Lucilla Finch
Dulcifer, Alicia	*A Rogue's Life*	Daughter of Dr Dulcifer
Dulcifer, Dr	*A Rogue's Life*	A forger
Dunboyne, Philip	*The Legacy of Cain*	In love alternately with the Gracedieu sisters
Dunross, Miss	*The Two Destinies*	Mysterious young woman on the Shetlands
Engelman, Herr	*Jezebel's Daughter*	German partner to Keller and Mrs Wagner
Eyrecourt, Stella	*The Black Robe*	Friend of Lady Loring; marries Lewis Romayne
Eyrecourt, Mrs	*The Black Robe*	Stella Eyrecourt's mother
Fairlie, Frederick	*The Woman in White*	Valetudinarian uncle of Laura Fairlie
Fairlie, Laura (Lady Glyde)	*The Woman in White*	Heiress married by Sir Percival Glyde for money
Farnaby, Emma (née Ronald)	*The Fallen Leaves*	Farnaby's wife, searching for her lost daughter
Farnaby, John	*The Fallen Leaves*	Villain and dishonest businessman
Farnaby, Regina	*The Fallen Leaves*	Farnaby's daughter, engaged to Goldenheart
Ferrari	*The Haunted Hotel*	Courier to Lord Montbarry and Countess Narona
Finch, Lucilla	*Poor Miss Finch*	Blind heroine in love with Oscar Dubourg
Finch, Revd	*Poor Miss Finch*	Lucilla Finch's pompous father
Fitz-David, Major	*The Law and the Lady*	'Don Juan' friend of Eustace Macallan
Fontaine, Madame	*Jezebel's Daughter*	Embezzler and poisoner
Fontaine, Minna	*Jezebel's Daughter*	Mme Fontaine's daughter, engaged to Fritz Keller
Fosco, Count Isidor Ottavio Baldassare	*The Woman in White*	Archetypal 'fat man' villain, conspires with Glyde
Fosco, Eleanor	*The Woman in White*	Fosco's wife; Laura Lairlie's aunt
Frankland, Leonard	*The Dead Secret*	Blind husband of Rosamond Treverton
Gallilee, Mrs	*Heart and Science*	Ovid Vere's formidable mother
Garth, Miss	*No Name*	Vanstone family governess and friend
Germaine, George	*The Two Destinies*	Childhood sweetheart of Mary Dermody
Glenarm, Mrs	*Man and Wife*	Rich widow set to marry Geoffrey Delamayn
Glenney, David	*Jezebel's Daughter*	Narrator; Mrs Wagner's English representative
Gloody	*The Guilty River*	Servant to the Lodger
Glyde, Sir Percival	*The Woman in White*	Friend of Laura's father, marrying her for money
Goisvintha	*Antonina*	Sister of Hermanric, determined to kill Antonina
Goldenheart, Amelius	*The Fallen Leaves*	Christian socialist hero; rescues Simple Sally
Gracedieu, Revd Abel	*The Legacy of Cain*	Retired prison chaplain
Gracedieu, Eunice	*The Legacy of Cain*	Good-natured daughter of Revd Gracedieu
Gracedieu, Helena	*The Legacy of Cain*	Spiteful daughter of Revd Gracedieu
Gray, Julian	*The New Magdalen*	Curate nephew of Lady Roy
Graybrook, Sir Joseph	*'Miss or Mrs?'*	Father of Natalie Graybrook
Graybrook, Natalie	*'Miss or Mrs?'*	Heiress in love with Launcelot Linzie
Graywell, Carmina	*Heart and Science*	Mrs Gallilee's niece from Italy; in love with Vere
Grice, Joanna	*Hide and Seek*	Mat Marksman's self-righteous aunt
Grice, Mary	*Hide and Seek*	See *Madonna*
Grosse, Herr	*Poor Miss Finch*	Eccentric German oculist
Gwilt, Lydia	*Armadale*	Villainess after Allan Armadale's money
Halcombe, Marian	*The Woman in White*	Resolute heroine; Laura Fairlie's half-sister
Hartright, Walter	*The Woman in White*	Drawing-master hero in love with Laura Fairlie
Henley, Iris	*Blind Love*	Wife of Lord Harry Norland
Hermanric	*Antonina*	Chieftain under Alaric the Goth
Holchester, Lord	*Man and Wife*	Geoffrey Delamayn's father
Holmcroft, Horace	*The New Magdalen*	War correspondent, friend of Lady Roy
Hynd, Major John Philip	*The Black Robe*	Old friend of Lewis Romayne
Idía	*Iolani*	Mother of Iolani's child

Ioláni	*Ioláni*	Evil high priest of Oro
Jennings, Ezra	*The Moonstone*	Opium-taking assistant of Dr Candy
Jervis (Jervy)	*The Fallen Leaves*	Fraudster, extorting money from Mrs Farnaby
Jethro, Sarah	*'I Say No'*	Teacher dismissed from Emily Brown's school
Jicks (Selina Finch)	*Poor Miss Finch*	Lucilla Finch's three-year-old half-sister
Kerby, Leah	*After Dark*	William Kerby's wife and amanuensis
Kerby, William	*After Dark*	Portrait painter and story-teller
Keller, Fritz	*Jezebel's Daughter*	Keller's son
Keller, Herr	*Jezebel's Daughter*	Business partner of Mrs Wagner
Kirke, Captain	*No Name*	Sea-captain in love with Magdalen Vanstone
Le Frank, Mr	*Heart and Science*	Music master to the Gallilee family
Lecount, Mrs	*No Name*	Noel Vanstone's formidable housekeeper
Leeson, Sarah (Mrs Jazeph)	*The Dead Secret*	Mrs Treverton's maid
Limping Lucy	*The Moonstone*	Friend to Rosanna Spearman
Linley, Catherine (Mrs Norman)	*The Evil Genius*	Herbert Linley's wife
Linley, Herbert	*The Evil Genius*	In love with Sydney Westerfield
Linley, Kitty	*The Evil Genius*	Five-year-old daughter of Herbert and Catherine
Linley, Randal	*The Evil Genius*	Herbert Linley's brother
Linzie, Launcelot	*'Miss or Mrs?'*	Young cousin in love with Natalie Graybrook
Lockwood, Agnes	*The Haunted Hotel*	Jilted fiancée of Lord Montbarry
Lodger, the	*The Guilty River*	Gerard Roylake's rival for Cristel Toller
Lord Harry (Norland)	*Blind Love*	Irish revolutionary; insurance fraudster
Loring, Lord and Lady	*The Black Robe*	Catholic friends of Lewis Romayne
Louisa	*No Name*	Magdalen Vanstone's maid
Luker, Septimus	*The Moonstone*	Dubious moneylender
Lundie, Blanche	*Man and Wife*	Sisterly friend of Anne Silvester
Lundie, Lady Julia	*Man and Wife*	Overbearing guardian to Blanche Lundie
Lundie, Sir Patrick	*Man and Wife*	Retired lawyer; head of the Lundie family
Lydiard, Lady	*'My Lady's Money'*	Owner of a missing £500 note
Macallan, Eustace	*The Law and the Lady*	Victim of Not Proven verdict
Macallan, Mrs	*The Law and the Lady*	Valeria's affectionate mother-in-law
Macallan, Valeria	*The Law and the Lady*	Detective wife of Eustace
Madonna (Mary Grice)	*Hide and Seek*	Adopted daughter of the Blythes
Mahíné	*Ioláni*	Tahitian chieftain
Mannion	*Basil*	Assumed name of Sherwin's confidential clerk
Marksman, Mat	*Hide and Seek*	Outlandish friend of Zack
Melton, Mr	*The Fallen Leaves*	Older suitor for Regina Farnaby
Mere, Fanny	*Blind Love*	Loyal maid to Iris Henley
Merrick, Mercy	*The New Magdalen*	Reformed prostitute posing as Grace Roseberry
Midwinter, Ozias	*Armadale*	Hero whose father murdered Armadale's father
Miller, Isabel	*'My Lady's Money'*	Adopted daughter of Lady Lydiard
Milroy, Anne	*Armadale*	Jealous wife of Major Milroy; Eleanor's mother
Milroy, Major David	*Armadale*	Armadale's tenant; Eleanor's father
Milroy, Eleanor (Neelie)	*Armadale*	The Milroys' daughter, in love with Armadale
Minerva, Miss	*Heart and Science*	Governess to the Gallilee girls, Zo and Maria
Mirabel, Miles	*'I Say No'*	Charismatic preacher in love with Emily Brown
Montbarry, Lord	*The Haunted Hotel*	Husband of Countess Narona
Moody, Robert	*'My Lady's Money'*	Lady Lydiard's steward, in love with Isabel Miller
Mool, Mr	*Heart and Science*	Family solicitor to the Gallilees
Morris, Alban	*'I Say No'*	Drawing master in love with Emily Brown
Mountjoy, Arthur	*Blind Love*	Hugh's brother; killed by Irish revolutionaries
Mountjoy, Hugh	*Blind Love*	In love with Iris Henley
Murthwaite, Mr	*The Moonstone, The Black Robe*	Renowned explorer and foreign traveller
Narona, Countess	*The Haunted Hotel*	Wife of Lord Montbarry
Norland, Lord Harry	*Blind Love*	See Lord Harry

Numerian	*Antonina*	Father of Antonina; Christian zealot
Old Sharon	*'My Lady's Money'*	Slovenly pipe-smoking detective
Oldershaw, Mrs Maria	*Armadale*	Shady beauty-shop owner; Lydia Gwilt's mentor
Oxbye	*Blind Love*	Danish victim of the insurance fraud
Peckover, Mrs	*Hide and Seek*	Circus woman who rescues Madonna
Pedgift, Augustus Junior (Gustus)	*Armadale*	Lawyer son of Pedgift Senior
Pedgift, Augustus Senior	*Armadale*	Lawyer to Allan Armadale
Pendril, Mr	*No Name*	Vanstone family solicitor
Penrose, Arthur	*The Black Robe*	Priest and friend to Lewis Romayne
Perry	*Man and Wife*	Geoffrey Delamayn's trainer
Pesca, Professor	*The Woman in White*	Friend of Hartright; Italian political refugee
Playmore, Mr	*The Law and the Lady*	Scottish lawyer to Eustace Macallan
Pratolungo, Madame	*Poor Miss Finch*	Narrator and companion to Lucilla Finch
Presty, Mrs	*The Evil Genius*	Catherine Linley's interfering mother
Ralph	*Basil*	Basil's elder brother
Rivar, Baron	*The Haunted Hotel*	Brother and co-conspirator of Countess Narona
Romayne, Lewis	*The Black Robe*	Owner of Vange Abbey; converted by Benwell
Rook, Mrs	*'I Say No'*	Former innkeeper of the Hand-in-Hand
Roseberry, Grace	*The New Magdalen*	Cousin by marriage to Lady Roy
Roy, Lady Janet	*The New Magdalen*	Society lady; adopts Mercy Merrick
Roylake, Gerard	*The Guilty River*	Owner of Trimley Deen; loves Cristel Toller
Sarrazin, Mr	*The Evil Genius*	Lawyer to Catherine Linley
Sebright, Mr	*Poor Miss Finch*	Staid English oculist
Sherwin, Margaret	*Basil*	The Sherwins' daughter; marries Basil
Sherwin, Mr	*Basil*	Linen-draper, insisting on the secret marriage
Sherwin, Mrs	*Basil*	Margaret's timid mother
Shrowl	*The Dead Secret*	Misanthropic servant to Andrew Treverton
Silvester, Anne	*Man and Wife*	Heroine compromised by Geoffrey Delamayn
Simple Sally	*The Fallen Leaves*	Long-lost daughter of Mrs Farnaby
Softly, Frank	*A Rogue's Life*	Hero and narrator
Spearman, Rosanna	*The Moonstone*	Tragic servant in love with Franklin Blake
Straw, Jack (Hans Grimm)	*Jezebel's Daughter*	Inmate of Bedlam rescued by Mrs Wagner
Sweetsir, Felix	*'My Lady's Money'*	Nephew of Lady Lydiard
Tegenbruggen, Mrs (Elizabeth Chance)	*The Legacy of Cain*	Lover of Eunice Gracedieu's murdered father
Teresa	*Heart and Science*	Carmina Graywell's old nurse
Theophile Leblond (Toff)	*The Fallen Leaves*	Eccentric French servant to Amelius Goldenheart
Thorpe, Mr	*Hide and Seek*	Zack's father
Thorpe, Mrs	*Hide and Seek*	Zack's devoted mother
Thorpe, Zachary (Zack)	*Hide and Seek*	Wild friend of Blythe and Mat Marksman
Toller, Cristel	*The Guilty River*	Miller's daughter
Tommie	*'My Lady's Money'*	Lady Lydiard's Scotch terrier
Treverton, Andrew	*The Dead Secret*	Rosamond Treverton's miserly uncle
Treverton, Rosamond	*The Dead Secret*	Capt Treverton's daughter; marries Frankland
Turlington, Richard	*'Miss or Mrs?'*	Older man; marries Natalie Graybrook for money
Ulpius	*Antonina*	Pagan priest; Numerian's steward
Vanstone, Magdalen	*No Name*	Actress heroine trying to recover family fortune
Vanstone, Noel	*No Name*	Cousin of Magdalen Vanstone
Vanstone, Norah	*No Name*	Passive sister of Magdalen Vanstone
Vere, Ovid	*Heart and Science*	Brilliant young doctor; loves Carmina Graywell
Verinder, Rachel	*The Moonstone*	Recipient of the Moonstone; in love with Blake
Verinder, Lady Julia	*The Moonstone*	Rachel Verinder's mother
Vetranio	*Antonina*	Wealthy Roman

Vimpany, Dr	*Blind Love*	Insurance fraudster with Lord Harry
Vimpany, Mrs	*Blind Love*	Clever wife of Dr Vimpany
Wagner, Mrs	*Jezebel's Daughter*	Widow of Ephraim Wagner and social reformer
Wardour, Richard	*The Frozen Deep*	Frank Aldersley's rival for Clara Burnham
Westerfield, Sydney	*The Evil Genius*	Governess to Kitty Linley; Herbert Linley's lover
Westwick, Henry	*The Haunted Hotel*	Lord Montbarry's brother
Wigger, Miss	*The Evil Genius*	Sydney Westerfield's brutal schoolmistress aunt
Wildfang, Thomas	*'Miss or Mrs?'*	Turlington's murderous accomplice
Winterfield, Bernard	*The Black Robe*	Bigamous first husband to Stella Eyrecourt
Wragge, Captain	*No Name*	Likeable rogue who assists Magdalen Vanstone
Wragge, Mrs	*No Name*	Simple-minded wife of Captain Wragge
Wray, Annie	*Mr Wray's Cash-Box*	Mr Wray's daughter
Wray, Reuben	*Mr Wray's Cash-Box*	Retired actor obsessed with Shakespeare
Wybrow, Dr Joseph	*The Haunted Hotel, The Black Robe*	Eminent Harley Street physician
Wyvil, Cecilia	*'I Say No'*	School friend of Emily Brown

APPENDIX C
THE COLLINS FAMILY TREE

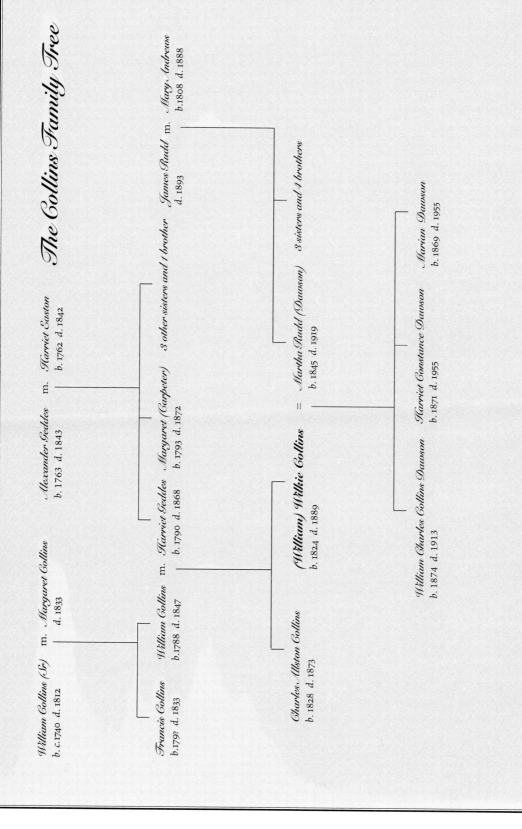

The Collins Family Tree

William Collins (Sr) b. c.1740 d. 1812   m.   **Margaret Collins** d. 1833

Alexander Geddes b. 1763 d. 1843   m.   **Harriet Easton** b. 1762 d. 1842

James Rudd d. 1893   m.   **Mary Andrews** b. 1808 d. 1888

Francis Collins b. 179? d. 1833

William Collins b. 1788 d. 1847   m.   **Harriet Geddes** b. 1790 d. 1868

Margaret (Carpenter) b. 1793 d. 1872   *3 other sisters and 1 brother*

3 sisters and 4 brothers

Charles Allston Collins b. 1828 d. 1873

(William) Wilkie Collins b. 1824 d. 1889   =   **Martha Rudd (Dawson)** b. 1845 d. 1919

William Charles Collins Dawson b. 1874 d. 1913

Harriet Constance Dawson b. 1871 d. 1955

Marian Dawson b. 1869 d. 1955

APPENDIX D

MAP OF MARYLEBONE
THE RESIDENCES OF WILKIE COLLINS

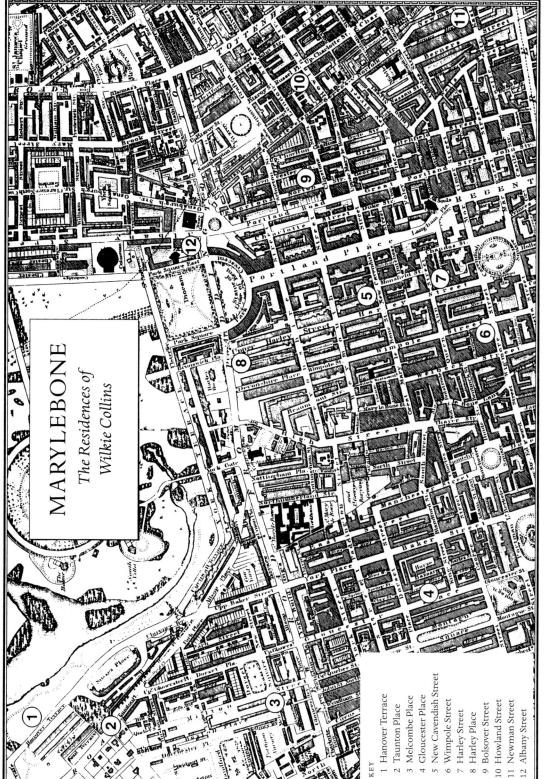

MARYLEBONE

*The Residences of
Wilkie Collins*

KEY

1 Hanover Terrace
2 Taunton Place
3 Melcombe Place
4 Gloucester Place
5 New Cavendish Street
6 Wimpole Street
7 Harley Street
8 Harley Place
9 Bolsover Street
10 Howland Street
11 Newman Street
12 Albany Street

Greenwood map, 1830 by permission of Westminster City Archives

⇾ APPENDIX E ⇽

SELECT BIBLIOGRAPHY

'All for knowledge. All for knowledge!' (*Heart and Science*)

BIBLIOGRAPHIES

Abbreviated Bibliographic Check List [Harlow, S.], *Wilkie Collins 1824–1889*, Canterbury 1990

Andrew, R. V., 'A Wilkie Collins check-list', *English Studies in Africa*, 3 (1960), 79–98; reprinted in *Wilkie Collins: A Critical Survey of His Prose Fiction, with a Bibliography*, New York 1979

Ashley, R., 'Wilkie Collins' in Lionel Stevenson (ed.), *Victorian Fiction: A Guide to Research*, Cambridge, Mass., 1964

Beetz, K., *Wilkie Collins: An Annotated Bibliography, 1889–1976*, Metuchen, NJ, and London 1978

Brussel, I. R., 'Wilkie Collins' in *Anglo-American First Editions, 1826–1900: East to West*, London 1935; reprinted, New York 1981

Gasson, A., 'Wilkie Collins: A Collector's and Bibliographer's Challenge', *The Private Library*, Third Series 3: 2 (Summer 1980), 51–77

Index of English Literary Manuscripts, iv: (1800–1900), compiled by B. Rosenbaum and P. White, London and New York 1982

Jarndyce, *Wilkie Collins*, Catalogue 93, Summer 1993

Lohrli, A., *Household Words: A Weekly Journal 1850–1859 Conducted by Charles Dickens. Table of Contents, List of Contributors and their Contributions*, Toronto 1973

Oppenlander, E. A., *Dickens' 'All the Year Round': Descriptive Index and Contributors List*, Troy, NY, 1984

Parrish, M. L., with Miller, E. V., *Wilkie Collins and Charles Reade: First Editions Described with Notes*, London 1940; reprinted, New York 1968

Sadleir, M., 'Wilkie Collins' in *Excursions in Victorian Bibliography*, London 1922; reprinted 1974

—— *XIX Century Fiction: A Bibliographical Record Based on His Own Collection* (2 vols), London 1951; reprinted, New York 1969

Todd, W. B. and Bowden, A., *Tauchnitz International Editions in English 1841–1955: A Bibliographical History*, New York 1988

Topp, C. W., *Victorian Yellowbacks & Paperbacks, 1849–1905*, i (George Routledge), Denver, Colo., 1993

The Wellesley Index to Victorian Periodicals 1824–1900 (5 vols); vols 1–3 (1966–79) edited by W. E. Houghton and E. R. Houghton; vol 4 (1987) edited by W. E. Houghton, E. R. Houghton and J. H. Slingerland; vol 5 (1989) edited by J. H. Slingerland, Toronto and Buffalo.

Wolff, R. L., *Nineteenth-Century Fiction, a Bibliographical Catalogue* (5 vols), New York and London 1981–6

See also sale catalogues in AUCTIONS.

BIOGRAPHIES

Ashley, R., *Wilkie Collins*, London 1952

Baker, W. and Clarke, W. M. (eds.) *The Letters of Wilkie Collins* (2 vols), London 1998

Clarke, W. M., *The Secret Life of Wilkie Collins*, London 1988; reprinted, Stroud 1996

Collins, W. W., *Memoirs of the Life of William Collins, Esq., R.A.* (2 vols), London 1848

Davis, N. P., *The Life of Wilkie Collins*, Urbana, Ill., 1956

Peters, C., *The King of Inventors: A Life of Wilkie Collins*, London 1991; paperback edition, London, 1992

Robinson, K., *Wilkie Collins: A Biography*, London 1951; reprinted 1974

Sayers, D. L., *Wilkie Collins: A Critical and Biographical Study* (unfinished), edited by E. R. Gregory, Toledo, Oh., 1977

Wolzogen, E. von, *Wilkie Collins: Ein Biographisch-Kritischer Versuch*, Leipzig 1885

DETECTIVE FICTION

Hubin, A. J., *Crime Fiction: A Comprehensive Bibliography, 1749–1990* (2 vols), New York and London 1994

Lambert, G., 'Enemy Country *Wilkie Collins*' in *The Dangerous Edge*, London 1975

Ousby, I., 'Wilkie Collins and Other Sensation Novelists' in *Bloodhounds of Heaven*, Cambridge, Mass., 1976

Petersen, A., 'Wilkie Collins and the Mystery Novel' in *Victorian Masters of Mystery: From Wilkie Collins to Conan Doyle*, New York 1984

Quayle, E., *The Collector's Book of Detective Fiction*, London 1972

Stewart, R. F., *. . . And Always a Detective: Chapters on the History of Detective Fiction*, London 1980

Symons, J., *Bloody Murder: From the Detective Story to the Crime Novel*, London 1972

THE DICKENS CONNECTION

Ackroyd, P., *Dickens*, London 1990

Adrian, A., *Georgina Hogarth and the Dickens Circle*, Oxford 1957

Ashley, R. P., 'Wilkie Collins and the Dickensians', *Dickensian*, 49 (March 1953), 59–65

Dickens, C., *Letters of Charles Dickens to Wilkie Collins, 1851–1870, Selected by Miss Georgina Hogarth*, edited by Laurence Hutton, London 1892; New York 1892

—— *Letters of Charles Dickens*, edited by M. Dickens and G. Hogarth (3 vols), London 1880–2

—— *The Letters of Charles Dickens*, vol 6 (1849–52), edited by Graham Storey and K. J. Fielding, Oxford 1988; vol 7 (1853–5), edited by Graham Storey and Kathleen Tillotson, Oxford 1993; vol 8 (1856–8), edited by Graham Storey and Kathleen Tillotson, Oxford 1995

Fielding, K. J., 'Dickens and Wilkie Collins: A Reply', *Dickensian*, 49 (June 1953), 130–6

Fitzgerald, P., *Memoirs of an Author* (2 vols), London 1895

—— *Memories of Charles Dickens*, Bristol 1913; reprinted, New York 1973

Forster, J., *The Life of Charles Dickens* (3 vols), London 1872–4; edited by J. W. T. Ley, London 1928

Johnson, E., *Charles Dickens, his Tragedy and Triumph* (2 vols), London 1953; revised, New York and Harmondsworth 1986

Kaplan, F., *Dickens: A Biography*, London 1988

Lehmann, R. C., *Charles Dickens as Editor*, London 1912

Ley, J. W. T., *The Dickens Circle: A Narrative of the Novelist's Friendships*, London 1919

Miller, W., *The Dickens Student and Collector*, London 1946

Newlin, G., *Everyone in Dickens* (3 vols), Westport, Conn., and London 1995

Page, N., *A Dickens Chronology*, London 1988; reprinted 1996

Shore, W. T., *Charles Dickens and his Friends*, London 1909

Slater, M. (ed.), *The Catalogue of the Suzannet Charles Dickens Collection*, London 1975

Stone, H., *The Uncollected Writings of Charles Dickens: 'Household Words' 1850–1859* (2 vols), Bloomington, Ind., 1968

Storey, G., *Dickens and Daughter*, London 1939

Tomalin, C., *The Invisible Woman: The Story of Nelly Ternan and Charles Dickens*, London 1990

PUBLISHING HISTORY

Downey, E., *Twenty Years Ago*, London 1905

Exman, E., *The Brothers Harper*, New York 1965

—— *The House of Harper: One Hundred and Fifty Years of Publishing*, New York and London 1967

Gettman, R., *A Victorian Publisher: A Study of the Bentley Papers*, Cambridge 1960

Griest, G. L., *Mudie's Circulating Library and the Victorian Novel*, Bloomington, Ind., and Newton Abbot 1970

Harper, J. H., *The House of Harper*, New York and London 1912

Huxley, L., *The House of Smith Elder*, London 1923

Law, G., 'The Serial Publication in Britain of the Novels of Wilkie Collins', *Humanitas*, 33 (20 Feb. 1995), Waseda University Law Society

Law, G., 'Wilkie in the Weeklies: The Serialization and Syndication of Collins's Late Novels', *Victorian Periodicals Review*, 30 (Autumn 1997)

Marston, E., *After Work*, London 1904

Nowell-Smith, S., *The House of Cassell 1848–1958*, London 1958

Sadleir, M., *Trollope: A Bibliography*, London 1928; reprinted 1964, 1977

Sutherland, J. A., *Victorian Novelists and Publishers*, London 1976

—— *Victorian Fiction: Writers, Publishers, Readers*, London 1995

Tinsley, W., *Random Recollections of an Old Publisher* (2 vols), London 1900

Vann, J. D., *Victorian Novels in Serial*, New York 1985

Wolff, R. L., *Sensational Victorian: The Life and Fiction of Mary Elizabeth Bradden*, New York and London 1979

THEATRICAL

Ainger, A., 'Mr Dickens's Amateur Theatricals. A Reminiscence', *Macmillan's Magazine*, 23 (Jan. 1871), 72–82; reprinted in *Lectures and Essays*, London 1905

Archer, F., *An Actor's Notebooks*, London 1912

Ashley, R., 'Wilkie Collins and the American Theatre', *Nineteenth-Century Fiction*, 8 (March 1954), 241–55

Bancroft, S., *Empty Chairs*, London 1925

—— and Bancroft, M., *Mr and Mrs Bancroft: On and Off the Stage* (2 vols), London 1888

—— *The Bancrofts: Recollections of Sixty Years*, London 1909

Berger, F., *Reminiscences, Impressions and Anecdotes*, London 1913

Brannan, R. L., *Under the Management of Mr Charles Dickens: His Production of 'The Frozen Deep'*, Ithaca, NY, 1966

Daly, J. F., *The Life of Augustin Daly*, New York 1917

Dexter, W., 'For One Night Only: Dickens's Appearances as an Amateur Actor', *Dickensian*, 36 (1 Sept. 1940), 195–201

Fitz-Gerald, S. J. A., *Dickens and the Drama*, London 1910

Nicoll, A., *A History of Late Nineteenth Century Drama 1850–1900* (vols 1 and 2), Cambridge 1946

Pascoe, C. E., *The Dramatic List: Actors and Actresses of the British Stage*, London 1879

Reeve, W., 'Recollections of Wilkie Collins', *Chambers's Journal*, 9 (June 1906), 458–61

Winter, W., *Old Friends*, New York 1909

—— *The Wallet of Time* (2 vols), New York 1913

OTHER CRITICISM AND MEMOIRS—PRE-1890

Anonymous, 'Wilkie Collins', *Appletons' Journal of Popular Literature, Science and Art* (3 Sept. 1870), 278–81

Anonymous, 'Mr Wilkie Collins', *Once a Week*, NS 217 (24 Feb. 1872), 196–7

Anonymous, 'Wilkie Collins', *Illustrated Review*, 6 (10 July 1873)

Anonymous, 'Wilkie Collins', *Harper's Weekly*, 17 (8 Mar. 1873)

Anonymous, 'Celebrities at Home, No 81, Mr Wilkie Collins in Gloucester Place', *The World*, (26 Dec. 1877); reprinted by Edmund Yates, 3rd series, London 1879

Cooper, T., 'Wilkie Collins, Esq, Novelist and Dramatist', *Men of Mark, Fifth Series,* London 1881

Forgues, É.-D., 'William Wilkie Collins', *Revue des Deux Mondes, 2e série,* 12 (Nov. 1855), 815–48

Frith, W. P., *My Autobiography and Reminiscences* (3 vols), London 1887–8

Jehu Junior [T. Gibson Bowles], 'Men of the Day, No 39, Mr Wilkie Collins', *Vanity Fair* (3 Feb. 1872), 39

Kosmos [T. H. S. Escott], 'Letters to Eminent Persons, No 72, Mr Wilkie Collins', *The World* (6 June 1883), 5–6

Lang, A., 'Mr Wilkie Collins's Novels', *Contemporary Review,* 57 (Jan. 1890), 20–8

Payn, J., *Some Literary Recollections,* London 1884

Quilter, H., 'A Living Story-teller', *Contemporary Review,* 55 (Apr. 1888), 572–93

—— 'In Memoriam Amici', *Universal Review,* 5 (Oct. 1889); reprinted in *Preferences in Art, Life and Literature,* London 1892

Reade, C. L. and Reade, C., *Charles Reade: A Memoir,* London 1887

Swinburne, A. C., 'Wilkie Collins', *Fortnightly Review,* 275 (1 Nov. 1890), 589–99; reprinted in *Studies in Prose and Poetry,* London 1894

Trollope, A., *An Autobiography,* London 1883

Yates, E. 'Men of Mark: No 2—W. Wilkie Collins', *The Train,* 3 (June 1857), 352–7

—— 'In memoriam—W. W. C., obit September 23rd 1889', *The World* (25 Sept. 1889), 12–13

—— 'The Novels of Wilkie Collins', *Temple Bar,* 89 (Aug. 1890), 528–32

OTHER CRITICISM AND MEMOIRS—POST-1890

Anderson, M., *A Few Memories,* London 1896

Ashley, R. P., 'Wilkie Collins Reconsidered', *Nineteenth-Century Fiction,* 4 (Mar. 1950), 265–73

—— 'The Wilkie Collins Collection', *Princeton University Library Chronicle,* 17 (Winter 1956), 81–4

Beard, N., 'Some Recollections of Yesterday', *Temple Bar,* 102 (July 1894), 315–39

Caine, H., *My Story,* London 1908

Caracciolo, P., 'Wilkie Collins's "Divine Comedy": the Use of Dante in *The Woman in White*', *Nineteenth-Century Fiction,* 25 (Mar. 1971), 383–404

—— 'Wilkie Collins and the Ladies of Baghdad, or the Sleeper Awakened', *The Arabian Nights in English Literature,* edited by Peter L. Caracciolo, London 1988

Compton-Rickett, A., 'Wilkie Collins', *Bookman,* 42 (June 1912), 107–22

de la Mare, W., 'The Early Novels of Wilkie Collins' in John Drinkwater (ed.) *The Eighteen Sixties,* Cambridge 1932

Eliot, T. S., 'Wilkie Collins and Dickens', *Times Literary Supplement* (4 Aug. 1927), 525–6; reprinted in *Selected Essays: 1917–1932,* London 1932

Ellis, S. M., *Wilkie Collins, Le Fanu and Others,* London 1931

Elwin, M., *Victorian Wallflowers,* London 1934

Gasson, A., 'Wilkie Collins, Edmund Yates and *The World*', *WCSJ* 4 (1984), 5–17

Hawthorne, J., *Shapes that Pass,* London 1928

Hayter, A., *Opium and the Romantic Imagination,* London 1968

Heller, T., *Dead Secrets: Wilkie Collins and the Female Gothic,* New Haven and London 1992

Hughes, W., *The Maniac in the Cellar: Sensation Novels of the 1860s,* Princeton, NJ, 1980

Hüttner, K., *Wilkie Collins's 'The Woman in White'—Analysis, Reception and Literary Criticism of a Victorian Bestseller,* Wissenschaftlicher Verlag, Trier 1996

Hyder, C. K., 'Wilkie Collins and *The Woman in White*', *Publications of the Modern Languages Association,* 54 (1939), 297–303

Kendrick, W. M., 'The Sensationalism of *The Woman in White*', *Nineteenth-Century Fiction,* 32 (June 1977), 18–35

Lehmann, J., *Ancestors and Friends,* London 1962

Lehmann, R. C., *Memories of Half a Century,* London 1908

Lonoff, S., *Wilkie Collins and His Victorian Readers: A Study in the Rhetoric of Authorship*, New York 1982

Maas, J., *The Victorian Art World in Photographs*, London 1984

MacEachen, D. B., 'Wilkie Collins and British Law', *Nineteenth-Century Fiction*, 5 (Sept. 1950), 121–39

Marshall, W. H., *Wilkie Collins*, New York 1970

Melville, L., 'Wilkie Collins', *Temple Bar*, 128 (Sept. 1903), 360–8; reprinted in *Victorian Novelists*, 1906

Millais, J. G., *The Life and Letters of Sir John Everett Millais* (2 vols), London 1899

Nayder, L., *Wilkie Collins*, New York 1997

O'Neill, P., *Wilkie Collins: Women, Property and Propriety*, London 1988

Page, N. (ed.), *Wilkie Collins: The Critical Heritage*, London 1974

Phillips, W. C., *Dickens, Reade and Collins: Sensation Novelists*, New York 1919

Rance, N., *Wilkie Collins and Other Sensation Novelists*, London 1991

Reeve, W., 'Recollections of Wilkie Collins', *Chambers's Journal*, 9 (June 1906), 458–61

Sehlbach, H., *Untersuchungen über die Romanskünst von Wilkie Collins*, Jena 1931

Six Letters of Wilkie Collins from the Charlotte Ashley Felton Memorial Library at Stanford University, with an introduction by J. Terry Bender, San Francisco 1957

Smith, N., and Terry, R. C. (eds.), *Wilkie Collins to the Forefront: Some Reassessments*, New York 1995

Smith, R. J., 'Margaret Carpenter (1793–1872): A Salisbury Artist Restored', *Hatcher Review*, 4 (Autumn 1993), 2–32

Taylor, J. B., *In the Secret Theatre of Home: Wilkie Collins, Sensation Narrative, and Nineteenth Century Psychology*, London and New York 1988

Thom, P., *The Windings of the Labyrinth: Quest and Structure in the Major Novels of Wilkie Collins*, Athens, Oh., 1992

Walford, L. B., *Memories of Victorian London*, London 1912

Walters, J. Cumming, 'Books and Their Makers: A Chat about Wilkie Collins', *Ideas* (22 July 1905), 11

Ward, E. M., *Memories of Ninety Years*, edited by Isabel G. McAllister, London 1924

Watt, G., *The Fallen Woman in the Nineteenth-Century English Novel*, London and Canberra 1984

Waugh, A., 'Wilkie Collins: And His Mantle', *Academy and Literature* (5 Apr. 1902), 364–5

For an annual listing of new works on Collins, see 'Victorian Bibliography', Summer Number, *Victorian Studies*.

⇥ PICTURE ACKNOWLEDGEMENTS ⇤

The author and publishers wish to thank the following who have kindly given permission to reproduce the illustrations on the pages indicated: **25** (right) While every effort has been made to secure permission to reproduce the illustration, we have failed to trace the copyright holder. Should the copyright holder be in contact after publication, we would be happy to include a suitable acknowledgement on subsequent reprints; **30** Ashmolean Museum, Oxford; **31** (left and right) Faith Clarke; **33** (bottom and top) Faith Clarke; **35** Reproduced by courtesy of the National Portrait Gallery, London; **41** (left) Reproduced by courtesy of the National Portrait Gallery, London; **46** (bottom) Faith Clarke; **52** Reproduced by courtesy of the Dickens House Museum; **61** © 1948 Turner Entertainment Co.; **85**, **86** Glen Horowitz, Bookseller, New York; **96** (bottom left) Faith Clarke; **130** Kent County Council; **135** Faith Clarke; **146** (top left) © BBC Picture Archives; **153** Reproduced by courtesy of the National Portrait Gallery, London.

CANTERBURY CHRIST
CHURCH COLLEGE